The Kidnapped and the Ransomed

The narrative of Peter and Vina Still
after forty years of slavery

Kate E. R. Pickard

*with an introductory essay on
Jews in the antislavery movement by*

MAXWELL WHITEMAN

Introduction to the Bison Books Edition
by Nancy L. Grant

University of Nebraska Press
Lincoln and London

♻ The paper in this book meets the minimum requirements
of American National Standard for Information Sciences—
Permanence of Paper for Printed Library Materials,
ANSI Z39.48-1984.

First Bison Books printing: 1995
Most recent printing indicated by the last digit below:
10 9   8   7   6   5   4   3   2   1

Library of Congress Cataloging-in-Publication Data
Pickard, Kate E. R.
The kidnapped and the ransomed: the narrative of Peter and
Vina Still after forty years of slavery / by Mrs. Kate E. R.
Pickard, with an introductory essay on Jews in the antisla-
very movement by Maxwell Whiteman; introduction to the
Bison Books edition by Nancy L. Grant.
p. cm.
ISBN 0-8032-9233-3 (pbk.: alk. paper)
1. Still, Peter, b. 1801. 2. Still, Vina. 3. Slaves—United
States—Biography. 4. Slavery—Kentucky. 5. Slavery—
Alabama. 6. Concklin, Seth, 1802–1851. 7. Afro-Ameri-
cans—Relations with Jews. I. Whiteman, Maxwell.
II. Title.
E444.P53   1996
306.3'62'092273—dc20
95-30735 CIP

Originally published in 1856 by William T. Hamilton as *The
Kidnapped and the Ransomed. Being the Personal Recollec-
tions of Peter Still and His Wife "Vina," after Forty Years of
Slavery*. Reprinted from the 1970 edition by the Jewish
Publication Society of America.

Contents

Introduction to the Bison Books Edition

Nancy Grant

Over the past fifty years, historians and general readers have developed a renewed interest in the slave narrative. It has become an important vehicle for understanding the cruelties of the slave system and the complex humanity of the slaves. The personal experiences of male and female slaves brought an immediacy to the study of slavery that has been missing in the scholarly debates on cliometrics, slave labor systems, and theoretical essays on the slave economy. The slave narrative also reminds the reader of the countless struggles of slaves for survival, for hope, for dignity, for control, for creativity and joy in that inhumane environment.

The Kidnapped and the Ransomed: The Narrative of Peter and Vina Still after Forty Years of Slavery is a well-crafted narrative that is a multilayered story of suffering, redemption, and rebirth for the Still family. There is also irony in the complex and sometimes hidden stories of their lives. For example, the emotional climax of the narrative is reached in the home of Peter's mother in 1850. In a classic, almost operatic scene, Peter is reunited with his aged mother whom he has not seen in over forty years. According to the narrative, Peter and his brother Levin were taken away from the peace and tranquility of their home on the Delaware River by a slave kidnapper who sold them in Kentucky. Levin died in slavery but Peter lived to retain the memory of his lost family. Persevering through hard work, faith, and good fortune, he was able to return "home."

However, this joyful moment was, in reality, much more problematic than presented in the narrative. The original and current texts do not reveal the fact that Peter, despite the well-publicized title, had not been kidnapped. He was abandoned by his mother when she escaped slavery in Maryland to join her husband who had bought his freedom several years earlier. Peter's mother, Sidney, decided to take her daughters with her and elected to leave behind her eight-year-old and six-year-old sons. For over forty years, the Still family had kept alive the memory of their two relatives lost in slavery, a tale recounted with much sadness and guilt by the mother and daughters. It is not clear whether Peter was aware of his slave status and chose to hide it or had been too young to understand his abandonment.[1]

The narrative recounts the journey of Peter as he is sold first in Kentucky and then to a plantation owner who lived in Tuscumbia, Alabama. Meeting and marrying Lavinia (Vina) in Alabama, Peter worked in a variety of trades and jobs in the area, successfully raising a family. After forty years of slavery, Peter managed to buy his freedom through the help of two German-Jewish businessmen. Coming to Philadelphia, Peter reunited with his mother and siblings and vowed to rescue his wife and children from slavery. After an abortive rescue attempt that resulted in the death of Seth Conklin, an underground railroad agent, Peter orchestrated a successful fund-raising campaign to purchase the freedom of his wife and children for $5000.

This narrative is essentially a joint autobiography with the remembrances and perspectives of both Peter and Vina Still as told to Kate Pickard. Peter Still is the principal voice of the narrative. It is his journey from slavery to freedom that is the focus. For Peter, the goal of freedom is clear. He defines freedom as the relinquishing of control by an owner, the opportunity to choose a career and earn a living, the maintenance and security of one's family, the right to travel and relocate, and the right to defend one's honor and sense of dignity. Peter's desire for freedom was fostered by an innate sense of independence and not from pamphlets, advisers, or external events. Apparently he was not driven to freedom by any particularly harsh event or treatment as a slave. An escape from slavery was not compatible with the planned, deliberate approach to life of this "hardworking, universally respected and loved" man. Purchasing his free papers allowed Peter an orderly, if secret, transition from slavery to freedom and permitted his family to prepare for his absence. Indeed, the laws of Alabama did not allow newly freed slaves to remain in the state, so Peter knew that he would have to relocate. Peter did observe a clear contrast between the behavior of African Americans in the North and those living under slavery in the South. He noted a greater sense of self and presence among his relatives, members of the well-known and accomplished Still family of Philadelphia. Implicit in this contrast is the sense that if Peter had been allowed the same opportunities as his siblings, he might have also become a physician, activist, or businessman. Instead, he remained in freedom a semiliterate farmer.

The narrative through Peter's voice also supports the conclusions of several scholars acknowledging the important role of men in the slave family. Although he lived away from his family under the control of a different owner, Peter visited his family frequently, bringing food, clothing, and extra furniture whenever possible. His children looked up to him as an authority figure and caregiver. His frequent visits also seemed to mitigate somewhat the harsh treatment of Vina by her owner and overseers and to help prevent their sexual advances. The devotion to his family was also demonstrated by his refusal to separate his wife from their children by purchasing their freedom one by one. He clearly did not want to repeat the horrible situation that had happened to him forty years earlier.

An exceptional aspect of this narrative is the role that the two Jewish merchants, Joseph and Isaac Friedman, played in the freedom aspirations of Peter and his family. There are very few narratives about the role of Jews in American slavery (see Maxwell Whiteman's introduction, 7–20). Indeed, fewer than thirty pages are devoted to the brothers, whose business is not described in detail. The narrative does provide a view of Jews living in a small town in the South. Local white inhabitants and perhaps a few of their slaves viewed the Friedman brothers with considerable suspicion, labeling them as outsiders and foreigners. As Jews, they were called moneychangers who "would sell their own children for money." Peter had carefully observed the brothers in their interpersonal relations and had not been influenced by the low opinion held by the town. He noted that Joseph had treated him like a man and not like a slave. It was that recognition of humanity that helped create a trust between Peter and Joseph. At Peter's insistence, Joseph bought him and made arrangements for a payment plan. When the local slave owners heard of Friedman's purchase, they expressed concern that Peter would be worked to death or treated poorly by the "non-Christian" who did not understand the proper way to treat such a reliable and loyal slave. Peter quietly purchased his freedom and received his free papers in April 1850, signed by Joseph Friedman. The brothers sold their business and relocated to the North where they remained in contact with Peter and his family. In a narrative tradition that elevates abolitionist activists as heroes, the Friedman brothers are given a positive, though secondary role in the fight against slavery. They, after all, accepted $500 from Peter and seemed to approach the purchase as a business transaction with an important social purpose (212–38).

Lavinia Still provides another voice to the narrative, a perspective different in region, occupation, and gender. Unlike the careful and unobtrusive Peter, Lavinia is more assertive and forceful, particularly as she protects her children and herself from the assaults by overseers and her owner. She is also portrayed as the victim of the "two-headed monster" of slavery, the lecherous master and the jealous mistress. In keeping with other narratives by Harriet Jacobs and Elizabeth Keckley, Lavinia reserves particular criticism for her slave mistress, who had a well-earned reputation for being extremely suspicious of her female slaves, particularly those who aroused the interest of her husband. Jealousy of his favored slave women drove the mistress to "seek solace in the wine cup." Lavinia, unlike Harriet Jacobs or Elizabeth Keckley, does not temper her critique of her mistress with a shared sense of victimization or suffering at the hands of white men. No victim of the pedestal, slave mistresses were "frail delicate ladies . . . [who could] strip and tie their slaves both men and women and beat them with the zest of a base-born overseer" (159).[2]

Lavinia also represents the story of those left behind after departure of one's spouse. She describes in considerable detail the loss of her husband and the punishment and banishment after her unsuccessful escape attempt. The enormous human suffering of those slaves left behind acted as a significant deterrent against escape from masters.

An appendix written by a prominent antislavery clergyman offers a third subject to the narrative. The life and martyrdom of Seth Conklin is given detailed treatment. Peter and Vina Still are quite heroic as slaves, but most of the whites are characterized as collaborators in an unjust system. There are no good masters in Peter and Vina's life. Only Joseph and Isaac Friedman are characterized as good, if somewhat conservative men. Seth Conklin is presented as a daring and unselfish abolitionist who was willing to make the ultimate sacrifice.

Our interest in the Still narrative is in part a reflection of the tension between blacks and Jews in the 1990s. The Friedman connection, the actions of two German-Jewish Americans, and not the martyrdom of Seth Conklin, a northern Irish-American, has captured the attention of the editors of the three twentieth-century editions of the narrative.

Slave narratives have always served social and political purposes as well as autobiographical expressions. In antebellum America, the narratives served as a means of persuasion and propaganda against the evils of slavery. The publication of most narratives was under the editorial and publishing control of abolitionists. Originally published in 1856, *The Kidnapped and the Ransomed* was just one of a large number of slave narratives in the decades prior to the Civil War.[3]

Kate Pickard, the editor, played a very active role both as a transcriber of the remembrances of Peter and Vina Still and also as an observer and commentator on events in their lives. Unlike most editors, Pickard had known Peter as a slave and had lived in Tuscumbia, where she worked as a teacher in the female academy that employed Peter for several years. She also knew Peter's owner and many of the whites who appear in the narrative. Her voice is most pronounced in the discussion of the views of the white community concerning Joseph and Isaac Friedman and in the intimate details of the relationships among slave owners.

It was the decision of Pickard and the publishers not to reveal the fact that Peter had been born a slave in order to protect his mother and sisters, who in 1856 would have been subject to fugitive slave laws. In a literary form given to authenticity and accuracy, the editor decided to fudge somewhat by advertising the narrative as based on the memory of Peter and Vina Still. In a similar attempt to conceal, the editor also omitted from the text a discussion of the network of underground railroad agents who helped Seth Conklin in his rescue attempt.

In 1941, a second edition of the narrative was published by the Negro Publication Society of America. On the advisory board of this organization were many of the most prominent black and white leftists, including Herbert Aptheker, Alain Locke, Theodore Dreiser, Dashiel Hammett, and Angelo Herndon. The preface for the 1941 edition was written by Angelo Herndon, a labor organizer for the American Communist Party.

The same edition carried an introduction by Lawrence Reddick. Highlighting the historical relevance of the narrative, he addresses two of the most important issues of time, the threat of war with Germany and the loss of human rights for European Jews and political dissidents.

He notes that "the Jewish or political refugee stealing across the border, hunted and haunted, yet finding unexpected, often silent, friends to help him on his way is astonishingly similar to the lone slave following the *North Star* through thicket and swamp, in his turn, befriended by the agents of the Underground Railroad to freedom" (11). Reddick used the Pickard narrative as a call to end terrorism—not only in Germany but also in America— as an important part of the fight against lynching and segregation in the South. Reddick did criticize the moralistic didacticism of Pickard and the foolhardiness of Seth Conklin, but applauded the richness of the characterization of slavery, which transcended stereotypes and exaggerations.

The 1970 edition published by the Jewish Publication Society of America chose to emphasize the role of the Friedman brothers in the life of Peter Still. The lengthy introductory essay by Maxwell Whiteman, "Jews in the Antislavery Movement," asks the question of what role, if any, did Jews play in the American antislavery movement. In an essay that predates the heated debates of the 1980s and 1990s on the degree of cooperation and conflict between African Americans and Jewish Americans, Whiteman provides an intriguing explanation for the relative absence of Jews either as individuals or members of congregations in the antislavery movement. According to Whiteman, the Christian religious base of some of the antislavery societies with Protestant clergy in prominent roles served to discourage Jews from membership. Whiteman calls for more research to be done in the area. It is interesting that, though markedly evenhanded and supported by extensive notes and sources, Whiteman's essay was harshly criticized in the *American Jewish Historical Quarterly* for missing important antislavery leaders in the Jewish community and for being too critical of the lack of an organized Jewish commitment against slavery. Twenty-five years later, there is a continued need for more research and writing on the subjects of Jews and the antislavery movement and Jews and the slave trade. Fueled by controversial interpretations and exaggerations by both African Americans and Jewish Americans, research and writing in these subjects should be returned to the reflective and scholarly environment of historical archives and universities and taken out of the hotly contested arenas of public forums and talk shows.[4]

The Kidnapped and the Ransomed is very much a story for the 1990s as well as for the 1850s, 1940s, and 1970s. It addresses the timeless issues of self-determination and self-empowerment in the face of racial oppression, the sanctity and centrality of the family, the cooperation between marginal groups for the greater good of freedom and security, and the recognition of the distinctive voices and experiences of men and women in history. It also reminds us that the lives of ordinary men and women can and should have an impact on the understanding of our history and our present society.

NOTES

1. The true circumstances of Peter's abandonment were not revealed until the publication of his brothers' books: William Still, *The Underground Railroad* (Philadelphia, 1872), and James Still, *Early Recollections and Life of Dr. James Still* (Philadelphia, 1877). Also, see Lurey Khan, *One Day, Levin . . . He Be Free: William Still and the Underground Railroad* (New York: Dutton, 1972).

2. There are not many narratives that feature the voices of women. The most famous are Elizabeth Keckley, *Behind the Scenes: Thirty Years a Slave and Four Years in the White House* (1868); Harriet Jacobs, *Incidents in the Life of a Slave Girl, Written by Herself.* For a discussion of the jealousy of the slave mistress, see Minrose C. Gwin, "Green-eyed Monsters of the Slavocracy: Jealous Mistresses in Two Slave Narratives," in *Black Women in America: An Historical Encyclopedia,* vol. 2 (Brooklyn NY: Carlson Publishers, 1993).

3. For a discussion of the slave narrative in American history see Jean Fagin Yellin and Cynthia D. Bond, *The Pen is Ours: A Listing of Writings by and about African-American Women before 1910 with Secondary Bibliography to the Present*

(New York: Oxford University Press, 1991); Charles and Henry Louis Gates Jr., *The Slave's Narrative* (New York: Oxford University Press, 1985); John Sekora and Darwin T. Turner, *The Art of Slave Narrative: Original Essays in Criticism and Theory* (Macomb: Western Illinois University, 1982).

4. For an example of controversial interpretations, see *The Secret Relationship between Blacks and Jews*, prepared by the Historical Research Department, Nation of Islam (1991), and *Jew-hatred as History: An Analysis of Nation of Islam's "The Secret Relationship between Blacks and Jews*," by the Anti-Defamation League (1993).

Introduction

Jews in the antislavery movement
by
Maxwell Whiteman

for

Elizabeth Delano Whiteman

whose ancestors from the day of the first settlement
on American soil were in the forefront of the
movement that made the United States the great
republic that it is

This introduction, built around the narrative of
Peter Still, is concerned with the attitudes and
the participation of Northern Jews in the antislavery movement prior to the Civil War.

In the broad context of a deeply troubled nation, immersed in complex problems that pre-
ceded the Civil War, the reaction of Jews to
slavery appears vague and insignificant; and yet
at times it was striking and volatile. Present-day
scholarship has given it little attention. The hundreds of works on the antebellum period contain
little or no mention of Jews in connection with the
antislavery movement. For evidence of Jewish
involvement in this crisis, which shook the founda-
tions of the United States, it is necessary to turn
to two diverse sources: writers of the school of

parochial Marxists, who engendered a "progressive" filiopietism, and to the contributions of the rabbinate, which explored the Jewish religious position on slavery. These writings require reexamination.

On the basis of sources newly examined, but long available to the investigator, a number of questions can be posed, and some answered. Why were not American Jews, an articulate and socially conscious people, in the forefront of a struggle that engaged the attention of every American household? Why, considering the abundant literature on the Pentateuchal view of slavery—which either upheld or distorted the Jewish position—were Jews absent from or in the background of a debate that extended over a century and a half?

One form of literature which the Jewish historian has overlooked, perhaps for good reason, is the slave narrative. The number of Jewish slaveholders was so small in the total picture of slavery that only one narrative, out of the approximately ninety that were published, records the "flight" of a slave from a Jewish slaveholder. This major exception is *The Kidnapped and the Ransomed,* the narrative of Peter Still, a slave whose redemption was made possible by two Jewish shopkeepers living in the South who conducted business in Cincinnati, Ohio, and Tuscumbia, Alabama.

Views on the worldwide condition of Jews, as expressed by the former slave Frederick Douglass and free Northern blacks of high literacy and scientific standing, such as Martin R. Delany and Alexander Crummell, have not been examined. Black men who denounced the "peculiar institution" carefully observed the "peculiar people" with whom they were frequently compared. The significant influence upon Negroes by Jews who found religious freedom in a land where slavery was constitutionally upheld seems strange indeed. Yet in the history of black thought, it was the pro-Zionist Edward Wilmot Blyden, a Liberian by adoption, who first recognized the mutual spiritual role of Negroes and Jews. Black literature of the nineteenth century presented the Jew in a positive light at a time when many white writers cast Jews and blacks in odious stereotypes.

The opinions advanced in the tremendous outpouring of the general sermonic and philippic literature of the times constitute the most intriguing aspect of the place of the Jews in the antislavery movement. However, these sermons and writings solved no issues, were in the end without lasting influence, and brought forth Jewish spokesmen only when the nation was on the brink of division or when a Jewish voice defended slavery from the pulpit.

A related historiographic problem that has also

suffered neglect is the attitude of Christian-dominated antislavery societies, and their failure to attract Jews in greater numbers than they did. Few of these questions have been posed in the vast literature of antislavery. Except for the recitation of obvious fact, these problems have been largely ignored. Only the abstract background of slavery in the Pentateuch and in rabbinic literature has been discussed.

Throughout the history of slavery, only a small number of American Jews were involved as owners or traders of slaves. In the New England colonies, there was one major Jewish shipping firm engaged in the African slave trade—Lopez and Rivera, merchants in Newport, R. I. Jacob Franks, a New York City merchant, occasionally handled a parcel of slaves, and in Philadelphia his son David also acted as an agent in the sale of slaves. The enterprising Michael Gratz kept a slave who managed a strictly kosher household; and a slave of Gratz's brother Barnard refused to be sold to another master. In colonial New York City a member of the prominent Gomez family owned a slave named Cuffee, who participated in the destructive New York City slave insurrection of 1741.

In the Middle Atlantic colonies, Jews who held slaves manumitted them or made other provisions for their freedom, paving the way for similar measures after the founding of the United States.

The census of 1790 recorded that out of a Jewish population of less than 1,000, there were 31 Jews holding approximately 73 slaves north of Maryland.

In the South no Jews are known to have been involved in the African slave trade, but there they were more inclined to hold slaves. In the South, as in the North, many blacks were benefited by manumission. Close association between black and Jew led to instances of miscegenation. An early example is Robert Purvis, a Negro who was of English and Jewish-Moorish ancestry. The plantation system required numerous slaves, but there were so few Jewish planters that whether Jews became slaveholders or not did not affect the system. For the eighteenth century, no study of Jews and slavery, North or South, exists. However, one examination of Jews in the antebellum South has opened the field for further scrutiny.

II

The story of Peter Still begins early in the nineteenth century on the banks of the Delaware River, not far from Philadelphia. He and his brother Levin were left behind when their parents made good their escape from slavery. The boys, unaware of their plight, were kidnapped and sold to a Kentucky slaveholder. Peter relates in detail all the cruelties of this most degrading period in American history. He first worked in a brick factory and then as a tobacco and cotton plantation hand. Religious teaching was forbidden to the slaves, and illiteracy was as prevalent as the overseer's lash.

For years Peter dreamed of his mother and how he could return to her. He planned to escape, but as he grew older he became increasingly aware of the dangers of failure: bestial lashing, a body bound in shackles, imprisonment in a dank hut designed for the torture of runaways, and separation from his growing family. Blind flight was not the answer.

After he was taken to Alabama, escape became even more difficult. He so distrusted his new master that he dreaded to approach him on any subject. When he came to know Joseph and Isaac Friedman, for whom he occasionally did odd jobs, he became convinced that he had a better chance to carry out his plan successfully with Jews than with Christians.

The extreme caution and trepidation with which he approached even the kindliest of white people was born of his instinct for self-protection. To those unfamiliar with the slave system, such fear is almost unbelievable. Many masters had betrayed their faithful, trusting blacks at the point of redemption. Once a master had obtained purchase money from his slave, knowing that such a transaction was illegal, the slave had no more recourse than a mule. Peter had seen what happened to his fellow slaves.

Before he approached the Friedmans, he studied their habits, listened to their conversation, and even had his services hired out to them so that he could observe them better. Each step was careful and deliberate. When he mustered enough courage to reveal his plan to them, he was still fearful of the outcome. The Friedmans agreed to help him, and Peter, still apprehensive, suppressed his joy.

The first step in putting the plan into effect was to convince his master that he was no longer worth his keep and that the Friedmans would be willing to purchase him in spite of any defects. He simulated a chronic cough to reduce his value in his master's eyes. He was nearing the age of fifty, and he pleaded that he was no longer as desirable as a younger slave. The Friedmans feigned indifference to the purchase, and after some deliberate haggling, Peter was sold to the Friedmans for five hundred dollars.

The shocked and dismayed community feared that Uncle Peter would be ill-used by his "Jewish master," for who else but a Christian knew how to treat a slave? Peter assured his Christian friends that "Mass'r Joe and Mass'r Isaac always has been good to me, and anyhow, I belong to him, and they can do what they like." This was the proper slave answer, which usually avoided conflict, and Peter knew it. The Friedmans went about their customary affairs, ignored all rumors, and kept Peter in their household as a handyman. He was given permission to earn what he could as the town's general factotum. These earnings were set aside for his redemption fund, according to the mutual agreement, for the Friedmans had no interest in expropriating his meager earnings. Castoff clothing and useful articles were given to Peter as gifts for his family, who belonged to a nearby plantation owner.

City slaves, like Peter, whose services were hired out could keep some of their earnings for the purchase of clothing. His wife, Vina, who was a plantation slave, had seldom been given this privilege and rarely saw a piece of shiny silver. Slaves who were permitted to raise and market a bit of cotton in which their masters had no interest were at the mercy of their masters when the product came to be sold. How they were deprived of the sparse fruits of their labor and denied the only opportunity they had to purchase something for themselves is described by Vina at the end of the narrative.

During the forties and fifties, when immigrant Jewish peddlers and shopkeepers came to Georgia and Alabama, plantation slaves had a greater opportunity to sell or barter the items they were permitted to produce. To do so without permission was illegal, but a clandestine trade flourished which was commonly known of though overlooked, except when slaves were caught selling pilfered goods. With the coming of the Jewish peddler, poor whites who had formerly sold to plantation slaves faced their first competition.

The Northern white observer and the European traveler who journeyed through the South reported that they saw "swarms" of Jewish immigrants enticing slaves into an illicit traffic, luring them to steal by extending them credit, to be paid for with stolen goods. Threats of denunciation forced them into further theft. In actual fact, however, while this was occasionally possible for poor whites to do, the mobile peddler had no time to linger for payment. Frederick Law Olmsted, considered to be a careful observer, described the petty trade of the Jew in uncomplimentary terms. Few contemporary Northerners challenged Olmsted on so unimportant a matter as accusing "Jew-Germans" of shady dealings. But when he stated the amount of meat alloted annually to a slave in some states, when actually none was provided at all, George McDowell Stroud, the legal historian and authority on slave law, commented: "If so intelligent a writer as Mr. Olmsted could be misled, what confidence is to be placed in the gleanings of anonymous correspondents . . . on transient visits."

But a number of these canards, many coming

from the pens of antislavery men, have traveled
through the past century and into modern literature; these allegations are claimed to be the
source of the "American Negro's sporadic anti-
Semitism." Even so prominent a Jewish editor as
Isaac Leeser accepted the validity of some of the
charges. Whatever significance these attitudes
and reactions may have had at the time, it is
known that the lives of Jewish peddlers and shopkeepers in the South were less than comfortable.
The Yankee peddler who left behind his wooden
nutmegs remained a romantic figure of the trade.
The Jew, no matter how straightforward he
acted, was looked upon as a speculator and a
sharp trader who benefited from slavery.

Within a year after Peter was sold to the
Friedmans, the brothers decided to close their
shop and return to Cincinnati. Peter begged to
go along, hoping to stop in Louisville. The Friedmans granted his request. When word of the move
leaked out, the Tuscumbians were full of consternation. Not only had a Jew bought Peter, but he
was ready to take him away to some unknown
place. Local gossipers concurred in the opinion
that the Jews, full of chicanery, had bought
Peter to resell him for a nice profit. This happy,
obedient slave, a symbol of abomination to Northern abolitionists, was in jeopardy. His Christian
friends advised Peter to let them know immedi-

ately if this was the case and they would buy him
back. Peter agreed pleasantly but placed his
trust in Joseph Friedman. Once in Cincinnati, he
knew he would be a free man. And Cincinnati, in
the mind of Peter, was the gateway to the East,
the road to Philadelphia, where he was determined to go and find his relatives.

Peter reposed little confidence in his pretended
friends, whose Lord he had embraced. They had
had their opportunity and failed. He recalled
that they had cheated and betrayed innumerable
slaves who had worked and saved pennies and
small pieces of silver with which to buy their freedom, only to be robbed and brutalized in the end.
Then they had been sent to the "low country" or
the dreaded New Orleans slave market. They
were refused the simplest gesture of human kindness and permanently separated from their families: their women were subjected to the lust of
the overseers and masters. Witnessing these
atrocities was enough to make Peter doubt his
Christian friends.

This theme is emphasized by Mrs. Kate E. R.
Pickard, the writer of Peter's narrative, by Rev.
Samuel J. May, the Unitarian clergyman who
wrote the preface, and by Rev. William Henry
Furness, who prepared the appendix. And more
than twenty years after the event, William Still,
the black abolitionist historian, added many con-
firming details in his history of the underground

railroad, that were not published prior to the Civil War.

The Kidnapped and the Ransomed differs from most slave narratives in that much of the content is corroborated by the writer, who had contact with Peter while she was a teacher at the Female Seminary at Tuscumbia. Most reporters seldom visited the South and merely copied down these narratives exactly as they were related. Mrs. Pickard, however, lived in the midst of slavery and was able to observe the conduct of Peter and write of him from firsthand experience. Beneath her pious and pedestrian style is a dramatic story of the "Christian wolves," as the slaveholders were described by Seth Concklin, a martyred abolitionist. Others in the narrative, such as the Gist family of Lexington, to whom Peter belonged as a boy, are readily identified in Kentucky annals. Benjamin Gratz, of the Philadelphia Gratzes, had married a Gist and had probably met Peter.

As characters in the narrative, the Friedman brothers are hard-working, hard-bargaining men who finally win the confidence of the community. They are depicted as tradesmen at heart, paying no more for Peter than the price he secretly suggested he was worth. Peter provided some of the funds for his purchase, and the shopkeepers advanced the balance without interest. The Friedmans were like the Jewish characters in the literature of the mid-nineteenth century. Kate Pickard transferred the fictional image of the Jew to the people whom she met in Tuscumbia. *"The Jew!* Yes, Joseph Friedman was a German Jew, who had resided in Tuscumbia for six or seven years. . . . He was small in stature, with the black hair and keen eyes peculiar to his race." They were "foreigners," with beady eyes set into shrewd faces. These same black eyes, even to the anti-slavery author, were bright, sparkling, and manly in the face of a slaveholder.

In the small Alabama town, the Friedmans, whose behavior was generally casual and who had no known allies among the townspeople, were the first to stake their lives for Peter. It was illegal for a slave to buy and redeem himself, and it was illegal to be an accessory to such a transaction in Alabama. If Peter risked his fate with the Friedmans, the Friedmans also risked severe punishment and imprisonment.

It is extremely interesting to note that the very language used on the two title pages of the book (and to this day it is not altogether clear why there are two title pages)—kidnapped, ransomed, redeemed—is inspired by the language of the Pentateuch and the daily Hebrew prayer book, to which the Friedmans, as traditionally observant Jews, were committed. But Peter had no way of knowing this; nor did he

know that the Friedmans were active members of
B'nai Jeshurun, the Cincinnati congregation. The
fact that they permitted their names to be used
in the narrative at the height of the antislavery
struggle, when so many other names in this and
in other narratives were disguised or had an
initial substituted, is additional testimony to
the courage of these men. Although the Friedmans did not return to Alabama, they continued to travel and conduct business in the slave
states.

On the journey north, Peter continued to act
like a slave. Not until he and his "Jewish master"
reached Cincinnati did he tell the story of how
he and his brother were snatched away as children and sold to a Kentucky man. Cincinnati was
infested with professional slave catchers, as were
most midwestern riverboat towns. Cincinnati
black men in the guise of abolitionists preyed on
free Negroes and fugitive slaves. These sinister
agents of the slave dealers have been described
in the narrative of Henry Bibb, a Kentucky fugitive. Bibb had traveled through the city ten years
earlier. Wearing false whiskers and passing as
white, he carried a pack on his back and followed
the familiar route taken by Jewish peddlers. In
spite of this disguise, he was apprehended by
the black slave catchers of Cincinnati and returned to Kentucky.

To avoid falling into the hands of these men,

Peter left Cincinnati as quickly as possible. The Friedmans asked him to stay until the cholera that was then prevalent in the Ohio Valley had subsided, but Peter preferred to risk cholera rather than remain. He reached Pittsburgh safely, greatly relieved. He boarded the stagecoach and later the train that took him to Philadelphia. Bewildered and uneasy, with a huge trunk as his only companion, he arrived in Philadelphia on August 1, 1850. After much hesitation he followed a black man to a boardinghouse, where he spent the night trembling in fear of slave catchers, unaware that he was in an antislavery home.

On the following day his newfound guide, an aide of Dr. James J. G. Bias, a leader in the black community, introduced him to the Anti-Slavery Office as Peter Friedman. To William Still, the secretary of the office, he revealed the story of his childhood kidnapping and described his parents and the fate of his brother Levin. Peter, full of distrust for both black and white people which had been instilled in him during a lifetime of slavery, was sure that a trap was being set to return him to Alabama. He longed for the advice of Joseph Friedman. Suspiciously, he faced William Still, who listened to his story with disbelief and amazement. In the course of this tense confrontation it soon became clear to Peter that he and Still were long-separated brothers. In a few days positive identity was established. On August 8, William Still wrote of their dramatic reunion for J. Miller McKim, the Presbyterian editor of *The Pennsylvania Freeman.*

The Friedmans had accomplished their purpose, but Peter Friedman Still, although free, had not accomplished his. He was now as determined to liberate his family, whom he left behind on a Franklin County, Alabama, plantation, as he had been to redeem himself earlier. At this time, Seth Concklin, a one-man abolitionist society, offered to go to Alabama and liberate the Still family. Peter was apprehensive about the plan but reluctantly agreed to it.

Shortly after he was reunited with his Northern relatives, Peter returned to Cincinnati. He called upon the Friedmans and discussed the possibility of purchasing his family rather than having them face the dangers of flight from the deep South. Joseph Friedman "readily promised to aid him, if possible, in negotiating for the purchase. . . ." Meanwhile, he obtained the official document of self-redemption. From the Friedmans he received a slave pass so that he could return to Tuscumbia, under the pretext that they would follow him by Christmas. The villagers were delighted to see him. Peter told them what they wanted to hear, that abolitionists were frightful people. Once again, he pretended to be the contented slave.

Finally, he was able to visit his family and instruct them as to Seth Concklin's plans for their escape. He then returned north.

The escape of Peter's family through the slave states succeeded, but the runaways were detected by slave catchers near Vincennes, Indiana, and imprisoned to await the arrival of their master. Concklin refused to leave the family and was taken with them on the riverboat trip to Alabama. It was alleged that he fell overboard and drowned in the Cumberland River while in chains and shackles. The subsequent details of this disastrous failure and the fate of Peter's wife, Vina, and of their two sons and daughter bring the narrative to a dramatic pitch.

When news of the abortive escape reached Philadelphia, Peter again went to Cincinnati. Two of the Friedman brothers were away. Levi, a third brother, offered to go to Tuscumbia "to try what could be done for the relief of the family," but he was warned by unidentified friends "that such a step would be hazardous and futile." The Tuscumbians were now highly incensed at the Friedmans, whom they regarded as instigators of the escape. In view of these intensely hostile feelings toward the Friedmans, who were not even known to be public champions of abolition, it is easier to understand Southern resentment of the newly arrived Jewish peddlers and storekeepers of Georgia and Alabama.

Peter was more resolved than ever before to liberate his family. The owner of Vina and Peter's children demanded a price of five thousand dollars for them, and negotiations for their purchase were begun. With the aid of many people who are now distinguished in American history, Peter toured the country for almost four years and collected enough money to redeem his family. A year after this was accomplished, *The Kidnapped and the Ransomed* was published.

The association of Samuel J. May and William Henry Furness with Still's narrative was not pure coincidence. Both were prominent Unitarian clergymen committed to the antislavery movement and interested in Jewish affairs. May's boyhood was spent in frequent company with the household of Moses Michael Hays, the head of the only known "family of the despised children of Israel resident in Boston." American and European Jews attracted May's attention, and in his introduction to the narrative he made clear that it was "through the generosity of a Jew" that Peter was liberated.

Rev. Furness, who came from New England, spent most of his life in Philadelphia. He was a topic of conversation in Jewish circles, which he frequented. His opposition to sectarianism and proselytizing won for him many Jewish admirers. When he preached on the subject of Jews, it was not unusual to find them present in his congregation, but whether he had any antislavery influence upon them has not been determined.

Mrs. Pickard's ability to turn Peter Still's life into a narrative that faithfully reflected the miseries and the horrors of plantation slavery places it among the outstanding accounts of slave life. Yet it did not receive the same acclaim that was given to other antislavery publications which appeared during 1856. William Lloyd Garrison's *Liberator* announced its publication with the single terse comment: "A remarkable and thrilling work." *The National Anti-Slavery Standard* published a lengthy review of the narrative reprinted from a Syracuse newspaper but added no comment of its own. In this review Seth Concklin is described as a martyr. Peter and Vina Still, whom the reviewer came to know, are treated with special dignity, but the Friedmans are not mentioned. Although the book could be purchased in any antislavery office, it was generally ignored by the press. Jewish journals are not known to have mentioned it either. Whatever contemporary Jewish reaction it may have aroused is still unknown.

In spite of the minimal publicity which the book received in a market glutted with antislavery and abolitionist literature, three editions appeared within six months. Until 1941 the book, like most slave narratives, was forgotten. The fact that Jews were instrumental in Peter's attaining his freedom remained unnoticed.

III

When Peter arrived in the summer of 1850, Philadelphia was a city divided on the subject of slavery and sectional politics. Its Jewish community appeared homogeneous to the outside, but its congregations were not denominationally cooperative except on matters that affected the total community. On the subject of slavery, however, it had the proudest record of any Northern community. For this reason, the Jews of Philadelphia command great attention.

When the Pennsylvania Society for Promoting the Abolition of Slavery was founded in 1774 and reorganized in 1787 under the leadership of Benjamin Franklin and Benjamin Rush, Jews were among the earliest members of this first abolitionist society in the United States. They were actively engaged in carrying out its work, encouraging if not compelling their fellow Philadelphians to manumit their slaves immediately. Although five Jews are on record as owning seven slaves in 1790, the records of the Pennsylvania Society carry many entries in which Jews figured, far beyond their proportion to the local population, as principals or witnesses in the freeing of slaves.

Benjamin Nones, one of the Jews active in the society, was equally active in the civic and political affairs of the city. In the summer of 1800, Nones, Benjamin Rush, Peter Stephen DuPonceau, and others met to express their views on the conduct of local Federalists. Among their company was Cyrus Bustil, a man prominent in the affairs of the black community. The Federalist press singled out Nones as a Jew and Bustil as "Citizen Sambo." With the same zeal with which he undertook other causes, Nones answered the slanders with dignity in the public press. He went beyond abolitionist activity in a quest for equality of human rights.

In New York City, Jews also took an active part in the local Society for Promoting the Manumission of Slaves, although they did not equal in numbers the participation of Philadelphians. Moses Judah, a merchant and a member of a large and influential family, was for two years on the Standing Committee of the society and active in many of its affairs. During the time that he served the Standing Committee (1806–1809), it was responsible for the manumission of approximately fifty slaves.

Following the slave uprisings in the 1790s in the West Indies, many Jews came to New York and Philadelphia from the islands. The slaves they brought with them were confronted with an entirely new situation. According to the astute black historian C. L. R. James, in the islands the great majority of Jews treated their slaves in accordance with the fundamentals of biblical law as found in the book of Exodus. James states that, "Except for the Jews, who spared no energy in making Israelites of their slaves, the majority of the colonists religiously kept all instructions, religious or otherwise, away from their slaves." In Philadelphia the Jewish islanders, surrounded by a libertarian antislavery environment, had little choice but to manumit their slaves.

What happened to these black converts to Judaism on the mainland is not known. Data on their activity as Jews is fragmentary, and references to black congregants in the synagogue are sparse. One Philadelphia congregation, Mikveh Israel, admitted them, although they were not permitted front-row seating, which was usually reserved for affluent members. Other congregations are silent on the subject. But there is no record of any incident of denial or exclusion of black worshipers similar to that which occurred shortly after the American Revolution in nearby Saint George's Methodist Episcopal Church. There black men kneeling in prayer were compelled to leave the church.

It is not known whether Lucy Marks, a member of the congregation Mikveh Israel, was a descendant of one of the black Jews who came up from the islands or was a former slave of Rachel Marks. She was a devout observer of the precepts of Judaism, and, following the traditional custom, she joined the ladies of Mikveh Israel in the separate seating assigned to women by practice and code. In the Philadelphia community there were no constitutional provisions similar to those in the island congregations which discussed equal religious privileges or intimated differences between black and white.

In the prominent Marks family, in whose household Lucy lived, she was an accepted member. Upon her death, the Marks family applied for the customary permit for burial in the historic colonial Spruce Street Cemetery. This was in accordance with congregational practice, which entitled Lucy to a place in the burying yard, provided that her induction into Judaism met with rabbinic dicta. Horrified that a black woman would lie eternally in consecrated ground among the old Jewish aristocracy, a number of members protested. But the Marks family and their supporters were successful in providing a Jewish burial for Lucy. Rumors spread that this had been accomplished only by a midnight ceremony and that the gates of the yard had to be broken down to let the mourners in; but this is latter-day legend. Lucy lies buried in an unmarked grave at the entrance to the cemetery, not far from the unmarked grave of the revolutionary war patriot Haym Salomon.

To fully understand this episode and the immutable criteria of rabbinic law, to which the congregation adhered, the case of Mary Gratz— who died in 1841, three years later—is illuminating. Miss Gratz, of an eminent family, was the daughter of a non-Jewish mother, and her conversion to Judaism, if there was one, did not conform to rabbinic standards. She was a faithful observer all her life, but it was to no avail. Upon her death, burial of her body in the old cemetery was forbidden, over the protests of the Gratz family. Rebecca Gratz, in ladylike fashion, reminded the board of Mikveh Israel that a black woman had been laid to rest there. But the board would not reverse its decision. This is the only controversy of its kind known to have taken place in Philadelphia. No evidence exists to indicate whether or not other Negroes were buried in denomination cemeteries other than their own in this period.

In the years prior to Peter Still's arrival in Philadelphia, the fragments of the Jewish antislavery record, when pieced together, provide sufficient evidence to overturn contemporary nineteenth-century views and dispel present-day aspersions about Jewish inactivity. As a matter of fact, proslavery thought among Northern Jews has not even been examined. It is of secondary importance whether Northern Jews were motivated individually or denominationally; the fact that a record of activity exists which requires further study and exploration is of greater significance.

Lucy Marks was still alive in January 1838, when "Mr. [Senator James] Buchanan presented a memorial from twenty-four Jews of Philadelphia" in favor of the abolition of slavery in the District of Columbia. The general press briefly noticed the independent Jewish petition; the antislavery press made no mention of it. Although their action was part of a citywide movement protesting the domestic slave trade, the Jews preferred to express themselves individually. Other memorials, containing 4,737 names, were presented by the senators from Pennsylvania about the same time. All the petitions were tabled by the Senate. For the Jews, who were still busy warding off Christian missionaries and were engaged in organizing their first immigrant aid societies, this public announcement of their views was a courageous step. Their small and vulnerable congregations, one of which was struggling to survive, did not yet have a membership totaling 350 persons.

Although universal freedom, as it was advocated by the antislavery movement, did not necessarily provide for Jewish rights, there were exceptional examples of men whose practices were not obscured by their beliefs. These included the Unitarians Samuel J. May and William Henry Furness, who opposed proselytizing. Joshua R. Giddings, a Congregationalist, shared a similar view. When Giddings attacked the Know-Nothing Lewis C. Levin for his anti-Free Soil position, Levin's Jewish background did not enter the debate. William Lloyd Garrison, the editor of *The Liberator*, never hesitated to remind his readers of an opponent who was Jewish. He distrusted the church hierarchy because it was on the side of the oppressor, and during the course of the conflict his views and those of others changed considerably as they moved away from orthodox Christianity. But the brotherhood of man remained a delicate matter when it interfered with the spreading of the Gospel.

Organized antislavery was connected with the temperance movement, moral reform crusades, and anti-Sabbatarianism. None of these causes appealed to potential Jewish members. Jews had no need for temperance or moral reform societies. And what had they to gain by fighting the Christian Sabbath in order to make possible the sale of antislavery literature on that day, when the spirit of the Sunday laws militated against them? Jews and Seventh Day Baptists were already being persecuted by sectarian groups, and for them to argue for the sale of antislavery literature on the Christian Sabbath could only add fuel to the fire.

Toward the end of the crisis, members of the Christian-dominated and -motivated societies, whose views were based on the teachings of the Gospel, also advocated Christianizing the Constitution, and argued that if the nation was declared Christian, sectional strife would diminish. Such an argument was not likely to attract Jews to the antislavery movement. The concept of universal freedom, in which antislavery men took great pride, meant different things to different people. New Englanders expressed their philosophy in a manner that could not be compared to that of Pennsylvania Quakers and Episcopalians, in whose libertarian society Jews found a warmer welcome. The abolitionist and antislavery press, while it engaged primarily in a war directed against Christian slaveholders and their supporters in the North, maintained its strong Christian tone. Despite its occasional overtures that appealed to all people, it did not convince many Jews to swell the ranks of the cause it espoused.

If the judgment of Frederick Law Olmsted, representing an extreme attitude, is accepted, no favorable conclusion could be drawn on the subject of Jews. Olmsted, the popular author of a series of books on conditions in the South, lost no opportunity to sneer at Jews wherever he met them. He described them as men without character in South Carolina and Georgia, and as profiteers who preyed on fugitive slaves in Texas. This great landscape architect, who contributed to the beauty of New York City's Central Park, was decidedly antislavery and just as decidedly anti-Semitic. His strong allegiance to the Union and his important position as general secretary of the United States Sanitary Commission in no manner softened his opinion of Jews. The diverse personal positions of those who as a group advocated universal freedom make it impossible to conclude that the antislavery movement was monolithic, for it neither seriously considered Jews nor deliberately rejected them.

Antislavery strongly appealed to the Jewish concept of the universal freedom of man. Hence, the hundreds of Jews who believed in the God of Israel and gave of their energies to the antislavery movement had to close their eyes to its christological influences. But practices which were perfectly in character for Christian-sponsored societies repelled many observant Jews. After the American Revolution, the door that was opened to Jewish participation in libertarian societies did not involve christological teaching. Where it was present, it was not directed to Jews. But with the increasing domination of the so-

cieties by clergymen, Jewish membership de-
creased. Equal participation in the struggle for
human freedom was gradually, almost impercep-
tibly, diminishing.

There were, however, many exceptions among
Jewish antislavery activists: the descendants of
the colonial Jewish families who remained faithful to the social manners of a previous generation
and maintained old associations enabled Benjamin Nones and his contemporaries to continue
in the work of the Pennsylvania Society; in the
twenties, Samuel Myers, breaking with Virginia
tradition, joined the Washington, D. C., Abolition
Society; in the thirties, Solomon Etting, who
believed that the future of blacks was in Africa,
became active in the Maryland Colonization Society; and in the forties, Rebecca Hart was present at the organization of the Quaker-inspired
Female Anti-Slavery Society in Philadelphia, of
which she was an officer for many years.

In New York City, Harmon Hendricks, one of
the wealthiest shipping merchants in the area, who
was not actively involved in the antislavery movement, ignored offers by his Charleston cousin
Jacob De Leon to enter the lucrative slave trade.

A totally new generation, represented by Moses
Aaron Dropsie of Philadelphia and Jonathan
Nathan of New York, serves as an example of
independent Jewish propagandists. To this group
also belongs Abram J. Dittenhoefer, a native

Charlestonian who moved to New York and adopted Republican party principles. Mingling freely in non-Jewish circles, these men worked in behalf of the newly organized Republican party and, as local spokesmen in their cities, condemned slavery and its evils.

From Liverpool, England, the steady flow of Jewish immigrants to the United States increased after the Napoleonic Wars. The newcomers brought with them the influences of the local English antislavery society. Members of the Tobias and Cohen families settled in New York; cousins of the Cohen and the Samuel families settled in Philadelphia. They were active in behalf of the freeman as well as the slave. Henry Samuel pursued this cause at the expense of offending some of his family, who were staunch Democrats, and at the risk of being socially ostracized. Jewish activity in antislavery, which still involved the descendants of colonial Jews, was gradually shifting to the newcomers. Jews from England were the first to wear the American antislavery mantle. Immigrants from Central Europe who followed were slow to adopt it. Language was not a barrier; the real obstacle in imbuing Jewish immigrants with the antislavery idea lay elsewhere.

What was there to attract Jews from Poland, Germany, and Hungary to societies that were made up of an exclusive, old-American family

Jewish audience but for German readers from the Pennsylvania Dutch country, whom he addressed in their own dialect. His career in journalism continued throughout the Civil War years, and his unflinching support of the Union was well known in the heavily populated German-speaking counties of eastern Pennsylvania.

A second Jewish editor who addressed non-Jewish audiences was Lewis Naphtali Dembitz, of Louisville, Kentucky. Three years after he settled in the United States, the uncle of Associate Justice Louis Dembitz Brandeis published one of the first translations into German of Harriet Beecher Stowe's *Uncle Tom's Cabin.* In the same border slave state where Mrs. Stowe had been active a decade before, Dembitz and his brother-in-law were ardent abolitionists in a proslavery environment. After resuming his law studies, Dembitz moved to Louisville.

On December 5, 1852, he became editor of *Der Beobachter am Ohio.* In the seven months that he edited this journal, his translation of *Uncle Tom's Cabin* appeared serially under the title of *Onkel Tom's Hütte, oder: Das Leben unter den Niedrigen.* It was one of three German translations of the book that appeared in the United States following the serialized version in English. No bibliographical precedence has been established. Dembitz's translation is of particular importance because it reached Germans who settled in the Ohio Valley. And unlike translations that appeared in the North, it faced the possibility of fanatical opposition from those who denounced antislavery literature in any form.

On June 7, 1853, Dembitz resigned his editorial post to enter the practice of law. He voted for John Frémont in 1856, subscribing to the platform of the Republican party, which spoke out against the evils of American civilization, Southern slavery, and Mormon polygamy, subjects which he also had discussed in the English press. In 1860 he was made a delegate to the Republican convention in Chicago, and he was an enthusiastic supporter of Lincoln. Throughout the course of the antislavery debate and during the years of war that followed, Dembitz was an agent for the distribution of controversial antislavery literature. Perhaps it was not a coincidence that many years later he was chosen to write the scholarly article on slavery which appeared in *The Jewish Encyclopedia*.

There were many Jewish editors and journalists identified with the German press of the fifties, some of whom took a strong antislavery stand in the columns of their publications. Of these, only two published Jewish journals, both of which appeared in Cincinnati. One was short-lived and parochial. The other, *Die Deborah*, founded in 1855 and edited by Isaac Mayer Wise, is a rich source for Jewish life in the Midwest.

Wise defies easy description. In addition to *Die Deborah* he also edited and published *The Israelite*, an English weekly. Each newspaper presented a different point of view on Jewish life in the United States.

Before the war his words were mainly directed against those who disagreed with him on religious grounds. He had little to say about the anti-slavery movement, and when he first wrote of Negroes it was usually in kindly terms. He published at least one article on black Jews, including an incident he witnessed of a black Jew worshiping in the Charleston, S. C., synagogue on the Day of Atonement in 1853; but he made no comment on this unusual occurrence in a slave state.

Toward the end of 1858, when news of the forced baptism of Edgar Mortara spread across the nation, he published an article about the affair in which he advised the Roman Catholic Church to employ Catholic nurses, send them South, and baptize young Negroes whom they could abduct and canonize. Wise, the Democrat, the bitter critic of the Protestant clergy, next turned upon the abolitionists. His screaming hatred of the clergy, whom he held responsible for the ills of the nation, and his fire-breathing sarcasm equaled Parson William G. Brownlow's contempt for Jews. Neither saw the weakness of his own sweeping generalities.

If Wise was deliberately careful to avoid voicing proslavery thoughts, his hostile condemnation of abolitionists—all of whom he indiscriminately regarded as Protestant clerics—his attack on the Republican party, which offered an antislavery plank, and his derisive description of Lincoln cannot possibly place him in the humanitarian ranks of the antislavery movement, no matter what their faults. His arguments on deleting political matter from a parochial paper were unconvincing, for the paper carried vast amounts of secular news, general advertising, and miscellaneous trivia—all of which indicates that he had no real scruples about publishing matters of non-Jewish interest.

Typical of his attitude was a lengthy article entitled "Illiberality in the United States." Much of it was justified and well-intentioned. The power of his arguments was somewhat diluted when he wrote of "the confounded questions of slavery and anti-slavery, Kansas, Utah, Walker," and other items which were looked upon with disfavor by "the new-fangled republicanism." But in writing of the Massachusetts law that required "the public worship of God" and, residence restrictions upon voters, he was able to

summarize his comments with the following tren-
chant words:

> Where are the abolitionists, freesoilers,
> republicans, negro worshippers and liberty
> jobbers of Massachusetts? Is this State in
> the United States, or in Russia? Men who
> embrace the distant negro, cry furiously for
> bleeding Kansas, are intolerant enough to
> sully their own Constitution and intolerant
> laws. . . . Where are all the abolition orators
> of Massachusetts? We want to advise them
> first to sweep their own door.

Wise was correct in belaboring the conditions
of the Massachusetts constitution, but his attitude toward abolitionists hardly brought him
to the forefront as a man interested in the universal freedom for which he so passionately argued.

V

As seen against this background, the account
of Jews in relation to slavery published by the
American and Foreign Anti-Slavery Society, in
its *Annual Report* for 1853, is pertinent.

> The Jews in the United States have never
> taken any steps whatever with regard to

the slavery question. As citizens they deem it their policy "to have every one choose which ever side he may deem best to promote his own interests and the welfare of his country." They have no organization of an ecclesiastical body to represent their general views; no General Assembly or its equivalent. The American Jews have two newspapers, but they do not interfere in any discussion which is not material to their religion. It cannot be said that Jews have formed any denominational opinion on the subject of American slavery. Some of the Jews who reside in slave states have refused to have property in man, or even to have slaves about them. They do not believe that anything analogous to slavery as it exists in this country ever prevailed among the ancient Israelites. But they profess to believe that "the belief of Abraham, enlarged by Moses, and now acknowledged by the Jews, is one of purity and morality, and one which presents the strongest possible support for civil society, *especially a government based upon principles of equality and liberty of the person!* They believe that the coming of the King Messiah will be a signal for universal peace, UNIVERSAL FREEDOM, universal knowledge, and universal worship of the One Eternal."

The objects of so much mean prejudice and unrighteous oppression as the Jews have been for ages, surely they, it would seem, more than any other denomination ought to be the enemies of CASTE, and the friends of UNIVERSAL FREEDOM.

In stating that Jews had never taken any steps with regard to slavery, the editor of the report was obviously wrong. He was correct in noting that they had no ecclesiastical body comparable to those of Protestant denominations, and that they "refused to have any property in man," even though a small number of Southern Jews were involved in slaveholding. But what view was more traditionally American than the one allegedly adopted by the Jew to "choose which ever side he may deem best to promote his own interests and the welfare of his country," even if that choice be wrong? While it was logically sound to conclude that Jews "ought to be the enemies of caste, and the friends of universal freedom," the editor, Lewis Tappan, made no mention of the fact that the American and Foreign Anti-Slavery Society, like so many other antislavery societies, directed its appeals to "Anti-slavery Christians."

If the antislavery societies had consistently appealed to all people, or if Jews had established a separatist Jewish antislavery society, then it would have been relatively easy to determine their stand. Aside from the fact that their population was small and that they did not always agree denominationally among themselves, they were forced to deal with the Christian-martyr complex of many abolitionists, the evangelism of others, and the exclusiveness of still others in order to participate in these groups as individuals. The observations published by the influential American and Foreign Anti-Slavery Society may also be considered as an overture to attract Jewish members, for at this time there was a marked increase in independent Jewish antislavery activity.

But it is probable that the editor of the *Annual Report*, which had reviewed antislavery activity for two decades, did not know of the bitterness expressed by Heinrich Heine when he contemplated coming to America.

> Thou knowest what I think of this accursed land, which I used to love before I understood it. And yet my vocation as liberator compels me publicly to praise and extol this country! Oh, you good German peasants, go to America! You will there find neither princes nor nobles: all men are alike there; all are equally churls—except, indeed, a few million whose skins are black or brown, and who are treated like dogs.

Heine's malignant and biting sarcasm only exasperated his American critics. But although the editor of the *Annual Report* was unaware of Heine's comments on slavery, the Garrisons were very much informed of his attitude and commented on it when slavery was no longer an issue. Many of the New England antislavery men were attracted to the writings of Heine, whom they admired as a poet but condemned, as did Theodore Parker, as a blasphemer. Thomas Wentworth Higginson, the graduate of Harvard Divinity School who led one of the first black regiments into battle during the Civil War, thought otherwise about Heine and described the positive influences of his views.

There was less reason for the American and Foreign Anti-Slavery Society not to know of the Frenchman Isaac-Adolphe Crémieux, who had addressed the World Anti-Slavery Congress in 1840. Crémieux was in London in the late spring of that year to obtain support for the victims of the Damascus blood libel. Describing himself as a "descendant of those Hebrews who first proclaimed the abolition of slavery as a necessity," he declared before this Christian society that "the Jews first among all peoples abolished the sacrifice of human blood, and yet on this very day, in the Near East . . . they are accused of sacrificing Christians in their religious ceremonies." His address was greeted enthusiastically.

Crémieux's views represented the historical position of Jews on both sides of the Atlantic. He was an intimate friend of Abbé Henri Grégoire, one of the first to recognize latent African genius; his work on the subject was popular in the United States for many years prior to the Civil War. At about the time of Grégoire's death, Crémieux prepared articles for the French government on the equality of *all* Frenchmen. Crémieux, who is perhaps better known as the spiritual guide of the Alliance Israélite Universelle, gave his time and energy to the cause of universal freedom throughout his lifetime. He was among the first Europeans to congratulate the United States when the Emancipation Proclamation was issued. How did information on the early career of Crémieux escape the American and Foreign Anti-Slavery Society, which gave close attention to events abroad? And why did it escape Lewis Tappan, the evangelical devotee of antislavery who founded Dun and Bradstreet?

Ernestine Rose, unlike Crémieux, was very well known to the antislavery publicists. In their journals they made such a fuss over this gallant libertarian atheist, with her Polish-Jewish background and her flamboyant and inciting manner, that any public appearance by Mrs. Rose was certain to excite attention. But her endorsement by the editors of *The Liberator* and *The National*

Anti-Slavery Standard was due primarily to her abolitionist beliefs and her championing of the cause of women's rights. Her position as a Jew in the antislavery movement gained the approbation of those who shared her views and aroused contempt for Jews in those who disagreed with the aims of antislavery. Mrs. Rose did not hesitate to identify herself as a Jew, but described herself as a secularist who had derived all the benefits of a religio-cultural heritage which she no longer upheld. Yet in the history of antislavery and abolition, she was the only person of Jewish origin whose activity was regularly reported by the press.

William Lloyd Garrison's warmth for Mrs. Rose was equaled by his frank hostility for another Jewish figure, Major Mordecai M. Noah. Noah was a dramatist, journalist, Tammany Hall sachem, and generally controversial character active in many Jewish affairs. Noah's differences with Garrison predate the entry of *The Liberator*'s editor into the antislavery movement. Their newspaper debates and political arguments were resumed by both men shortly after *The Liberator* was founded, and it is difficult to separate their personal disagreements from their public statements. Garrison's view, shared by many abolitionist and antislavery people, was that Jews should have been in the forefront of the struggle for liberation. The fact that Christian-dominated societies made such activity difficult was not even considered.

Noah's rebuttals were highly inflammatory and added fuel to the journalistic war. While Noah was quick to argue and to challenge any man on the subject of religious principles, he made certain that these exchanges were never injected into his views on slavery. His frequent pro-Southern statements drew forth angry answers from Garrison and Horace Greeley. Noah's bark was worse than his bite, but up to the time of his death in 1851, he was still engaged in political and journalistic duels that offended. antislavery people.

VI

From the European side of the Atlantic came strong and determined men who, in addition to articulating their views on slavery in the press, in the pulpit, and as spokesmen for the fledgling Republican party, participated in a number of diverse activities related to the conflict. In sharp contrast to the war of words in the North, the most controversial activity in the new West, attracting national attention, was the border warfare in 1856.

When John Brown went forth on his divine mission to keep Kansas free of slavery, three

Jews were among his followers. Their presence
in Kansas was coincidental; Brown's was deliberate. He had followed his sons to Kansas with
the object of crushing proslavery forces and
preventing them from dominating the politics of
the future state. His Kansas exploits brought him
out of obscurity and into national prominence
overnight. He was believed to be demented, but
his fanatical devotion to antislavery cannot be
dismissed on this account. His mission was further
motivated by an intense Christian zeal. Yet he
never attracted a nucleus of more than forty men,
some of them his sons. To this band were drawn
the youthful adventurer August Bondi, the "big
savage, bloodthirsty Austrian" Theodore Weiner,
and the seemingly inconspicuous Jacob Benjamin.

Weiner had gone to Kansas to deal in cattle
and manage a country store. When challenged
to a fight by one of the proslavery Sherman
brothers for no obvious reason, he beat off his
attacker with an ax handle. Thereafter Weiner,
who originally had been a proslavery man,
changed his views and joined Brown's militia.
Weiner's store became a proslavery target. The
Free State settlers of the area were given notice
by the "Border Ruffians" to leave in thirty days;
the Jews, Bondi, Weiner, and Benjamin, were
given a choice between leaving in three days
or being lynched.

In retaliation against the proslavery forces that sacked Lawrence, Kansas, in May 1856, Brown and his small company launched their bloody crusade near the Pottawatomie Creek. Without warning, John Brown and seven men, four of them his sons, invaded the area and literally hacked their opponents to pieces. Weiner was present at the massacre and was identified by Brown's son-in-law, Henry Thompson, as the man who murdered Dutch Bill Sherman, his earlier opponent.

It is not clear whether Weiner and Benjamin, both of whom left Kansas shortly after the raids, were involved with John Brown as a matter of self-defense or out of belief and conviction; in the case of Weiner, who never turned away from a fight, the motive may have been vengeance. Benjamin's ideas are not known. After the death of his wife, Kansas lost its allure and he moved to Saint Louis. August Bondi, not yet twenty-three, was by temperament a rolling stone, an adventurer swept into the mainstream of the western movement. Of the three, he alone remained in Kansas, became an antislavery propagandist, and later fought in the Union army. Bondi published an autobiography fifty years after these events took place, and it is difficult to separate his hindsight from his on-the-scene experiences.

To those who saw Brown's Kansas campaign as a step toward the abolition of slavery, Weiner,

Bondi, and Benjamin were heroes. They were the only Jews who came under the influence of the Christian whose demented state they could not have suspected and whose hatred for slavery was dictated by fanaticism. Although information about Brown's Jewish followers was known to few, at least one contemporary easterner looked upon Brown's Kansas exploits as still another Jewish plot, masterminded by the French Rothschilds!

Far from the border warfare, in the nation's capital, the issue of Kansas sovereignty was hotly debated. Henry M. Phillips, the second Jew to be elected to Congress from Pennsylvania, would have writhed had he known of John Brown's Jewish followers. He argued strongly for the admission of Kansas as a slave state. One of his speeches was widely circulated as representative of Northern opinion on the admission of the new state to the Union. Phillips was an active Democrat, a warm advocate of President James Buchanan, a close friend of former Vice-president George M. Dallas, and a volatile opponent of the young Republican party. In these activities he was joined by John Samuel, a brilliant lawyer who was widely known for his adherence to a strict interpretation of the Constitution. Both men belonged to that segment of socially prominent Philadelphians who were later associated with the Peace Democrats and the Copperhead philosophy. It was these men, insignificant as their number was, that Sabato Morais, the Italian-born humanitarian minister of Mikveh Israel, addressed from the city's oldest Jewish pulpit.

In 1856, five years after Morais arrived in Philadelphia, his sonorous voice could be heard denouncing the evils of American slavery. Morais appears to have been the first to discuss from a Jewish viewpoint the biblical provisions of slavery and their context in antiquity. His ability to relate the biblical view to the American system and point out the differences brought him to the forefront of the argument. His allegiance to the Republican party, which opposed the extension of slavery, was closely related to his condemnation of slavery as an inhuman institution. This view was also similar to the philosophy of the Garrisonians, who believed that opposition to the extension of slavery was not enough; it had to be abolished.

Morais was in the thick of the battle as a voluntary citizen, inspired by the social and ethical teachings of Judaism. But he did not seek membership in any of the antislavery societies to further his work, although during the Civil War he was active in a number of pro-Union organizations. His opposition to slavery, his Republican convictions, and his sermons found favor with most of his congregants and offended only an influential minority. The attitude of the Phillips-

Samuel clique with their Southern ties through marriage and business—at least one relative was known to have been an extensive slaveholder—was typical of that of many non-Jewish Philadelphians. Samuel was so strict a constitutionalist that he was still arguing the virtue of the Dred Scott decision when the Civil War was over. Eventually these differing social and political attitudes led to a sharp cleavage among many Philadelphians.

If Morais had opposition from Phillips and Samuel and their supporters, he gained uncommon strength from the support of other families. Abraham Hart, the publisher; Edward L. Mawson, a staunch Republican and a charter member of The Union League of Philadelphia; and members of the Hyneman, Lazarus, and Liverpool Cohen families were only a few who upheld Morais in his position. Perhaps the most contrasting example was Henry Samuel, a brother of John, who aligned himself with the antislavery movement, opposed his brother, and was a key figure in the organization of the United States Colored Troops, Pennsylvania's first black regiments.

The conflict over slavery, which agonized so many Protestant denominations, fragmenting them along sectional lines, did not affect Jews owing to the fact that the stands they took were along individual rather than denominational lines.

Jews were split on the subject of traditional observance and the introduction of religious reform; the issue of slavery, which also challenged the minds and hearts of Jews, did not disrupt their religious structure.

In spite of internal congregational differences, resentment toward Morais did not really increase until the national argument turned into open hostilities. Conflict within the congregation did not occur until the disaster of war had taken its human toll, after members of Mikveh Israel had perished at Andersonville Prison or died on the field of battle. By this time Morais's sermons were a regular feature in the pro-Union press of Philadelphia.

Meanwhile the sermon had been recognized by some as a patriotic vehicle. Antislavery preachers no longer confined themselves to the concept that slavery was a political matter, as some proslavery Protestants insisted; it had become a spiritual matter. The traditional mode of Jewish sermonizing, the two yearly sermons delivered on the occasion of special Sabbaths, had been transformed into a regular weekly sermon in English or, in some congregations, in German. In many instances, congregational permission to preach had to be obtained in advance. The subject of slavery was soon given maximum attention in the pulpit. Most of the rabbis were recent immigrants with diverse views on the practice of Judaism,

but the most articulate were inflexbily bound to
the spirit of universal justice.

In Baltimore, Morais's equal was David Einhorn, who went to that city a year before Peter
Still's narrative was published. In the border slave
state which was his first American home, Einhorn
declared his uncompromising opposition to slavery.
Although he offended many Jews by his interpretation of traditional Jewish religious practice,
his knowledge of the Bible and of rabbinic literature could not easily be contested. Nor was his
use of the Bible as a weapon against slavery
easily challenged. Unlike Morais he had not
mastered English, and his congregants were
German-speaking immigrants.

To spread his theological views and further
publicize his condemnation of slavery, Einhorn
established a monthly journal, *Die Sinai*, shortly
after he arrived in Baltimore. Unfortunately his
heavy German style and his theological arguments did not attract a wide circle of readers, and
Die Sinai had a limited appeal. It is not possible
to estimate how many of his congregants were
committed to antislavery principles. His antislavery appeals were as forceful as his appeals
for the revision of traditional Jewish practice,
and it is safe to assume that Einhorn influenced
many of his congregants.

The fact that *Die Sinai* attracted attention
among a non-Jewish reading public is evident

from the columns of the Republican Baltimore
Wecker. In the restless proslavery environment,
Einhorn found an ally in the editor of that paper,
who shared his views and always spoke of him
with respect. This was not the case in most other
cities with predominantly German populations,
where newspaper editors were liberal on the subject of antislavery but, at the same time, were
anti-Semites.

Morais the traditionalist and Einhorn the
reformer were able scholars who shared a common
hatred of slavery. Their failure to unite the voice
of the rabbinate in a common cause was due to
the fact that, for a variety of reasons, Jews were
at that time unable to unite denominationally on
any subject. Reformers challenged traditionalists
and treated one another with scorn. Jewish
sectionalism, between East and West, hindered
attempts at unity. Immigrants of the antebellum
period were only gradually being admitted to the
circle of older families, and many were struggling
to obtain an economic foothold. These internal
divisions in Jewish life, which were national in
scope, militated against any possible united effort
to oppose slavery as a group. Morais, Einhorn,
Bernhard Felsenthal of Chicago, and a few
others maintained the theme of independent
action that had characterized Jewish conduct
since the antislavery petition of Philadelphia
Jewry in 1838.

A strong response was evoked only when Rabbi Morris J. Raphall of New York rose to the pulpit to preach on the National Fast Day on January 4, 1861, and defended slavery as sanctioned by Jewish biblical thought. Yet the negative reactions which this sermon provoked were still in the form of voluntary and independent expressions.

There exists neither a bibliographical record nor an exegetical examination of the many hundreds of sermons coming from Protestant pulpits that used the same biblical defense of slavery which Raphall expounded. Were such a study available it would show that the logic of many preachers was on a plane equal to that of Raphall's literal theology. The artifices used by Raphall to show that slavery came about through divine decree are found in the sermons of others. Up to this time only one biblical argument supporting slavery, C. Blancher Thompson's book *The Nachash* . . . , had received a Jewish endorsement—from Rabbi James Gutheim of New Orleans. In spite of its pretentious recourse to the Hebrew text to prove that Negro slavery was established by divine authority, the book's dull and repetitive arguments attracted little attention outside of Saint Louis, where it was published in 1860.

When a Jew recognized by his contemporaries as a historian, critic, and lecturer on biblical literature used similar sources and identical arguments to uphold slavery, it attracted wide attention. In New York City, where the sermon was delivered, the *Herald* considered it important enough for front-page publication. One of the claims made by Raphall was that the Pentateuch did not present slaveholding as sinful and that not a line could be found in the Scriptures to controvert his view. Even his apologetic statement expressing disagreement with American slavery was unconvincing.

Negative reaction to Raphall's sermon was immediate, "from newspaper paragraphs of a few lines up to elaborate articles of many columns." One of the "elaborate articles" was the first major Jewish refutation, which came from the layman Michael Heilprin, the scholar and editor of Appleton's *New American Cyclopedia*. It was published in Horace Greeley's *Tribune* on January 16, 1861, almost two weeks after Raphall's sermon was delivered. Greeley, who had a ready pen to denounce Major Noah for any intimation of proslavery thought, called attention to Heilprin as a "learned Jew of this city, who, in historical, philological, and biblical knowledge has few living equals. . . ." Heilprin's reply, one of force and depth, condemned both Raphall and his sermon. He denounced Raphall's misinterpretation of the Bible and at the same

time engaged in biting and satirical comparisons
between the South and its proslavery proponents
in the North. Raphall's "proofs" were dashed to
pieces under the critical hammer blows of Heilprin.

Heilprin's letter was quickly followed by a
statement from David Einhorn. Written in
German, translated into English, and issued as a
pamphlet by three Jewish booksellers of New
York, it does not appear to have attracted the
kind of attention given to Heilprin's article in
the *Tribune*. Einhorn was not content with this
refutation, and early in February a fuller version
appeared in *Die Sinai*. Here the full range of his
anger was displayed in the eloquent German of
which he was a master. Einhorn cut deeply into
Raphall's statement that slavery existed in the
South through the sanction of Divine Providence.
To these two critics of Raphall, this was a denunciation of the spirit and practice of Judaism.

In the twenty-two pages which he devoted to
Raphall's sermon, Einhorn left no idea or
citation unexamined, either in biblical or rabbinic
sources. He disposed of one argument after
another in what became the lengthiest response
to Raphall that appeared in any of the Jewish
journals. Fortunately, the editor of the Baltimore *Wecker* discussed Einhorn's rebuttal extensively in three successive issues, taking it out of

its parochial confines and presenting it to a non-Jewish German reading public.

Throughout the North, the independent voice of the Jewish pulpit was heard denouncing Raphall and his proslavery exhibition. It was an occasion when the Jewish pulpit could have united in a common condemnation of slavery; but the opportunity was not grasped by the rabbis.

Meanwhile, two other sermons were delivered in Manchester, England, by Gustav Gottheil, who later became the rabbi of Temple Emanu-El in New York City. Perhaps without knowing of Heilprin's response or Einhorn's two retorts, Gottheil also attacked Raphall for stating that "slaveholding is no sin according to the Scriptures." Raphall's words were sacrilegious, a distortion of the spirit of Judaism and a debasement of Moses, a lowering of the great lawgiver to the level of an American slaveholder.

On the following Sabbath, Gottheil's second sermon (coinciding with the reading of the weekly portion of the Law containing the Ten Commandments) made it clear "that there never *existed* among the Hebrew people any social usage or institution bearing even the least resemblance to the slave system in America." To bring his views into the perspective of the nineteenth century, Gottheil drew upon the admonition of Exodus 21.16, "He who kidnaps a man—whether he has sold him or is still holding him—shall be put to death," and pointed to the role of Christians in establishing slavery in the Americas:

> How *came* a slave population to exist in the Republic? Have we not to answer it by saying that it was primarily by importation of slaves from Africa—men in the first instance torn from their homes and families, and shipped across the Atlantic? There is no need that I attempt describing to you the appalling horrors of the slave passage— these are familiar to every Englishman. Pity that the law of the Hebrew legislator had been forgotten or trampled underfoot by Christian nations professing to hold it as of divine authority! Had it been in force among them, the slave trade would have been put to an end with swift retributive justice. The first perpetrators of the abomination would have expiated their crime with the forfeiture of their lives.

Gottheil challenged the Fugitive Slave Law on the basis of Bible and Talmud, and described American slavery as an institution totally inconsistent with biblical teaching. He was deeply vexed by Raphall's notion that the Ten Commandments could serve as the justification of slavery. And finally he castigated Judah Touro, the New Orleans merchant and benefactor, as a slaveholder whose eyes were shut to the greatest of human evils. Of all the published sermons critical of Raphall, Gottheil's, delivered far from the scene of battle, came closest to relating the Bible to the true conditions of slavery. Yet it received little attention on the American side of the Atlantic. It is interesting to note that its publication was requested by the members of his congregation.

From Europe there also came "a work of sterling merit, of candor and simplicity" written by the rabbi of Copenhagen, Moses Mielziner. It was brought to the attention of *The American Theological Review*, a Christian journal, by the antislavery publicist Francis Lieber. There is no evidence to indicate that it was published to counteract Raphall's sermon. When the first installment appeared in April 1861, under the title *Slavery among the Ancient Hebrews from Biblical and Talmudical Sources*, it probably had more influence upon the Christian antislavery clergy than it did in offsetting whatever influence Raphall's sermon had among Jews. Mielziner's study was a strict historical interpretation and analysis of slavery in Jewish law, written without reference to American slavery.

Other Jewish voices were either weak, like that of Isaac Leeser, or refrained from any outright

condemnation of slavery, like that of Isaac M.
Wise, who resorted to abstract subterfuges about
the Canaanites and Ham. The controversy over
the biblical view of slavery continued throughout
the Civil War. The trite and wearisome defenses
of slavery as ordained by God erupted into a
fierce pamphlet war when Episcopal bishop John
Henry Hopkins of Vermont permitted his defense
of slavery to be used as political campaign literature in Pennsylvania in 1863. It immediately
drew down the wrath of the Episcopal Diocese.
One rebuttal came from the convert Rev. Louis
Newman, who argued the subject effectively on
Hebrew philological grounds; but his conclusions
were based on the theology of the New Testament.

Less than a year later, a movement was organized under the leadership of The Union League
club of Philadelphia to declare Christianity and
Judaism to be the enemies of slavery and disunion
—in fact and in deed. Toward this end, the
Episcopalians not only set aside their differences
with the Methodists, they invited the black rector
of a Philadelphia church to join them in the
common goal; Presbyterians united among themselves in the antislavery cause; and Protestants
invited Roman Catholics to join them in a
patriotic statement. Jews were invited to meet
religiously to denounce slavery—the first such
occasion of which we know. It is all the more

remarkable that this step in bringing together various denominations was taken by a secular institution.

The controversy over the biblical interpretation of slavery before and during the Civil War has not received sufficient examination. The ambivalence toward Jews displayed by the Protestant antislavery clergy remains undefined and requires careful scrutiny. Frequently a preacher would cite Genesis and Exodus to uphold an antislavery argument and in the following passage of a sermon, if not in the same breath, speak of Jews as "now a corrupt people and guilty of hypocrisy, deceit, and craftiness. . . ." The impact upon Jews of such contemptuous assertions is not fully known. That it may have contributed to bringing a latent anti-Semitism to the foreground during the Civil War years is a likelihood that ought not to be overlooked.

Jewish rights were secondary to the overwhelming issues of slavery; but it is difficult to separate the social responsibility of the Church toward slavery from the conscience of Christians toward Jews. The hundreds of Jews that were involved in the conflict, as Bernhard Felsenthal reported in 1862, are a credit to the determination of Jewish participants who refused to be held at a distance. That American antislavery literature eluded the czarist censor and reached Yiddish-speaking Jews in the interior of Russia is an intriguing fact that challenges investigation.

If the seemingly limited role of Jews in the antislavery movement is to be understood, the professional historian interested in the tragedy of American slavery must carefully examine the manner in which Christian attitudes toward Jews affected Jewish attitudes toward the antislavery conflict.

Notes and Sources

The pioneer investigation into this subject is represented by two articles in the *Publications of the American Jewish Historical Society*—No. 5 (New York, 1897), 137–155, and No. 9 (New York, 1901), 45–56, by Max J. Kohler, titled "Jews and the American Anti-Slavery Movement." Many references to Jews in relation to slavery and antislavery appear in the *Publications* cited. Most of them are merely documents and lack the interpretative quality necessary to understand the problems that confronted Jews.

Following World War II new attempts were made to present Jews as a people active in the antislavery struggle. The Marxist approach was taken by Philip S. Foner in *Jews in American History* (New York, 1945), 51–62, "Jews and the Anti-Slavery Movement." A more thoroughgoing historian, offering the same Marxist interpretations, is Morris U. Schappes, in his *A Documentary History of the Jews in the United States* (New York, 1952). Schappes introduced a tremendous amount of new material on various aspects of Jews in the struggle against slavery. Both Foner and Schappes will be referred to later. Samuel Sillen's *Women against Slavery*

(New York, 1955), 88–92, briefly recounts the activity of Ernestine Rose in Marxist parlance. The impact of Christianity and Jewish reaction escapes all these authors.

The rabbinical approach is discussed by Bertram W. Korn in his *American Jewry in the Civil War* (Philadelphia, 1951), 15–31, "The Rabbis and the Slavery Question," where the Jewish sermonic debate over slavery is presented. Recognition of the absence of rabbinical participation in the Christian slavery debate, and the fact that rabbinic reluctance to interpret the Pentateuch stemmed from bitter European memories that caused Jews to avoid biblical discussion with Christians—these matters are not discussed by Korn.

The numerous references to Jews in black writing throughout the nineteenth century have been ignored, and a brief essay would be required to enumerate them and establish their position. Some of the observations by Frederick Douglass, Martin R. Delany, and Alexander Crummell can be found in the collection prepared by Howard Brotz: *Negro Social and Political Thought, 1850–1920* (New York, 1966), 38, 41, 185–186, and 241–242; in Frank A. Rollin's *Life and Public Services of Martin R. Delany* (Boston, 1883), 33, 45–46, 334; and in *Minutes of the State Convention of the Coloured Citizens of Pennsylvania Convened at Harrisburg December*

13th and 14th, 1848 (Philadelphia, 1849),
18–19, on the disfranchisement of Jews and mis-
treatment of other American minorities. Many
of the convention proceedings contain various
references to the persecution of Jews. Hollis
Lynch, in his *Edward Wilmot Blyden: Pan-
Negro Patriot, 1832–1912* (London, 1967), 63–
64, discusses briefly the impact of Jewish experience, which is compared to the history of the
Negro. Blyden's Zionist views are of considerable
importance.

The study of Jewish stereotypes in American
literature prior to the Civil War is confined to
a few novels in Leslie A. Fiedler's *The Jew in
the American Novel* (New York, 1959), 5–8. A
thorough study of the period is not available. A
lengthier treatment by Sterling Brown, in *The
Negro in American Fiction* (Washington, D.C.,
1937), is useful for a comparative examination of
stereotypes.

Sermonic and theological literature concerned
with the theme of American slavery is still a
neglected aspect of study. It has been partially
examined from a Southern viewpoint by William
Sumner Jenkins, in *Pro-Slavery Thought in the
Old South* (Chapel Hill, 1935). For a present-
day treatment of the complex ambivalent Christian attitude, which includes Jewish biblical and
rabbinic sources, the excellent study by Winthrop
D. Jordan, *White over Black: American Atti-*

tudes toward the Negro, 1550–1812 (Chapel Hill, 1968), should not be overlooked.

The Christian-inspired and Christian-dominated zeal characteristic of the abolitionist and antislavery societies has not been examined. Phases of this aspect are recognized in such works as Hazel Catherine Wolf's *On Freedom's Altar: The Martyr Complex in the Abolitionist Movement* (Madison, 1952). With the single known exception of Louis Ruchames's "The Abolitionists and the Jews," *Publication of the American Jewish Historical Society*, vol. 42 (New York, 1952), 131–155, which is both a critical response to Korn's *American Jewry* and a defense of the humanitarian stand of the abolitionists, no attempt has been made to define the many positions taken by abolitionists toward Jews. It is obvious that Ruchames and Korn have not read the vast press of the abolitionist and antislavery movement. The views presented here only indicate the need for such a study. Non-Jewish scholars like Winthrop D. Jordan have critically considered the general role of Christianity, but Jews have not scrutinized Christian attitudes except in instances where overt anti-Semitism was present.

The picture of colonial and eighteenth-century Jewry in regard to slavery awaits piecing together. Jacob R. Marcus, in *Early American Jewry*, vol. 1 (Philadelphia, 1951), 126–127, discusses briefly the trade of Aaron Lopez, Jacob R. Rivera, and others. The Franks family and others of New York City are also discussed by Marcus, 64–65. In Daniel Horsmanden's *A Journal of the Proceedings in the Detection of the Conspiracy Formed by Some White People, in Connection with Negro and Other Slaves, for Burning the City of New York* . . . (New York, 1744), 32 ff., one of the West Indian Gomezes is said to have been involved. This important, well-known work has long been neglected by Jewish historians. Marcus's *American Jewry. Documents. Eighteenth Century* (Cincinnati, 1959) contains a good number of interesting documents. These await further analysis. References to the Gratzes, David Franks, and others are in *The History of the Jews of Philadelphia from Colonial Times to the Age of Jackson*, by Edwin Wolf, 2nd, and Maxwell Whiteman (Philadelphia, 1957), 47, 168, 190–192, *et seq.*

Morris U. Schappes, in his *Documentary History*, indicates that Francis Salvador was the "owner of a plantation of 7,000 acres and many slaves" in South Carolina. Manumission writs from Jews are extensive and are more indicative of an attitude than any other documentary source. These are found in the documentary histories cited above. Marcus's *Early American Jewry*, vol. 2, is useful for its introduction of material on Jews and slavery in the South.

William Still, in *The Underground Rail Road* (Philadelphia, 1872), 711, describes the Jewish background of Robert Purvis: "His maternal grandmother was a Moor; and her father was an Israelite, named Baron Judah."

The slave narrative as biography and autobiography first received attention in *The Negro Author: His Development in America* (New York, 1931), by Vernon Loggins, 212–232. Charles H. Nichols, in *Many Thousands Gone: The Ex-Slaves' Account of Their Bondage and Freedom* (Leiden, 1963), 74, 76, 129 f., and 133, mentions Peter Still but does not take into account the Friedmans. Much of the dramatic horror in the narratives is not conveyed in this work, which treats some eighty-odd narratives.

Details of the Still narrative are drawn from three sources: the narrative itself, William Still's letter to *The Pennsylvania Freeman*, August 22, 1850, and William Still's *The Underground Rail Road*, 23–38. The manner in which slaves sold the crops they were allowed to produce, and how they were cheated, is recounted by Vina Still and is in part corroborated by Frederick Law Olmsted, in *A Journey in the Seaboard Slave States in the Years 1853–54* . . . vol. 2 (New York, 1904), 68. The conditions which he describes prevailed in South Carolina as well as in Alabama. However, he makes no comment on the ruthless designs to rob slaves of their meager crops.

Olmsted's *Journey in the Seaboard Slave States,* 70, is also the source for the stories about illicit trade of Jews with slaves. In his book *A Journey through Texas . . .* (New York, 1860), 329, Jews are referred to as "Jew-Germans." George McDowell Stroud, in *A Sketch of the Laws Relating to Slavery . . . ,* second edition (Philadelphia, 1856), 7, note, questions the accuracy of Olmsted's observations. But on the basis of Olmsted's comments, J. C. Furnas, in *Goodbye to Uncle Tom* (New York, 1956), 108, makes the following statement: "Some investigators trace the American Negro's sporadic anti-Semitism to slaves' experience with petty Jewish traders." Who the investigators were and how this was transmitted over generations is nowhere indicated by Furnas. Nor is such a view found in the discerning writings of contemporary black sociologists.

Leeser's reaction to Jews engaged in trade with slaves appeared in *The Occident,* November 8, 1860, where he cautioned that "we must warn all our brothers residing in the Southern states against making themselves obnoxious by violating the ordinances against dealing with the bondman of that part of the republic." Jews were ordered to leave because, according to Leeser, "they offended the public sense of propriety." Should this be interpreted as meaning that they offended the slaveholder? It mattered not to Leeser, the foremost Jewish journalist of his age, whether the charges were "founded or unfounded. . . . There is no need of becoming martyrs to political notions. . . ." If it occurred to Leeser that Jewish tradesmen were providing slaves with items they could not otherwise obtain, he did not mention it. Korn, in *American Jewry*, 24, does not recognize the deeper implication of this order.

C. Vann Woodward, in *The Burden of Southern History* (New York, 1960), provides a description of the South's extreme attitude to critics, opponents, and those suspected of holding views contrary to slavery, among whom were "ten peddlers [who] were driven out of the village of Abbeville, Mississippi." Rev. Isaac W. K. Handy, in his sermon on the National Fast Day, *Our National Sins: A Sermon Delivered in the First Presbyterian Church, Portsmouth, Va. . . . January 4, 1861* (Portsmouth, Va., 1861), 14, presents the typical concept of the roving Yankee peddler: "Even the shrewd, jogging pedlar, from 'the land of wooden nutmegs,' was not respected less because he knew how to make a bargain, but was often anxiously looked for, by many a rural housewife, who had carefully laid by her 'chores and fixings,' for the day of his coming." It has frequently been pointed out that the peddler, both Yankee and Jew, was the bearer of news from city to town and village, but that he may have carried abolitionist literature in his pack has not been mentioned.

For the Gist-Gratz and Clay family connections and descendants in Lexington, see William Vincent Byars, *B. and M. Gratz, Merchants in Philadelphia* . . . (Jefferson City, Mo. 1916), 267.

The religious and commercial activity of the Friedmans is noted by Maxwell Whiteman, in "The Kidnapped and the Ransomed," *American Jewish Archives*, April 1957, 31—an excerpt in which only the relevant Jewish aspect was reprinted. See also *Narrative of the Life and Adventures of Henry Bibb*, an autobiography (Philadelphia, 1969), 60–62, a reprint with an introduction by Maxwell Whiteman. Dr. James J. G. Bias, who had directed Peter to the Anti-Slavery Office, was active in the Negro convention movement; see *Minutes of the State Convention*, where his name appears throughout the proceedings. See also *The Pennsylvania Freeman*, August 22, 1850.

William Still, in *The Underground Rail Road*, 23–38, presents a sketch of the life and activity of Seth Concklin, including the material that Furness was unable to use in the appendix. Still says of his brother that by extreme economy and by doing overwork, he saved up five hundred dollars, the amount of money required for his ransom, which "with his freedom he, from necessity, placed unreservedly in the confidential keeping of a Jew, named Joseph Friedman, whom he had known for a long time and could venture to trust. . . ."

For the early Jewish associations of May, see *Memoir of Samuel Joseph May* (Boston, 1873), 15–17 and 205–206; for his fuller activity, see his *Some Recollections of the Anti-Slavery Conflict* (Boston, 1869).

The biographical account of Furness by Elizabeth M. Geffen, "William Henry Furness, Philadelphia Antislavery Preacher," in *Pennsylvania Magazine of History and Biography,* vol. 82 (Philadelphia, 1958), 259–292, is an excellent source; Miss Geffen's *Philadelphia Unitarianism, 1796–1861* (Philadelphia, 1961), 176, presents Furness's views and his relationship to Jews. The Still narrative is not mentioned in either of these sources. David Philipson, in *Letters of Rebecca Gratz* (Philadelphia, 1929), 131 f., refers to Furness, but otherwise this is an incomplete version of the Gratz correspondence.

Notice was first taken of *The Kidnapped and the Ransomed* in *The Liberator,* June 13, 1856; publisher's advertisements appeared in the issues of September 12 and October 17, 1856, *et seq.* The review in *The National Anti-Slavery Stand-*

ard, July 5, 1856, appeared under the heading
RECOLLECTIONS OF PETER STILL. It is taken from
The Syracuse Journal and is signed "Quincy,"
who is otherwise unidentified. (Samuel J. May
was living in Syracuse at this time.)

During 1856, antislavery literature reached
its peak, with the appearance of some of the following books: *Anthony Burns* by Charles Emory
Stevens; *My Bondage and My Freedom* by Frederick Douglass; and *Archy Moore, The White
Slave* by Richard Hildreth. The publisher's cata-
log of antislavery literature, following the appendix to Still's narrative, is indicative of the
tremendous interest in this literature.

In the 1941 reprint of *The Kidnapped and
the Ransomed,* the editor's note was prepared by
Angelo Herndon and the introduction by Lawrence D. Reddick. Reddick used the occasion to
compare Jews, "hunted and haunted" in their
efforts to flee Nazi Germany, to fugitive slaves.
In his introduction, written about two months
before America's entry into World War II, Reddick anticipated by almost three decades the
reprinting of other outstanding slave narratives.
With the belated discovery by white trade publishers of a market in black literature, Reddick's
perceptive insights into the crucial year 1941
came to be recognized retrospectively. The present edition contains May's introduction and Fur-

ness's appendix and includes the publisher's list of antislavery literature, none of which is in the 1941 reprint.

There were four Jewish congregations in Philadelphia in 1850: Mikveh Israel, founded in 1740; Rodeph Shalom, founded in 1795; Beth Israel, founded in 1839; and Keneseth Israel, founded in 1847. The two latter congregations, each observing a different ritual and seeking an intraethnic identity, seceded from the first two congregations.

The Pennsylvania Society for Promoting the Abolition of Slavery, while it came under multiple religious influences, had a secular base.

The first investigation of Jewish antislavery and abolitionist activity in the eighteenth century appeared in *The History of the Jews of Philadelphia,* by Wolf and Whiteman, 190–192 and 436–437, based on the Pennsylvania Abolition Society's Manumission Books in the Historical Society of Pennsylvania. For Benjamin Nones and Cyrus Bustil (Bustill), see Wolf and Whiteman's book, 209. Descendants of Bustil are represented today by the Griffin, Mossel, and Tanner families of Philadelphia; see "The Bustill Family," by Anna Bustill Smith, in *Journal of Negro History,* vol. 10 (Washington, 1926), 638–647, and vol. 11 (Washington, 1927), 82–

87. Moses Judah's abolitionist record is in Morris U. Schappes's *Documentary History*, 118–121 and 596–597. Schappes was obviously unaware that Jews "participated in an organized manner" in the Pennsylvania Society. C. L. R. James, in *The Black Jacobins* (New York, 1963), 16, compares Jewish conversionist activity with that of Christians.

The incident at Saint George's Methodist Episcopal Church is recounted by Richard Allen in *The Life, Experiences, and Gospel Labours of Richard Allen* (Philadelphia, 1833), 13, but it is not found in most standard white Methodist histories and encyclopedias.

Rachel Marks is listed in *Heads of Families at the First Census of the United States Taken in the Year 1790. Pennsylvania* (Washington, 1908), 243. She died in 1823, according to the death records of Congregation Mikveh Israel. (She is not to be confused with another woman of the same name who died in New York City in 1797. Only the latter is noted by Malcolm Stern in *Americans of Jewish Descent* [Cincinnati, 1960], 132.) The provisions of the various constitutions of Congregation Mikveh Israel are summarized in Wolf and Whiteman's book, *The History of the Jews of Philadelphia*, 229 f. Compare with *By-Laws for the Government of* קהל קדוש נדחי ישראל [*Kahal Kadosh Nidḥe*

Israel] *Which Were Finally Passed and Unanimously Agreed to, at a Meeting of the Vestry* . . . (Barbados, 1821), 20–21.

Henry S. Morais, in *The Jews of Philadelphia* (Philadelphia, 1894), 203, describes the Gratz burial incident as a "mere speck from the collection of anecdotes surrounding" the cemetery. He had examined the records of the congregation and knew better, as the following documents reveal. Rebecca Gratz wrote to Lewis Allen, president of Mikveh Israel, on May 31, 1841, stating that Mary Gratz "has been brought up strictly, and is in faith and practice a pious conforming Jewess." Lewis Allen, in his reply to her of the same date, wrote "that a Daughter not born of Jewish parents . . . [is] not allowed the Privileges or rights of our Burial Ground." Rebecca Gratz responded: "If Mr. Allen will consult the register of the Congregation he will find that a person 'not born of Jewish parents' but a Negro servant in a Jewish family living a religious life was allowed the privilege of burial in our ground." Her reference to the register and the use of the word "privilege" lead one to dismiss Morais's statement, which aimed at respectability.

In all, Rebecca Gratz and Lewis Allen exchanged four letters during the course of the day, between the hours of 9 A.M. and 6 P.M. Lewis Allen dismissed the precedents cited by Miss Gratz and relied upon the final justice of "Providence."

Mary Gratz died at 7 P.M.; one hour later the Board convened and resolved that she had failed to meet the requirements of Jewish law and could not be interred in the burial ground. Rebecca Gratz's appeal, based on "humane" needs, failed. Although the death of Lucy Marks appears in the congregational register, as Rebecca Gratz noted, Rev. L. H. Elmaleh and J. Bunford Samuel, in *The Jewish Cemetery, Ninth and Spruce Streets, Philadelphia* (Philadelphia, 1906) and in an untitled supplement published during the same year, make no note of it.

A notice of the antislavery memorial appeared in *The Philadelphia Gazette* on January 30, 1838; the *Journal of the Senate of the United States of America . . . Second Session of the Twenty-fifth Congress . . .* (Washington, 1837), 185 (January 29, 1838), reads: "Mr. Buchanan presented a memorial of a number of youth of the City and County of Philadelphia, praying the abolition of slavery and the slave trade in the District of Columbia and Territories of the United States." Unlike the newspaper account, the Senate document does not state that the memorialists were Jews. *The National Enquirer*, on January 18, 1838, reported that within one week, memorials from Pennsylvania "representing 4,737 members, were presented to Senator S. M'Kean for Congress on the subject of abolition of Slavery. . . ." *The Enquirer*, edited by

Benjamin Lundy, was published by the Anti-Slavery Society of Pennsylvania.

Conversionist activity directed toward Jews had increased tremendously between 1820 and 1840, coinciding with the rise of the various Jewish mutual aid and philanthropic societies. On the vast extent of missionary activity, no matter how unproductive, Nathaniel Willis's *Boston Recorder* for the twenties is a fruitful source; for subsequent decades, the publications of the American Society for Ameliorating the Condition of the Jews are equally important. For the conduct and attitude of May and Furness, see works on them cited above. George W. Julian, in *The Life of Joshua R. Giddings* (Chicago, 1892), 283 and 402, provides additional evidence of the changing religious views of abolitionists and antislavery Christians.

Lewis C. Levin's support of African colonization complemented his Know-Nothing, antiforeigner position. For the former, see *Report of the Naval Committee to the House of Representatives, August 1850, in Favor of the Establishment of a Line of Mail Steamships to the Western Coast of Africa* . . . (Washington, 1850), 3, where he is listed as one of the nine petitioners; for the latter, see John A. Forman's "Lewis Charles Levin, Portrait of an American Demogogue," in *American Jewish Archives*, October 1960, 150–194.

Garrison's views of Jews have not been assessed
and cannot be until the contents of *The Liberator*
and his personal papers have been searched carefully for references to Jews. He chastized Mordecai Manuel Noah and extolled Ernestine Rose
(see below). An interesting example of Christian
missionary work by a Jewish convert who did not
wish to become involved in antislavery is brought
out by antislavery editor Benjamin Lundy, who
criticized Joseph Wolff in *The United States
Gazette* of October 21, 1837, and *The National
Enquirer* for October 26, 1837.

Temperance and moral reform occupied much
of the attention of the antislavery press; moral
reform as a solution to American problems swept
the Philadelphia area in particular. Interesting
evidence of this is found in William Whipper's
*The Minutes and Proceedings of the First An-
nual Meeting of the American Moral Reform
Society* (Philadelphia, 1837). Whipper was a
Negro.

Discussion of the anti-Sabbath movement appears in *William Lloyd Garrison, 1805–1879.
The Story of His Life Told by His Children*,
vol. 3 (New York, 1889), 178, where the observation is also found that "the scripture was clear
against Puritanico-Judaic Sabbath." Two contemporary studies by a Quaker author, William
Logan Fisher, provide a good account of the
legal proscriptions of the time: *The History of*

the Institution of the Sabbath Day, Its Uses and Abuses; with Notices of the Puritans and the Quakers, the National and Other Sabbath Conventions, and of the Union between Church and State (Philadelphia, 1845) and *History of the Institution of the Sabbath Day, Being a Plea for Liberty of Conscience in Opposition to Sabbath Conventions* (Philadelphia, 1846).

No adequate study on the relation between Protestants and Jews is available to provide even a glimpse of those public expressions that went beyond Christian missionary work. Activity of the Episcopal Diocese in Philadelphia throughout the nineteenth century indicates more than a friendly façade toward Jews: see *Mikveh Israel and Christ Church, Friendship without Ecumenism,* by Maxwell Whiteman, an unpublished lecture delivered at the combined annual dinner of Christ Church and Mikveh Israel in Philadelphia in April 1967. To a lesser degree, evidence exists for Quakers and Presbyterians. Ruchames, in "The Abolitionists and the Jews," supplies only limited evidence to support his view that Christian antislavery leaders were also concerned with rights for Jews.

In *Frederick Law Olmsted, A Critic of the Old South* (Baltimore, 1924), xi, Broadus Mitchell describes Olmsted as one who calmly presented facts pertaining to slavery in the South. Garnering information from slaveholders, Olmsted wrote in *A Journey through Texas*, 329–331:

> There are a few Jew-Germans in Texas, and in Texas the Jews, as everywhere else, speculate in everything—in popular sympathies, prejudices, and bigotries, in politics, in slavery. Some of them own slaves, others sell them on commission, and others have captured and returned fugitives. Judging by several anecdotes I heard of them, they do not appear to have made as much of it as by most of their operations.

In the appendix to this book, 494, he cites Jacob De Cordova, a Texas land developer and a known Jew, in relation to the history of land titles to prove a positive point, but does not mention that De Cordova was a Jew. On pages 497–516, under the heading SCRAPS OF NEWSPAPER, dealing largely with published items on slaves and slavery, Olmsted does not introduce a mite of evidence to support the anecdotes that came from the mouths of Christian slaveholders.

Olmsted's journeys through the South were prompted by William Lloyd Garrison. If his *A Journey in the Seaboard Slave States* had not attained the popularity of *Uncle Tom's Cabin* and Helper's *Impending Crisis*—these three are probably the outstanding books on slavery that appeared in the decade before the war—then his anti-Semitic statements would not have to be taken seriously. But Olmsted's books did contribute to the shaping of American opinion, and his comments on Jews in the old South and in Texas cannot be dismissed as "tall tales." Mitchell, in his book on Olmsted, 105, note, appraises his attitude as follows: "Though a man of strong dislikes, Olmsted had a few unreasoning prejudices to counterbalance his catholic sympathy. That against Jews was one of them."

For Samuel Myers of Norfolk (1790–1829), see *Letter Book of the Pennsylvania Society for Promoting the Abolition of Slavery*, vol. 10, 1827–1838, for a letter from Washington on October 31, 1828, in which he was appointed a delegate of the Washington Abolition Society. See the subsequent volume, 1847–1916, a letter of December 30, 1852, for another Jew, Frederick Kohn. For the information on Solomon Etting, see Wolf and Whiteman's *The History of the Jews of Philadelphia*, 192 and 437.

Records of the participation of Rebecca Hart are in the various annual reports of the Philadelphia Female Anti-Slavery Society (Philadelphia, 1859 to 1870). It is important to note that this society had a broad secular base despite its Quaker influence. On the Harmon Hendricks incident, see the letter of Jacob De Leon to Hendricks, from Charleston, S. C., of August 20, 1807, in the Hendricks Collection of the New York Historical Society.

The intriguing figure of Moses Aaron Dropsie awaits biographical study. Cyrus Adler's *Lectures, Papers, Addresses* (Philadelphia, 1933), 51, is thus far the most reliable, but Dropsie's political and antislavery commitments have only been skimmed. See *Chronicle of The Union League of Philadelphia* (Philadelphia, 1902), 481, for his membership admission. It is important to note that Dropsie was an early advocate of eliminating religious, national, and color bars.

Schappes, in *Documentary History*, 349–351, presents interesting documents on Jonathan Nathan's support of Republican principles and politics in 1856. Abram J. Dittenhoefer, in *How We Elected Lincoln . . .* (New York, 1916), 1, briefly summarizes his background: "Born in Charleston, South Carolina, of Democratic pro-slavery parents, I was brought in early youth to New York; and although imbued with the sentiments and antipathies of my Southern environment, I soon became known as a Southerner with Northern principles." Samuel I. Tobias was the first of his family to emigrate to the United States. He arrived in New York City after the War of 1812 (see *Tobias Letter Book* in the New York Historical Society). Lewis I. Cohen and

Samuel L. Cohen, manufacturers of playing cards at 184 William Street, New York City, were cousins of Henry Cohen, who came to Philadelphia from Liverpool in 1837 and entered the stationery business.

The Samuel family noted here is descended from David Samuel of London. Henry (1828–1893) and John Samuel (1829–1913) were brothers (see Stern, *Americans of Jewish Descent*, 188). Charles J. Cohen, in *Memoir of Rev. John Wiley Faires . . . Founder and Principal of The Classical Institute Philadelphia . . .* (Philadelphia, 1926), 697–698, presents brief sketches of the Samuel brothers. Bunford Samuel, a son of John and librarian at the former Ridgway Branch of The Library Company of Philadelphia, was the author of a much-neglected work, *Secession and Constitutional History* (New York, 1920).

Leeser, unquestionably the most prominent Jewish editor and publisher of the middle decades of the nineteenth century, has been widely referred to but no critical biography of this prolific author and editor is available. The absence of a clearly stated position toward slavery is attributed to his five formative years in Richmond in the 1820s. This view, suggested by Korn in *American Jewry*, 44, is interesting but doubtful. Abram J. Dittenhoefer rejected his proslavery upbringing; Samuel Myers of Virginia became an active abolitionist; and Septima Levy of Charleston, whose brothers fought for the Confederacy, "became a Union woman" when she married Major General Charles H. T. Collis (see Septima M. Collis's *A Woman's War Record* [New York, 1889], 1–2.) Leeser's argument against admitting into a Jewish journal material that was not of direct Jewish interest was maintained for the twenty-five years that he edited *The Occident* and was not limited to the subject of slavery. For his statement comparing Jewish disabilities with slavery and the Maryland law, see *The Occident* for April 1847, 56–57.

Robert Lyon looked upon slavery as a political issue but saw no reason why he should not write of it. He gives the impression of discountenancing slavery on account of its Christian proponents rather than of upholding proslavery ideology. This was typical of the editorial stand of most of the Jewish editors of English-language journals.

The German-language press and the German press for Jews during the nineteenth century has been ignored. The present introduction is the first attempt to utilize the sources relevant to slavery. For one of Loeb's antislavery comments and editorials, see *Morgenstern* for August 8, 1849; and January 22, May 7, 21, 28, 1851. The influence of Loeb (1812–1887) is noted by Ralph Wood in *The Pennsylvania Germans* (Princeton, 1942), 143 and 153. A factual obituary is in the Norristown, Pa., *Daily Register* for December 22, 1887.

Although the journalistic record of Lewis Naphtali Dembitz (1833–1907) is not comparable to that of Loeb, it is outstanding on its own account. His brief association with *Der Beobachter am Ohio* was first noted by John J. Weisert in "Lewis N. Dembitz and Onkel Tom's Hütte," in *The American German Review*, vol. 19 (Philadelphia, 1953), 7–8. His brother-in-law Adolphe Brandeis's interests are described in Alpheus Thomas Mason's *Brandeis, A Free Man's Life* (New York, 1946), 24. Dembitz appears in the *Publications Distribution* records for 1862–63 in the archives of The Union League of Philadelphia. The article on slavery is in *The Jewish Encyclopedia*, vol. 11 (New York, 1916), 403–407. Dembitz was one of the founders of the present-day Jewish Publication Society of America and one of its first American writers.

Some of the Jewish editors involved with the German press were C. Behrens, publisher of the San Francisco *Abend-Zeitung* in 1857; Julius Loewy, who in association with Leo Elsesser launched the San Francisco *Abend-Post* in 1858; Moritz Mayer (1815–188?), who published the *New Yorker Handelszeitung* in 1851 (see *Buch der Deutschen in Amerika* [Philadelphia, 1909], 495 and 574). G. M. Cohen, in December 1858, began the monthly publication *Der Israelitische Volksfreund*. It lasted about a year.

Isaac Mayer Wise's stature as a bilingual journalist awaits further investigation. See *The Israelite*, April 3, 1857, for an article on Negro Jews and Wise's recollections of Charleston; *The Israelite* of December 31, 1858, contains his comment on Mortara, Catholics, and Negroes. For Wise on Brownlow of Tennessee, see *The Israelite* for January 18, 1860, where Wise defends Jews against Brownlow; also see "Illiberality in the United States," in *The Israelite* of June 19, 1857. Bertram W. Korn, in "Isaac Mayer Wise on the Civil War," in *Eventful Years and Experiences* . . . (Cincinnati, 1954), 125–150, presents the most useful study on Wise during the war years. Although the items cited above are not included in Korn's evaluation, he arrives at the same conclusion, perhaps without intending to do so. Ruchames, in his refutation of Korn's analysis of Wise and abolitionists in "The Abolitionists and the Jews," appears to have missed the key point of Wise's attack—as did Korn—that officeholders had to declare themselves to be of the "Christian Religion" (see *The Israelite* for June 19, 1857). The naturalization restriction followed later.

The Thirteenth Annual Report of the American and Foreign Anti-Slavery Society, Presented at New York, May 11, 1853; with the Addresses and Resolutions (New York, 1853), 114–115, was just noted by Max J. Kohler, in *Publications of the American Jewish Historical Society*, vol. 5, 143–144. The document was republished by Schappes in *Documentary History*, 332–333, and again by Korn, in *American Jewry*, 15, with minor deletions. Each accepted the report uncritically. See also *An Address to the Anti-Slavery Christians of the United States* (New York, 1852). Dwight Lowell Dumond, in *A Bibliography of Antislavery in America* (Ann Arbor, 1961), 7, attributes almost all the reports to Lewis Tappan. See also Wolf's *On Freedom's Altar*, 8–10, 16–17, 61 ff.

Heine's reaction to slavery in the United States is in *William Lloyd Garrison*, vol. 1, 254. Eight lines of the letter, which was written from Helgoland under the date July 1, 1830, are quoted in German. It is evidently the same letter cited by H. B. Sachs in *Heine in America* (Philadelphia, 1916), 11–12 and 30–31. This letter does not appear in the most recent editions of Friedrich Hirth's *Heinrich Heine Briefe . . .* (Mainz und Berlin, 1965). See Thomas Wentworth Higginson's *Cheerful Yesterdays* (Boston, 1898), 80, 90, 120; other references to Jews appear on 289 and 314. Higginson's *Army Life in a Black Regiment* (Boston, 1869) is a classic on the military history of American Negroes.

Kohler was the first to note Crémieux's European antislavery position in "Jews in the Anti-

Slavery Movement," 53–56. It was briefly noted by Foner in *Jews in American History*, 51, but treated more extensively by S. Posener in *Adolphe Crémieux, A Biography* (Philadelphia, 1940), 58–59 and 106–107. None of these writers appears to have examined this source for his speech: *Proceedings of the General Anti-Slavery Convention, Called by the Committee of the British and Foreign Anti-Slavery Society, and Held in London, from Friday, June 12th to Tuesday, June 23rd, 1840* (London, 1841), 149 and 166–169; the editors comment on "a child of the house of Israel" who was as good an abolitionist as any Christian. *The Jewish Encyclopedia*, vol. 4 (New York, 1916), 347, reproduces his letter on the Emancipation Proclamation.

Ernestine Rose, the heroine of Marxist historians, has attracted less attention in other circles. In the works we have cited by Foner, Sillen, and Schappes, she is particularly glorified. Her reaction to the World Bible Convention and the biographical sketch which appeared in *The Liberator* on March 7 and May 16, 1856, are both useful and important. See also *William Lloyd Garrison*, vol. 3, 133, 297, and 385. Schappes, in *Documentary History*, 655–656, provides important biographical data on her women's suffrage activity.

Garrison's contest with Noah (1785–1851) is first noted in *The Liberator* for August 20, 1831.

Much has been written about Noah's Ararat scheme, in 1825, to settle Jews in the wilderness of Grand Island, but only one biography can be turned to in order to follow Noah's tumultuous career in journalism and his reactions to slavery: Isaac Goldberg's *Major Noah: American Jewish Pioneer* (Philadelphia, 1936) 86; 251–252; 264–268—a book that hardly satisfies the needs of the present-day investigator. There are also references to his pro-Southern leanings and Greeley's attack upon him. See *William Lloyd Garrison,* vol. 1, 53–55, for Noah's reaction to the Garrisonians' proposal for the "Dissolution of the Union" on account of slavery.

Legend, myth, and glory have been draped over the history of John Brown and the two great episodes of his career: the Kansas warfare and the Harpers Ferry raid. His Jewish associates in Kansas assume importance because he had so few followers. The sources used in this brief evaluation are Oswald Garrison Villard's *John Brown, 1800–1859. A Biography Fifty Years After* (Boston and New York, 1910); *Autobiography of August Bondi, 1833–1907* . . . (Galesburg, Ill., 1910); and C. Vann Woodward's "John Brown's Private War," in *The Burden of Southern History* (New York, 1960). Villard's book, 151–164 and 178–213, contains the most reliable documentation on Bondi, Weiner, and Benjamin.

Many of the relevant sections of Bondi's *Auto-biography* have been reprinted in such diverse studies as Jacob R. Marcus's *Memoirs of American Jews*, vol. 2, (Philadelphia, 1955), 165–213, and Schappes's *Documentary History*, 352–364 and 666–670. Although the latter work is carefully documented and suggests that Bondi's account "may not be fully accurate," the Marcus book looks upon Bondi's activity as "a real juicy slice of American life!" No attempt was made by either to scrutinize the relation between Brown and his Jewish associates. See *Details of an Unpaid Claim on France* . . . (Philadelphia, 1869), 4–5 (this appeared anonymously but was written by R. A. Parrish).

Henry Meyer Phillips (1811–1884) was an active Democrat, locally and nationally. He became a close political associate of George M. Dallas, a leader of the Democrats in Pennsylvania and Vice-president of the United States in 1844; see the *Dallas-Phillips Papers* in the Historical Society of Pennsylvania. Phillips was elected to the House of Representatives in the Thirty-fifth Congress, 1857–59; see Henry S. Morais's *The Jews of Philadelphia*, 402–404, and Henry M. Phillips's *Admission of Kansas. Speech of Hon. Henry M. Phillips of Pennsylvania, in the House of Representatives, March 9, 1858* (Washington, 1858). Perhaps the only biographical account of John Samuel (1829–1913) is in the Philadelphia *Legal Intelligencer* for September 5, 1913, written by Norris S. Barratt. Barratt was a staunch Republican, and his objective praise and respect for Samuel's association with Philadelphia Copperheads is all the more interesting. The Philadelphia Athenaeum holds the Samuel papers, which contain the following items of unusual interest: a letter from J. Paul Cobbett to Joseph L. Moss, Manchester, on March 31, 1864, expressing opposition to the slave trade (the Moss family and other relatives of the Samuel family were largely antislavery); a letter from Ellis Yarnall to John Samuel, no address given, on April 29, 1865, arguing Justice Taney's famous decision on the Dred Scott Case (Yarnall, a friend of the English Coleridge family, was the author of two books relating to them); a letter from James Buchanan to John Samuel, Zionesta, on November 5, 1865: "at the same time the nigger seems likely to be kicked by both parties, and is booked for slavery again with the inevitableness of fate. . . ."

Sabato Morais (1823–1897) was born in Leghorn, Italy. He came to Philadelphia from London and in 1850 succeeded Isaac Leeser in the pulpit of Mikveh Israel. His earliest identified sermon, "Some Remarks on the Institution of Slavery among the Hebrews," was delivered in 1856. It was a succinct review of biblical provisions in relation to slavery. Its only comment on the American system reads:

> But what shall we say of nations that boast of civilization and religious enlightenment, and yet until within a few years [with the abolition of the slave trade in 1808] sanctioned a nefarious slave traffic which subjected innocent creatures to indescribable evils? Indeed, when we read of the cruelty, the barbarity, the inhumanity practiced in the prosecution of that abominable trade, we doubt whether it is the history of men or that of tigers that we peruse. But such records do not stain the annals of the Jews.

Abraham Hart (1810–1885) was the president of Mikveh Israel from 1841 to 1876, with the exception of two years during the Civil War. He published a number of books of antislavery interest, supplied background slavery literature for the Cinque case, and was accused—along with his partner, Edward L. Carey—by Hinton Rowan Helper, in *Compendium of the Impending Crisis* (New York, 1860), 166–167, of expurgating the antislavery content of Longfellow's poems so that they could be distributed in the South. He was an early Republican and a member of The Union League; see *The Chronicle of The*

Union League, 490, for Hart's admission to The Union League on May 2, 1863. Edward L. Mawson (see the *Chronicle*, 502) was a charter member of The Union League and active in many of its affairs. For background on the Hyneman family, see Morais, *The Jews of Philadelphia*, 327–331.

The Lazarus family was directly related to Moses Aaron Dropsie. Aaron Lazarus was a Republican, a member of The Union League and served in the Twenty-eighth Regiment, Pennsylvania Volunteers. See *Address at the Funeral Service of Henry Cohen* . . . , June 23, 1879 (Philadelphia, 1879), 20, and Elinor Gleaves Cohen's *Family Facts and Fairy Tales* (Wynnewood, Pa., 1953), 84–90. Henry Samuel, brother of John, was involved in the organization of Negro regiments in the United States Army; see *Free Military School, for Applicants for Commands of Colored Troops* . . . (Philadelphia, 1863), outer wrapper, where Samuel is listed as one of a committee of sixty-nine for recruiting "colored soldiers." The manuscript scrapbook *Philadelphia Supervisory Committee* . . . , in the Historical Society of Pennsylvania, contains Thomas Webster's note of April 5, 1864, describing Samuel as "an ardent practical colleague." Webster was chairman of the committee; Henry Samuel, secretary.

A discussion of Morais's conflict with the board

of Mikveh Israel is in Korn's *American Jewry*, 38. The story of Morais's position, while basically correct, requires revision on a number of points. David Einhorn went to Baltimore in 1855, delivered his inaugural sermon on September 29, and founded *Die Sinai* in February 1856. Criteria for judging Einhorn's influence can be based on the support he received from his congregants. See Dieter Cunz's *The Maryland Germans* . . . (Princeton, 1948), 307.

Bernhard Felsenthal (1822–1908) emigrated to the United States in 1854 and settled in Chicago in 1858. A fuller study of his activity than any written so far is essential for the understanding of the antislavery work of Jews in this section of the Midwest.

Morris J. Raphall (1798–1868) of Stockholm, Sweden, lived and ministered in England for many years prior to coming, in 1849, to New York, where he was appointed rabbi of B'nai Jeshurun. Soon after, he toured many cities of the East, giving a series of lectures on "The Post-Biblical History of the Jews," the text of which was published in *The Saturday Evening Post* for November 9, 1850, *et seq*. The lectures were collected and published in two volumes under the title *Post-Biblical History of the Jews* (Philadelphia, 1855). The publishers Moss & Brother distributed antislavery literature from their Philadelphia book and stationery shop. Raphall's *Bible*

View of Slavery. A Discourse . . . (New York, 1861) was published by Rudd and Carleton, a recognized trade publisher.

Sermonic literature pertaining to slavery, dating from the early colonial period through the Civil War, is mentioned by innumerable writers. No study is known to have examined proslavery and antislavery thought as it was expressed from the pulpit. Its value would be considerable in determining the christological interpretation of the Pentateuch, and the totally unrelated system of American slavery, to the laws set down by the ancient Hebrews.

The curious work by C. Blancher Thompson, הנחש *The Nachash Origin of the Black and Mixed Races* (Saint Louis, 1860), 3–4, contains Rabbi James Gutheim's endorsement, which was forwarded through Samuel A. Cartwright, M. D., of New Orleans. The work is of bibliographical interest; one edition appeared with ten pages of front matter, under the title of *The Nachashlogian*, vol. 1, no. 1, (Saint Louis, August 1860). A subsequent edition eliminated the front matter. If Thompson escaped notice, Cartwright did not. His independent work as an ethnologist was criticized in *Die Sinai* for July 1861, 180–186, in "Die Herkunft der Neger." It is signed "H.," possibly Michael Heilprin. For the newspaper publication of Raphall's sermon, see the New York *Evening Express* of January 5, 1861, and

Schappes's *Documentary History*, where numerous other newspaper references are provided.

Michael Heilprin (1823–1888) came to the United States in 1856 and settled in Philadelphia. His antislavery interest is briefly noted by Morais in *The Jews of Philadelphia*, 323; a lengthier notice is in *The Jewish Exponent* for October 27, 1899. On the basis of the latter, Gustav Pollak, in *Michael Heilprin and His Sons* (New York, 1912), 169, writes more extensively of Heilprin. For the text of Heilprin's reply, see *The New York Daily Tribune* for January 16, 1861. Foner, in *Jews in American History*, 54, where he denounces proslavery hoodlums, writes of Heilprin as a Jew who "would not sit by and calmly watch a progressive cause disrupted by the paid agents of the reactionaries," and so "was only following in the footsteps of another great Jewish fighter for liberty." In applying recent Marxist parlance to Heilprin, Foner implies that proslavery people were agents of slave ideologists. No matter how wrong the disrupters were, the comparison between Rose and Heilprin makes no sense. Each was motivated by entirely different forces and circumstances. Rose lacked Heilprin's scholarship, and Heilprin did not share the secularist thought of Rose. Schappes, in *Documentary History*, 685, was the first to note the English edition of the Einhorn pamphlet: *The Rev. Dr. M. J. Raphall's Bible View of Slavery*

Reviewed by the Rev. D. Einhorn (New York, 1861). See *Die Sinai* for February 1861, 2–22: "Dr. Raphael's Rede über das Verhältniss der Bibel zum Sklavenkunde"; and March 1861, 45–50: "Noch ein Wort über Dr. Raphael's Prosklaverei Rede"; on 60–61, under the heading NACHRICHTEN, Einhorn publishes the reaction to Raphall's sermon by Jews in the New York press. Einhorn's responses were discussed in the Baltimore *Wecker* on February 5, 6, 7, 1861.

See Gustav Gottheil's *Moses versus Slavery: Being Two Discourses on the Slave Question* (Manchester, England, 1861), 18, 28. Gottheil's views on Judah Touro are completely at variance with those of Korn in *The Early Jews of New Orleans* (Waltham, Mass., 1969), 74–90.

See Moses Mielziner's "Slavery among the Ancient Hebrews" in *The American Theological Review*, vol. 3 (New York, 1861), 232–260 and 423–438. Lieber's comment appears on the first page of the article. *The Occident*, on January 24, 1861, contains Leeser's summary of "The National Day for Humiliation": "We preferred prayer over political speeches"; and he expressed his vexation over the dispute. He had not read Raphall's sermon and "could not sanction the tone of bitterness which pervades Mr. H.'s [Heilprin's] remarks." In the following issue, January 31, 1861, Leeser gave his views on the sermon and with the exception of minor points agreed with it, but thought it unwise to have preached it in the synagogue.

Isaac M. Wise briefly gave his opinion in *The Israelite* for January 18, 1860, but confined his statement to biblical views. The Bishop Hopkins controversy was extensive. Ronald Levy, in "Bishop Hopkins and the Dilemma of Slavery," *Pennsylvania Magazine of History and Biography*, vol. 91 (Philadelphia, 1967), 56–71, gives the background of the controversy. See the Philadelphia *American and Gazette* for October 6, 1863, *"Slavery and the Old Testament."* More than twenty-five pamphlets were issued in Philadelphia attacking Hopkins's views. See Louis C. Newman's *The Bible View of Slavery Reconsidered* . . . (Philadelphia, 1863), issued under the pseudonym "Biblicus"; and *Christianity versus Treason and Slavery. Religion Rebuking Sedition* (Philadelphia, 1864). Rev. J. R. Shanafelt's *The End to the Slavery Controversy* (Philadelphia, 1864), 2–3, contains an acrimonious view of Jews.

Die Sinai for July 1862, 158–163, reprinted Bernhard Felsenthal's article, which first appeared in the *Illinois Staats Zeitung*. He pointed to evidence that Jews in the South were caught in a system for which they had no sympathy and that hundreds of Jews living in the North supported the antislavery ideas of William Lloyd Garrison. He emphasized the important role of

Charles Bernays, editor of the *Anzeiger des Westens*, one of the finest German newspapers in America, and the antislavery Republican members of the Missouri legislature, Meyer Friede and Isidor Busch (Bush). Kohler, in *Publications of the American Jewish Historical Society*, vol. 9, 52, was the first to note these items.

Felsenthal's contemporary statement is quite different from that made by Bertram W. Korn in *American Reaction to the Mortara Case: 1858–1859* (Cincinnati, 1957), 109:

> The abolitionists were far more eager to give support to this Jewish cause [protest against the Mortara baptism], which involved the principle of freedom of conscience, than Jews were to give support to the abolitionist cause, which involved every kind of freedom. Only a handful of Jews were actively or publicly associated with the antislavery movement. . . .

Other evidence contained in this introduction does not support Korn's statement. For Friede and Busch, see also *Die Deborah*, February 15, 1861, *et seq.*

Yiddish antislavery literature is an open field for study. Isaac Meir Dick (1807?–1893) was a virtual contemporary of Harriet Beecher Stowe

(1811–1896). Dick was acquainted with *Uncle Tom's Cabin* and produced a Yiddish paraphrase of it entitled *Di Shklaveray*. Mendel Raffel's *Amerika, oder der ungliklikher don. Bilder ois dem sklavenlebn* . . . (Czernowitz, no date) is also a free translation of *Uncle Tom's Cabin* and was turned into a pamphlet to encourage emigration to the United States. Two copies of this rarity have been located in the United States: in the Library of Congress and in **YIVO**.

Acknowledgments

Without the magnificent resources of The Historical Society of Pennsylvania, The Library Company of Philadelphia, The Presbyterian Historical Society, and The Philadelphia Athenaeum, this introduction would not have taken on its present shape.

I am indebted to Clarence L. Holte of New York City for making available material from his collection of rare Afro-Americana, and to Charles Blockson of Upper Gwynedd, Pennsylvania, for listening patiently to my views on blacks and Jews, past and present.

The warm interest of Chaim Potok, editor of The Jewish Publication Society, in this neglected aspect of American history and the careful attention given to the manuscript by Kay Powell are deeply appreciated.

Facsimile Edition of

The
Kidnapped
and the
Ransomed

THE KIDNAPPED

AND

THE REDEEMED

N. ORR–Co. N.Y

THE KIDNAPPED

AND

THE RANSOMED.

BEING THE PERSONAL RECOLLECTIONS OF

PETER STILL AND HIS WIFE "VINA,"

AFTER FORTY YEARS OF SLAVERY.

BY

MRS. KATE E. R. PICKARD.

With an Introduction,
BY REV. SAMUEL J. MAY;

And an Appendix,
BY WILLIAM H. FURNESS, D.D.

SYRACUSE:
WILLIAM T. HAMILTON.

NEW YORK AND AUBURN:
MILLER, ORTON AND MULLIGAN.
1856.

E. O. JENKINS,

𝔓rinter and 𝔖tereotyper,

No. 26 FRANKFORT STREET.

To the Memory

OF

LEVIN STILL;

AND OF

ALL THE BRAVE-HEARTED MEN AND WOMEN,

WHO LIKE HIM HAVE FALLEN, EVEN WHILE LONGING TO BE FREE,

AND

WHO NOW LIE IN NAMELESS, UNKNOWN GRAVES,

The Victims of American Slavery,

THIS VOLUME

IS DEDICATED.

CONTENTS.

CHAPTER I.

THE KIDNAPPER.

CHAPTER II.

EARLY EXPERIENCE IN SLAVERY.

CHAPTER III.

MASTER NATTIE.

CHAPTER IV.

THE TOBACCO FACTORY.

CHAPTER V.

THE SEPARATION.

CHAPTER VI.

MASTER NATTIE'S DEATH.

CHAPTER VII.

THE JOURNEY TO ALABAMA.

CHAPTER VIII.

FIRST FOUR YEARS IN THE SOUTH.

CHAPTER IX.

LEVIN'S MARRIAGE.

CHAPTER XVI.

LEVIN'S DEATH.

CHAPTER XVII.

THE JAUNT TO FLORIDA.

CHAPTER XVIII.

A SLAVE-MOTHER'S GOOD BYE.

CHAPTER XIX.

THE MISTRESS' SECOND MARRIAGE.

CHAPTER XX.

THE PLANTATION "BROKEN UP."

CHAPTER XXI.

BABY-LIFE IN THE CABINS

CHAPTER XXII.

FACTS.

CHAPTER XXIII.

PETER'S YEAR AT McKIERNAN'S.

CHAPTER XXIV.

BURTON'S REIGN.

CHAPTER XXV.

FIRST FOUR YEARS IN TUSCUMBIA.

CHAPTER XXVI.

PETER HIRES HIS TIME.

CHAPTER XXVII.

PETER BUYS HIMSELF.

CHAPTER XXVIII.

JOURNEY TO PHILADELPHIA.

CHAPTER XXIX.

THE KIDNAPPED BOY RESTORED TO HIS MOTHER.

CHAPTER XXX.

PETER'S FAREWELL VISIT TO ALABAMA.

CHAPTER XXXI.

THE ESCAPE.

CHAPTER XXXII.

THE CAPTURE.

CHAPTER XXXIII.

PETER PLANS TO REDEEM HIS FAMILY.

CHAPTER XXXIV.

" HOW DID HE GET THE MONEY ?"

CHAPTER XXXV.

EXPERIENCE OF THE RETURNED FUGITIVES.

CHAPTER XXXVI.

" THEY TAKE GOOD CARE OF THEIR PROPERTY."

CHAPTER XXXVII.

THE RE-UNION.

INTRODUCTION.

WITHIN the last four years, many hundreds, probably thousands, of persons in our nominally free States,
have seen Peter Still, a neat, staid black man, going
from city to city, town to town, house to house, asking
assistance to enable him to purchase the freedom of his
wife and children. He has always been grateful for the
smallest favors, and never morose when utterly denied.
He has not obtruded himself or his story; but those
who have shown curiosity enough to make any inquiries, have been soon led to suspect that he was no
common man; that the events of his life had been
thrillingly interesting—some of them even more wonderful than we often meet with in works of fiction.
Kidnapped, in his early childhood, from the door-step

of his home in New Jersey; more than forty years a slave in Kentucky and Alabama; his unsuccessful appeal to the great Henry Clay; his liberation through the generosity of a Jew; his restoration to his mother by the guidance of the slightest threads of memory; the yearning of his heart for his loved ones; the heroic but disastrous attempt of Concklin to bring his wife and children to him—wherever these incidents of his life were detailed, they seldom failed to draw from the hand of the listener some contribution towards the exorbitant sum demanded for the liberation of his family.

Words of discouragement, even from his warmest friends, fell without weight on the heart of Peter Still. Arguments, sometimes urged against the propriety of paying, especially an exorbitant price, for liberty, were parried by him with a skill not to be acquired in "The Schools." His soul was intent upon a great purpose. He could not be withheld; he could not be turned aside. His perseverance, his patience, his exactness, his tact, everywhere attracted attention, and often commanded respect. In less than three years, his wife and children were restored to him; and, after a few weeks spent in seeing and being seen by friends and relatives, they all settled themselves in employ-

ments, by which they are earning comfortable liveli-
hoods, and laying the foundation of future independence.

It was thought, by most of those who had heard the
histories of Peter Still and Seth Concklin, that such
histories ought not to remain unwritten or unpublished.
It was believed that good narratives of both of these
remarkable men, would give to the people of the
Northern States some new illustrations of the horrors
of that "peculiar institution," which has well-nigh
subjugated to itself our entire Republic.

It so happened that a lady was at hand, singularly
qualified for the former and larger part of the task,
not only by her ability as a writer, but by her personal acquaintance with Peter Still, while he was in
bondage.   Mrs. Pickard had lived several years in the
very town, or neighborhood, where most of the events
transpired that would come into the narrative.   She
knew personally many of the individuals, who had
acted conspicuous parts in the tragedy she was called
upon to write.   Moreover, she had conceived a very
just appreciation of the character of this man and
woman, who, under the laws of our country, had been
subjected to all that domestic servitude can do to
imbrute human beings, and yet retained so much that

is distinctive of the best specimens of our race. She was therefore persuaded to undertake the work, which is now given to the public.

The writer of this narrative was a highly esteemed teacher in the Female Seminary of Tuscumbia, Alabama. There Peter Still was employed in several menial offices, and was subject to her observation every day for many months. She often admired his untiring diligence, his cheerful patience, his eagerness to get work rather than to avoid it, and his earnest gratefulness for the perquisites that were frequently bestowed upon him by the many, whom he served in various ways, and served so well. Little did she suspect what was the mainspring of the intense life that she witnessed in the poor slave-man, who seemed to her to have so little to live for. She did not know that (as he has since told her) he was "hungering and thirsting after liberty," which had been promised him by a compassionate Jew, who then owned him, for a sum that it seemed possible for him to accumulate. It was that hunger and thirst which filled "Uncle Peter" with all the graces, and brought him all the gifts, that he needed to attain the object of his heart's desire. He had long been known, and universally respected and loved, in the town where he lived. Everybody believed that what

Uncle Peter said was true; and that every duty imposed upon him would be faithfully discharged. But the amount of labor that he was then accustomed to perform had come to be a matter of frequent remark and admiration. Some attributed his severe toil to the requirements of his Jew master. They had yet to learn, that there is a harder driver than any Jewish or Christian slaveholder, even the man's own spirit, when the priceless boon of liberty is set before him, as an incitement to exertion.

We can promise the lovers of exciting adventure very much in the ensuing volume to gratify their taste; and all those who really desire to fathom the heights and depths of that Iniquity which is threatening the destruction of our Republic, may turn to these pages, in the assurance that they will find in them a great amount and variety of information, derived from the most authentic sources, and given with the strictest regard to truth.

In this narrative will also be found, incidentally, but very clearly given, intimations of many excellences that are latent, as well as lively sketches of some that are patent, in the negro variety of our race—indeed, all the qualities of our common, and of our uncommon humanity—persistence in the pursuit of a desired object; ingenuity in the device of plans for its attainment; self-possession and self-command that can long keep a cherished purpose unrevealed; a deep, instinctive faith in God; a patience under hardship and hope deferred, which never dies; and, withal, a joyousness which, like a life-preserver, bears one above the dark waves of unparalleled trouble

The latter and smaller portion of this volume—the Sketch of the Life of Seth Concklin—was written by a gentleman who has long held so high a place among American authors, that we shall not presume to give him our commendation. That Dr. Wm. H. Furness, of Philadelphia, deemed the merits of Seth Concklin to be such as to deserve a tribute from his pen, must be a sufficient assurance that the subject of this sketch had evinced traits of character, and done deeds, or endured trials, worthy of commemoration. Those who know that Dr. Furness never touches anything that he does not adorn, will go to the perusal of his portion of this book, in the confident expectation of being delighted with the unaffected beauty of the sketch, and of having their sympathies and better feelings made to flow in unison with those of the true-hearted author. They will close the volume with gratitude to Dr. F., for having rescued from oblivion, and placed before his countrymen, another well-authenticated example of successful conflict with appalling difficulties in early life; of unwavering fidelity to right principles, in the midst of great temptations; and of heroic, disinterested self-sacrifice in the cause of suffering humanity.

SAMUEL J. MAY.

SYRACUSE, Feb. 14, 1856.

KIDNAPPED AND THE RANSOMED.

CHAPTER I.

THE KIDNAPPER.

LATE in the afternoon of a pleasant summer day, two little boys were playing before the door of their mother's cottage. They were apparently about six or eight years old, and though their faces 'wore a dusky hue, their hearts were gay, and their laugh rang out clear and free.

Their dress was coarse, and in no wise restrained the motions of their agile limbs, for it consisted merely of a cotton shirt, reaching no lower than the knee.

How they ran races down the road, and turned summersets on the green grass! How their eyes danced with merriment, and their white teeth glistened in the pleasant light!

But as the day wore on they grew weary, and with childhood's first impulse, sought their mother. She was not in the house. All there was still and lonely. In one corner stood her bed, covered with a clean blanket, and the baby's cradle was empty by its side. Grandmother's bed, in another corner of the room, was made up nicely, and every article of the simple furniture was in its accustomed place. Where could they all have gone?

"I reckon," said Levin, "mammy's gone to church.

The preachin' must be mighty long! O! I's so hongry! I's gwine to meetin' to see if she's thar."

The "church" stood in the woods, about a mile off. It was an old white building that had formerly been occupied by the family of S. G., who now lived in a large brick house close by. The boys had often been at the church with their father, who kept the key of the building, and opened it for worship on Sundays, and prayer-meeting nights.

"You better not go thar, I reckon," replied Peter, the younger of the two boys, "Mammy 'll whip you well if you goes to foller her to meetin', and all about."

"Mammy! O Mammy!"

Thus they called their mother, and cried because she did not answer, till their eyes were swollen, and their pleasant play forgotten.

Soon the sound of wheels diverted them for a moment from their childish grief, and looking up the road, they saw a handsome gig approaching. Its only occupant was a tall dark man, with black and glossy hair, which fell heavily below his white hat.

He looked earnestly at the little boys as he approached, and marking their evident distress, he checked his horse, and kindly asked the cause of their sorrow.

"Oh! Mammy's done gone off, and there's nobody to give us our supper, and we're so hongry."

"Where is your mother?"

"Don't know, sir," replied Levin, "but I reckon she's gone to church."

"Well, don't you want to ride? Jump up here with me, and I'll take you to your mother. I'm just going to church. Come! quick! What! no clothes but a shirt? Go in and get a blanket. It will be night soon, and you will be cold."

Away they both ran for a blanket. Levin seized one from his mother's bed, and in his haste pushed the door against his brother, who was robbing his grandmother's couch of its covering.

The blanket was large, and little Peter, crying all the while, was repeatedly tripped by its falling under his feet while he was running to the gig.

The stranger lifted them up, and placing them between his feet, covered them carefully with the blankets, that they might not be cold. He spoke kindly to them, meanwhile, still assuring them that he would soon take them to their mother.

Away they went very swiftly, rejoicing in their childish hearts to think how their mother would wonder when she should see them coming.

After riding for some time,—how long they could not guess—they suddenly upset in the water with a great splash. The strange man had, in his haste, driven too near the bank of the river, and the slight vehicle had thus been overturned. He soon rescued the children from the water. They were much frightened, but nothing was injured by the accident, and in a few minutes they were once more covered with the blankets, and flying along the river bank faster even than before.

When the gig stopped again, the sun was just setting. They were at the water side, and before them lay many boats, and vessels of different kinds. They had never seen anything like these before, but they had short time to gratify their childish curiosity; for they were hurried on board a boat, which left the shore immediately.

With the assurance that they should now find their mother, they trusted implicitly in their new-made friend; who strengthened their confidence in himself by gentle words and timely gifts. Cakes of marvellous sweetness were ever ready for them, if they grew impatient of the length of the journey; and their childish hearts could know no distrust of one whose words and acts were kind.

How long they were on the boat they did not know; nor by what other means they travelled could they afterwards remember, until they reached Versailles, Kentucky. Here their self-constituted guardian, whom they now heard addressed as Kincaid, placed them in a wagon with a colored woman and her child, and conveyed them to Lexington.

This was the first town they had ever seen, and as they were conducted up Main street, they were filled with wonder and admiration.

Kincaid took them to a plain brick house where dwelt one John Fisher, a mason by trade, and proprietor of a large brick yard.

After some conversation between the gentlemen, which of course the children did not understand, they were taken out to the kitchen, and presented to Aunt Betty, the cook.

"There, my boys," said Kincaid, "there is your mother—we've found her at last." ·

"No! no!" they shrieked, "that's not our mother! O, please, sir! take us back!" With tears and cries they clung to him who had abused their guileless trust, and begged him not to leave them there.

This scene was soon ended by John Fisher himself, who, with a hearty blow on each cheek, bade them "hush!" "You belong to me now, you little rascals, and I'll have no more of this. There's Aunt Betty, she's your mammy now; and if you behave yourselves, she'll be good to you."

Kincaid soon departed, and they never saw him again. They learned, however, from a white apprentice, who lived in the house, that he received from Mr. Fisher one hundred and fifty-five dollars for Levin, and one hundred and fifty for Peter.

Poor children! what a heavy cloud now shadowed their young lives!

For the first few weeks they talked constantly of going back to their mother—except when their master was near. They soon learned that they must not mention the subject in his presence.

He was, in the main, a kind, indulgent man—but were they not his money? Why should he allow them to prate about being stolen, when he had bought them, and paid a right good price?

"Father," said John Fisher, junior, "isn't Philadelphia in a free State?"

"Certainly—it is in Pennsylvania."

"Well, then, I reckon those two boys you bought *were* stolen, for they lived with their mother near the Delaware river; and Aunt Betty says that is at Philadelphia. It was too bad, father, for that man to steal them and sell them here, where they can never hear from their mother!"

"Pooh, boy! don't talk like a fool! Most likely they were sold to Kincaid, and he told them he would take them to their mother, in order to get them away without any fuss. And even if he did steal them—so were all the negroes stolen at first. I bought these boys, and paid for them, and I'll stop their talk about being free, or I'll break their black necks. A pretty tale that, to go about the country—just to spoil the sale if I should happen to wish to get shut of them! Free, indeed! And what is a free nigger? They're better off here than if they were free, growing up in idleness, and with nobody to take care of them."

Before night the young offenders were thoroughly kicked and beaten, and received the assurance that they should be killed outright if they dared to tell such a tale again. So they grew cautious; and spoke those sweet memories of home and mother only in whispers to each other, or to some fellow-slave that knew how to sympathize with their sorrows.

CHAPTER II.

EARLY EXPERIENCE IN SLAVERY.

THE long, hard lesson of slavery was now fairly open before our young students. In vain they shrank from its dreadful details. In vain they appealed for pity to their hard-handed master. Page after page of dark experiences shadowed their boyish eyes, and their young hearts, so merry hitherto, grew sad and anxious.

The necessity of concealing the true feelings is among the rudiments of slavery's lore. A servant should be merry. A gloomy face is a perpetual complaint, and why should it be tolerated?

To this necessity the temperament of the African is most happily suited. Cheerful and warm-hearted, with an innate love of light and harmony, the slightest sympathy awakens his affection, and the faintest dawn of happiness provokes a smile.

Levin and Peter were not long in divining, with the tact of childhood, their exact position, domestic and social.

Their master was a large, fine looking man, with a free, hearty manner, and much real kindliness of disposition. He never allowed this latter quality, however, to interfere in business matters; and as, in addition to the business of brickmaking, he rented a large plantation about a mile out of town, he had no time to waste in unprofitable sentimentalities. How to get

the most work done with the least expense he regarded
as a problem worthy of his attention, and his success
in business proved that he considered it well.

Mrs. Fisher was a stout, freckle-faced lady, plain
and unpretending in her dress and manner, and perfectly devoted to her husband and children. She had,
at the time of which we speak, two boys, John and
Sydney; and for the first three years that he lived
with them, Peter was their constant playmate. Levin
was sent to the brick-yard the second year after Fisher
purchased them, he being at that time only nine years
old.

At night the little slave boys rolled themselves up
in their blankets, and slept on the floor in their mistress' room. They often waked in the morning under
the bed, or the bureau, where Mrs. Fisher had shoved
them with her foot, the night previous—that they
might be out of the way. They were comfortably
clothed, well fed, and—if they said nothing of their
mother's house on the Delaware river—kindly treated.
But if a word on that forbidden subject reached their
master's ear, he became a monster. By stripes and
kicks he taught them that they had no right to that
blessed memory, that they were his property, and that
he possessed the power to quiet their restless tongues.

The plantation which was rented by Mr. Fisher belonged to Mrs. Russell, a widow lady, and lay about a
mile from the city, across the road from the residence
of Henry Clay. Here, while Peter was too young to
work in the brick-yard, he was sent daily for the cows,
and for vegetables from the garden; and as he had
plenty of leisure, he spent many happy hours in playing with the little colored children at Mr. Clay's.

Frequently the merry group was joined by young Masters Theodore and Thomas Clay, and then the sport was liveliest.

The heart of the little new-made slave glowed with love for these noble boys, and he soon confided to them his sad history; and one day, when Mrs. Clay, as was her custom, spoke kindly to the dusky playmate of her sons, he simply recited to her the story of his sorrows, and asked her if she did not think some one would send him back to his mother.

She quieted him with cakes and other delicacies, to the palate of the child exceeding grateful, and then gently dismissed the children to their play.

But the brave-hearted *boys* were young enough to long *to do* something for their little favorite, and bade him tell his story to their father, who, they assured him, would send him back. There was true Kentucky generosity in their breasts, and they felt sure their honored father could not fail to do his utmost to redress such a cruel wrong.

"O Levin!" whispered Peter, the first time he was alone with his brother. "I reckon we'll go back to-reckly!"

"Go back! whar?"

"Why home, to see mother! Mass' Theodore Clay say, his father so good to everybody, he know he'll send us back if we tell him how we got stole—says his father allers *hope* folks whar gits in trouble."

"Mass' Theodore say so? Reckon then we will, kase Mr. Clay mighty good to all his people. Hi! Mars John Fisher! you's gwine lose these chillerns!"

And with comical grimaces, Levin cut a series of

shuffles, indicating the confusion that awaited "Mars John."

Not long after this conversation, Peter saw Mr. Clay standing near the court-house with a letter in his hand. His little heart bounded with hope as he ran towards him.

"O Mr. Clay!" he exclaimed, "I'm stole!"

"Stole? Who stole you, and where were you stolen from?"

"I's stolen from my father and mother on Delaware river—folks say that's Philadelphia—but I don' know. Please, sir, won't you send me back to my mother?"

"To whom do you belong?"

"I 'long to Mars John Fisher, on Main street, and I wants to go back to my mother."

"Well, my boy, I have no time to talk to you now; you carry this letter to Major Pope—you know where he lives—and then come back and I'll attend to you."

Away ran the child dancing with delight, and crying, "I's free! I's free! I's gwine to my mother!"

"What is that you say?" asked a gentleman who met him. "I's gwine to be free! Mr. Clay gwine to send me back to my mother, kase I was stole away from her!"

"Now look here, you little negro," said the man, who knew the child, and understood the temper of his master, "you'd better not talk about that to Mr. Clay, for he will tell your master, and then old John Fisher will be sure to skin you."

The bright vision that Hope had held before the trusting boy faded away. With drooping head and tearful eye he returned to tell his brother of their disappointment, and after that they both avoided Mr. Clay.

Yet Hope did not desert them; but whispered often in their eager ears—"You shall return; your friends will come to seek you. You were born free, and slaves you shall not die!"

When Peter was about nine years old, he too was employed in the brick-yard, as "*off-bearer.*" Three thousand brick a day was the task for two boys; and if one of them chanced to be by any means disabled, his companion must "*off-bear*" the whole. The moulder must not be hindered.

These moulders—slaves themselves—were cruel tyrants. The boys, though seldom abused by the master himself, were subject to all *their* caprices and passions. If one of inferior station failed to perform his task, they knew no mercy; and their master *permitted* any punishment they chose to inflict.

Their favorite mode of chastisement was called "*standing in the wheelbarrow.*" The offender was placed with a foot on each side of the wheel, and compelled to reach over and grasp a handle in each hand; and then the youngest boys—the "*off-bearers*"—were compelled to whip him with cowhides. If he would lie still, and take twenty-four lashes without attempting to rise, that was deemed sufficient proof of his humility. But if he made an effort to change his position before that number was inflicted, the moulder who presided over the ceremony, and who counted off the strokes, commenced again at "*one,*" and caused the twenty-four to be repeated.

One day a large man, named Charles, was put into the wheelbarrow, and received over three hundred blows before he was sufficiently subdued to lie still, and take twenty-four without moving. The boys that were selected to inflict this horrible punishment (of whom Peter was one) were all trembling with terror; but if one of them, through pity, failed to strike with his utmost strength, the moulder, who stood aside with a cowhide, punished his merciful folly by a violent blow upon his own back.

Amid such scenes passed the childhood of these hapless boys. Their natural cheerfulness and mildness of temper made them universal favorites. In their own person, therefore, they endured few such sufferings as they were forced to witness. A "Boston clergyman," carefully observing their every-day life, would have pronounced them happy, careless boys; so ardently attached to their young masters and their fellow servants, that it would be really unkind to set them free. They were well fed—their clothes were comfortable—all they needed was supplied without their thought or care.

CHAPTER III.

MASTER NATTIE.

WHEN Peter was about thirteen years old, Mr. Fisher planned a removal to Cincinnati, where his brother had recently gone. He disposed of his brick-yard, and intended to sell all his servants, except Aunt Betty, the cook, with her daughter and grand-child. These he could not spare, as they were indispensable to the comfort of the family.

Levin and Peter were overwhelmed with grief at the news of the intended sale. There was degradation in the thought of being trafficked for like horses; for, with all their apparent humility, and their submissive, gentle manners, there was a principle deep in their hearts that claimed the birthright of humanity.

Besides, they had, through all these years, cherished the hope that they should yet be sought by their parents; and they knew that if they changed owners, the chances of their being discovered would be lessened.

But their destiny was fixed. Mr. Fisher found some difficulty in disposing of them, for their old story of being stolen was remembered, and men hesitated to buy where there was a shadow of uncertainty in the title. Their master, however, so confidently asserted that he had conquered them, and it was so many years since they had been heard to say anything on the subject, that a sale was at last effected.

The purchaser was Mr. Nat. Gist, of Lexington, and he paid four hundred and fifty dollars for each of the brothers.

Mr. Fisher did not, as he had anticipated, go to Cincinnati, but remained in Lexington for several years, and then he removed with his family to Louisville, Ky.

The change of owners was far from being an agreeable one to Levin and Peter. Nat. Gist, their new master, lived in a small brick house on Dutch street, or, as it was sometimes called, Hill street. He was a short, stout, gray-headed man, about fifty-six years of age, a Virginian by birth, and had been a revolutionary soldier. He swore hard, and drank to intoxication every day; therefore, as he was a bachelor, his home was seldom visited by any humanizing influence.

He owned a brick-yard of about five acres, and had, in all, twenty slaves. These he fed sparingly, clothed scantily, and worked hard. In the winter, when they could not make brick, he was accustomed to hire them out wherever he could get the highest price for their services.

Mr. Gist had now among his people four boys—Levin and Peter, with Alfred and Allison, who were also brothers. They had been brought from Virginia, where their parents still remained.*

* The mother of these two boys, who belonged to one George Lewis, in Virginia, has recently, with several of her other children, escaped from slavery, and travelled, by the "underground railroad," to Canada.

Peter was not long in becoming a special favorite with his new master. Yet the strange old man never evinced his preference by any peculiar kindness of word or act. That would contradict his theory. He believed there was nothing so good for a *nigger* as frequent floggings; and while he kept Peter near him as much as possible, and always chose him to wait upon him, he never abated towards him a jot of his accustomed severity. An incident that occurred soon after he purchased the two boys of Mr. Fisher, will illustrate his method of governing them.

He had come home from town, as usual, much intoxicated, and ordered Peter to scatter a couple of bundles of oats on the ground, for his horse. The boy obeyed, but strewed them over rather more space than was necessary. In a few minutes, his master appeared.

" Did you feed Ned his oats?"

" Yes, sir."

" I'll see if you have done it right." And, muttering curses as he went, he proceeded to the yard, where the horse was eating.

" What the d—l did you throw them all about for?"

" Why, mass'r, you told me to scatter 'em."

Quick the old man's cane descended on the offender's head. "I did'nt tell you to scatter them all over the yard. Follow me to the house. I'll give you a lesson."

Peter walked slowly behind him to the door.

"Now take off your shirt, you rascal, and cross your hands."

The boy obeyed; and his master, after tying his hands together, drew them down over his knees, where he confined them by means of a stick thrust under his knees. He then beat him with a cowhide, first on one side, and then on the other, till his drunken rage was appeased. "There, you black *cuss*," cried he, when he had finished, "I mean to make a good nigger of you, and there's no way to do it, only by showing you who's master."

This method of confining a negro for punishment is called "*bucking*" him, and it is much practised in slave-land. The culprit is frequently left in the "*buck*" several hours—sometimes, indeed, all night—and, in such cases, the protracted straining of the muscles causes intense pain.

A few benevolent individuals, about this time, established a Sabbath School in Lexington, for the instruction of such slaves as might be permitted by their masters to learn.

At this proceeding Master Nattie was indignant. He would not have *his* niggers spoiled by getting learning—no, indeed! Niggers were bad enough, without being set up by such rascals as these Sunday School teachers. They'd better not meddle with *his* property; and if he heard of one of *his* boys going near the school, he'd give him such a flogging that he'd never need any more education.

But in the breast of one of these slave boys burned a thirst for knowledge so intense, that even this terrible threat could not deter him from making one effort to learn. Peter went to the school.

The teacher received him kindly, and inquired for his "*pass.*"

"Ain't got none, massa."

"I am sorry," said the teacher, "for we are not permitted to instruct any servants without the consent of their masters."

Peter knew this very well; and he also knew that to ask his master for a pass would be only to apply for a whipping; but he did so long to learn to read, he could not go away. He looked around on the pupils. Their masters allowed them to come, and surely not one of them could learn so quick as he. He determined to make a desperate effort to stay that one day, at least. So he told the teacher that his master *didn't care nothin' 'bout his comin'*—he'd get a pass next Sunday; and he was permitted to remain.

The next Sabbath, when the school was opened, Peter stood among the pupils. The other boys presented their passes—his did not appear. *He had forgotten to ask his master*, but would be sure to remember it the next Sunday.

But on the third Sabbath he was no better off. *His master had gone from home early in the morning*, and of course it was impossible for him to get a pass in his absence. The teacher once more allowed him to remain, but assured him that no such excuses would be taken in future.

The fourth Sabbath came, and Peter walked boldly into the school. "Pass, boy!" as usual, was the first salutation.

"Ain't got none," replied he. "Mass' Nattie say, don't need none; no use, no how."

The teacher began to suspect the true state of the case, and though he would gladly have aided to illumine that eager intellect, that was "stretching forward to the light," yet he was forced to thrust it back into the darkness, lest a prejudice should be aroused which would palsy all his efforts. So he positively forbade Peter's future entrance to the school without a pass, and he was thereafter obliged to seek for amusement on Sundays in some other direction. He had, in these four Sundays, learned the alphabet, and could spell a few words, and hard and bitter was the fate that consigned him thenceforward to ignorance.

"Oh," thought he, "if I could only learn to read! I could find out the way to write myself. Then I might write letters to Philadelphia, and let our mother know what's 'come of her chilluns. There's white boys in town that goes to school every day, that would a heap ruther play in the street. I's seen 'em runnin' off to keep clar of the mas'r in the mornin'. Reckon, if I could go to school, nobody wouldn't cotch me runnin' off that way."

CHAPTER IV.

THE TOBACCO FACTORY.

AFTER Levin and Peter had worked for four summers in the brickyard, their master hired them, with Alfred and Allison, to Mr. George Norton, a tobacconist, who at that time carried on an extensive business in Lexington.

They had been hired out before to different persons during the winter. Peter had, one winter, served as waiter, a cousin of his master, Mr. Sandford Keene. This was his first introduction to house service, as well as his first experience, since he became a slave, of genuine kindness. Mrs. Keene was a noble-hearted lady, who delighted to promote the happiness of all around her, and Peter loved to serve her acceptably.

But to this Mr. Norton they were hired for the whole year; and violent as was Master Nattie in his phrensied hours, and carefully as he avoided every indulgence towards them which might seem to recognize their humanity, they dreaded to exchange him for this new master, for of him report spake never kindly.

Mr. George Norton—ah! how grand he looked as he stood near the shop door conversing with his overseer! His broad-brimmed hat seemed conscious of its *elevated* position, and his hair descending in a cue behind was stiff and stately. The very smoke from his cigar ascended with a consequential puff, and his cane thumped on the sidewalk in exact accordance with the great man's varying moods. It had a gentle tap to answer words of compliment, or salutations from the rich or beautiful. But when a breath of contradiction came, or any sable menial hesitated to obey his slightest wish, the expressive staff beat furiously upon the pavement, in token of the vengeance that should fall upon the offender's head.

A fit foil to his pompous superior was the overseer, Mr. Kisich. Small and pale, awkward in his manners, and "slightly lame," he seemed totally indifferent to his personal appearance, and gloried only in the force and accuracy with which he could execute his employer's plans.

He was a native of the Emerald Isle, as his "rich brogue" plainly indicated; and, like some of his more distinguished countrymen in these later days, claimed liberty *for Irishmen*, and equality with the noblest in every land. But when

> " He found his fellow guilty of a skin
> Not colored like his own."

he could see him bought and sold, and tasked, and beaten, without a single impulse of pity.

About thirty men and boys were employed in Mr. Norton's establishment. Of these, three were white men, who were hired to do that part of the work which required more experience and skill than the negroes were supposed to possess. These acted as spies and informers; making the privilege of tyrannizing over their dark-skinned fellows, a sort of compensation for the degradation which is inseparable, in slave-land, from the necessity of labor.

Peter and Allison succeeded admirably in pleasing Mr. Norton. He liked their ready obedience, and their sprightly, nimble movements. When he gave an order, he could not wait with patience its dilatory execution, and they loved to surprise him by returning from an errand, or by finishing a task earlier than he expected. Yet by this they won no praise. It was but their duty, and they had reason to rejoice if, by performing it, they escaped the cow-hide.

For several months they thus succeeded in avoiding any outbreak of his wrath. They had been accustomed to no mild exercise of authority, and the angry strife they often witnessed, seemed to them, if not quite necessary, unavoidable at times. *Force* was their law, and *force* their motive to obedience; and but for their brother-love, and the warm memory of their mother, their hearts must have grown callous and incapable of affectionate response.

For Levin and Peter there was ever a bright morning in remembrance, and they were young—could they live without the hope of returning once more to that mother-home? Humble was the cabin which they delighted to remember, but the sunshine came freely in at the open door, and no harsh word was ever heard within the lowly walls.

How sweet, how soothing, was the influence of these cherished retrospects! How often, when their tasks were finished, the two brothers strolled away from the noisy mirth which their companions were beguiling the twilight hour, and in low tones discussed the possibilities of an escape from slavery—a return to the dear home where they had known no care nor fear.

A hundred plans they at different times suggested to each other, but the execution of any one of them required more knowledge than they possessed, or could acquire. And then there were so many that failed in such attempts. The jail was always tenanted by captured fugitives. No—they could not run away.

But perhaps, some day, they might buy their freedom. They could work nights and Sundays, and earn the money, and then they would be safe. This was their favorite aerial abode, and here they enjoyed many bright anticipations. But alas! they soon learned by the sad experience of others, that such a plan was all uncertain. The history of one man of their acquaintance in Lexington, taught them a lesson of caution on that point, that chilled their ardent hopes, and deepened their distrust of *seeming friends*.

Spencer, a fine-looking intelligent mulatto, belonged to a Mr. Williams, who kept a lottery office in Lexington. His master, having no need of his services, hired him out; usually to the keepers of hotels or livery stables, and sometimes to Spencer himself. He was a great favorite with the white people, and had excellent opportunities of making money; not only by extra services about the hotels or stables, but also by doctoring horses, in which he had much skill.

He sometimes speculated in lottery tickets, but here his success availed him little. He drew at one time a house and lot in Lexington, valued at $30,000, and although many white people declared that it would be a shame to deprive him of the benefit of his good fortune, yet it was on the whole deemed an unsafe precedent to allow a *negro* to acquire so much property. So the prize was finally awarded to a getleman in Philadelphia, who stood second in the list of successful competitors.

Soon after this, Spencer conceived the idea of buying his freedom, and proposed the subject to his master. Mr. Williams received it favorably, and fixed the price at one thousand dollars.

Spencer, habitually industrious, had now a new animation in his labors; and so untiring was his diligence, that in a few years he had paid his master within twenty-five dollars of the whole sum. The goal of all his hopes was just in sight, when lo! the perfidious tyrant denied ever having promised him his liberty, and bade him never mention the subject more.

Spencer was sorely disappointed, but not discouraged, and when not long after a gentleman who had heard the history of this deception offered to purchase him, and to give him his freedom as soon as he could earn the price which he must pay to Williams, the hopeful slave eagerly accepted the offer.

The bargain was soon concluded, and with new zeal, the bondman commenced his labors. He took the precaution this time, to ask for a receipt whenever he made a payment. This was readily given, and Spencer deemed himself safe. But behold! when he had paid all but seventy dollars, his new master suddenly left town; and before the poor slave was aware of any approaching change, an agent to whose care he had been consigned, had sold him to another master. He was indignant at this outrageous fraud, and produced his receipts, which he had carefully preserved. But these availed nothing. They did not show to whom the money had been paid. And even if they had been properly written they would have profited nothing—for does not a slave's money as well as his person and his labor, belong to his master?

Still hope died not in Spencer's breast. Again he tried a man who had been lavish of his sympathy, and loud in his denunciations of the baseness by which he had suffered. Into his hands—for the third time—he paid the hard-earned price of his redemption; and when he should have received his free papers, and a pass out of the State, he was chained in a gang, and sent to the cotton and sugar fields of the south.

To the ears of Peter and his brother came many tales like this, and in their inmost hearts were treasured the lessons of caution which they imparted. Surely there was none *they* could trust. It were far better, by apparent contentment, and by cheerful manners, to win the confidence of those in whose power they were placed, than to become objects of suspicion and dislike, by ill-timed efforts to be free. So they toiled on, their genial sunny natures, and the warm heart-love ever fresh within their breasts, preserving them from despair.

Half the year at Mr. Norton's had passed away, and neither of the boys belonging to old Nattie Gist had fallen into any serious difficulty. They had witnessed many exhibitions of their employer's cruelty, and one which occurred about this time, filled their hearts with horror.

Mr. Norton's body-servant, a large black man, chanced one day to offend his haughty master. He was immediately put in a buck, and in the presence of all the men and boys, Norton inflicted on his naked back three hundred lashes with a cowhide. The blood gushed out, and ran in streams upon the brick floor of the shop.

When the stick was removed from under his knees, the poor victim was unable to rise. At this his tormentor was enraged. He seized a board that lay near, full of shingle nails, and with it struck him several violent blows; every one of which brought the blood in streams, as though he had been pierced with lancets.

The slaves who witnessed this horrid deed were paralyzed with fear, but the white men swore it was just right. The cursed niggers—they must be conquered, or they would not be worth a d—n.

Here young Peter's caution for a moment failed. His eyes, usually so mild, flashed fiercely, and he declared in a low voice to his brother that George Norton should never strip *him* and put him in a buck to whip him—*he would die first.*

Poor boy! his rash speech was overheard, and reported to the tyrant, who from that day waited only an excuse to punish his presumption.

The next Saturday evening, as the boys were sweeping the shop, an old woman came in and asked for some tobacco. Peter, being nearest the door, gathered up a handful of the sweepings, and gave them to her.

On the following morning, it was Peter's turn to make a fire in the sweat-room; and when he had performed this duty, he locked the door of the shop and went to his old master's, where he usually spent his Sundays. Here he played marbles, and enjoyed such other sports as are proper for the Sabbath-rest of slave-boys, while their young masters are at the Sunday-school or in the billiard-room—according to their tastes.

Peter had been absent from the shop but a short time when Mr. Norton himself took a fancy to go in and look at the tobacco. He tried the door, but it was locked, and the key was nowhere to be found. His anger rose. Ah! Peter, a heavy cloud is gathering, and there is no shelter for thy defenceless head!

Early Monday morning, Mr. Norton came into the shop. His eyes looked darker and brighter than usual, and the smoke from his cigar came in quick passionate puffs. His cane, too, beat an ominous march upon the floor. Something was wrong.

The great man spoke. "Whose business was it to make a fire in the sweat-room yesterday?"

"Mine, sir," said Peter.

"Did you attend to it?"

"Yes, sir."

"*You did!* where were you when I came here?"

"Don't know, sir,—recken I was up home."

"Where is your *home*, your rascal?"

"Up to Mars Nattie's, sir."

"I'll let you know, nigger, that this is your home, and that I am your master!" and with a furious thumping of his cane, the mighty man strode out of the shop. He was in a rage. It always made him angry for one of his *hired* servants to call his owner, "*Master;*"—*it was his law* that in his shop no one should receive that ennobling title except himself.

Before sunrise the next morning, just as the work of the day was commenced, Mr. Norton appeared at the door. He stood a few minutes perfectly still, and then taking out his knife, he commenced trimming a switch—whistling meantime a beautiful march.

The sweet notes woke no answering melody in the hearts of those within, for well they knew the spirit of their master. Only when about to inflict some cruel punishment did George Norton utter sounds like these.

His march ended, he spoke—

"Peter!"

"Sir."

"Where were you, yesterday?"

"Here, sir, strippin' tobacco.

"Well, Sunday, where were you?"

"Home, to Mars Nattie's, sir."

"The hot blood mounted to Mr. Norton's face. "*I* am your master, rascal, and I'll let you know you are to go to no other *home* than this! Who swept the shop on Saturday?"

"We boys, sir, all of us."

"Who gave tobacco to an old woman?"

"I gave her a handful of sweepings, sir,—no 'count, no how, sir."

"Well, you'll find *I* am your master, and you are to obey me. Come here, and lie down across this box."

Peter obeyed, wondering at the same time that he had not been ordered to strip. It was not Mr. Norton's custom to whip his servants over their clothes, and the boy had on a new suit of blue linsey. But he had heard of the expression he had made a few days before, and perhaps thought best to avoid an unnecessary contest.

No sooner was the boy extended across the designated box, than Norton struck him a violent blow.

Peter raised up. "Lie down you nigger!" and he renewed the blows with greater force. Peter raised up again. "Lie down!" cried the fury, with a curse. Peter obeyed the third tie, and them blows fell hard and fast.

Once more he raised up. "Lie down! I say, you cursed nigger—if you move again till I bid you, I will beat you till you cannot rise."

The boy stood upright, and looked his tormentor steadily in the face. "I have laid down three times for you to beat me, when I have done nothing wrong; I will not lie down again!"

Instantly Norton seized him, and attempted to force him across the box—but was unable. "Here, Mr. Kisich! Tadlock! all of you! help me conquer this nigger!"

Quick to his aid came the overseer, and the three other white men that worked in the shop, and all fell upon him at once, while Peter screamed "*Murder!*" and fought with his utmost strength.

People in the street heard the tumult, and gathered about the doors of the shop; when Norton ordered them closed and fastened. Among those thus excluded was Sandford Keene, the nephew of old Nattie Gist. He listened to the uproar with anxious ears, but could not determine from which of the boys the cries proceeded. Had he known that it was Peter, his special favorite, to whom also his wife was much attached, he could hardly have refrained from rushing in to his rescue.

The ruffians tried to bind his hands, but he struggled so fiercely that they were in danger of breaking his bones. That would have been too costly an amusement. But they succeeded in throwing him upon the floor, and there he struggled, and screamed, and bit their legs and ankles, till they despaired of holding him in any position, unless they could succeed in tying him.

One of them, accordingly, prepared a slip noose, and threw it over his head when he rose up—with intent to choke him. He perceived their purpose, and quickly raising both hands, thrust them through the noose and slipped it down below his arms.

Thus baffled in one scheme, they resorted to another. Dragging him along by the rope now fastened around his waist, they proceeded to the back part of the shop where stood five or six presses, each about eight feet high. If they could hang him up on one of these he would be entirely at their mercy. But he foiled them here. As they raised the rope to fasten it to the top of the press, he sprang one side, and crept into the narrow space between it and the wall.

Here he remained for some time. Bleeding and panting—his bloodshot eyes glared at his persecutors, who, on both sides, were engaged in beating him over the head with cowhides and hoop-poles, and thrusting sticks and pieces of iron against his bruised flesh.

At last they dragged him from his partial hiding place; and now he made no resistance—he had not strength to struggle. Norton threw him across a keg, and with fiendish curses, whipped his bleeding back with a cowhide; swearing he was the first nigger that ever tried to fight him, and that he should be humbled if it took his life.

When this correction was finished it was nearly ten

o'clock; and, commanding the other slaves, who stood
agape with horror, to go to work, Mr. Norton, followed
by his aids, went to the house for breakfast. They
had exercised sufficiently to eat with good appetites;
and while they were enjoying a plentiful repast, and
discussing in their own peculiar style, the "obstinacy
of the nigger," their poor victim, bruised and torn,
with only a few shreds left of his new suit of linsey,
crept out of the shop, and with his little remaining
strength, succeeded in gaining the residence of his
master, on the hill.

Old Nattie Gist had, according to his morning custom, gone down town. Aunt Mary, the cook, however, received him kindly, pitied him, and dressed his
wounds. She had a human mother's heart, *and her
two boys were slaves.*

Peter guessed rightly, that his old master, cruel as
he was himself, would not like to see his property thus
damaged by others. Yet he spoke no gentle word to
the sufferer. He would not intimate to a "*nigger*"
that a white man could do him wrong. But he sought
Norton, and cursed him roundly for inflicting such
abuse upon a boy of his.

For a week he allowed Peter to stay at home, and
then he sent him back to the shop. Here he remained
till the end of the year. Norton was evidently either
ashamed of his previous violence, or afraid to repeat
its exercise, for never after that did Peter receive an
unkind word from him or either of his satellites.

Just before Christmas, Mr. Norton went to old Master Nattie, and, assuring him that the boys were all
perfectly satisfied with the past, and anxious to remain

with him, hired them for another year. But when their time expired, they all ran off together to their master, and he did not force them to go back.

This was a merry Christmas-time to these four boys. They had been accustomed to severity before, and had lived on poor and scanty fare. Yet even their old master, heartless as he seemed, was not systematic in his cruelty. When he went down town in the morning, there was none to watch them till he returned. They could talk, and laugh, and sing; if they but finished their tasks, they had little to fear.

But, at Norton's shop, there was scarcely a minute of the day that evil eyes were not upon them. Not a laugh, a gesture, or grimace, but was remembered, and and quoted as a token of disrespect to the lofty master, who could ill brook a jest reflecting on his dignity.

CHAPTER V.

THE SEPARATION.

In the fall of this year (1817), the community of which old Nattie Gist was the centre and the head, became greatly agitated.

The old man had two nephews, Levi and Andrew Gist, of whom he was very fond. They were both sons of his brother William, who resided on a farm a few miles out of town.

These young men, after much discussion, and notwithstanding some opposition from their friends, determined to seek their fortunes in Alabama. They had heard tempting reports of the fertility of the valley of the Tennessee, and of the ease with which a fortune could be made by raising cotton; and besides, they were Kentuckians, and loved adventure.

Their uncle liked the spirit of enterprize that impelled them; he liked money too, and he foresaw that they would have fine opportunities in that new country of amassing wealth.

Levi Gist, the elder of the two brothers, had always been a special favorite with his uncle, and to him he intrusted six of his negroes. These he was to take with him to Alabama, to assist him in putting in his first crop. The old man promised to go himself the next year, if they should like the country, and decide to settle there.

The command to prepare to go with Master Levi, fell with crushing weight upon the hearts of the doomed slaves. Old Frank and his wife Peggy, were the first to learn their sentence. They were indignant at the word. Long and wearily had they toiled in their master's service. Patiently had they endured hunger. Stripes and cursings had been their frequent portion, and these they had learned to receive without complaint. Now they were growing aged, and to be torn from the old place, and from all the friends in whose society the Sundays passed so pleasantly, seemed too hard a trial.

Their two children were to go with them. That was some comfort, but a deeper sorrow, for they would be forced to work in those great cotton fields, where venemous snakes would hiss at them, and cruel overseers watch their toil.

Yet old Frank and Peggy had not the deepest cause for grief. Levin and Alfred were destined to accompany them, and they must each leave behind his brother, dearer to him than life itself.

The young men intended to take with them every thing that would be needed to stock a new plantation. To collect and arrange in travelling order all their goods, required much time and labor, and every hand, at home, and at their uncle's, was enlisted in their service.

At Master Nattie's, particularly, all was now excitement and confusion. The old man hurried to and fro, administering curses and stripes to all who failed to execute his plans. The boys who had been hired out, were brought home to aid in these unusual labors, and thus the brothers, that must so soon be separated, were allowed to spend the last few days in each others society.

The thought that his brother must go to the South was agony to Peter. In all their sorrows, thus far, they had been together. They had shared the same little pleasures—their hearts had been as one. And now, to be sundered so wide—could they live apart?

"O Levin, Levin! if they take you 'way off there, I sha'n't never see you no more, sure!"

"O yes," sobbed Levin, his heart almost broken, while yet he strove to speak cheeringly to his weeping brother—"O yes, Mars Nattie say he gwine bring ye all next year when he come."

"Mars Nattie! He never gwine 'way off there! He'll stay here long as he can get breath enough to curse. He's too old to go to a new country, any how."

"Well, he have to die some day—he can't live a mons's long time, sure."

"Yes, and if he dies, we'll all be sold—they allers has an auction when folks dies—and then their people's scattered all about. O 'pears like 'taint no use livin' in this yer world. I sha'n't never see you no more!"

The preparations for the journey were at last completed, and one pleasant afternoon in October, the little company of slaves had orders to repair to Master William's, in order to be ready to start with their young masters the next morning.

"Mars Nattie," said Levin, as they were all assembled in the yard to say good-bye, "please, sir, give me something 'fore I go, to 'member you by."

"Well," said the old man, "go in and bring me the

cowhide, and I'll give you something you'll never forget. If I should give you a coat or a shirt, you would wear it right out, but if I cut your skin to pieces, you will remember this parting as long as you live. And mind, you rascal, when I come out next fall, I'll bring the cowhide, and if you don't behave yourself, I'll give you enough then—d'ye hear?"

Such, interspersed with numerous curses, was the kind farewell of old Nattie Gist. The servants all shook hands, and strove to speak in cheering tones to their departing friends; but great tears stood in their eyes as they watched the little company slowly marching down the hill.

Sadly they returned to their work, but their thoughts crept on toward the dim future. Which of them should go next? Master Nattie had sold, during the past year, more than half his servants; and none could tell what caprice might seize him before another year should pass. They might all be chained in a gang, and driven away by some barbarous trader. Heavily throbbed their hearts as these gloomy fancies floated before them; and while they tried to repress the tears that *would* scald their aching eye-balls, they pursued their task in silence.

Peter returned no more to his work at Mr. Hudson Martin's, where he had spent the former part of the year, but was sent by his master to take Levin's place as waiter at Mr. John D. Young's.

Mr. Young was not a rich man—indeed he had failed in business, and now inhabited a small brick house on the plantation of his father-in-law. He was an intelligent gentleman, of pleasant manners, and great kindliness of heart. Had his wife resembled him in amiability and gentleness, their home would have been happy; but she was unfortunately destitute of that true independence and dignity of character, that can meet worldly reverses with composure. She felt humiliated by their comparative poverty, and the comforts with which she was surrounded looked hateful in her eyes, because the splendors wealth might purchase, were beyond her reach. Her servants endured most in consequence of this unfortunate peculiarity. From morning till night they were scolded, till they came to heed the shrill voice of their mistress, no more than they would heed the rain-drops an the roof.

During the few months which Peter spent in the service of Mr. Young, he passed many pleasant hours at Mr. Clay's. His childish fear of the great statesman had changed to deepest reverence; and, though young masters Theodore and Thomas Clay, no longer played, as had been their childish custom, with their colored favorite, they treated him ever with perfect kindness.

But with the servants, every one of whom was privileged beyond the common lot of slaves, he was always at home; and many a pleasant winter evening did he spend at Ashland.

Among the slaves that gathered there at night, one of the merriest was Aaron the coachman. He was the father of Mr. Clay's body servant, Charles, who, during the last years of his master's life, was ever at his side.

Aaron was an excellent servant—quick and energetic, and his mirthfulness and genuine good feeling rendered him a favorite with all; while his stories, songs and merry jests, made the warm kitchen ring again.

But he had one fault. He loved a dram, and when

tempted by the sight or smell of his favorite liquor, he could seldom resist the entreaties of his appetite.

This weakness was peculiarly annoying to Mrs. Clay, as it frequently unfitted him for business at a time when she had most need of his services.

He one day drove her carriage into town, and while she was making a visit, he improved the opportunity to indulge in a glass of his loved beverage; and by the time his mistress was ready to go home, he was wholly incapable of driving her carriage. She was, therefore, obliged to hire a man to take his place, and she then resolved that Aaron should be punished. But it could not be done without Mr. Clay's consent, as the overseer was forbidden to strike one of the house servants, without consulting him.

So to her husband she recited the story of her mortification, and, as he had tried various mild means to cure the slave of this unlucky propensity, he decided that it was best to use more severe measures.

The next morning he sent for the overseer, and directed him to take Aaron into the carriage-house, and give him a slight whipping. "Now do it quietly," said he, "and be sure not to cut his skin. I don't want to hear any disturbance. Do it as gently as possible."

The overseer respectfully assented and went out. Instantly one of the maids, who had chanced to overhear this conversation, stole out of the house, and sought Aaron.

"Look yer," said she, "you know what massa say?"

"Know what massa say? No! How I know what he say, when he never spoke to me this mornin'?"

"Well, he say to the overseer—'Aaron must be punish—for he take a dram when Mrs. Clay want him to drive for her—you may take him to the carriage-house and whip him, but don't cut him up.'"

"Don't cut him up! Massa say so? Well, well, reckon this chile be ready. Overseer mighty good—he talk so clever—'pears like he thinks I's white sometimes, but the devil in his eye   He done wanted, this long time, get a cut at me. I knows what overseers means when they gets too good. Yah! yah! he thinks now his gwine give this chile all he owes him."

The girl's astonished eyes followed Aaron as he leaped over the fence, and ran toward a small grocery that stood at a short distance on the road to town. Here he had no difficulty in procuring a dram; and, having thus fitted himself for the anticipated contest, he walked home, and resumed his work.

Soon the overseer called from the carriage-house door—Aaron!"

"Sir?"

"Come here."

In a moment the slave stood before him.

"Aaron, Mr. Clay says you must come into the carriage-house and be whipped."

"Did Massa say so?"

"Yes—he says your habit of drinking annoys your mistress so often, that you must be punished for it. He says he has tried to persuade you to leave it off, but it does no good. I don't like to whip you, Aaron, but it is Mr. Clay's orders."

"Well, if Massa says so, then it must be so," and he walked quietly into the carriage-house, followed by his

Mr. Clay's Overseer outwitted.   See page 62.

kind friend, the overseer, who fastened the door on the inside.

"Now, Mr. ——," said Aaron, "you may whip me, if Massa says so, but you needn't tie me—I wont be tied."

"Very well," replied the overseer, throwing down the rope which he had in his hand, "you needn't be tied, if you will stand still; but you must take off your coat."

"Yes sir; but if I take off my coat to be whipped, you ought to take yourn off first to whip me."

The man perceived that he had been drinking, and knew he must indulge his whim, if he would obey Mr. Clay's orders to *keep quiet*—so he pulled off his coat, and Aaron quickly laid his beside it on the floor. Then followed the vest—the slave insisting that Mr. —— should first remove his own. "Now your shirt, Aaron," said he.

"Yes sir, but you must take off yourn first."

This was going further, for quiet's sake, than the overseer had intended; but he hesitated only a moment. It would be best, he thought, to humor him. He had, in truth, long wished for a chance to humble Aaron, and now the time had come.

But, behold! no sooner had he lifted his arms to pull his shirt over his head, than Aaron seized the garment, and twisting it around his neck, held him fast. Then catching the whip, he applied it vigorously to the overseer's naked back, raising the skin at every stroke. His victim screamed, and threatened him with vengeance, but all in vain; the blows fell hard and fast.

Mr. Clay heard the outcry, and grew very angry.

"I told him," said he, "to make no noise, and to be sure not to whip the poor fellow severely. He must be cutting him to pieces."

He hastened to the carriage-house. The door was fastened within, but he could hear the whizzing of the whip, as it descended on the sufferer's back. "Open the door!" he cried. "Didn't I tell you not to whip him hard? Open the door, I say!

"O, Mr. Clay! it's Aaron whipping me! I haven't given him a blow."

"Aaron," cried the master, "open the door."

Instantly the slave obeyed. With his right hand, in which he still held the whip that he had used to such good purpose, he opened the door, while with his left he retained his vice-like grasp of the twisted shirt. His face was all complacency, yet his eyes twinkled with mirth, and a roguish smile lurked at the corner of his mouth.

Mr. Clay stood for a few moments mute with astonishment. But when he fully comprehended the strange scene, he burst into a hearty laugh, and although the overseer, as soon as he was released, proceeded to explain to him the manner in which he had been caught, and insisted that he should now be allowed to whip Aaron, his arguments were lost. The master quietly expressed his opinion that there *had been whipping enough*—it was not necessary to go any further.

CHAPTER VI.

MASTER NATTIE'S DEATH.

IN April, 1818, Mr. Young having no further need of Peter's services, Master Nattie sent him to his brother, William Gist, to be employed on his plantation. Here Allison was his companion once more, and the pleasure of being together was, in part, a compensation to each for the absence of his brother.

But this joy was transient. Early in the ensuing summer, young Master Andrew came from Alabama for a short visit. He brought news of the health and prosperity of those who had gone with him the year before, and gave glowing descriptions of the beauty of the country. The rich bottom lands, with their grand old trees, the clustering vines and graceful flowering shrubs, and, above all, the abundance of game in the forests, afforded exhaustless topics of discourse.

When he returned, he took Allison with him.

Peter was left all alone, and his heart was very heavy. There was no one now to whom he could communicate all his little trials; none that would sympathize with his griefs. He had nothing but work to divert his thoughts during the day; and at night his dreams, sleeping or waking, were all of that dear brother, that had for so many years trod by his side the rugged path to which they two were doomed.

Soon after the departure of his nephew, Master Nattie's health was observed to fail; and though for a long time he struggled against disease, and would not own that he was ill, yet he was at last obliged to yield. His constitution was worn out by intemperance and the indulgence of evil passions; and now, no medicine could retard the steady approach of the Death Angel.

Twice a week, during the summer, Peter was accustomed to go to market. Then he never failed to visit his old master; and as he saw his sunken eye and hollow cheek, and noted his vacant wandering stare, his heart sank within him.

He did not regard his master with affection. Who could love old Nattie Gist? But the sale, ah! if he should die, there would, of course, be an auction, and the traders would be there, and then, adieu to the last hope he had cherished, of one day joining his beloved brother.

The unhappy old man continued to fail. Death stays not at the behest of kings or generals; how then should the faint prayer of a poor slave-boy impede his progress?

In loneliness and gloom passed the last days of the wretched man. His housekeeper and cook, Aunt Mary, was his constant nurse. She understood all his wants, and she had learned patiently to bear all his caprices. Her will—her very womanhood—had been crushed into submission to his authority; for though a slave called her his wife, she had for years been forced to disregard her marriage ties, as well as her own honor, in order to indulge the base passions of the tyrant.

Now, in the death-hour, the down-trodden woman moistened his parched lips, all heedless of the curses which they uttered. Her hand smoothed his pillow, administered his medicine, and surrounded him with all possible comforts.

Death advanced. On Saturday morning, the thirteenth of September, when, according to his custom, Peter went in to see him, the final struggle had commenced. His brother William and the doctor were standing by the bed. Silently they witnessed his agony as he strove with the King of Terrors. There was no light of Christian hope in his glazing eye, no love in his obdurate heart. He would resist—he would live! Why should he die? This world had been gloomy. No love-light had shone upon his path—no gentle hand had led him through the labyrinths of evil to the Author of all good. And as his lips had loved cursing, why should he look for blessings now? Could he hope for a better life than he had chosen here? Fearful was the frown upon his face as he was forced to yield to the great Conqueror. He struggled—groaned—gasped—he was gone.

Silently they closed his eyes, and horror sat upon every countenance.

They buried him, and raised a stone to his memory. Ah! he chose his own remembrancers! Poor Levin and his fellows need no stone to tell them that a monster lived.

After the funeral Mr. Wm. Gist conveyed the greater part of his brother's property to his place for safe keeping. A will was found conveying to his favorite nephew, Levi Gist, the house and lot in Lexington, as well as all the servants. Whatever money he possessed he left in legacies to his other relatives.

At the time of his death, Master Nattie owned but eleven slaves—the six that went first to Alabama. Aunt Mary, with her two sons, and Allison and Peter. The others he had sold some time before.

Aunt Mary was left in town to take care of the house, till young master Levi should come to take possession of his property. As she went through the familiar rooms, and arranged and re-arranged the furniture, she had time to think. The past rose before her—the dark repulsive past. She had been young, but it was so long ago—it was hardly worth her while to think of all the hopes that cheered her youth. She was married—and her husband's love shone for a brief time on her pathway; too soon, alas! to be shadowed by the dark passions of her absolute master. Two babes had nestled on her bosom, and they, too, were branded with her humiliation.

Now, *he* was dead—he would curse her life no longer. Ha! what a pang came with that half-uttered gratulation! Dead—and she who had served him so faithfully—who had meekly borne his wrathful curses, and patiently endured the degradation to which he had reduced her—she to whom he was indebted for all the comfort his home had known for years—who had attended him by day and night till the grave closed above his head—*she was coolly given to his nephew*, to be transported hundreds of miles away. How her great eyes flashed at the thought, as, with her hand upraised, in the solitary room where her master died, she swore she would not go!

Her husband, a native African, named Sam, who still spoke but broken English, was soon to be free, according to contract with his importer. Sam had the spirit of a prince. To live always as a slave he would not consent; and, lest he should ·kill himself or his master, his liberty was promised him at a stipulated time.

Mary was fully determined that she would never leave him nor Lexington; and when in the December following his uncle's death, the young heir came from the South to remove his goods, and desired Aunt Mary to prepare for the journey, she revolted. They might kill her, she said, but she would not go—she indeed, would hang herself, and that would end it.

The young man coaxed, and threatened, but in vain. She liked Mars Levi—everybody liked him—a heap better than old Massa; but as to leaving "Kaintucky," and going away to the South, she could not.

At last, finding that it was useless to attempt to remove her, Master Levi sold her, with her two boys, to his father,—and she was left to spend the evening of her days in her beloved Lexington.

CHAPTER VII.

THE JOURNEY TO ALABAMA.

On a cold Sabbath morning, December 20, 1818, Peter started with Master John Gist, a younger brother of "Mars Levi," for his new home in Alabama.

He wore his old master's broad-brimmed hat, and had his shot-gun lashed upon his back. Miss 'Maltha, the youngest daughter of Master William, came out just as they started, and with a kind smile gave him a handful of biscuits. Heaven bless her for the kindly thought! The memory of that simple gift is still warm in the heart of him who was then but a poor slave-boy, going forth to meet his uncertain fortunes amid scenes strange and new.

The farewells were all said, and the young men rode away—silently at first, for there were last words and affectionate charges from his parents, still ringing in the ears of Master John; and Peter's heart was full.

He left Lexington with few regrets. It had never seemed to him like home: though among the many families in which he had served, there were some who had treated him with great kindness. Yet the memory of his mother haunted him, and a sense of injustice and wrong, a consciousness that he had been stolen from home, and that the power to which he had been forced to submit was all usurped, prevented his forming a strong attachment to the place itself.

Now he had little hope of ever seeing any of his kindred except the dear brother that had gone before; and his heart grew lighter, as hour by hour the distance diminished between them. Alfred and Allison, too, he soon should meet, and they were very dear to him—for had they not suffered together?

Then came a heavy sinking of the heart at the thought, that he must thenceforth be exposed to all the reputed hardships of the South. The constant toil in the great cotton fields, the oppressive heat, the danger of fearful sickness, and the deeper dread of cruel overseers—all these fell upon his hopes like snow upon the violets that have peeped out too soon.

And oh! if after all these years his parents should come in search of their children, and they both be gone! No, no! he would not think of that—and giving old master's riding-horse a smart cut with his whip, he galloped on to overtake Master John.

Hour after hour the youths rode side by side; now conversing pleasantly about the country through which they were passing, or reviewing little incidents connected with their departure from home; and again, their thoughts grew busy, and forgot to shape themselves in words. Day after day they still rode on; one anticipating a pleasant visit with his brothers, and a speedy return to all the endearments of a happy home—the other, hopeful, and yet half afraid to meet his destiny.

They spent the nights at houses of entertainment, which they found scattered here and there along the roadside. At these, they were received more like family visitors than guests at a hotel. Master John sat in the parlor by the blazing fire, and told the news from Lexington to his kind host, or listened to the history of the last year's crop. Peter, meanwhile, in the kitchen made himself no less agreeable. He had come from town, and could tell wonders to his less privileged auditors, who had seldom been out of sight of home.

The travellers arrived at Hopkinsville on Christmas morning. Here dwelt Dr. William Teagarden, whose wife was a maternal aunt of Master John, and at his house they spent the holidays.

This was a merry time. All the usual Christmas festivities were enjoyed, and Mrs. Teagarden, in addition to these, gave a large evening party in compliment to her nephew.

Here Peter had a fine opportunity to display his skill and grace as a waiter, and so highly pleased was Mrs. Teagarden with his expertness in this vocation, that she made several efforts during the next three years, to purchase him of his young master.

"Look yer, Peter," said a gossiping old woman, who stood among the other servants just outside the parlor-door, and who had been watching the dancers with intense interest, "your Mars John gwine fall in love wid dat young lady, I reckon. How you like her for missus?"

"What young lady you mean? I reckon Mars John ain't in no hurry to fall in love, no how."

"Why, Miss Agnes Keats. Dear! he's leadin' her to a cheer by her sister, Miss Francess. He's danced a'most all night wid her, and 'pears like he thinks she's mighty porty."

"She is that," said Peter, "does her father live about yer?"

"Yes, he's a livin' now; but he come wons's nigh gwine to de bad man where he 'longs. Didn't you hear 'bout it in Lex'n'ton? He's got a heap o' people on dem dar two big plantations, and he does 'em mighty mean. But it wasn't none o' de field hands 'at killed him."

"Killed him? You said he was a livin' now."

"So I did; but I'se gwine tell you how he kep' clar. You see, he allers keeps three or four to de home place to wait on de family—well, he was *dat mean* dey couldn't live in no sort o' fashion; so two big men what staid round de house and garden, dey 'trive a plan to get enough to eat, for one day, leastways. Dey got hold de gun, and when de ole massa done got settle nice in his bed, dey ris de gun up on de winder bottom, and pint it to his heart. But de ole cook 'voman—she hope um, kase she fotch out de gun, an' lef' de winder open; she got mighty skeered 'bout her missus, and kep' tellin' 'em all de time dey's fixin' de gun, 'Now min' you don't hit missus—keep it clar o' missus.

"When dey got all fix, dey pull dat dar trigger— Hi! didn't it pop? but it didn't kill de ole massa— struck his ribs, I reckon. Well, de minute de ole cook 'voman year de gun, she lif' up her hands and fotch a big scream. 'O Lor'! I'll lay you's done kill missus, now!'

"Every person on de place year dat yell, and all come a runnin' to see who's kill."

"What 'come of the men?" asked Peter, his blood chilled at the thought of the horrid deed.

" De men—O dey 's hung. Dey had a little court ; did n't take long to prove dey's guilty, kase you see dey got cotch, so dey hung 'em mons's quick."

" Did they hang the 'voman, too ?"

" No, dey sol' her way off to de Coas'. Reckon she won't never hope no more sich work as dat. 'Pears like, it's mighty hard to have sich a mean massa as ole Keats, but it's a heap wuss to try dis yer killin' business. De Lor' don't 'low dat dar, no how.

" Dar ! dat set's up. Mars John gwine lead Miss Agnes up for de nex'. How nice dat pa'r does look ?"

On the morning of the third of January, Master John and Peter resumed their journey southward. They spent one night at Nashville, and one at Columbia, Tenn., and on the morning of the sixth, at eleven o'clock, they reached Bainbridge.

Peter's heart beat fast as he approached the spot that was thenceforth to be his home. Everything he saw looked strange and uncouth. The town, if such indeed it might be called, consisted of about thirty small log cabins, scattered here and there among the tall old forest trees. Groups of white-haired, sallow-skinned children were playing about the doors, or peeping slyly at the strange gentleman as he passed. Now and then, between the trees, were seen the bright waters of the Tennessee sparkling in the sunlight; but even they pursued their pleasant way in silence, as if reluctant to disturb the quiet of the place.

" Well, Peter," said Master John, "this is Bainbridge—how do you like the looks of the place?"

" Looks like 'taint a town, Mars John; I never knowed folks have a town in the woods."

Oh ! the woods will be gone in a few years. Don't

you see, many of these trees are dead now? They
girdle them that way, and the next year they die."

"Whar's the store? Mars Levi say he got a store
yer."

"Yonder it is—where that gentleman is sitting on
the porch?"

"That the store! Don't look no bigger'n a kitchen!
Whar Mars Levi live?"

"Here we are at his house, now." Master John
sprang to the ground, and gave his horse to Peter,
who with wondering eyes, was looking toward the
house.

He could hardly believe that those two log cabins,
with an open passage between them, constituted Master Levi's residence in Alabama. "Ha!" thought he,
"ole Mars Nattie say, they all gwine get rich out yer.
What he say now, if he see his young gentlemen
alivin' in a cabin in the woods 'among pore white
folks."

He followed Master John into the house. No one
was there. They went on to the kitchen, and with an
exclamation of joy, old Aunt Peggy ran forth to meet
them. "Mars Levi gone out huntin'," said she, "but
I reckon Mars Andrew in de store—he's dar mostly.
O, I's so glad to see somebody from de ole place!"

"Dar Peter!" cried she, as the sound of wheels was
heard, "dar's my ole man with his wagon; he's gwine
to de mill whar de boys is all to work."

A moment more, and Peter was in the wagon beside old Frank, hastening to the embrace of his brother
Levin. He could hardly wait to answer all the old
man's questions about home, and the dear friends *he*
had left behind.

Very joyful was the meeting between the brothers. Few were the words they uttered—their hearts were too full for speech. Alfred and Allison, too, were there; the little group of true friends was once more complete.

After two weeks spent about the house, in assisting Aunt Peggy to cook, and in forming a general acquaintance with the premises, Peter was sent to the cotton field.

CHAPTER VIII.

FIRST FOUR YEARS IN THE SOUTH.

HERE a new world opened before the young slave. The brick-yards in which his boyhood was spent, the fields of corn, tobacco, and hemp, around Lexington, presented no picture that could equal this. Far away stretched the brown plain, covered with the frosted cotton shrubs. Here and there stood a girdled forest tree, leafless and grim, yet mighty in its very desolateness. Gloomily its wasted shadow fell across the pathway trod by its destroyers, like the mysterious dread of ill that ever haunts the footsteps of the guilty.

The crop was now about half picked out. The business was all new to Peter, and though it did not look difficult, yet he worked diligently all day, and at night had only twelve pounds and a half. The other boys were greatly amused at his awkwardness, and played many jokes upon him, telling him he must first break off the boll, and then pick out the cotton.

At night, when Master Andrew weighed the cotton, he told them he would give a new pair of shoes to the one who would pick fifty pounds the next day. Allison was nearly barefoot, and he worked hard for the prize, but in vain. Peter, however, had learned wisdom from one day's failure, and, to the surprise of all, he had at night, seventy-five pounds. After this, he was seldom excelled in the cotton field. His fingers were long and nimble, and he could pluck the fleecy treasure from the frost-browed boll almost without effort.

Bainbridge, though mainly settled by poor people, who gained a scanty subsistence by hunting and fishing, was at that time surrounded by the estates of wealthy planters. Some of these were of good Virginia or Carolina families, but more were ignorant and vulgar men; overseers, or even negro traders, formerly, who had gained wealth in these refined pursuits, and were thereby entitled to stand in the ranks of the aristocracy of North Alabama.

The store of the Messrs. Gist was a favorite resort of these neighboring planters. It contained not only the usual assortment of dry goods, groceries, &c., with which country stores are usually supplied, but what was more essential to the social enjoyment of the gentlemen there congregated, excellent liquors of every kind. There too, was the Post Office; and to the patriots of Bainbridge there was never lack of interest in the great subjects of politics, and —— the cotton market. Upon these they conversed day after day, as they sat on the porch at the store door, and night after night the discussions warmed, as the brandied flush crept over cheek and brow of the staunch vindicators of their different party chiefs. Sometimes, indeed the arguments ran so high that the disputants went home with visages slightly disfigured by contact with opposing fists; but these wounds soon healed, and over a bottle of good old wine, such trifling episodes were quite forgotten.

For two years, this little family quietly pursued the regular avocations of the farm. They made excellent crops in proportion to the number of hands employed; and the business of the store was at the same time very lucrative. The brothers bought and shipped cotton, corn, and bacon,. and kept for sale, at a good profit, all kinds of goods that were required by their various customers.

During the winter the slaves had many opportunities of earning pocket money. Flat-boats loaded with cotton, while coming down the river, were frequently stove on the rocks in the Muscle Shoals, at the foot of which Bainbridge is situated. The cotton, becoming wet, was thus rendered unfit for market, unless the bales were opened and thoroughly dried. This furnished employment for the negroes on sundays. Carefully they spread the damp cotton on boards or rocks in the sunshine, turning and shaking it frequently till it was perfectly dry, and fit to be repacked in bales for market. For this labor, they sometimes received a dollar a day— thus supplying themselves with the means of procuring many little comforts.

In the year 1821, Mr. Levi Gist bought a plantation of four hundred and eighty acres, about seven miles south of his home. He also built a large brick house in Bainbridge, the lower story of which he intended to occupy as a store. In the fall of this year, he removed all his servants, except Peter, to the new plantation. Him he retained to wait on himself, and on the beautiful young bride whom he brought home in December.

This lady, whose generous and uniform kindness to himself Peter still delights to remember, was Miss

Thirmuthis Waters, formerly of Nashville. She had come out to Alabama the previous spring with her sister, Mrs. McKiernan, who, with her husband, had settled on a plantation near that recently purchased by Mr. Gist.

Peter had now to perform the duties of cook, house-maid, and waiter, there being no other servant in the house, except a little boy about twelve years old, that assisted him in performing some of the lighter labors.

These were the brightest days that had ever fallen to the lot of the young slave. His time was all occu-pied, but he succeeded in performing his various duties to the satisfaction of his mistress, and he felt not the want of leisure. Her approving smile shed sunshine on his lowly path and her gentle kindness filled his heart with gratitude.

Now, but for the one cloud that shadowed his spirit, he would have enjoyed comparative content. But the thought of his mother far away, who could never hear from him, and whom now he might not hope to see, isolated him, in some sense, from his companions in bonds. It is true, that no intelligent slave can feel that his thraldom is just, because his mother was, perforce, a chattel; and yet, the knowledge that he was born a slave, like those he sees around him, and the total ignorance of a different structure of society, go far to reconcile the unfortunate bondman to his lot.

A few weeks after the wedding, Mr. Gist accom-panied his bride and her sister, Mrs. McKiernan, on a visit to their friends in Nashville.

The journey—one hundred and twenty miles—was performed on horseback; and as the party rode away through the woods on a fine January morning, they formed a beautiful group. Mr. Gist—a well-formed Kentuckian—his fine brown features enlivened by splendid black eyes, and glowing with health and vigor, rode proudly at his lady's side. She was very beautiful. Her large, dark eyes sparkled with animation, and her tall, erect figure, and graceful dignity of carriage, rendered her, in her husband's eyes, an embodiment of womanly perfection.

Near the fair bride rode her sister—a graceful, matronly lady, several years her senior, whose slight. delicate figure presented a marked contrast to her own queenly proportions.

At the distance of a few paces followed Peter, and while he gazed admiringly at the dear forms of his young master and mistress, he was far from being forgetful of his own fine points. He was now nearly twenty-one, and his pleasant, lively face, and obliging manners, won him friends wherever he went. Then, his new suit was very becoming, and he rode as fine a horse as he could wish. Not one of the party was better mounted.

He was proud, too, of his young master, and determined, in his own mind, that the Nashville folks should be impressed with the dignity and consequence of the family into which Miss Thirmuthis had married.

Swiftly flew the two weeks of their stay in Nashville. Several parties were given to the young couple by the family and friends of the bride, and before the plans which their friends had formed for their pleasure were half accomplished, the time that they had allotted to the visit was spent, and they were obliged to set out upon their return.

At the age of twenty-one, Peter began to think

more seriously than he had ever thought before, of establishing a character for life. He saw the moral degradation that prevailed among those of his own color, and he could not but discover that many of their masters failed to keep themselves pure. The vulgar and blasphemous oath, the obscene jest, and the harsh tone of angry passion, he often heard proceeding from the lips of *gentlemen ;*—yes, even the low jargon of drunkenness was not seldom uttered by the lordly master of scores of crouching slaves.

All this the young man saw, and heard—and loathed; and now that he had reached the age of manhood, he resolved to shun the insidious advances of every vice. He abandoned the use of tobacco, which he had commenced when but a boy; and though he had sometimes taken a dram with his companions, he determined that he would thenceforth touch no intoxicating drink. Thereafter, profanity dwelt not upon his lips, and falsehood was a stranger to his tongue. His character for integrity and honesty became firmly established, and though but a slave, he won the entire confidence of all with whom he was connected.*

With these noble resolves of his opening manhood, came ardent desires for freedom. He reviewed his past life—there was nothing there—in feeling, thought, or act—that proved him unfit for liberty. The curse of slavery had embittered his heart, and with every power of his soul aroused, he resolved that he would struggle to escape it. By flight or purchase—*some*

---

* Of Peter's integrity and honesty, the writer speaks from personal knowledge; having been acquainted with him for several years of his slave-life in Alabama.

means must offer—he would yet win back his human birthright.

With this goal of all his hopes, somewhere in the hidden future, he pursued his daily round of humble duties—patiently waiting till he should perceive some opening in the dense, dark cloud that enveloped his fate.

In October, 1822, Mr. Gist relinquished his share in the store to his brother, who had been his partner; and removing to the plantation, devoted his whole attention to agricultural pursuits.

Here they lived in true Southern country style. The "great house" on the plantation consisted of two cabins, built of hewn logs, and whitewashed within and without with lime. A covered passage connected the rooms, over each of which was a small, low chamber. A log kitchen and smoke-house in the rear, with the usual potato-house, saddle-house, and other small, shed-like buildings, each appropriated to the shelter of a single article or class, completed the establishment.

At dawn of day, the master was up and away with his hounds to the woods, and woe to the unlucky fox or rabbit whose trail they chanced to discover.

The overseer, meantime, marshalled his forces; and as there were so few hands on the plantation, he was, by his contract with the master, obliged to take his hoe and work with them.

The domestic arrangement of the household was perfect. The young mistress was fond of order and regularity; and, through her kind and constant discipline, those desirable qualities soon became manifest in the habits of her servants.

Thus, on the plantation of young master Levi, peace and happiness established their dominion. One acquainted with the neighborhood in which he lived, would have pronounced his place an oasis in the desert—a solitary star in a midnight sky.

CHAPTER IX.

LEVIN'S MARRIAGE.

IT is a pleasant Sabbath evening in early spring.
The air is filled with perfume from hosts of new made
flowers, and vocal with the merry notes of birds.

Master Levi rises from his seat on the porch, and
walks slowly to and fro in the yard. He is stouter
and handsomer than he was two years ago, when he
came out on the farm to live. Aye, and happier too;
for the lovely little Mary, that stretches out her tiny
hands towards her papa, and sweetly lisps his name,
has unsealed a new fountain of joy in his bosom.

Yes, he is happy and prosperous. His crops all
look well, and his negroes are healthy and obedient.

"O mass'r!" says a voice at his side. He turns. It
is Levin. He has grown tall and manly since we remarked him last—of course, for he is now about
twenty-five years old, and a fine stout fellow.

"Well, Levin, what do you want?" responds the
master. "What is the matter?"

"O, nuthin's the matter, sir; only I wanted to ax
you if you's willin' I should get married, sir."

"Get married? Why, yes—you're old enough, I
suppose—over twenty, aren't you?

"Yes, sir, I's twenty-five."

" Well, where's the girl you want to marry? You can have a wife as soon as you wish, if you will get one of the right sort."

" I wants Fanny Hogun, sir; and ole Mars Jimmy, he say I may have her if you's willin', sir."

" Fanny Hogun! Old Jimmy Hogun's Fanny! The very worst place in the neighborhood for a fellow to be running! Fanny—let me see—her mother's Linsey, old Jimmy's housekeeper—a regular she-devil. What put into your stupid head to go there to hunt for a wife? No, you can't have Fanny. You may have a wife, and welcome; but no boy of mine shall be spending his nights and Sundays at old Jimmy Hogun's—d'ye hear?"

" But, mass'r, Fanny's a good girl, and 'pears like 'twont do no hurt to go and see her, sir. I don't want nary nother wife, sir."

" But I tell you, Levin, I can't let one of my boys have a wife at such a place as that. So don't talk any more about it. You can hunt up another girl that will suit you better."

Poor Levin walked away. He was sadly disappointed. He knew his master had good cause for disliking to have his people associate with old Jimmy Hogun's negroes; but he and Fanny loved each other so dearly that he could not give her up.

Mr. James Hogun was a bachelor—an eccentric man—silent and unsociable. He was seldom seen from home, even within the circle of his own family connections.

But though as an individual, he was little known, his place was famed in all the country around as the scene of most disgraceful proceedings. No white woman inhabited the premises, but many beautiful slave girls embellished his demesne. Here "patrollers" and other wild and reckless characters were wont to resort at night, and, free from all restraint, to give the rein to every evil passion.

All this was well known to Levin—but Fanny, he was sure, was not like her companions. She was good and true, and she loved him.

He disliked exceedingly to offend his master who had always been so kind to him, and yet he could not decide to sacrifice his deepest, truest affection. For some time he hesitated, but at last love conquered; and without the approbation of his master, he took the lively Fanny for his wife.

Mr. and Mrs. Gist were both displeased. They had reasoned with Levin, and sought by every kind method to dissuade him from this measure, and his disobedience gave them real pain.

Levin had hoped that, once married, all his troubles would be past, but he soon ascertained that they had but just commenced.

He could seldom go to see his wife, for the overseer, aware that his master was opposed to his going, placed every possible impediment in his way. Once, indeed, he went so far, the day after one of these stolen visits, as to strip him and tie him up, intending to whip him well. The master, however, forbade the execution of this design, and the disappointed ruffian could only avenge his wounded pride by crushing his intended victim with heaps of curses.

But when Fanny dared to come to see her husband, she was under no such friendly protection. In vain Levin begged that she might be spared, and threatened to tell his master. The overseer knew that Mr. Gist did not favor her visits, and as he seldom had an opportunity to exercise his disciplinary talents, now— " *Gist was so devilish careful of his niggers*"—he could ill afford to lose such opportunities for sport.

Soon after his marriage, Levin's health failed, and he became unable to continue his labors in the field. He could, however, do light work, and his mistress took him into the house.

His master now renewed his efforts to persuade him to refrain from visiting his wife, but all in vain. His love for Fanny was warm and true, and no argument could move him.

Mr. Gist's patience at length gave way. His anger rose. He would not thus be baffled by a servant—he would force him to obey his wishes! He accordingly bound the astonished slave, and whipped him severely. Three hundred and seventeen lashes fell upon his naked back.

A little later, and the master's passion had subsided. He was astonished at himself. Remorse and bitter sorrow filled his heart; and with his own brave frankness he confessed—even to the victim of his wrath— that he had done a grievous wrong. "I have acted hastily," said he, "while in a passion, and I am very sorry."

After this no force was used to prevent the intercourse of the true-hearted pair, but they were permitted peaceably to enjoy their transient visits to each other.

CHAPTER X.

VINA'S EARLY HISTORY.

In Edgecombe county, N. C., about seven miles from Tarboro', lived a respectable planter, named William Foxall. He was handsome in person, and in manners most agreeable; a kind master, and a true-hearted friend.

At the time of which we speak—1817—he was a widower with two children. The eldest, a lovely and accomplished young lady, named Mary Ann, the fruit of his first marriage, resided with her father; but the little boy, a final parting gift from his last wife, was adopted by her grandmother immediately after her daughter's death.

Mr. Foxall was not a wealthy man; indeed he had never been ambitious to accumulate great riches. He had chosen rather to live in the enjoyment of the competency bequeathed him by his ancestors, and to leave it, together with an untarnished name, as an inheritance to his children.

But the quiet he had chosen was destined to be interrupted by the entreaties of an old schoolmate, who had resided for a few years in Lawrence county, Alabama.

This gentleman, whose name was Allen, wrote frequently to Mr. Foxall, and always begged him to sell what he termed his meagre old plantation, and to come to the Tennessee Valley. "Here," said he, "you will find a country beautiful by nature, and rich as beautiful. The soil seems eager to yield its increase, and wealth waits but the planter's bidding. Come to this charming valley, where, with the forces now at your command, a few years' crops will make you independent, and insure wealth to your children after you are gone."

The alluring prospect tempted even the unambitious Foxall; and he sold his old plantation, endeared as it was to him by a thousand tender associations. His servants, old and young, he resolved to take with him.

Among these, there was one woman named Sally, who, with her three children, properly belonged to his daughter; she having been given to the first Mrs. Foxall on her marriage.

Sally was an excellent servant, and devotedly attached to her young mistress. She had waited on her departed mother when she too was a blooming maiden, and had arrayed her in her bridal robes. All her cares and sorrows she had shared; and when their beloved mistress was passing away, she it was that smoothed the dying pillow, and folded the meek hands to their long repose.

Then the deep love of her nature was transferred to the sweet infant left wholly to her care; and though when her own children were born, a new fount of tenderness was opened in her heart, it was scarce deeper than that which had welled forth for the motherless babe she had cherished.

Her own poor children, alas! were now fatherless— though *death* had spared the husband of her love.

His name was Silas; and his owner, a Mr. Sisson, lived a few miles from Mr. Foxall's plantation. Silas was a carpenter, a fine energetic fellow, and was highly esteemed by his owner. He was also full of affection for his wife and babes; and was unhappy only when by some arrangement beyond his control, he was prevented from enjoying their society at the stated season.

When the youngest of his three children was but an infant, a branch of the Sisson family removed to Alabama, and as they would be obliged on arriving there to build themselves a house, they took Silas with them.

Sad was his heart when he came to say "Good bye" to Sally and her little ones, but he was hopeful. He was not *sold;* and when the new house should be built in that strange wild place where they were going, he could return. They would not keep him there, away from all he loved—ah, no!

But a year passed, and no permission came for Silas to return to the old place. He had been patient, but his endurance could not last forever; and one night, when all was still about the new house he had built, he rose up quietly, and bade a silent farewell to the kind friends that seemed so unwilling to let him go.

He was not long in returning to his old home, and there he spent one more happy year. His little children learned to watch for his coming, and Sally's eyes regained their wonted brilliancy.

Ah! when he had ceased to fear, then was his danger nearest. The man from whom he had fled came again, and carried him away in heavy chains.

Where he was conveyed, his wife knew not. Only once more she saw his face. After she had for months deplored his sad fate, he came to see her. Three days his "pass" allowed him to remain with her. How swiftly did they pass?

He had been working at his trade, he said, but they were about to send him to the Potomac river, to be employed upon a boat; and when he could come again, he did not know.

Never more did Sally's eye rest upon the form of her husband; never more did his pleasant voice delight her ear. Year after year she watched for his coming, till her heart grew sick with waiting, and she knew that she must give him up.

At last, the news that the Foxall family was about to remove to Alabama, reached his ears, and though he could not visit his dear ones, he found an opportunity to send them some little presents, as farewell tokens of his love.

The grandparents of Miss Foxall insisted that if her father went to Alabama, she should remain with them. That rude new country would be no place for her, destitute as she was of a mother's care; and though Mr. Foxall longed for her cheering presence, he felt that they were right; and with a father's blessing, he left his daughter to their guardianship.

Sally, too, and her children, should have remained, but he needed all his forces to make his first crop; and as he promised to send them back when he should be able to dispense with their services, his daughter and her friends consented to his taking them.

Sally's oldest child was named Jerry. He was a fine healthy boy, nine years old. Lavinia, or Vina, as she was usually called, was seven, and Quall, the youngest, a bright merry boy, was nearly five. These were the light of her eyes; and though she grieved at the thought of parting with her young mistress, and wondered who would now perform for her all the little services that had never yet been entrusted to less careful hands than hers, yet she felt that, so long as she could keep all her own children with her, she should not repine.

Dr. Allen, the friend who had urged Mr. Foxall's emigration, was settled near Courtland, Lawrence county. Here he had a fine plantation, and his friend bought one adjoining. Then with the idea that they could thus work their hands to better advantage, they entered into partnership, working all the land together, and sharing equally the profits.

Year after year passed in his new home; yet the bright visions of wealth that had enticed Mr. Foxall thitherward, vanished into thin air.

Not that his friend had exaggerated the fertility of the soil, or any other of the peculiar natural advantages of the beautiful valley in which he had settled. No; the rich bottom lands near the river teemed with vegetation, and the broad plains for miles back brought forth abundant crops. Nature's work was all perfect; and the laborers performed their duty well.

Cotton was "made" and sold; and corn, in quantities that astonished the Carolinians, who had all their lives been accustomed to tilling a less prolific soil.

Yet, notwithstanding all this apparent prosperity, the coffers of the planters were not full; and as years passed on, though crops were regularly gathered in and sold, great debts accumulated, and ruin stared them in the face.

Ah, William Foxall! could you hope to grow rich,

when your fortune was linked with that of a drunkard and a gambler?

With the cowardice characteristic of the votaries of dissipation, Dr. Allen, when he saw that a crash was inevitable, privately quitted the country, leaving his partner to endure alone the consequences of his own criminal self-indulgence, and to arrange the business as he could.

Poor Mr. Foxall was overcome with grief and humiliation. The debts had been contracted by his partner, but as his share of their wasted property was insufficient to pay one-third of them, he was obliged to turn out all his own. Even the trusting servants, more his friends than slaves, that he had brought with him from the dear old home, must go to satisfy the gambler's creditors.

Oh! what a wave of sorrow rushed over the spirits of those doomed slaves, when they learned their destiny! Even Sally and her children, who should have been sent back to their young mistress, to whom of right they still belonged, they, too, were given up.

As many as could be sold at private sale were thus disposed of. That was better than to be put up at auction, where they might fall into the hands of traders, and thus become so widely scattered that they could never more hear from each other.

Vina was the first of all the number to be sold. She had been hired out as a nurse for two or three years, and was now in the service of Mrs. Smith, at the hotel in Courtland.

It was Sunday morning, and Aunt Sally was coming in that day from the plantation, to see her children.

Vina had dressed the baby, and was just finishing the arranging of her mistress' room, when Dr. P——, of Cortland, entered.

"Your name is Vina," said he, "and you belong to Mr. Foxall?"

"Yes, sir."

"Well, I have bought you, and you must be ready to go with me in an hour."

He left the room, and Vina gazed after him like one bewildered. It was so sudden, only one hour, and her mother had not yet come.

She looked up the street. There was no one in sight that cared for her. A thought struck her. She would go and see her master, and learn from his own lips her fate. She would beg him to let her stay till her mother shold come; she could not go away without bidding her "Good-bye."

Mr. Foxall lived in the village, in a large brick house, near the hotel. Thither the excited girl ran. "Is Mass'r in the house?" asked she of the first servant that she met.

"I reckon so; I aint seen him gwine out."

But the master, well-nigh broken hearted at the necessity of parting with his servants, could not be found. Vina ran through the house, searching every room that was unlocked. He had expected this, and he could not bear to meet her, after he had sold her to a stranger.

The poor girl returned to the hotel. She had learned from some of the servants that Dr. P. had not bought her for himself; but that, being indebted to Mr. McKiernan, of Franklin county, and his former partner, Mr. Stout, of Nashville, he had, at their request, bought her and a young girl named Rosetta, for them.

With an aching heart, she stood watching for her mother. There was no tear in her eye, and her features were fixed and rigid. Ah Sally ! came there no spirit-voice to thee, bidding thee hasten to thy child, whose heart was breaking ?

" Ready, girl ?" shouted a coarse voice. " Come ! can't wait. Bring along your traps, if you've got any, but you can't take a big bundle, seein' there's two on you to ride."

Vina gazed a moment at the speaker, an ill-looking young man on horseback, and then, seeing that Rosetta stood by his side, holding another horse by the bridle, she silently picked up the little bundle she had prepared, and went out. One long look she cast up the street, with a faint hope that she might yet see her mother's form approaching.

That hope was vain. She saw many happy mothers with their children, walking to the house of God ; and maidens of her own age tripped by, unconscious alike of grief and care. No tearful pitying eye rested upon *her* face, no heart sighed at the utter desolation of *her* hopes.

She mounted the horse mechanically, as one in a dream ; and Rosetta sprang up behind her.

Silently, hour after hour, they followed their rough guide. Now, blooming fields, on either side, smiled on them as they passed ; and then, their road crept through thick gloomy woods, that hid the darkness in their shadowy depths through all the bright Spring days.

CHAPTER XI.

VINA'S FIRST YEAR AT McKIERNAN'S.

LATE in the evening, the two young maidens reached their destination, and were conducted to the kitchen. Bashfully they crept into the darkest corner, while curious eyes stared at them from every side, and wondering whispers passed from lip to lip.

The cook alone seemed not surprised at the arrival of the strangers, but with a wise look that well became her elevated station, bade them come closer to the fire; for "'Pears like," said she, "de evenin's sort o' cold. Missus 'll be home to-reckly; she went to Tuscumby to church, to-day, wid her sister, Miss 'Muthis. Dar, warm yerself, honey, you looks sort o' chilly like," continued the old woman, as she drew Rosetta towards the blazing fire, at which she was preparing supper.

Rosetta had left neither father nor mother behind, and though she was sad at leaving her young companions, and above all, her master, whom she almost adored, yet these slight regrets soon subsided, and she readily glided into conversation, with the new associates to whom she had been so unceremoniously presented. The iron had not entered her soul.

But Vina crept further back into her shadowed corner, where, heedless of the numerous visitors that love to assemble on Sunday evening in a planter's kitchen, she yielded to the influence of her desponding thoughts. Yet no tear moistened her eye-lid, no sob gave vent to the choking anguish of her heart.

" Missis come : say, bring in supper;" said a young girl, appearing for a moment at the kitchen door.

Supper was carried in, and, one by one, the dark visitors to the kitchen went out; some to prepare their own scant evening meals, and others to collect again in little groups for confidential chat.

"Hi! dem's nice gals in yon!" said the tallest in one of these groups—a kind hearted fellow, that had pitied the confusion of the young strangers.

" Not over an' above nice, I reckon; dat little un's sort o' fa'r, but t'other looks like she don't know nuthin'. She aint much 'count, no how."

" You don't know 'bout dat dar," rejoined the first speaker, "she mought 'a' lef'—her sweetheart—'way yon'—pears like she feels mighty bad."

" Missus say, come in de house; she want to see what ye all looks like;" cried the same young girl at the kitchen door.

" Dar, go 'long honey," said the old cook, as she drew Vina from the shaded corner, and placed her beside Rosetta. "Hol' up yer heads now, children, and look peart like when ye goes in to see Missus; go 'long."

" De Lor' help 'em, poor little critters," sighed the kind old woman, as she watched them from the kitchen door, "dey's got a she wolf to deal wid now. 'Pears like dey aint used to hard times, no how, but nobody cant say dat dar 'bout em, arter dey's done staid on dis yer place one year."

Timidly the two girls advanced into the presence of their future mistress. She fixed her keen cold eyes on them for a moment, and then addressed herself to Vina.

"What can you do, girl?"

"I's been used to nursin', ma'am, and waitin' in the house."

"Did you never work in the field?"

"No, ma'am."

"Ah! you've been raised quite a lady! Can you *round corn?*"*

"I don't know what that is, ma'am."

"Can you *chop through cotton?*"†

"No, ma'am."

"You're such a lady, I suppose you never saw any cotton grow."

"Yes ma'am, I's seen a plenty of cotton a growin', but I never worked it."

Mr. McKiernan then approached, and unfastening her frock behind, examined her back. "Have you ever been whipped?" asked he.

"No, Sir."

"So I thought, your back is as smooth as mine."

He then proceeded to make a more minute examination of her person, inspecting her limbs, to see whether she were well-formed and sound.

Rosetta then underwent a similar examination, and the master and mistress both seeming satisfied, they were dismissed.

"See that you behave yourselves," said the master,

---

* Weeding around the hills.

† Thinning the cotton by removing all superfluous stalks, so as to leave only enough for a stand.

as they went out,—"if you do well, you'll find that we shall be good to you."

Martha, the young girl before mentioned, accompanied them back to the kitchen. "Your coat is unfastened," said Rosetta, as they went out, "stop a minute till I button it."

"O no," whispered Martha, "I can't have it fastened, my back's so sore."

"What's the matter with your back?"

"Why, whar missus cuts me up. She's allers a beatin' me. O I wish I's dead!"

The strangers exchanged mournful looks, but not another word was spoken.

After they went out, a consultation was held in "Missus'" room, concerning the most profitable disposition that could be made of the two girls. "Mr. Stout will not be on for his till some time in the summer," said the mistress; "there will be time enough before that to ascertain which will make the most valuable servant; but it isn't best to let them know that either of them is to go to Nashville. We will try them, and keep the one that we like best."

They were both unaccustomed to field labor, and after due consultation .it was decided best to send Martha out, and to keep both of the new ones for the present in the house. Accordingly, the next morning, Martha was sent to the field. She was glad of the exchange, for she was not strong, and her mistress had taxed her powers of endurance to the utmost. To Vina was assigned the post of housemaid and waiter; and Rosetta was installed as nurse of Bernard McKiernan, Junior, then but a few months old.

Mrs. McKiernan was much pleased with her two

new maids, and with good reason, for they were quick and careful, and attentive to all her instructions. Poor Martha's bruised back had filled their hearts with terror; and from the conversations of their fellow-servants in the kitchen, they gained no impressions of their new mistress that tended to dispel their fears.

For three months the young girls quietly pursued their monotonous round of daily duties; and thus far, they had scarcely given occasion to their mistress for a reproof.

Rosetta had become quite happy and contented; but poor Vina's heart pined for her mother. All night she lay very still, wrapt in a blanket, on the floor of her mistress' room, and wondered if her mother and brothers had been sold, and wished she knew where they had been carried. When she fell asleep, her heart was wandering still through strange, lonely places, in search of those whose forms, alas! she might never more behold. But after all, they might be very near her—Oh! if she could only hear who had bought them!

This perpetual anxiety could not fail to impair her health. She lost all appetite for food; and though she uttered no complaint, one could plainly see, by her wasted figure, and by the look of melancholy that never left her face, that she was wretched.

One morning in June, as Mrs. McKiernan, according to her custom, was making a tour of discovery through the house, to be sure that everything was in order, she chanced to spy a silver ladle in the kitchen, that must have remained there since dinner-time of the preceding day. It was the first instance of carelessness or neglect that had occurred in Vina's department since she had been in the house; and with quick anger, the mistress seized the cowhide.

Vina had never in her life been whipped, except when, for some childish fault, her mother had corrected her; and now, when her mistress called her in an angry tone, saying *she* could make her remember to take care of the silver, the thought of Martha's lacerated back sent a shudder through her frame. But she did not weep, nor beg for mercy.

With her own fair hands the *delicate lady* chastised her trembling slave. She did it *very gently*, for she was not half as angry as she oftentimes became at smaller provocations. Yet the blood oozed through the bruised skin that was swelled in ridges across poor Vina's back; and she imagined—ignorant creature that she was—that she had been severely punished. Ah! the day was coming, when she would designate such a whipping as "*only a slight bresh.*"

From that morning, she determined, if possible, to escape from the immediate jurisdiction of her mistress; and soon after, seeing her master alone, she went to him, and asked him if she might go to the field.

"Why?" said he, "what the devil put that into your head? You don't know anything about field work, do you?"

"No, Sir, but I reckon I could learn; and I mought as well take my chance in the field as to stay in the house. But, please Sir, don't let missus know I axed you."

"Yes, yes; well, I won't tell her. I'd like to have you in the field, any how, for Martha's sickly, and not much account. Go along now; I'll talk to your mistress about it."

"Look here," said he to his wife, soon after this conversation; "Martha don't do much in the field; she's sickly, you know, and she can't keep up with the others. I reckon we'd better bring her back into the house, and take Vina in her place. She seems to be well, and willing to work."

"Well," replied the lady, in her characteristic asperity of tone, "I'd rather have Vina in the house; but if you can't manage Martha, send her in. I can make her work; she will never conquer me with her sickly complaining."

The next morning Vina went to the field, where, though at first all was strange, she soon learned to "round corn," that being then the work in season.

About midsummer, Mr. Stout came on from Nashville, to see the girl that had been bought for him, and to take her home.

Both the girls were shown him. He seemed to prefer Vina, but Mr. and Mrs. McKiernan both assured him that as he wanted a house servant, it would be much better for him to take Rosetta; for she was a very bright girl, and was becoming every day more useful. They could make Vina do very well in the field, but she was exceedingly ignorant, and withal quite deaf, so that it would be utterly impossible for her to learn the duties of a waiter or a nurse.

Mr. Stout, having been for many years a partner of Mr. McKiernan in a carriage factory in Nashville, understood his habits and principles of action. He had also some idea of the prevailing characteristics of his wife; and, suspecting that their advice was not entirely disinterested, he improved an opportunity to go alone to the field where the hands were all at work. He talked awhile with the head-man, Nelson, about the weather and the crops; and then, noticing Vina at her work, he carelessly asked the man what sort of a girl she was.

"Oh! she is a good hand, Sir, fus rate, Sir."

"Can she hear well?"

"Yes, Sir," replied Nelson, with a puzzled look.

"Your mistress told me she was right deaf."

"Well, call her, Sir, see if she can't hear. Yah! yah! Dat little gal deaf."

"O, Vina!" said Mr. Stout. She looked up from her work. "How do you get along, Vina? Would you like to go and live with me?"

"Whar you live, sir?"

"I live in Nashville. Would you like to go there?"

"Oh! I don't know, sir. I's fur enough from my mother now. I reckon I don't never want to go no furder."

Mr. Stout returned to the house. He saw the true state of the case, but it would be of no use to *seem* to understand it; so when a few days after, he left for home, he took Rosetta with him. She had no ties to bind her here, and was well pleased with the idea of living in Nashville; of which city she had heard glowing descriptions from the old servants. They were "raised" there, and still remembered the place with true home-love.

Towards the last of August, when the crop was laid by, Vina, who still pined for her mother, received from her master a "pass" to Courtland. She had some clothes there, which she wished to get; and even if her mother were sold, she hoped at least to learn where she had gone.

She started on Thursday morning ; and, as she rode alone on horseback over the road that a few months before had seemed so dark and lonely, the shadow that ever since that day had rested on her heart, was lifted. She was young; and Hope, though crushed and silent long, revived again; and whispered in her fainting spirit's ear, sweet promises of brighter days to come.

It was noon when she reached Courtland. How her heart beat as she rode up the familiar street!

Soon her eager eyes rested on an old acquaintance, and she inquired in trembling accents for her mother.

"La! honey," replied the old woman she had accosted, "whar you been all dis time, and never knowed yer mammy sol'? Mr. Peoples done bought her; dat Peoples whar live off yon' east o' town 'bout four mile. He got ole Moses and Jerry too; yer mammy's mighty lucky—got sol' 'long o' her ole man, and one o' her boys. Mr. Peoples mighty good massa too; leastways so all de folks say whar lives out dar. But yer mammy to Mr. Mosely's now. Mr. Peoples done hire 'em all out for de balance o' dis year."

Vina could listen no longer. Her heart was throbbing wildly; and tears, that despair had long forbid to flow, were standing in her eyes. She turned her horse in the direction of Mr. Mosely's;—he must not stop to rest till she should arrive at that goal of all her hopes—her mother's side.

Aunt Sally was at work in the field, at a short distance from the house, and little dreamed that she should that day behold the daughter for a sight of whose features she had so earnestly prayed.

Vina left her horse at the house, and walked to the field. She came very near the group of slaves at work before she was perceived. Suddenly her mother raised her head :—" My chile ! my chile !" she cried, as with uplifted hands and streaming eyes she ran to meet her daughter, and pressed her closely to her breast.

Mrs. Mosely had bidden Vina to tell her mother that she might " have holiday" while she remained ; and when the first gush of emotion had subsided, they walked together to the house.

" O Vina !" said her mother, " how I did mourn when I come to town dat Sunday, and you was gone. I reckon I skeered 'em all a screamin' and takin' on. I didn't know what to do, so I went right to mass'r. He felt mighty bad too ; but he say he can't hope it ; he's 'bliged, he say, sell every thing—and de Lord knowed he wouldn't part wid his servants if dar was any way for him to keep 'em. He cried a heap while I was dar. O 'pears like, gentlemen mought keep out o' debt when dey knows what trouble it 'll all come to at las'. He couldn't tell me nuthin' 'bout de place whar you done gone ; all he said, he done sol' you and Rosetta to Dr. T. ; and he's gwine send one to a gentleman in Franklin, and t'other to Nashville. O Lord ! how my heart did ache ! and 'pears like it never stop achin' 'till I see your blessed face. Is you got a good mas'r and missus, chile ?"

" Not over and 'bove ; but they 'aint troubled me much yit. They's mighty tight on the rest. O how some o' the people thar does git cut up ! 'Pears like they will kill 'em sometime."

" Poor chile ! poor chile ! May de good Lord keep de wolves off o' your flesh ! Der aint no way to live wid dem kind, only to pray to de Lord to keep de lions' mouths shut up."

Aunt Sally had married a man named Moses, since she came to Alabama, and having been sold with him and her oldest son, she felt that her lot was far better than that of many of her companions. She possessed a kind and grateful disposition, and her trust was in the arm of her Redeemer. " We's poor critters in dis yer world," she would remark, " but dars a crown for us yon', if we minds de word of de Lord, and keeps patient to de end."

" Now," said Aunt Sally, as they all sat round the door, enjoying the cool air of evening, " if Quall only knowed you was yer, Vina, and if mass'r could spare him, we'd be altogether once more. Poor Quall! mass'r say he gwine keep him ; but I don't know—I 'spect I shall hear he's sol', too."

Swiftly passed the hours till Sunday ; when, as her " pass" specified, Vina must return. She lingered as long as she dared, and when she *must* go, and Jerry had saddled her horse, and brought him to the door, she tore herself from her mother's arms, sprang into the saddle—and was gone.

Vina returned safely to her master's house. The old light came back to her eye, and the accustomed elasticity to her step ; and the old cook remarked that little Vina had " gone mighty peart like since she tuck dat dar jaunt to de ole place."

CHAPTER XII.

THE MARRIAGE.

DURING the first months of Vina's residence at Mr. McKiernan's, she formed no intimacies with her companions. Her heart was too heavy to sympathize in their transient griefs, or to join in the merry sports with which they sought to enliven their brief intervals of rest.

Mr. Gist's plantation lay very near, indeed, the dwellings were not more than a mile apart, and from the near relationship of the two families, a greater intimacy existed between the servants than is usual between the slaves even of near neighbors.

Peter was at this time a fine, cheerful fellow, in the first fresh vigor of manhood; and, being a special favorite with his mistress, he was always a welcome visitor at the plantation of her brother-in-law. Mr. and Mrs. McKiernan liked him, for he was always respectful and obliging; and to their servants, his bright, good-humored face brought ever a gleam of the heart's sunshine.

Even the lovely little Vina felt the genial influence of his presence, and her shyness and reserve gradually melted away in the warmth of his smiles. At the first sight of the desolate stranger his heart was moved to pity ; and, as he never failed to speak kindly to her, she soon began to look for his coming, as a weary watcher waits for the morning.

Thus, week after week, and month after month, grew and strengthened the sympathy between the brave-hearted youth, and the timid, shrinking maiden; and when Vina had been a year in her new home, they had confessed their mutual love, and only waited for a favorable opportunity to be united in marriage.

True, Vina was but fifteen years old, but she was very destitute and helpless, and there was none but Peter to care for her.

Her master and mistress were pleased to observe this growing attachment. Mr. McKiernan had always fancied Peter, and longed to own him; and, as he knew it would be inconvenient for him to have a wife away from home, he determined to encourage him to marry Vina, that then he might perhaps be able to induce his brother-in-law to sell him.

To his master and mistress, Peter dreaded to communicate his wishes. He had seen poor Levin's sufferings in consequence of having formed a connection which they did not approve; and he was conscious of the difficulties that would attend his caring for a wife on any neighboring plantation. His mistress always wanted him at home. She depended on him; and he knew that she would object to having his attention diverted from her business by family cares of his own.

Yet, while he understood all this, he felt that he was, himself, a man. Was he not twenty-five years old, and had he not a right to marry? Surely, when he had waited for so many years upon his master's family, without ever indulging a wish that could interrupt their pleasure, they might be content to spare him now and then on a Sunday for the cultivation and enjoyment of his own affections.

Still he knew they would oppose him, and he could not bear to vex them; so he postponed speaking to them of his wishes till something should occur that would naturally open the way for the communication.

Thus the matter was suspended, when, early in May, Mr. and Mrs. Gist announced their intention of visiting Lexington. They had for several years been talking of going there, and had promised Peter that when they went, he might drive the carriage. He had anticipated much pleasure in the visit; and when, year after year, circumstances had rendered its postponement necessary, he had keenly felt the disappointment.

But now, to the surprise of all, he did not wish to go. " Not go !" cried his master, " I thought there was nothing you would like so well !"

" Well, so I would," replied Peter, " but it's so long now, that I 'm 'feared everybody there done forgot me. There would 'nt be nobody glad to see me, no how."

" Well, well, then old man Frank can go—he'll not want to be asked twice."

Uncle Frank was wild with delight at the intelligence that Peter was to stay at home. There were so many old friends there that he would be glad to see— " yah ! yah ! Reckon all de folks in Lexington ain't forgot ole Frank."

Mrs. Gist had a brother living near; and to him, while he should be away, Mr. Gist entrusted the care of his servants. The overseer was to be under his authority ; and no slave was to be whipped, or in any way abused, during the master's absence. He knew that some of them might do wrong, and might even deserve whipping; but he chose to be there himself when they were punished, in order to be sure that justice was administered; and so, whatever might be the offence, the execution of the penalty should be postponed till his return.

On a fine May morning, the carriage drove up to the door. The trunks were strapped on behind, and a dozen little baskets and bundles were stowed away inside. The mistress, with her sister-in-law, Miss Mary Gist, was handed in by Master Levi, and the nurse followed with her little charge, the precious baby, Mary. Uncle Frank mounted the box; he was dressed in a new suit, and as he bowed good-bye to all his colored friends that stood about the door, his white teeth gleamed in the sunshine, and his black face shone with delight.

With a grand flourish of the whip he gave the signal to the spirited horses, and away they went; while loving eyes looked a fond adieu from the carriage windows, and many a dark hand from the crowded porch waved an affectionate response.

Master Levi's horse was ready; and, after shaking hands all around, and charging the servants again and again to take good care of everything in his absence, he sprang into the saddle, and galloped on to overtake the carriage.

Many were the warm wishes for a pleasant journey to "young Mass'r and Missus" that followed the travellers from that sable band; and many a fear was breathed that "Miss 'Muthis" or the sweet baby would "git mighty tired a ridin' off so far."

Soon they dispersed to their necessary labors—all

but Peter. He remained upon the porch alone. His eyes were fixed on the spot where the carriage had disappeared, and lo! they were dim with unshed tears. Ah! it was a great pleasure he had sacrificed. Now he should never see Lexington again. There he had suffered much; but, after all, he loved the old place. His boy-friends were, doubtless, scattered; yet he would like to learn their history—he hoped they were all happier than he.

" Ha! what a fool I am!" thought he, as some sound of busy life within the house roused him from his regretful reverie; " here I stand, and they're gone. I'll be married to Vina 'fore they come back, and then it'll be too late to make a fuss about it."

He walked quietly away to his work, and all day long, his thoughts were busier than his hands. When his task was done, his plan was laid; and with a light step he trod the path to Aunt Lucy's cabin, which, since Vina went into the field, had been her home.

It was easy to win her consent to immediate marriage; for she was but a lonely girl; and her young heart, so long unused to sympathy, bounded at the approach of the footsteps of love.

Her master readily assented to the plan proposed by Peter; and, on the evening of the twenty-fifth of June, all preliminary arrangements having been completed, they were married.

Old Cato Hodge, a Baptist preacher belonging to one of the neighbors, performed the ceremony. That over, a merry company, consisting of all Vina's fellow-servants, and a few of Peter's best friends from his master's plantation, enjoyed a substantial supper in the kitchen.

The bride was very pretty, notwithstanding her grotesque attire, which consisted of an old white dress and a few quaint old-fashioned ornaments, that she had gathered from the discarded finery of her mistress.

Vina was very poor. The clothes she had brought with her from Courtland were worn out, or had been stolen by the negroes; and a white linsey frock, which her mistress had given her the preceding fall, was minus the front breadth. This was the only article of clothing she had received since she had been on the place; and, as there was no immediate prospect of her getting another, Peter gave her a black surtout coat of his own with which she patched it; and though it was now half black and half white, it was quite comfortable.

She had driven four forked sticks into the ground in Aunt Lucy's cabin, and laid poles across from one to the other. On these she placed four clapboards, four and a half feet long. This was her bed; and her only covering consisted of a piece of an old blanket, which the kind Aunt Lucy had been able to spare to her. Other property she had none.

Peter, however, had good clothes; and when he found that Mr. McKiernan would supply them with no comforts, he sold many articles from his own wardrobe, that he might provide decent clothing for his wife.

Not long after her marriage, Vina again obtained permission to visit her mother.

She found her now at Mr. Peoples' place, and though there was, perhaps, less rapture in their meeting than at her former visit, there was more unmingled joy. Long and earnest were the conversations they held together, and many times the "Good Lord" was thanked for all the kindness he had shown them.

Aunt Sally had now a kind, considerate master, and her husband and her oldest child were with her there. Her former master had gone back to North Carolina; but he had sold Quall in Courtland to a Mr. Bynum. The poor boy had lost in the exchange of masters; but he was still near his mother, and for that she rendered thanks to Him who reigns above.

It were needless to detail the thousand items of advice and instruction which the young wife at this time received from her mother. The few days allotted to the visit passed all too soon, and the beloved daughter was forced to say " Good-bye." This time, however, there was less of anguish in the parting—*all* she loved was not left behind.

The Mistress' welcome home   See page 115.

CHAPTER XIII.

THE NEW CABIN.

THERE was an anxious gathering of dark faces just after sunset. Earnest eyes were peering through the trees in the direction of the great road, and long fingers shook threatfully at each little sable urchin, that could not stand still, and listen for the carriage wheels. The cook bustled about—now in the kitchen, watching her biscuits lest they should bake too brown; now in the house, to be sure that nothing was wanting on the neat supper table, and then her steaming figure came puffing through the crowd before the door, that she might be the first to welcome "Missus."

There! the faint rumble of wheels is heard approaching. A joyous shout rises from the excited throng, and a score of tiny feet fly in the direction of the sound. There is a merry strife between the proprietors of all these little feet for the high privilege of opening the gate for "Missus," but it lasts not long. The carriage comes in sight, and all the little eager hands are laid at once upon the gate, which flies wide open at their touch.

Here they come! Old Frank's smile is brighter, even in the twilight, than when last it beamed upon us in the full morning sunshine, and as he wheels proudly up before the door, his old heart warms at the kindly smiles that beam upon him.

How quickly is the carriage door flung open, and the steps let down! and how lightly the beautiful mistress is set down in the midst of her delighted servants, every one of whom pushes forward to offer a warm welcome home. The fair hand she presents is reverently shaken or tenderly kissed, and "How d'y' Missus?" "Oh! you's pertier 'an ever!" "How glad I is you's come home once mo'!" greet her on every side, as she passes into the house.

Nurse tenderly lifts the little Mary from the carriage. She is fast asleep, and as she lays her in her late deserted cradle, the dark faces steal along, one by one, to get a peep at her sweet baby-face.

"Bless my life! if dar aint Mass'r! Hi! we all's so glad see Missus, we done forget Mass'r gwine come too!" The hearty welcomes are repeated, the extended hand is duly shaken, and by the time Missus, with the aid of a dozen eager hands can be prepared to sit down at the table, supper is brought in.

"Well Peter, so you've stolen a march on us since we've been gone—been getting married, hey?"

"Yes, Sir, I's been gettin' married."

"Ha! ha! you thought the folks at Lexington had all forgotten you. Well, since you have been so smart, I must try and buy your wife for you. You'll not be worth much if you have to be running off every week to see your family. Besides, Mr. McKiernan intends to move to Bainbridge about Christmas, and then you'll have a long road to travel.

But Vina's master had no intention of selling her.

She was one of the best servants he had. He would, however, be glad to buy her husband—very glad.

That was out of the question. Neither Mr. Gist nor his wife would consent to sell him, and if they had been willing to part with him, Peter himself would have remonstrated. He knew too well the difference between the two masters to wish for an exchange.

Thus matters stood till Christmas. Peter went frequently to see his wife, as it was so near, and neither his master nor his mistress endeavored to dissuade him from doing so. They had tested their influence with Levin, and they had no desire to repeat the strife.

The brick house that had been built at Bainbridge was now occupied by Mr. McKiernan. He had bought a large plantation there,—much of it new land, and to clear it, and fit it for corn and cotton, required the utmost diligence.

There was no time to build cabins, though there were not half enough for the numerous families of slaves that he carried with him. Every family, therefore, that wished a house to themselves, were obliged to spend their Sundays in building it.

Peter immediately commenced preparations for building a cabin for his wife. Every Saturday he walked to Bainbridge—a distance of seven miles; and early on Sunday morning, he was at his work. All the holy day he toiled, and often when the moon shone, his work ceased not till late at night. Then by the first peep of Monday's dawn, he was up and away, to commence his weekly labors for his master.

Peter was obliged to cut the timber for his house, himself, and then to haul it across the creek. When that was all prepared, he hired men to help him raise it; and though he did his best, it was April when he had the little building finished.

The roof was made of boards, and the chimney of sticks and clay. Puncheons (slabs) formed the floor, and the ground itself made an excellent hearth. Peter was more extravagant than many architects of kindred edifices, in that he had a floor at all. The bare earth is generally deemed sufficient, and it becomes at length, by constant treading, almost as hard as brick.

The house completed, it was empty. Peter had worked nights and holidays, and had earned all he could, but, alas! that was very little; and now he was forced to sell more of his clothes to buy the most necessary articles of furniture. Two or three cooking utensils, two chairs, and a trunk, he procured at first. Then he cut a walnut tree, and "hauled" it to the mill for a bedstead, and when that was done, a straw bed was prepared and laid upon it.

Every Sunday morning, at Mr. McKiernan's, the weekly allowance was weighed out. This was generally practised by the Kentucky planters. Their servants all ate together, and usually a plentiful supply was cooked for them. But here, a peck of unsifted meal, and three and a half pounds of bacon, was the weekly allowance. The piece might be more than half bone, yet no additional weight was allowed on that account. No vegetables were provided for them, if they wished any they might raise them for themselves; and then, if they had any desire for decent or comfortable clothes, or any little articles of furniture, they could *sell* the few vegetables which their patches produced, in order to procure them.

Mr. Gist had bought a shoemaker, not long before,

and he had cheerfully imparted instruction in his art to his friend Peter. The slight skill he acquired in this branch of industry was now of great use to him, as he was able to make his own shoes, and those of his wife; thus saving many a dollar that must otherwise have been expended. He also earned many comforts for his cabin by making shoes at night for his fellow slaves.

After a while, *as the wealth of the young couple increased*, they bought a cupboard, and afterwards a chest. This latter article was very necessary, that Vina might lock up her week's provisions, and any little comforts which Peter brought her; as, if they were exposed, some of the half-clad hungry slaves were sure to steal them.

A flour barrel, too, the provident young husband bought, thinking it would be useful in their humble housekeeping; but before he had a chance to take it home, Mr. Gist's overseer took the liberty to appropriate it to his own use.

"That's my bar'l, sir," said Peter, as he saw him removing it, "and I want to use it myself."

"D—n you! hush your mouth, you nigger! I'll let you know you're not to forbid me to use a bar'l when I want it."

"But it's mine," persisted Peter; "I bought it, and I's gwine carry it to my wife."

The overseer was enraged; but he dared take no vengeance except the weak one of showering upon the offender his most terrible curses. When he had exhausted his stock of these, he was forced to wait till the master returned from town.

He then complained to Mr. Gist that one of his

niggers had been impudent to him, and swore he would have revenge. "And if," added he, "I aon't whip him now, I'll give him something that will hurt him a heap worse."

The master hesitated, but finally, judging from the fellow's temper, that such a course would be safest for his slave, he gave him permission to whip him very slightly. Accordingly, Peter was taken to the stable, where twenty-five lashes were inflicted on his naked back.

CHAPTER XIV.

THE YOUNG MOTHER.

On the twelfth of September, 1826, the wailing of a tiny voice was heard in Vina's cabin. A new fount of love gushed up in her mother-heart, to bless the little trembler; and her frame thrilled with a delicious joy, as she proudly placed in her husband's arms his first-born boy.

Oh! how happily to his mother passed the first four weeks of the existence of this little one. Quietly Vina sat in her cabin; and, as she gazed upon the innocent face of her child, and saw his little eyes learning to seek hers in loving trustfulness, her cup was not *all* bitter. She knew her babe was born to slavery—and sorrow; but oh! so dearly did she love it! And, perhaps, after all, it might fall into kind hands, and be far happier than its parents.

Now, with her joy, her care was doubled. As soon as she was able to sit up, she toiled to the extent of her strength to put everything in order in her cabin, before *her month* was up.

Peter had managed to provide materials for a comfortable wardrobe for the little stranger; and she now took great pleasure in making up the tiny garments. They were certainly not very fine, nor traced with elegant embroidery; but when she had them all finished, and laid, neatly folded, in the trunk, she could not help lifting the lid, now and then, to see how nice they looked.

Then she washed and mended all her own and Peter's clothes; for she knew she should have but little time after she went to the field again.

When she did go out, poor little Peter (for the baby bore his father's name), was left all alone upon her bed. Four times in the day, while yet he was very young, she was permitted to go in and minister to his little wants. But she had then only a few minutes to stay; and, though in her heart she longed to lull him to sleep upon her breast, and though he cried so hard when she laid him down, yet she must go.

How tenderly, when she was employed as nurse in Courtland, had she cared for the little ones entrusted to her care! How anxiously had she watched every indication of uneasiness, lest they should be sick! And when the moan of pain fell on her ear, how well she knew the simple remedies for all their little ailments! Now that her own babe needed her constant care, she could not be spared. *The cotton must be picked.*

How her heart ached when she heard him crying, as she often did, when she was at work in the field near the quarter. And if the overseer chanced to be at a distance, so that she thought he would not observe her, how suddenly she darted between the trees that sheltered the cabins, and entered the house! How she pressed her baby to her breast, while her tears fell on his little face! And when she dared not stay a minute longer, how gently she laid him down again, and imprinted one fond kiss upon his cheek.

When she came in at night, she built a bright fire on the clay hearth, and cooked her supper. Then she brought water from the spring, and having undressed her boy, she washed him thoroughly. How he enjoyed the nice cool bath! and how he kicked and laughed in token of his gratitude! But his mother had no time to play with him, for it grew late. So when she had arrayed him in clean clothes, she tied him in a chair, and hastened to her work. There he sat and watched her till his eyelids drooped, and he sank quietly to sleep, while she washed all the garments he had worn that day, and hung them up to dry. Then, after making her cabin as neat as possible, and preparing her food for the next day, she threw off her clothes, and with her baby on her bosom, laid her down to rest.

Many times when she had some extra work to do, her own and her husband's washing, for instance, or an old coat to mend, the morning of another day dawned in the east before her task was done. But the overseer's horn blew not a minute the later, because she had not slept. With aching eyes, and weary limbs, she went forth to the field; and through all the long day, her feet lagged not, though sometimes " 'pears like," to use her own expression, she could not keep awake. " But I wouldn't see my child go dirty and raggety," added she, "if I didn't never git a wink o' sleep."

How welcome to poor Vina was the approach of the Sabbath day! How her eyes brightened, and her heart grew light, as its morning beams filled her little cabin, and revealed her husband playing with his boy.

Sometimes they dressed in their best clothes, and, taking little Peter in their arms, walked to meeting on that day; but oftener they were busy through all its precious hours, working in the patch, or performing some necessary labor about the house.

A large field was divided into as many little patches as there were field hands on the plantation; and every slave could here work nights and Sundays to cultivate his crop. Some raised cotton, others corn; and many planted their patches entirely to water-melons. If the overseer chanced to be "far'ard" with his work, and there was not much grass among the corn and cotton, they could sometimes have a half holiday on Saturday to work for themselves. But chiefly they depended on their Sundays. Early in the morning they were out with mules and ploughs, and till late at night they toiled to raise their little crops. When the moon shone brightly, if they were getting "in the grass," they often remained at work all night.

The corn and cotton that they "*made*," they were obliged to sell to their master—*at his price*, which was seldom more than half the market value. But the water-melons they were allowed to carry to town. This was the most profitable crop they raised, if they could get the fruit into market at the right time; but, as Saturday was the only day on which they could go, and as all that had fruit to sell could not have wagons at the same time, they frequently lost portions of their crops.

They also raised chickens; and for these there was always a ready market in the neighborhood. Mrs. McKiernan, herself, frequently bought them of her servants, and *she* never failed to pay them *a fair price*.

When little Peter was about a year old, his mother had a severe illness. The disease was inflammation of the brain, and the cause thereof we give in her own words.

" I never got a heap o' whippin' no how, but when Bill Simms was oversee' he give me one mons's hard beatin', bekase I would n't s'mit to him 'bout everything he wanted.

" He pestered me a heap, but I told him I would n't never do no such a thing; I told him I'd got a husban' o' my own; and I was n't gwine have nothin' to do with nobody else. He tried to starve me to it— many a Sunday, when he weighed out the 'lowance, he never give me half my sheer, and I could n't git no more for a week; but I did n't mind that.

" At last he told me if I did n't 'bey him, he'd whip me nigh 'bout to death. I told him he might kill me, but I would n't never do it, no how. So when I's in the field one day, he tuck and whipped me—I did n't call it whippin'—I called it beatin'. He tied my hands with his hand'chief, and pulled my coat off o' the waist; and then he beat me till I could n't hardly stand. He struck me over the head mos'ly, and tried to knock me down with the butt end o' his bull-whip. My head was cut in a heap o' places, whar the scars is on it yit.

" I reckon he would n't 'a' give me so much, but I tried to fight him at first, and he had to call two o' the men to help him tie me. By that time he got so mad that he jist went 'cordin' to his own mercy. I knowed I's in his power, but I's determined to die in the cause.

" The other people was all in sight, and he made out like he's beatin' me 'bout my work; but he told me it's all bekase I would 'nt 'bey him.

" When he done beatin' he curse me powerful, and

say, if I ever tole this yer to mass'r, or to any person else so it would get to him, he'd give me a heap more; and if that did n't do, he'd shoot me.

"I was determined he should n't never conquer me, no how; but he was that mean, I was feared he mought kill me sly; so I never said nothin' 'bout it, to nobody but Peter. He came home a Sunday, and when he's sittin' by me, he sort o' put his arm 'round me. 'Oh!' says I, 'don't put yer arm thar, you hurt my back!'

"'What's the matter o' yer back?' says he.

"'Oh, it's mighty sore whar ole Bill Simms done beat me,' says I, 'but don't you tell nobody, for if he finds out I done tol' the tale, he'll kill me, sure.'

"Peter felt mighty bad when I told him what I got the beatin' for—'peared like, he could 'a' gone right out and killed ole Bill Simms on the spot. He never liked him, no how—they had a fallin' out, afore, when he was overseein' for Mars Levi Gist.

"But 'twas n't no use gittin' mad 'bout it, nor tellin' mass'r nuther; bekase he allers say if any person come to him with complaints 'bout the oversee's, he'd give 'em worse, hisself.

"The next Sunday, Simms come up afore my house, and spoke to Peter, whar was a standin' in the door.

"Peter answered him mighty low, and that made him mad, bekase he 'lowed I done told him how I been 'bused. 'Seems to me,' says he, 'you're gettin' mighty grand. You're too great a gentleman to speak to a white person with respect. Never mind, I'll do you a kindness some o' these days. I owe you something this long time.'

"'Well,' says Peter, 'that debt never will be paid till the judgment day.'

"I tremble every minute, for I 'lowed I should have to take more next day; but I reckon he thought how 't was n't no use, for he never said nuthin' to me 'bout it no more.

"I had a heap o' misery in my head all the time for two weeks arter I tuck that beatin', and then I got right sick, and they said I's out o' my senses for a week. They sent for the doctor, but I did n't know nuthin' 'bout it, and he said I'd tuck some mighty hard blows on the head. He left medicine, and missus, she stay by me all the time. She sent for Peter to come—she reckoned I'd know him—but 'twas n't no use. They all 'lowed I's gwine to die; and then Peter, he told 'em all 'bout what done make me sick.

"Mass'r was mighty mad. 'Why the devil didn't she tell me this afore?' says he.

" 'Bekase,' says Peter, 'she knowed your rule, that you don't keer how hard an oversee' beats your servants, if they comes to you, they shall git worse.'

"Mass'r felt mighty bad then, but he 'lowed I might knowed he'd protect me in that.

"I reckon I should n't never got well, if they all had n't tuck such good care o' me. When I got so I could talk, mass'r ax me why I never told him what a beatin' old Simms done give me.

" 'What I come to you for,' says I, 'you allers told us never to do that, without we wanted more. If I'd 'lowed 'twould done any good I'd 'a' come to you, sir, mons's quick.'

"Soon as I's able to walk from the bed to the fire, mass'r come in to see me, and brought old Simms with him. Then he axed me 'bout that beatin' right afore him, and I told it to his face. 'Twas so true, he couldn't deny it. Mass'r cursed him mightily, and told him he should pay my doctor's bill, and pay for every day whar I was sick. I never knowed 'bout the payin' whether he done it or not, but mass'r drove him off the place, and he never come on it agin.

"I see him twice after that. The first time we's all gwine to meetin'. I see him comin', and says I, 'Thar comes the devil; I ain't gwine to look at him.' So I pulled my bonnet down over my face; and when he come 'long, and say how d'y' to the rest, I never look up.

"The next time I met old Simms, look like he's the picter o' Death. He been mighty sick, and jist got able to ride out.

"That thar was the last o' his ridin'. He took a 'lapse arter that, and then he died in a mighty short time.

"When I heard he's dead, I's so glad! My heart could n't help from shoutin', though it oughten't."

CHAPTER XV.

DEATH OF A KIND MASTER.

THE sunshine of prosperity beamed steadily upon the peaceful home of Mr. and Mrs. Gist. Gradually their worldly substance increased; and the dearer treasures of their hearts were multiplied.

The Spring of 1830, when she had waked the delicate flowers of the forest, came noiselessly on, and with careful ·hand, unfolded the rosebuds that climbed on the porch.

Near the half-open door sat the young husband and his still beautiful wife. Not a line of care or sorrow had stolen across their foreheads; not a shade of coldness or distrust had fallen on their hearts. Their children sported before them—two lovely girls and a brave boy, the youngest, and the pet of all.

Ah! came no whispering voice to bid them prize these golden moments? Entered no dread of change into all the plans they formed together? None! The sweet Spring smiled on them from without—the parching Summer drought she never heralds.

They were planning a visit to Kentucky. It was five years since they had enjoyed the hospitalities of that endeared home of other days; and the beloved parent, from whom they had been so long severed, were growing old. Yes; they would go to Lexington.

On a bright May morning, a few weeks after, the family carriage rolled away from the door, with its precious burden of gentle trusting hearts. Tears gathered in dark eyes that gazed fondly after the travvellers; and fond adieus to loving favorites were tossed back by tiny hands.

" 'Pears like," sobbed Aunt Ceely, " somethin's gwine happen. I's had mighty bad dreams dese las' nights."

" Oh! you's allers a dreamin'; reckon yer dreams aint much 'count," replied a cheerful girl at her side.

" I reckon nuthin' aint gwine hurt dem, no how; dey's been to Kaintucky 'fore dis," said another, who, though sad herself, would fain dispel Aunt Ceely's gloom.

The old woman turned towards the kitchen, and her croaking was soon forgotten. But when at night she smoked her pipe before her kitchen door, the shadow of impending ill darkened her heart.

Summer came with its heat, and wearying toil, and September passed away, and still the house was closed. Now and then, for a few hours the windows were thrown open, that the fresh air of morning might wander through the deserted rooms. But it would not tarry long; for it missed the merry children, to whose radiant eyes and blooming cheeks it had been wont to lend a deeper glow. So, after kissing lovingly each little couch, and chair, and scattered toy, the soft air flew away, to dally with the summer leaves that danced at its approach.

Early in October, new life seemed to have awakened

on the plantation. The laborers stepped more briskly out at morning, and the house servants went bustling through the lonely rooms, "clarin' up, and putting things to rights for Missus."

There were no gloomy faces now—no dark foreboding of approaching woe; Aunt Ceely herself forgot her dreams, she was so busy planning a nice supper, such as she knew suited "Mars Levi when he come home hongry."

The last day of September was the time appointed for the family to leave Lexington, and though the summer had passed most pleasantly in the society of valued friends, yet not one of the little group wished to remain longer.

On the day previous to their intended departure, a few friends sat down with them to a farewell dinner, at the house of an uncle of Mr. Gist.

The party were in fine spirits, albeit a shadow of regret that they were so soon to part, did now and then steal over them. Plans of future re-unions, however, were proposed, and promises of more frequent visits interchanged.

"What is it?" whispers with bloodless lips, the beautiful young wife, as her husband sways towards her, and she sees that his face is ashy pale. Quickly his friends spring to his assistance. They bear him from the table, and support him in their arms upon the sofa.

Ah! they saw not the Death Angel, as with white wings he approached, and gently scaled those loving eyes and stilled that throbbing heart. No! they saw him not. They did not know how vain were all their agonized endeavors to restore the warm breath to that manly form. " He has only fainted—give him air !"

Vain hope! The warm hands grow rigid—cold. The features become fixed. Can it be he is dead ?

God pity thee ! fond wife—and grant thee tears— that thy young heart break not.

In the parlor, at his childhood's home, was laid all that was mortal of Levi Gist. His father and mother, with great tears on their aged cheeks, gazed tenderly upon the face of their first-born son ; and his little children stole up on tiptoe to look at dear papa; and wondered that he lay so still, when only yesterday, he told them they should start for home to-day. Dear little ones ! too soon shall ye learn the full meaning of that cold word—fatherless !

The funeral was over. Fond eyes had gazed for the last time on those dear features, and to the earth had been consigned the sacred dust. Words of condolence had been duly uttered—Oh ! how they rent *her* heart ! —and curious eyes had scrutinized the widow's face and manner, to ascertain how keenly she felt the stroke. All these were satisfied. They saw her glazed eye, and pallid cheek ; and even their morbid jealousy for grief could exact no more.

The desolate woman returned, with her children to her thenceforth darkened home.

No smiles greeted her coming now ; but great hot tears glistened on the dark cheeks of the faithful band that came forth to meet her.

Well might they weep that their only protector had fallen ! Where, in all the country round, could be found another such master ? His servants had been, in some sense, his children; subject, it is true to his passions and caprices—and who is free from these? Still he had ever protected them from the violence of overseers and other ruffians, and their supply of wholesome food and comfortable clothes had not been scant.

Equally kind, and even more indulgent, had been their mistress, and she was spared to them. But now the government would, partially, at least, fall into other hands; there was no will, and the estate must be settled according to law.

Deeply, notwithstanding her own grief, did the kind mistress sympathize with her people in their peculiar sorrow; and earnestly did she resolve to do her utmost to alleviate the hardships of their lot.

Mr. John Gist, a brother of the deceased, proceeded to administer upon the estate, while Mrs. Gist remained on the place, and preserved, as far as possible, the accustomed order of affairs.

She was now a stately woman, of somewhat haughty presence, and with an eye whose lightning few would dare to brave. Usually, her voice was gentle, and her manners mild; but when the helpless were outraged, she summoned all her powers to awe and to command —for their relief. One instance will suffice to show her spirit.

It was Sunday evening, and Peter and Allison, who had been to visit some of their friends on a neighboring plantation, were returning home, when, to make their road shorter, they crossed a field belonging to Col. John D——.

Now, the gallant Colonel had made a law that no negro belonging to his neighbor, should cross his field on Sunday; and his overseer, named S——, by chance spying these trespassers, ran after them cowhide in hand.

They heard him on their track, and made all speed for home. Bounding over the door-yard fence, they imagined themselves safe; but in an instant, their pursuer leaped over after them, and even followed them to the kitchen, where they hastened to take refuge.

Here the slaves determined to do battle, and one of them had seized the rolling-pin, and the other a large knife, when their mistress, hearing the tumult, came to the door.

The overseer quailed beneath her haughty eye. "What is your business here, sir," said she, in a voice steady and brave.

He explained his errand; with much trepidation, however, for her great eyes were fixed upon him, and her majestic form seemed to grow taller every instant.

"Well, sir," said she, when he ceased speaking, "leave these premises immediately, and let this be the last time your foot approaches my house on such an errand. My boys are not subject to your authority; if they do wrong, it is not your business to punish them."

The overseer departed in silence, seeming much smaller in his own eyes than he had appeared an hour before.

CHAPTER XVI.

LEVIN'S DEATH.

JUST a year after the death of his master, Levin's health, which had been poor for several years, began rapidly to decline; and it was soon plain to all who saw him that his work was done.

His sufferings soon became intense, but he endured them with great patience. Levin was a Christian. His intellect, it is true, had possessed few means of development, but he had heard of the Lamb that was slain. Upon that bleeding sacrifice his hopes had long been fixed; and though in much ignorance and weakness, yet earnestly had he sought to follow his Redeemer. Now as the death-hour approached, he heard a voice, saying, "My peace I give unto you, not as the world giveth, give I unto you;" and, calmly resigning himself into His arms who is a Saviour of the weakest and the lowliest, he waited quietly the coming of the last Messenger.

Poor Fanny was permitted to spend the last days by his side. This was a great comfort to both, for they had suffered much for each other, and it was very hard to part so soon. But Levin talked so sweetly of the green fields and still waters of that better land, that she could not wish to prolong his painful sojourn here.

It was the twenty-eighth of December. Peter had gone to Bainbridge, to make his usual Christmas visit to his wife and little ones, and by the bed-side of her dying husband sat the devoted Fanny. Yet, though her eye watched every sign of change, she knew not that he was departing.

Sadly she gazed upon his placid face. Ah! did he not look happy? Why should she weep?—and yet the tears *would* flow.

"Call Peter, Fanny," said he, suddenly waking from a gentle sleep.

"Peter's gone to Bainbridge."

A shade of disappointment passed over his face— for a few moments he remained silent. Then suddenly, with all his strength he cried, "Peter! Peter! O, Peter!"

But the loved brother answered not. Ah! little thought he, as he sat fondling his children, and holding pleasant converse with their mother, that poor Levin's heart, even at that hour, was breaking.

There was but a slight struggle,—a faint gasp,—and the freed spirit of the lowly slave was carried by the angels into Abraham's bosom.

They placed the lifeless form in a rude coffin, and bore it to its lowly grave. No stone marks his resting place; no fragrant flowers adorn the sod that covers his silent house. Yet he sleeps sweetly there. The loud horn of the overseer reaches not his ear at dawn; the harsh tone of command and the bitter blasphemous curse break not his peaceful slumbers.

The death of this dear brother cast a heavy gloom

upon Peter's spirits. He felt that he was now alone. The memories of their early childhood, of their mother's love, and of the sad, sad day when they were stolen from their home, there was now none to share. And the fond hope, which through all their years of bondage had lived far down in some hidden recess of his heart—even that one hope went out—and all was dark.

CHAPTER XVII.

THE JAUNT TO FLORIDA.

PATIENTLY, month after month, Aunt Sally pursued her labors on the plantation of Mr. Peoples. She had a kind master, and her boys were near her, as was also Uncle Moses, the husband of her latter years. Of poor Silas, to whom her heart's young affections had been given, she never heard. He might be dead, and—oh! what torture in the thought!—he might be enduring sufferings compared with which, even death itself were naught. She could only pray for his weal; and trust, as she ever found it sweet to do, to that compassionate father, who loves the prayers of the humble, while "the proud he knoweth afar off."

But it was concerning her daughter that Aunt Sally's spirit was most deeply troubled. She was so young to be taken away—and alone among strangers too—how often would she need her mother's sympathy and counsel!

"Well," said she to Uncle Moses, at the close of one of their frequent conversations on the subject. "I's mighty glad de pore chile done got married. 'Pears like she wont be so lonesome now. I'd like to see her ole man. But her missus—she's a screamer. Laws! Vine say de little gal whar waits in de house gits her back cut up powerful, and she's a sickly little thing. Hi! wont dem kind o' ladies cotch it mightily when de bad man gits 'em? Reckon he wont think dey's so mons's nice, kase dey's white. De Lord years all de screams o' his chilluns, and he aint gwine put harps o' gold in dem dare hands, whar allers a playin wid de cowhide yer."

There were at this time two sets of slaves on Mr. Peoples' place; his own, and those belonging to the estate of a deceased brother, with whom he had been in partnership. Many of these were united by family ties, and all were strongly attached to each other, as they had lived together for many years.

Suddenly, late in the autumn of 1827, the gloomy tidings came among them that they were to be separated. Their master, having heard tempting accounts of the beauty and fertility of Florida's fair plains, had determined to remove there with his working hands: while those belonging to his brother's estate, as well as the children and any that were unfit for labor, should remain on the home place, in the guardianship of an overseer.

Aunt Sally was overwhelmed with sorrow. She was more fortunate than many of her companions, for her husband and her oldest son were to go with her; but poor Quall must stay behind, and Vina—she had not seen her for two years. She longed to make her a farewell visit, but such was now the haste to secure the crop, and to complete the needful preparations for the journey, that she could not go even to "tell" her darling child "good-bye."

The master strove to comfort them by the promise that they should some day return; or, if he liked the country so well as to wish to remain in Florida, then their friends should come to them. But the dim hope in the distant future could not dispel the present gloom: and with bitter lamentations fond mothers pressed their weeping children to their aching breasts, and loving husbands turned back for one more look on those dear faces which they never more might see.

They have gone! Their friends stand mournfully watching the sad procession till it passes out of sight, and their stricken hearts breathe earnest prayers for the safe keeping of their dearest treasures.

Vina did not hear of Mr. Peoples' intended removal till his family had already arrived in Florida; and her grief was then extreme. To lose her mother thus, without receiving so much as a parting message, was harder far than all her previous trials. Not even the laughing prattle of her little Peter could dispel this heavy sorrow; not even her husband's love could soothe her aching heart.

But a kind Providence was better to them than their fears. Mr. Peoples did not like Florida; and when he had "made one crop," he returned with all his slaves in glad procession, to his former home.

Ah! earth is not all gloomy, for there be sometimes glad reunions, when the partings have been dismal— hopeless. There be transient gleams of joy, though misery hath hung her heavy clouds over all the sky. There is an Infinite Father who looketh down in love on the weakest of his children; and though he suffer them to drink a bitter cup, he often mingles therewith rare drops of sweetness.

The summer following her return from Florida, Aunt Sally paid a visit to her daughter.

What changes have been wrought during the four years that had passed since she had seen her child·

Vina had grown quite tall, and her face, instead of the timidity and sadness that then marked its expression, now wore a careful *mother-look*. Poor child! she was not strong, and the fatiguing labor of the hot summer days, together with the care which her two children claimed at night, taxed her exertions to the utmost.

Aunt Sally had not been long on the plantation, before she learned the policy pursued by Mr. McKiernan towards his slaves. Their lot was truly hard. Not an article of furniture or clothing did they receive from their master, except, that once a year he gave a coarse plantation suit to such as were old enough to work. Even this, however, was sometimes withheld, and then those who had no means of procuring garments for themselves, went to their daily tasks in such a ragged filthy state, that the more respectable of the overseers could not endure their presence. Several of these, at different times, left the plantation, for no other reason than that they could not stay in the field with such a miserable gang of negroes.

Little cared the master for their departure. Others were always ready to be hired, who heeded not such trifles, so that they could have full power over the half-naked wretches that instinctively recoiled at their approach.

But Vina and her children, thanks to Peter's industry and self-denial, had always decent clothing, and their cabin boasted many convenient articles of furniture, such as slaves seldom possess. They had also better food than most of their companions, for to the scant allowance of bacon and corn meal which was doled out to Vina on Sunday mornings, Peter often found means to add a little coffee and sugar, or a few pounds of flour.

All this Aunt Sally learned during her short stay, and for each kindness thus bestowed upon her child, she rendered thanks to Him, whose hand she recognized in every good.

Too soon the time allotted to this precious visit passed away; yet much of hope lingered in the sad farewell. "Dat dar jaunt to Florida," Aunt Sally thought, had cured her master of his thirst for novelty; and now, she trusted, she should never more be widely separated from her daughter.

Vina's eyes were dim, as from her cabin door, she watched her mother's departing form. A heavy sadness oppressed her spirits; and the kind voice of her husband, who stood beside her, could scarce dispel her gloom. But many little motherly duties claimed her thoughts. Young Peter wanted his supper, while little Levin raised his pleading voice to beg for her attendance; and soon the pleasure of contributing to the comfort of those she loved restored her accustomed cheerfulness.

CHAPTER XVIII.

A SLAVE MOTHER'S "GOOD-BYE."

AUNT SALLY rode briskly homeward. She had not felt so happy in many years as now. Her children were all comfortably situated; even Vina, about whom she had been so anxious, had now so kind a husband, and such fine "peart" children, that she could no longer repine at her lot.

A few weeks glided calmly on. Summer stole noiselessly away, and Autumn came with quiet steps, to cool the parched earth.

The cotton fields grew brown with age, and snowy tufts burst from the ripened bolls. Tremulous they hung—those fleecy tassels—and the cool breeze, as with mock sympathy it sighed among the withering leaves, lingered to whisper softly to these fair strangers, and toss in amorous sport their dainty tresses.

The crops were all gathered in. Beside the gin-house lay great heaps of hoary cotton-seed, and the mighty press had uttered the last creak of the season. Under a shed hard-by, the old-fashioned, tight-laced bales were huddled close together, and yet it was not winter.

The hands upon the place were very proud. There was not another plantation in all the country round, but had great fields, where still in fleecy clusters the precious cotton gleamed.

It is night—and the people are all in their cabins. The smiles of triumph which but a few hours since brightened their faces have departed, and a wail of anguish resounds through all the quarter. Mr. Peoples has bought a sugar farm away down on the dreadful Gulf Coast, and thither his slaves are all to be conveyed, as soon as they can make the necessary preparations for the journey.

Look! Aunt Sally comes forth alone from her cabin door. Tears are upon her cheeks, and her breast is convulsed with sorrow.

She walks slowly and with drooping head along a narrow footpath leading to the woods. She kneels upon the rustling leaves. Oh! with what humble trustfulness she offers her agonized petitions! Has she heard that it is written, "Like as a father pitieth his children, so the Lord pitieth them that fear Him?"

The preparations for emigration were conducted with the bustle and confusion usual on large plantations. There were full three hundred slaves; and their master intended to carry along provisions sufficient for one year's consumption, as well as corn for the horses, mules and cattle. Then all the utensils of the farm were collected and repaired; and each family had to arrange its own little store of clothes and furniture.

During the day, the constant occupation of the slaves prevented the contemplation of their gloomy prospects. At night, however, they had time to think; and then the torrent of their grief broke forth afresh. In every cabin might be heard the voice of weeping;

and the rude pallets, on which reposed their weary limbs, were wet with bitter tears.

When all was ready, and the cattle and stores had been conveyed to the river's bank, then came the final leave-taking. Husbands and wives, brothers and sisters, parents and children, who belonged on neighboring plantations, came with sobs and tears to say "farewell" to those whose hearts were breaking.

Aunt Sally came hurriedly, with a small bundle in her hand, from her empty cabin. Hastily she walked along the road to Courtland, and paused not until she reached the residence of Mr. B——, where dwelt her youngest child.

Poor Quall! henceforth he would be motherless! He saw her form approaching, and ran to meet her. Oh! the tender agony of that last long embrace.

He was her darling boy, how could she leave him? He clung around her neck. She felt his warm breath on her cheek. O Saviour! pity them! It is their last fond meeting—their last heart-crushed "good bye."

With desperate strength she tore herself from his arms; and with one prayer to Heaven to bless and keep her boy, she thrust the little bundle into his powerless hand, and hastened on to join her gloomy comrades.

The rendezvous was Bainbridge. To this point some came on foot, and others on the boats over the shoals. Here they were obliged to wait till all the boats arrived; and now a faint hope sprang up in Aunt Sally's heart that she might yet see her daughter. She determined at least to make one effort.

A gentleman on horseback was slowly riding by. It was Andrew Gist. Hastily she approached him.

He pitied her evident distress, and listened kindly to the recital of her sorrows.

"So your daughter is at McKiernan's. What is her name?"

"Her name Vina, Sir."

"Vina? why that is Peter's wife."

"Yes, Sir, her man name Peter. He belongs to Mars Levi Gist."

"Well, I'll find her myself, and send her down to see you. Come, cheer up, Auntie, you'll have good times yet."

The field where Mr. McKiernan's people were at work was three miles from the landing, but the Kentuckian's fine horse soon bore him there.

"Which of you all has a mother at Peoples'?" said he, as he rode up to a group of women.

"It's Vina's mother whar lives dar, Sir:—yon's Vina," replied a young girl, pointing as she spoke, to the object of his search. She was working alone, at a short distance from her companions, and did not look up till she was addressed.

"Howd'y' Vina, does your mother belong to Peoples?"

"Yes, Sir."

"Well, if you go down to the landing, you'll see the last of her, I reckon, for she's going down the river. Peoples is moving down to the coast."

He rode away, and Vina gazed after him in speechless terror. Her mother—the coast—could it be? One moment she started towards the overseer to ask permission to go to the river—the next her courage failed her, and she felt sure he would not let her go. She tried to work, but her limbs seemed palsied, and her eyes were full of blinding tears.

After nearly an hour had passed, she summoned all her strength, and left the field. With fearful steps she walked to the house, and fortunately her master and mistress were both at home. She told them what Mr. Gist had said, and touched with pity, they bade her go immediately to the landing, and stay with her mother as long as the boats remained.

A strange picture met her eye as she approached the river. Along the bank in the dim twilight, gleamed the blaze of numerous fires, and around these were gathered groups of unhappy slaves. Some were cooking their simple suppers, and others close huddled together, warmed their benumbed limbs, while they bewailed, in low sad tones, their gloomy destiny. Mothers hovered tenderly over the dear little ones that never more might hear their fathers' voices, and here and there, like a majestic tree by lightning blasted, stood a lone father, who had left all—wife, children, hope, behind.

Vina paused, and listened, but in the sad murmur that met her ear she heard not her mother's voice. She passed on. Four large flat boats were tied to the bank, and one of these she timidly entered.

A great fire was glowing at the further end of the boat, and dark figures were moving slowly about in the uncertain light. She heard no mirthful voices, no gay laugh; but heavy sighs and mournful wailings filled her ears.

On a low stool near the fire sat a female figure. Her bowed head rested on both her hands, and her body swayed to and fro, in unison with the melancholy

measure of her thoughts.   Vina came very near.   She
paused.   Aunt Sally raised her head, and with a cry,
half joy—half anguish, she clasped her daughter to
her breast.

"O my chile! I's studyin' 'bout you, whether I's
ever gwine see you agin or not," and she sobbed aloud.
"Oh! how can I go and leave you, honey? I shan't
never come back no more! 'Way down on de sugar
farm I shall die, and der wont be no daughter dar to
see 'em lay me in de grave!"

Long sat Vina and her mother close together, conversing in low tones, and weeping over their sad doom.

The slaves who had been gathered around the fires
upon the bank came in, and wrapping themselves in
their blankets, lay down to sleep.

As midnight approached, it was announced that the
boats would probably not leave Bainbridge until Monday morning; and Aunt Sally obtained permission of
the overseer who had charge, to go home with her
daughter, and spend the next day which was Saturday,
at her cabin.   Immediately they left the boat, and
hastened home.

The hours of that short Saturday passed swiftly by,
and at night Vina accompanied her mother back to the
boat.   There she left her, promising to come again in
the morning, that they might spend one more day
together.

The dawn of the Sabbath-day saw the affectionate
daughter on her way to the river.   She walked rapidly,
for every minute of that day was precious.

She comes in sight of the landing.   Why does she
pause? and Oh! what means that heavy groan?

The boats have gone!   The fires are smouldering

on the bank. Here and there lies a fragment of hoe-cake or a bit of an old blanket that has been forgotten. All is silent.

Slowly the freighted boats pursued their way between the lonely banks of the Tennessee. The trees that overhung the stream shivered as they saw their leafless branches in the still clear water, but the bright mistletoe clung closely to the desolate trunks, and strove, with its rich green, to hide their rigid outlines.

Slowly they floated on. The broad Ohio bore them on her breast to the Father of Waters, and still they stayed not. The tall cotton-woods that guard the Mississippi's banks listened to the murmur of the slaves' sad voices; and every breeze they met went sighing past as though it sorrowed with them.

Their fears were all too true. The sugar farm upon the coast was to them as the "Valley of the Shadow of Death."

So many of his slaves died during the first year, that Mr. Peoples, when he had made one crop of cane, sold his plantation and left the coast. He could not endure to see his faithful servants dying there, even though he knew the profits of the business would enable him to buy others in their stead. So he purchased a plantation in the north part of Mississippi, and returned, with the remnant of his people, to the culture of corn and cotton.

Here, after several years, Aunt Sally sank peacefully to her last, long slumber. She had no dread of Death. Long had she waited for his coming; and now that she knew he hovered near, her heart was filled with holy joy, and all who saw the light of love and hope that beamed from her faded eye, knew well that she had been with Jesus. And when her pulse was still, and her cold hands lay meekly folded across her breast, a heavenly smile still lingered on her face; blest token that her weary spirit had reached at length that happy home where she had so longed to rest.

Her master, who, during her sickness, had done all in his power for her comfort, wrote to inform her absent children of her decease. He told them of her faith and patience, and of her final triumph over the terrors of the grave; and added that he provided a neat shroud and coffin for her sleeping dust, and buried her with every token of respect.

Happy Aunt Sally. She had never known other than the "sunny side" of slavery. Neither of her masters had been capable of wanton cruelty, and her excellent character had made her a favorite with both. Yet the *system* of slavery cursed her life. It bereaved her of the husband of her youth, and robbed her of her beloved children. It tore her from scenes endeared by association with all her pleasures, and dragged her away into strange lands, of which, from her childhood, she had heard nought but tales of horror.

And for all these, what compensation reaped she from the *institution*. Verily, none—save such as is bestowed upon the faithful ox. Even the unusual kindness of her master could grant no other boon than a shroud, a coffin, and a promised letter to tell her children that they were motherless.

Such is a "*South Side View.*"

CHAPTER XIX.

THE MISTRESS' SECOND MARRIAGE.

On the twelfth of November, 1833, Mrs. Gist was married to Mr. John Hogun, a man more than twenty years her senior. He possessed few personal attractions, and still fewer intellectual or social accomplishments. But he owned two large plantations, one in the neighborhood of Mrs. Gist's residence, and another in Mississippi. Both of these were well stocked, the slaves numbering more than one hundred.

The marriage of their beloved mistress caused great grief among the slaves on the plantation, for it foreshadowed the partings that must come.

The servants, thirty-four in number, were to be divided equally between the mother and her four children (one daughter was born after her father's death). In order to this, they were placed in five lots, and these were so arranged as to keep the families together. These lots were not of equal value; but the discrepancy was to be made up by a corresponding difference in the distribution of the other property, so that the revolting scenes of an auction might be avoided.

The mistress drew first. Old Frank, and Aunt

Peggy, with their three daughters, together with a yellow boy named Nelson, fell to her share. She felt disappointed, for she had always hoped to retain Peter in her service; but notwithstanding he loved and honored his mistress, he was grateful that he had not fallen under the dominion of her husband. The remaining lots were not drawn at that time, as the children were still very young.

About a month after the marriage—a sad and gloomy month to all upon the place—Mrs. Hogun, with her children and servants, left the quiet home where she had spent so many happy hours, and went to the residence of her husband.

This was a large framed house, situated on a rich plantation, about four miles from her late abode, and four and a half miles from Tuscumbia. The former Mrs. Hogun had been dead four or five years, and her eldest daughter, Miss Louisa, had since her decease, presided at her father's table. This young lady was married soon after her father, and there were then three children left at home, John, Robert, and Thirmuthis.

Mr. Hogun was emphatically a hard man. His heart knew no mercy to those upon whom the laws of his State, as well as the customs of surrounding society allowed him to trample. To his own children he was ever indulgent; to his neighbors and acquaintances, smooth-tongued and polite; but he had a will that could not brook resistance, and a temper which, when roused, was capable of inflicting any cruelty. He considered his servants as *his*, body and soul, and strove to compel them to make his wishes their law in all things. He allowed none of them to marry off the

the place, and by watching them carefully, and pursuing prompt measures, he usually managed to bring them together according to his mind.

When he saw a young man and woman engaged in any little sport together, or noticing each other in any way, if he thought they would make a good match, he ordered the overseer to build them a house. Accordingly, on the first convenient day thereafter, a sufficient number of the hands were called to the work, and the cabin was erected. It was but a small task to complete the structure—one little log-room, having a door on one side, a small unglazed window with a wooden shutter on the other, and at one end a chimney, built of sticks and smeared with mud. Nothing further was considered necessary. The ground sufficed for all the purposes of floor, bed, table, and chairs; unless the inmates, by working on holidays, or by selling eggs or chickens, managed to procure some little comforts for themselves.

When the house was finished, the master ordered Bob, the head man to bring Joe and Phillis, and put them into their house. Then, putting a small padlock on the door, he gave the key to Bob, saying, " Here, Bob, I have put my seal on this door; now here is the key; you keep this nigger and this wench together, or, *by jings*, you'll pay for it. Do you make Joe build a fire for Phillis, and see that Phillis cooks for Joe, and washes his clothes; and, mind, Bob, I shall look to you."

No expostulations from either party could alter his decree. *He had been to the trouble of building a house for them*, and now they should live in it, or take the consequences of braving his authority.

When such were the marriage rites, what must have been the morals of the place?

The slaves on this plantation were worked very hard. Before the dawn of day the horn was sounded to call them to the field, and in hurrying times, they were not allowed to go to rest till late at night. "Cotton,"—"cotton"—was ever the watchword and reply; and the great crops which they "made" brought wealth into the master's coffers, while they drained the life-founts of the toiling slaves.

One year, however, they had, providentially, a little rest. The crop was nearly destroyed by the early frost, very few bolls ripening at all.

Late in this "*unlucky*" year, a gang of slaves were one day repairing the fence around a large field, and a few were picking the cotton from the scattering bolls.

"Well, boys," said the overseer of a neighboring plantation, who chanced to pass, "aint you sorry you've got no cotton to pick this year?"

"Ah! no, mass'r," replied one of the oldest men, "we's mighty glad in place o' bein' sorry. De Lord has done a mon's good work for us, mass'r; if he'd on'y sent de fross a little sooner, we wouldn't had none to pick at all."

The overseer, angered by the old man's "impudence," cursed him bitterly.

"Yah, yah, mass'r, 'taint no use bein' mad, I reckon, kase nobody aint to blame but de Lord, and it wont do no good to be mad wid him; can't skeer him a cussing, no how."

For six years after the marriage of their mistress, the slaves belonging to the Gist estate were kept upon the plantation. The overseer with his family took possession of the house that had so long been the abode of peace and happiness; and everywhere on the place a new order of things was established.

Peter was made foreman of the hands, which position he retained as long as the family of slaves was kept together. The overseer gave him his orders at night, with particular directions concerning the next day's work. In the morning he was obliged to rise first, to call his fellow-servants from their slumbers, and to see that each was in his place, and that his his work was properly commenced. All day he took the fore-row and led his gang. At night it was his business to see that the tools they had used were safe and in order, and the people were all in their cabins, before he could go to bed. In picking time, he also was obliged each night to weigh the cotton, and to report to the overseer the number of pounds which each of the hands had picked. His extraordinary memory was now a great advantage to him, for though he could not write, he was never known to report erroneously the contents of the baskets.

The loss of their kind master was keenly felt by the slaves during all these years. The overseers, always men of the lowest stamp in intellect and morals, had full sway. If they succeeded in making a good crop, they satisfied their employers, the administrators of the estate; and why should they hesitate to use any means that might advance this end? The slaves, men and women, were therefore required to labor at their utmost strength; and when over-wearied, they found no sympathy. The kind word of encouragement was wanting, the voice of commendation became strange unto their ears.

In the year 1839, it was thought best, by the guardians of the estate, to sell the plantation and to hire out the negroes. The tidings of this approaching change in their condition spread a panic throughout the little community. They had suffered much since their master died, but they had suffered together. Now to be scattered—they could not bear the thought!

Many were the consultations which they held together over their gloomy prospects; but none could suggest a plan of escape from the ills that threatened them. They could only submit to their fate, and meet whatever awaited them with patience—since hope had fled.

"Oh!" thought Peter, "what's the use in livin'? Mass'r Levi's gone, and Levin; and then missus, she must go too, and leave us all without nobody to care whether we lives or dies. Here I've served the family so many years; and now I must go to wait on some strangers, that wont care for nuthin' only to git all the work they can for their money. Oh! if they send me off where I can't go to see Vina, it 'll kill her, sure."

CHAPTER XX.

THE PLANTATION "BROKEN UP."

THE last Christmas came which these doomed people were to spend together at the old place, and instead of the mirth which usually reigned at that season, mourning and weeping filled its hours. The slaves had all been hired out here and there, and, after the holidays, they were to go to their new homes. Fourteen of the number, including Peter, were destined to spend the ensuing year on the plantation of a Mr. Threat, about four miles from Bainbridge.

The one great dread, that of being conveyed still further from his wife, was now removed, but otherwise his situation was not bettered. Mr. Threat had immigrated from Virginia, about four years before, and had bought a small plantation. He owned no slaves, and was therefore obliged to hire them year by year.

Peter, having led the hands on the old place, was still retained as *head-man*, and his labors were in no degree diminished. His fare too, was scanty, for the young master was just beginning in the world, and could ill afford an abundance of wholesome food to other people's negroes.

The Threat family, as we have said, came from Virginia, and though the young man to whom Peter and his companions were hired, was not rich, yet his parents, who resided in the neighborhood, possessed a competency. *His mother*, we should have said, for the elder Mr. Threat had failed in business in Virginia, and his property was all sold under the hammer. Two brothers of his wife, men of great wealth, bid it in, and settled it upon their sister and her children; giving to her the entire control during her lifetime. The family then removed to Alabama, where Mrs. Threat assumed the reins of government. Her husband lived with her, and she permitted her servants to wait upon him, but in business matters, he was not consulted.

Mrs. Threat kept no overseer, and hesitated not to show her subjects that the sole authority over them was vested in herself, and that her arm was strong to punish their transgressions. She frequently rode over her fields with cowhide and rope at hand, and inspected the labor of her slaves. If she found one of them dilatory or otherwise remiss, she quickly dismounted, and ordered him to strip. Then after commanding one of his fellow slaves to tie him, she vigorously applied the cowhide to his naked back, until she deemed that he had expiated his offence.

One spring morning, while Peter was hired to her son, she mounted one of her carriage horses, a large bay, and rode to the field. She had, the day before, whipped a large, powerful negro, and on this morning she started with her rope and cowhide, intending to inflict the same punishment upon another who had incurred her wrath. But when she had nearly reached the spot where her people were at work, her horse took fright, and springing aside, threw her to the ground. The slaves hastened to her assistance. They bore her home, and a doctor was soon summoned. Her hip was badly injured, and it was a long time before she recovered. Ever after, she used a crutch, and dragged one foot after her when she walked. Her good right arm, however, was not weakened, as the scarred backs of many of her slaves could testify.

This may be regarded as an extraordinary instance of female "chivalry," but in truth, similar cases are not rare. Frail, delicate ladies, whom one would instinctively shield from a rude breath of the free air, can strip and tie their slaves, both men and women, and beat them with the zest of a base-born overseer.*

During the summer which Peter spent at Mr. Threat's—1840—the well remembered political excitement of "Tippecanoe and Tyler too," spread through that vicinity. A Convention was held at Tuscumbia, and party men on both sides were loud in the defence of the liberties of their country. Speeches were made, songs were sung; and each busy patriot seemed to imagine himself destined to save the nation from misrule and consequent destruction. The excitement was contagious. Ladies' fair hands embroidered banners, and their soft voices joined in the exciting songs of the times.

The slaves could not remain uninterested listeners to the conversations concerning liberty that were held everywhere—at the dinner-table, and on the street. They interpreted *literally* the language of their masters, and in their simple hearts imagined that the dawn of liberty had come. What else could it mean? The white people were already free; and if liberty was to

* In making this assertion, the writer relies not wholly upon information derived from Peter, but speaks also from personal knowledge.

become universal—and people on each side declared it
would become so, if their party should succeed in the
election—then the "black folks" would enjoy its
blessings, "*sure*."

On Sundays the slaves from "town" met their
plantation friends at their fish-traps on the river, and
there the joyful news was communicated—in whispers
at first—but as they became more certain that their
hopes were well-grounded, they gradually grew bolder,
till at length they dared to discuss the subject in their
religious meetings. The preachers were inspired by
this bright hope of freedom, and as it grew nearer its
imagined fulfilment they preached it to their people
with thrilling eloquence.

" 'Taint no dream, nor no joke," cried one of these;
"de time's a'most yer.   Der won't be no mo' whippin',
no mo' oversee's, no mo' *patrollers*, no mo' huntin' wid
dogs; everybody's a gwine to be free, and de white
mass'r's a gwine to pay 'em for der work. O, my
brudders! de bressed time's a knockin' at de door!
De good Lord 'll *ramshackle* de devil, and all de people
in dis yer world, bof white and black, is a gwine to
live togedder in peace."

Alas! their bright visions were speedily shadowed.
Their masters learned the subject of their earnest discussions, and then a system of espionage was established, which pursued its objects with a vindictive
energy worthy of the best days of the Inquisition.

The black preachers were silenced; all assembling
of the slaves forbidden; and patrols established
through all the country.   Every negro encountered by
the patrols was whipped, if he had no pass; and even
that important slip of paper often lost its magic, if the

bearer chanced to have the reputation of being a man of spirit.

A panic pervaded the whole community. "The negroes intend to rise," was whispered with white lips by timid ladies in their morning visits; and every sigh of the night-wind through the lofty trees was interpreted by the fearful into the rush of black assassins. Old stories of negro insurrections were revived, and the most faithful and attached servants became objects of suspicion.

This excitement, however, like that to which it owed its origin, at length passed away. The few old privileges were restored to the slaves, and the services of the patrols were no longer in constant requisition. Yet the confidence of the slaveholder is always imperfect, and easily shaken. When injustice constitutes the base of the system, how can faith adorn the superstructure?

Some of the better class of servants about Tuscumbia have not to this day recovered from the effects of the suspicions which they then incurred. Many, in their joyful excitement, had run after the wagons that bore in procession the log cabin with its admirers, and cried, "The year of jubilee is come! We all's a gwine to be free!" These were almost crushed by the disappointment, and by the sufferings consequent on too frank an expression of their hopes. They were scourged and persecuted *in a manner befitting the nature of their offence.*

Toward the close of 1840, Peter was hired for the ensuing year to Mr. McKiernan. To this he was greatly opposed, even though he would by such an arrangement be able daily to enjoy the society of his family. He loved his wife and children most fondly, but their master had long sought to buy him, and Peter feared that if he went there, he might succeed in accomplishing his wish. The idea of becoming the property of such a man was dreadful to him, and this fear shadowed the otherwise bright prospect of living constantly with his beloved Vina. Yet he carefully concealed his feelings on the subject from any that would report them to Mr. McKiernan. His wife was in the tyrant's power, and he dared not offend him.

CHAPTER XXI.

BABY LIFE IN THE CABINS.

WE left Vina at the landing straining her weeping eyes to retain the images of the flat-boats that were bearing the *goods* of Mr. Peoples down the river. Long she stood gazing there; even till the last faint outline of a boat was lost, and then with swollen eyes and aching heart she returned to her cabin.

She had then two children. Peter, the eldest was a little more than three years old, and Levin, who was born on the twenty-fourth of June previous, had seen about six months. They were '*peart*,' healthy little fellows, and they received much better care than is usually bestowed upon the children of a field woman.

At that time there was no *old woman* on the place to take care of the children; and every mother, when she went to the field in the morning, locked her little ones in her cabin, leaving some bread where they could get it when they became hungry. Or, if there was one too small to help itself to bread, the thoughtful mother tied a little mush in a rag upon its finger, so that when, as babies will, it thrust its finger in its mouth, it could suck the mush through the rag, and that would keep it quiet.

Sometimes, when the day was very hot, the mothers

left their cabin doors open, that the little ones might have air. Then those that were able would creep out over the low threshold, and perhaps fall asleep on the hot ground. "Many's the time," says Vina, "I come home and find my baby sleepin' with the sun a beatin' on its head, enough, 'peared like, to addle its brains."

Very few infants lived on this plantation. The mothers were obliged to work so hard before their birth, and so often suffered cruel beatings while in a situation that required the utmost kindness, that most of the children, if born alive, died in spasms when a few days old.

When Vina's children were small, not an article of clothing was provided for them by the master, till they were old enough to be employed in some light work about the house. Their mother might manage to clothe them, or let them go naked. But for the last few years, they have lost so many in consequence of the total lack of necessaries, that now they give each mother clothing for her child. But if the baby dies, every little garment must be carried back to the mistress, not even excepting a covering for the tiny corpse. If the mother cannot provide something to shroud her baby, she may have it buried without. *Those clothes* must be laid by for some future necessity.

In 1831, October twenty-fifth, another little voice was heard in Vina's cabin, pleading for care. She called the baby William, and he was a fine brave boy. His little brothers gave him a joyous welcome, and so did his fond parents; though, in truth, they scarcely knew how they were to supply his baby wants. "But 'pears like," says the mother, "every baby I had I growed smarter, so 't when I had three, I tuck just as good care of 'em all as I did of the first one."

When little William was a few months old, a child belonging to a woman named Ann, was burned to death while its mother was away in the field at work. It was winter, and the mother, as was necessary at that season, had built sufficient fire to keep her half-naked children comfortable; and then, locking her door, had left them to amuse themselves during her absence. When she came in, her child was lying lifeless upon the clay hearth. It had crept too near the pretty blaze, and had probably fallen on the burning coals.

The burning of Ann's child brought about a new order of things on the plantation. Thereafter, every mother was required to leave her little children at the kitchen when she went to the field, and then the cook could mind them.

One morning, not long after this law was made, Vina was "pushed" to get out in time. She had slept but little during the night, and she did not wake as early as usual. So she thought she would leave the children in the cabin till she came in to nurse her baby, and then she would carry them to the kitchen.

The other little ones were crowing and crying about when the mistress's eye missed Vina's. She counted them all over.

"Where are Vina's children?"

"She never brought 'em dis mornin', ma'am."

"Well, I'll settle with her when she comes. I've told them all not to leave their children at home—they don't care whether they're burnt up or not."

When Vina came at breakfast time to her cabin, (all but the mothers of young children ate their breakfast before they went out) she took her three little ones to the kitchen, and sat down there to nurse the baby Soon the mistress came in, holding the cowhide partly behind her.

"How's this, Vina?" said she, "I thought I told you that you was n't to leave your children in your house of a morning."

"Well, Missus, I's pushed this mornin'. I had n't time ——"

"I don't care how much you was pushed. I told you to bring them here; and if the sun was an hour high you should obey me. Lay down your child; I'm going to whip you now, for I said I would do it. If your children had got burnt up, you would have blamed me about it."

"No, ma'am, I would n't——"

"Lay your child down. I'll let you know you are to obey *me*."

Vina obeyed; and when her weary shoulders had received twenty hard lashes, she went out to her work. Verily, as a lady in that neighborhood remarked, not long since, to a Northern friend: "*The negroes ought to be very thankful to us for taking care of them: they make us a great deal of trouble.*"

CHAPTER XXII.

FACTS.

AMONG the slaves on Mr. McKiernan's plantation were a number of handsome women. Of these the master was extremely fond, and many of them he beguiled with vile flatteries, and cheated by false promises of future kindness, till they became victims to his unbridled passions.

Upon these unfortunate women fell the heavy hatred of their mistress; and year after year, as new instances of her husband's perfidy came to her knowledge, her jealousy ran higher, till at length reason seemed banished from her mind, and kindliness became a stranger to her heart. Then she sought a solace in the wine-cup; and the demon of intoxication fanned the fires of hatred that burned within her, till they consumed all that was womanly in her nature, and rendered her an object of contempt and ridicule, even among her own dependents.

The master was, at the time of which we are writing, not far from fifty years of age. He was short and burly in person, with a large head, and a very red face. His hair was quite grey, and as he walked towards the quarter in the morning with his hat on one side, cursing and spitting with equal zeal, he looked, as some of his slaves remarked, "like a big buzzard just ready to fly."

Vina thoroughly understood her master's character; she knew also the temper of her mistress; and she strove by her prudence and correctness of demeanor, to avoid exciting the evil passions of either. But one day, when William was a baby, her trial came. The following is her own account of her contest with her master, and it shows that she possessed a brave, true spirit:

"I was in my house a spinnin' one rainy day, and firs' I knowed, Mass'r he come to the door, and ax me what was I doin'. I told him I's a spinnin' fine yarn. 'Who's thar with you?' says he, 'Thar aint no person yer but my chillerns,' says I; and so he come in and sent Peter and Levin out. I knowed what was a comin' then, for his eyes looked mighty mean.

"He sot down and talked till I got tired a hearin', and I told him I wished he'd go 'way and leave me alone. I told him he got a wife o' his own, and I didn't never want no fuss with her. Well, he 'lowed she wouldn't never know nothin' about it, no how, so it wouldn't do her no hurt.

"I told him that thar wasn't my principle, to wrong any person behind their back, thinkin' they wouldn't know it. I wouldn't like any body should do me so. At las' I told him I got a task to do, and if he wouldn't go off, and let me do it, I'd go myself;——so I started for the door.

"He sprung after me, and cotch me by the neck of my coat, and tore it half way down the skirt behind. That made me mad, and I fell at him, and tore his shirt mighty nigh off his back. I pulled his hair too, right smart, and scratched his face, and then tripped and flung him on the floor.

"He was powerful mad when he got up, and he say he gwine whip me well for that. I told him just so sure as he give me a lick, I'd tell Missus what it's for; and he knowed he never'd git no chance to whip me 'bout my work, so he neeedn't make no such pretence. 'You tell her one word,' says he, 'bout this yer, and I'll cut your two ears off close to your head!' 'No, sir, you wont,' says I, 'you know you dares not crap one o' your servants.'

"Then he went up to the house, and slipped in sly, and put on a clean shirt. But that thar raggety one never was seen. His wife missed it, though, for she knowed he put on a clean shirt that day. She axed all the house servants had they seen it, but none of 'em didn't know nuthin' 'bout it. Then she 'lowed some of 'em done stole it, and she laid it to Jinny,— she was cook then. She 'lowed she done give it to Jacob her husband. They both 'clared they's innocent; but the missus and the overseer give 'em more'n three hundred lashes to make 'em own they got it.

"'One of your best shirts is gone,' says she to the Mass'r, 'and I'm determined to whip the servants till I make them tell where it is. I've had Jinny and Jacob whipped well, but they wont own any thing about it. I shall have to try the others.'

"'Jinny,' says Mass'r, 'what about that shirt of mine?

"'Missus has whipped me 'bout that shirt, sir,' says Jinny, 'an' I don't know no more 'bout whar it is an' you does yourself.'

" ' Well, go 'long,' says he, ' but mind, Jinny, you've got that to find.'

" All the house servants got whipped 'bout it, but none of 'em didn't take so much as Jinny ; and they had every house in the quarter searched. There was more'n five hundred blows struck 'bout that shirt, and they never found no sign of it.

" Two or three weeks after, old Mass'r come into the field to whar we's plowin' ! He tried some o' the other women's ploughs, and then he come to me. ' Well, girl,' says he, ' how does your plough run ?"

" ' Oh ! it runs well enough,' says I.

" ' Let me try it,' says he.

" ' I don't want nobody a holdin' my plough', says I.

" ' The devil you don't !' I see he's gittin' mad; so I stepped back and drapped the line. He cotch it, and ploughed a few rods. ' What you think now,' says he ' of a servant fightin' her master ?'

" ' What you think, sir, 'bout a Mass'r doin' his servants that way ?' says I. ' You see 'em misbehave with any body else, and you'd whip 'em sure !"

" ' Yes, but *I'm* your *master.*'

" ' That don't make no difference to me, sir,' says I. ' How could you see your poor house servants cut up so 'bout that shirt, and you knowin' whar it was all the time ? I b'lieve I'll go up this very night, and tell 'em all about it.'

" ' By G—d,' says he, ' I wish you would. I'd like to have you tell it. I'd give you the devil.'

" But I didn't have no notion o' tellin' ! They had storms enough without havin' any 'bout me; and I knowed I could allers keep him away by fightin' him. I liked to fight him a little, anyhow, he's so mean. If I'd

told, I'd allers had Missus agin me, and they mought
'a' sold me away from my family, and that would 'a'
been the end o' me."

Vina's wisdom in refraining from reporting to her
mistress, may be inferred from the following incident,
with the circumstances of which she was well acquainted.

Jinny, the cook, had a young daughter named
Maria. She was small of her age, a bright mulatto,
and uncommonly pretty; and her mistress had always
kept her about the house.

One morning, when Maria was about thirteen years
old, the mistress called her to perform some little
service, but she did not answer. She sent to the
kitchen, but she was not there, and, thinking she had
perhaps fallen asleep somewhere in the house, the lady
proceeded to look for her in the different rooms. She
opened the parlor door, and there was the child ——
with her master.

All the fierceness of her nature was aroused. Her
husband immediately mounted his horse and rode off
to escape the storm; though well he knew that its full
fury would fall upon the young head of his victim.

The enraged woman seized the trembling child and
put her in a buck. Then she whipped her till she was
tired, but not satisfied; for as soon as she had rested
her weary arms, she flew at her again, and after beating her till she had exhausted her own strength a
second time, she shut her up in the brick smoke-house.

The matter was no secret, for she told the story to
all the servants, and to every one else who chanced to
come to the house while her wrath was burning.

For two weeks she kept the poor girl constantly imprisoned there, except that every day she took her out long enough to whip her. She gave her nothing to eat or drink, and all the light or air that could enter the gloomy place came through the small holes that were left by the builders to admit air to the bacon. Through these, Jinny, when she could steal an opportunity, passed small pieces of bread, and a little water in a vial, that her child might not die of hunger.

Some of the elderly servants expostulated with their mistress, and even hinted that Maria was but a child, and that it was "mass'r" that was to blame. "She'll know better in future," was the stern reply; "after I've done with her, she'll never do the like again through ignorance."

"But she'll die, missus, if you keeps her shut up thar much longer."

"That's just what I want; I hope she will die."

The poor child grew very thin and pale, and sometimes, when she was taken out to receive her daily whipping, she could hardly stand. "O missus," said she one day, "if you whips me any more it will kill me."

"That's just what I want; I hope it will;" was the only reply. But some merciful angel restrained her cruel arm for that one day, and she thrust her back without beating her.

"Please, missus, wont you let me have a drink of water?" said the child, as the door was once more about to close upon her.

"No; not a drop of water shall you have, nor a mouthful to eat;" and she shut the door upon the youthful sufferer.

After she had kept her thus imprisoned for two weeks, her eldest son, Master Charles, came from Louisiana on a visit. To him his mother told the story of *Maria's depravity*, and begged him to take her away with him. " Sell her," said she, " to the hardest master you can find, for, if she stays here, I shall certainly kill her."

Master Charles readily assented to his mother's proposal, and proceeded at once to the smoke-house to let Maria out. Poor child, how changed was she from the bright young girl of two weeks before! Her face had now an ashy hue, and her large eyes were dull and sunken. Her flesh, too, was all gone; so that she was indeed frightful to look at.

"Why, mother," said the young man, "you must have this girl fattened up or she will never sell. I should be ashamed to offer her for sale looking as she does now."

The mistress went to the kitchen. "Jinny," said she, "I want you to feed *my young mistress* well, and fatten her for the market."

Poor Jinny was greatly distressed, and as soon as she could find him alone, she begged young Master Charles not to sell her child.

"O Aunt Jinny," said he, "I am not going to sell her. I want to take her home with me, to get her away from the old lady. I shall keep her myself, and I'll take good care of her.

The young man kept his word. He took her to Louisiana, and kept her till she had recovered her health and her good looks. Then he hired her out to a lady of his acquaintance, who taught her to sew, and she became an excellent seamstress. A few years after, when he came home on a visit, he brought her with him that she might see her mother. She was then a large, fine looking woman, so changed from the poor persecuted child that left them, that her friends could scarcely credit her identity. Yet, though years had passed, she dared not come into the presence of her angered mistress. Master Charles left her at his sister's; and only when her enemy had left the plantation for the day, did Maria venture to steal a visit to her early friends.

CHAPTER XXIII.

PETER'S YEAR AT McKIERNAN'S.

On the first day of January 1841, Peter commenced his labors on the plantation of Mr. McKiernan. Now came his most intimate acquaintance with the realities of slavery. He had witnessed much suffering both in Kentucky, and also since his removal to Alabama; and had even endured, in his own person, enough to give him some idea of the meaning of the word *slave*, but never did he comprehend its full, fearful import till he learned it here.

Not that he suffered personal abuse, for aside from two or three violent cursings, he received during the year, no unkind treatment. This exemption he owed partly to his own cautious avoidance of any act or word that could annoy his irritable master; and partly, no doubt, to the fact that Mr. McKiernan wished to buy him, but was well aware that he could not be purchased from the estate of his late master without his own consent. Mrs. Hogun, his former mistress, was still his kindest friend; and though she had now no real authority over any of the slaves except the six that had been allotted to herself, she still possessed great influence with those who managed the estate; and she would never sanction the sale, against his will, of one of her favorite servants.

So Mr. McKiernan was wondrous kind to Peter. He employed him during part of the year as moulder in making brick, with the professed intention of building new brick cabins for his people; but to this day the old log huts remain their habitations.

It was not in personal sufferings or privations that Peter found the bitterest woes of slavery. It was the stifling influence of the deep degradation of his race that most oppressed his spirit. The moral malaria of the place filled his blood with hatred of the oppressions by which it was engendered; and his own consciousness of higher aspirations than those indulged who called themselves his masters taught him that, though his skin was black, they were, in truth, beneath him in all that constitutes a man.

But though Peter found much to sadden his spirit while he remained on Mr. McKiernan's place, his constant presence there was a rich blessing to his family.

Vina had now, in addition to the three children we have previously named, a little daughter about three years old. She had, during the autumn of 1833, buried a baby a week old; and little Silas, after remaining with her just one year, was borne away to the hill-side in August, 1836. Again in March, 1840, a little daughter, five months old, was strangled by the croup.

In July, 1841, another little boy was welcomed to their humble cabin. They called him Bernard, and for three years he remained the pet of all the little household. Then he was seized with spasms—and soon his merry voice was hushed, and his little form grew cold and stiff in death.

The three boys, Peter, Levin and William, were now old enough to work on the plantation, and their obedience and kindness to their mother fully rewarded all the care she had bestowed upon them. Yet she was forced even now to labor very hard to keep them comfortably clad. She made all their clothes herself, and washed and mended them by night. Their stockings, too, she knit, though she was obliged first to card the wool and spin it. Of this the slaves had usually as much as they needed for stockings, *if they could get time to manufacture it.* The master had plenty of sheep, and was not in the habit of selling the wool.

All the fragments of their worn-out clothes the careful mother saved, and pieced them into bed-quilts. She managed to get help to quilt these, by inviting in the other women on Saturday nights. They were not allowed to leave their cabins after the blowing of the horn for them to go to bed; but they were welcome to sit up and work till morning, if they could furnish themselves with lights.

Thus, in exhausting and continual toil, had passed the years of Vina's motherhood. Her husband had been unable to share her cares, except on Sundays, when he had done all he could to aid her in her labors. No wonder she was glad when every night his smile brightened her cabin, and his pleasant voice beguiled her hour of toil; and yet, in her unselfish heart, she wished his lot had fallen elsewhere.

Peter, as we have seen, had been long accustomed to plantation life; and, during the ten years that had elapsed since his master's death, he had seen many hardships. But still, the kindness of his mistress had never failed him; and even when she no longer possessed the power to ameliorate his condition, the knowledge that she pitied him, and exerted all her influence in his behalf, endued him with new strength to bear his troubles. But on this plantation a phase of slave-life was presented for his observance, new, and more revolting than any he had elsewhere witnessed; for here the women suffered most, and oftenest by their mistress' hand, or in obedience to her orders.

The main house-servant, at this time, was Ann Eliza, whom with her husband, Edward, Mr. McKiernan had bought several years before in Mississippi. She knew how to read well, understood all the branches of good housewifery, and was withal possessed of excellent sense and real piety. Yet, although her services in the house were invaluable, and her conduct was above reproach, her mistress hated her. *She was too handsome, and had "such a tongue!"*

Ann Eliza was not impudent or bold; but when her mistress violently upbraided her, and accused her falsely, she threw back her head, and fixed her large, clear eyes upon her face, while with a steady voice she declared her innocence. This dignified defence the passionate lady could only answer with the cowhide, and she frequently exhausted her own strength in fruitless efforts to subdue the spirit of her slave.

Once, during the year that Peter spent there, the mistress, as a punishment for some offence, sent Ann Eliza to the gin-house, to assist in moving a quantity of cotton. After she had gone, a messenger was despatched for a man named Anderson, who was in the habit of attending to any necessary business on the place during the master's absence.

"Look here, Mr. Anderson," said the lady, when that personage presented himself before her. "I want you to go to the gin-house, and get Ann Eliza, aud give her one good whipping. I have whipped her myself till I am tired, but it does no good. She needs bringing down, for she is the torment of my life. Lay it on well; you needn't be afraid. It is a good time now, as Mr. McKiernan is away from home. He is mighty careful of the pretty girl, himself, and that is what makes her so impudent."

"Yes, ma'am," replied Anderson, "I'll give her a lesson she'll remember;" and he departed to the gin-house.

Ann Eliza saw him coming, and she knew her doom. She cast one imploring look at her husband, who was working at her side. Edward returned it with a glance so full of terror, pity, and an intense longing to avenge her wrongs, that all her powers were roused, and she felt strong to endure the worst.

She stood calmly by her husband's side, while, with his rope, the ruffian bound her hands; and then, at his command, she followed him towards the house, leaving poor Edward gazing after her in silent terror. One moment a flash of vengeance gleamed from his dark eyes; and then he realized his utter helplessness, and his head drooped low, while great tears fell upon the heap of cotton.

Peter stood in the shelter of one of the out-buildings, and watched Anderson as he led his victim to the orchard. There he "staked her out" upon the ground, and, with a zest unknown to *uncultivated natures*, he applied the cowhide to her naked back and limbs. Her screams of agony only excited his demoniac mirth. "That's right," he cried, "I like to hear you shout;

that's the way ye all shout at the camp-ground. Shout away! you're gittin' happy now."

He beat her there, mocking the while her cries of pain, till she became too much exhausted to utter another sound; and then, untying her, he delivered her to her mistress. "Thar, ma'am," said he, "she ain't got use for no more this time. She's got the devil in her, but I reckon he'll keep still till she gits over this ere."

Much religious excitement existed at this time among the slaves in the neighborhood, and particularly upon the plantation of Mr. McKiernan. An old Baptist preacher, named Archie Eggleston, had been hired here the preceding year; and he had zealously preached to his brethren in bonds the love and compassion of Jesus; and had sought, in his simple way, to encourage them to hope for a home among "the spirits bright." His language, it is true, was full of the quaint idioms of his race; but it spoke to the hearts of his unlearned auditory; for the little which he could tell them of the blessed Saviour was just what they loved to hear. They "received the word with gladness," and, with its warm and cheering rays, it illumined their darkness, and strewed the thorny path they trod, not with the roses of content, but with the trembling violets of hope.

Sweet, when their daily toil was done, was the hour which, borrowed from their needed rest, they spent alone in prayer; and, as the breath of their humble souls ascended on the soft air of evening, their trusting hearts were filled with heavenly consolations.

But even these few precious moments were not un-disturbed, if the overseer or young Master Charles discovered their retreat. "Ye all needn't pretend to be praying, when you're just hiding around to get a chance to steal; take that—and learn to stay at home of nights!"

CHAPTER XXIV.

BURTON'S REIGN

THE overseer on Mr. McKiernan's place was usually a representative of the lowest order of his profession. The master could tolerate no other, and those of the better class would not remain in his employ. If, by chance, he hired one of a higher grade than the brutish fellows to whom his business was wont to be intrusted, his stay was short.

"Why don't you put on some decent clothes?" said such a one to a half-naked negro, soon after he entered upon his duties in the field.

"Ain't got none but dese yer, sir."

"Where's the clothes your master gave you this fall?"

"He ain't never give us no clothes, sir, in more'n a year."

"Humph! I'll not have anything to do with his lousy niggers; I shall get lousy myself."

"Mr. McKiernan, I can't do business for you; your niggers are too filthy and ragged; I can't oversee such a gang."

"Well, I'm going to get them new clothes soon; I've been intending to get some this long time, but it has been neglected."

Nothing more was heard of them, however, and the scrupulous overseer found another situation, leaving his place to be filled by one whose tastes accorded better with those of the old master.

One of this latter class was employed upon the place a few years after Peter's sojourn there, who had so keen a relish for the varieties of his profession that a few instances of his reign should be related here.

His name was Burton. He was a tall, dark man with grey hair, and shaggy eye-brows, as fierce and disagreeable in countenance as he was cruel and hard of heart.

He came on Saturday, and commenced business on Sunday morning by summoning all the hands to listen to his rules.

"D'ye all hear? Every man of you must get your axe and saw, and go to the woods, and chop and saw logs for boards. And you girls, get your mattocks and handspikes, and go on the new ground and grub; and, d'ye hear? mend every log-heap, and every brush heap there. And mind; the same's to be the law for every Sunday morning. Ye all are to work till noon, and after that you may go the devil."

The sable company gazed at each other in blank amazement. They had been "pushed" when they had been allowed to wash and mend, and work their patches on the holy day, but now ———

The silence was interrupted by one of their number, named Lewis, a very black man with a round face and heavy figure, who stepped forward, and said, as he looked the new overseer firmly in the face,———"Well, Sir, de res' cun do as dey likes, but dis chile aint gwine to do it."

"You tell me," cried Burton, "that you're not going to do it?"

"Yes, Sir, I tell you I wont do it. I aint gwine to work a Sunday for no man."

"Very well—v-e-r-y w-e-l-l." The enraged over-seer turned his fiery eyes upon the other slaves, and saw that they obeyed his orders. With rolling eyes and pouting lips they all went in their dirty clothes to work.

Till noon they labored; none dared a moment to lag; for the monster with his heavy whip was near. At twelve they returned tired and angry to the quarter. They were unwashed, their cabins were untidy, but they had no heart to move; and there they sat in sullen silence.

Presently the overseer summoned five or six of the strongest men to go and help him "take that gentle-man that would'nt work on Sunday."

They dared not disobey. Burton took a rope, and, attended by these unwilling aids, entered the cabin of Lewis. He did not look up as they went in, but sat with his head inclined, and with a look of fierce de-cision on his face. They approached to bind him. Instantly he sprang to his feet, and fought like a tiger.

For half an hour the uproar in the house continued; and then they brought poor Lewis out, wound up in ropes.

The cabins were built in a hollow square, one side of which was formed by the overseer's house and gar-den. Into the centre of this square Burton led his victim, and there in sight of all the slaves, he stripped him entirely naked, and then whipped him till the blood streamed from his back. Then commanding, as before, other negroes to his aid, he led him to the smoke-house, and put him in the stocks.

These consisted of two heavy timbers, with mortice hole cut in each, through which they thrust the hands and feet of the offender, securing them by heavy iron bolts at each end of the timbers.

Thus the pitying slaves confined their mangled brother. Alas! they had no power to aid him, and they dared not refuse to obey the orders of the overseer, though every appealing look of their suffering companion wås a dagger to their hearts.

After supper that night, a light was seen gleaming through the small apertures in the smoke-house wall; and some of the slaves peeped in. Burton sat composedly in a chair which was kept there for the convenience of overseers on like occasions, and as his cowhide, with a sharp twang fell on his prostrate victim, they heard his muttered curses mingle with the sufferer's groans. "Well," whispered one of these curious listeners, "I gives it up. Der aint no use talkin' 'bout de Lord's orderin' all things; kase its plain to my comperhendin' dat nobody sent dat dar ole feller yer but the devil himself. De Lord knowed we done seen hard times enough on dis yer place; we didn't need no more o' dat sort."

The next day at noon, Burton let the offender out, and ordered him to go to work.

"I aint able to work," growled Lewis.

"But you shall work," rejoined the overseer, "or I'll give you more of the same sort."

Notwithstanding this threat, Lewis went to his cabin, and there day after day he sat brooding over his injuries.

"How long are you going to sit there, you d—d sulky nigger?" cried Burton at the cabin door.

"I's gwine stay yer till I gits well, and den I's gwine to de woods."

Lewis kept his word. A day or two after this, he rose in the morning at the sound of the horn, and went out. Soon after Burton appeared at the door. "Where's Lewis?" demanded he, of Lucy, his wife, who was preparing to go to her work.

"I don' know, sir, I reckon he's some're 'bout de yard."

The day wore on, but no Lewis appeared. "I tell you, my lady," said Burton to Lucy, "I'll fetch the truth out of you." So saying, he seized her, and tying her arms around a stump, whipped her cruelly. But thus he gained no knowledge of her husband; for she still protested that she supposed he had only gone into the yard.

Week after week passed on, and yet no tidings came of Lewis; but he was not alone, for soon a man named Frank, and "old man John," were driven by Burton's cruelty to join him in his "den."

Yet the cowhide of the overseer had no rest; for so dearly did he love its music, that a day seldom passed on which he could find no occasion for its use.

Young Peter was one day suffering from a severe toothache, and he quit his work, and sought his mother's cabin. It was a busy time, for they were to kill hogs the next day.

He had been in the house but a short time, when Burton came to the door and bade him go and help to make the necessary preparations for the morrow. "I can't work, sir," said he, "my tooth aches too bad."

"Well," said the overseer, "come along to my house, d—n you, and I'll cure it, or knock it out—one."

"If that be the case, sir," said Peter, "I wont go; for I aint gwine have my teeth knocked out like I was a horse or a hog."

"So you tell me you wont, young man—v-e-r-y w-e-l-l."

The next morning, Peter, having been kept awake nearly all night by his tooth, did not go out till sunrise, though he was called soon after midnight. Meantime, the master visited the scene of slaughter.

"Master Peter is laid up with the tooth-ache," said Burton to his employer, "and I told him yesterday if he would come to my house, I would give him something to ease it; but the young gentleman told me he would not."

Vina stood near, and as she had heard the conversation the day before, she determined, if possible, to shield her son from the impending storm. She had always been a most useful servant; and since the time when the overseer Simms had so nearly murdered her, the master had not suffered her to be beaten. So with a consciousness of her own high standing in his esteem, she boldly repeated, in his presence, the precise language which the overseer had used to Peter.

"You told him," said she, "to come to your house, and you'd cure it or knock it out; and he said, if that was the case, he wasn't gwine come, kase he didn't want his teeth knocked out like he was a horse."

Burton gave her an angry scowl. "Was I talking to you?" said he.

"No, sir, but you's tryin' to git Peter whipped, just for nuthin?"

"Hush your mouth!" cried her master.

"I told the truth, sir," said she, nothing daunted, and looking him earnestly in the face.

After a while, Peter came out. "What's that impudence you were giving to Mr. Burton last night, telling him you wouldn't?" said the master.

The young man repeated the conversation.

"Well," said Mr. McKiernan, turning to the overseer, "you can tie him up to that apple tree."

Burton needed nothing further. He quickly tied Peter to the tree, and gave him a hundred lashes, after which he ordered him to go to work.

This scene was highly amusing to the master, who often told the story with great glee; swearing that the best cure he ever knew for a nigger's tooth-ache was to tie him up to a tree, and "give him the devil."

For three months no trace was found of the three runaways, though many days were spent in hunting them, and no means were left untried to induce their fellow-slaves to betray them to their foes. Their wives, from the time of their flight, received weekly but half their usual allowance of meat, that they might have no surplus "to feed the rascals." "Go out and hunt them," said Burton, when they complained of the scanty fare, "and when you bring them in, your allowance shall be made up to you."

The master at last despaired of taking them by ordinary means, and he resolved to try a desperate measure; one that should frighten all the others who might thereafter be tempted to try the woods.

About half way to Courtland lived a negro-hunter, named Elliott, and Mr. McKiernan now sent for him to come and catch his runaways. Elliott promptly obeyed the summons; bringing with him his trained dogs—seven hounds and a bull-dog.

He arrived just before supper, and early the next morning the hunt was to commence. That night Frank came to the quarter. His friends informed him that the dogs had come, and bade him haste to flee beyond their reach. But he was very swift of foot, and he felt sure he could outrun them. He however, hastened back to the "den" which the three occupied together, and told the news to his companions, Lewis, and "old man John."

Lewis lost no time in fleeing beyond their scent. The dawn of the next morning found him in the woods near La Grange, distant from their rendezvous about seven miles.

Early in the morning the party, composed of Mr. McKiernan, Elliott, and a slave named Vollen, started on the hunt. They were mounted on the swiftest horses the place could boast, and the dogs with their noses to the earth, silently followed them.

They passed the gang of slaves just going out to work, and from many a heart the fervent prayer went up to Heaven that they might miss their prey.

Late in the afternoon the baying of the dogs was heard. "Thar," said Vina to the woman who was plowing next her, "I'll lay anything they's started one o' the poor fellers."

The horrid sounds came nearer—the hunters' yells mingled with the dogs' loud baying; and as all eyes were turned in the direction of the woods, a man bounded over the high fence, and ran with desperate speed into the midst of the excited slaves. The fright-

ened mules set up their ears, and ran furiously through
the field, dragging the plows behind them over the
young corn.

"Hold on! Hold on!" cried the master, who rode
close behind poor Frank; "don't let 'em run!"

But few tried to obey, and those few were dragged
at full length along the ground, adding by their shouts
and cries, to the confusion of the scene.

"Take off de dogs! call 'em off! dey's killin' me!"
cried Frank.

"Let 'em go!" shouted his master; "who cares if
they do kill him! He's made me more expense and
trouble than his neck's worth."

The bull-dog, with the ferocity of his race, kept
close to the poor fellow's legs, and tore great pieces of
flesh out of them as he ran. At last Frank seized a
stick that lay across his path, and attempted to beat
him off. Up rode Elliott. "You d—d rascal! how
dare you strike my dog?" So saying, he gave him
several blows over the head and neck, that sent the
blood gushing out.

"Mercy! Mercy!" cried the slave, "you're killin'
me!"

"I mean to kill you, you black cuss."

When they called off the dogs, and started for the
house, poor Frank, faint with fatigue and loss of blood,
could walk no further; so the master commanded one
of the men to take his mule out of the plow and carry
him to the house.

They lifted him, all covered with blood, upon the
mule, and when they reached the quarter Mr. McKiernan delivered him to the overseer. "Here, Burton, is

one of your runaways—Elliott says he'll bring in the
other two to-morrow, if they're any where this side of
h—ll."

Burton ordered the slaves to go on with him to the
smoke-house, and put him in the stocks.

The next day the overseer went in to "take his
satisfaction." He first fastened the hands of his victim
in their mortise; and then, sitting down, whipped him
till his demoniac rage was "satisfied."

For several days thereafter, Frank was left in the
stocks. His wounds inflamed, his bruises festered, and
at last he told the overseer, who daily paid him a visit,
that if he did not have his legs dressed where the dogs
had bitten him, he should die, "sho 'nough." Burton
made no reply, but the next day he took him out of
the stocks, and let him go.

For two months he remained in his cabin; and
though his wife had dressed his wounds with the greatest care, five of them were still unhealed. Then the
order came for him to go to work; and though he was
still very weak, he dared not refuse obedience. " *He
had lost a heap o' time, but mass'r 'lowed his example
would skeer the others, so't they'd keep out o' the woods.*"

Burton swore, when he released him, that he should
work every Sunday in the year to make up lost time;
and for five Sundays, he kept him all day in the field,
visiting him occasionally, to see that he was not idle.
After that, however, he was released at noon with his
companions.

The next day after Frank was taken, " old man
John" was brought in. He was not torn by the dogs,
for on their approach he climbed a tree, where he re-

mained till Elliott called them off. No trace of Lewis was discovered, and the hunter, with his dogs, went home.

About a fortnight after this, at midnight, Lewis came to Vollen's house. This was a cabin, near the kitchen; Vollen's wife being one of the house servants.

"Is you come in to stay?" said Vollen.

"Don' know; think I better?"

"Yes, I reckon you mought as well, for de dogs done tore Frank a'most to pieces."

"What you reckon dey'll do if I comes back?"

"Don' know; best ax ole mass'r—I'll go tell him you done come in."

Soon the master came to the door. "Well, Lewis," said he, "you had your race? Come back to stay, eh?"

"I don' know, sir, I'll stay ef I can be left alone, and not git whipped to death."

"Well, you go to the kitchen and wait till morning."

The slave obeyed, though with many misgivings. Something within urged him to flee; but then he could not believe his master would allow him to be beaten more. It surely would not be for his interest to render him unfit for labor at a season when all the the forces he could summon were needed in the field.

The master rose at dawn; and sent a note to Burton, saying that Lewis had come in, and desiring him to come up "soon."

Promptly, with rope in hand, the overseer presented himself at the kitchen door. Lewis threw at him a glance of angry defiance. "No!" cried he, as Burton attempted to tie him, "my mass'r 's yer;—he cun kill me if he will; but you shan't tie me, nor whip me—nary one. You's done enough o' dat dar."

"Cross your hands!" shouted Mr. McKiernan.

"Very well;" responded the slave, "If mass'r says so, you cun do it; but if he was n't her, I'd die fus."

"Lewis," said his master, "I want Mr. Burton to make me a crop; and how can he do it, if you all are off to the woods?"

"I'se willin', sir, to help make you a crap," replied the slave, "but when you gits such a mean oversee', whar whips all de time, I can't stand it."

"Burton," said the master, "you take your satisfaction out of him, and then give him an extra fifty for me, to make him tell who fed him when he was out."

With a grim smile upon his repulsive face, the overseer led Lewis to the smoke-house, and put him in the stocks; then, leaving him there to meditate upon the manifold benefits ensuing to his poor heathen race from being allowed to dwell in a Christian country, he went out to see that all his other subjects had commenced their daily toil in accordance with the orders he had given them.

After dinner, he went in to chastise his victim. He fastened his wrists in their appropriate mortise, and then, lighting his pipe, sat down to his delightful task.

Burton was in his element. He wasted not his strength by violent exercise or undue excitement, for his long arms swayed leisurely in unison with his *pleasant thoughts*. He had plenty of time to "take his satisfaction," and at every cut of the cowhide that forced an extraordinary groan from the prostrate wretch before him, a gleam of fiendish exultation flitted across his savage face; and through his closed teeth he hissed : " Ah! that's a good one; it takes me to break a nigger in."

When he had given him enough for once, he called two of the boys, and ordered them to make " a bucket of strong pickle." and carry it to his house. " My wife," said he, " will put in some spirits of turpentine, and then it will do to rub down this gentleman."

They soon brought the brine, prepared according to his directions ; and then, by his command, they washed poor Lewis from head to foot. Oh! how he shrieked and writhed as the stinging fluid penetrated every bleeding gash the cruel whip had made ! Then, after giving him a few more cuts, as he said, " to beat the medicine in," Burton loosened his wrists, and, leaving his feet still in the stocks, went out and locked the door.

For four days, the slave remained fast in the stocks; his loneliness unbroken, save by a daily visit from the overseer, who came in " just to give him a few cuts to wake him up." By this time his wounds were much inflamed, and he begged to be allowed to go to his cabin and put on clean clothes.

Burton granted this request; but placed him in charge of two other slaves, who were informed that if they did not bring him back when he had changed his clothes, they should take " the same bounty."

They led him to his cabin, and his wife called in several of the other women to see his back. Vina was one of these. She says: " When I went in the door, Lucy was a wettin' his shirt with warm water to loosen it from his back; and his two children, Charles and 'Muthis, was a cryin' like their hearts was done broke. Lucy soak the shirt a long time, till she think it done got loose; but a heap o' times, when she tried to pull it up, it fotch up welts o' flesh about the size o' my finger 'long with it. Then the blood *trinkle* down his back, and 'peared like, he'd faint, constant. She wash his back till it done stop bleedin', and then she kivered it all over with tallered plasters. Then, when he got his clean clothes on, the men whar fotch him from the smoke-house, they carried him back. Lucy and her children stood in the door, and watched him till he done got out o' sight; and 'peard like, they all would sob theirselves to death."

This was Sunday. Early the next morning Lewis was taken out of his prison, and led by two men to the blacksmith's shop, to receive "the runaway's irons." An iron ring, weighing fourteen pounds, was welded on his ankle; and to that was fastened one end of a heavy log-chain, the other end of which was brought up and passed twice around his waist, where it was secured by a lock. A collar was then put around his neck, from which an iron horn extended on each side nearly to the point of the shoulder.

He was then sent to the field, and forced to work, though he could hardly drag himself along. Through all the long hot summer days those heavy irons galled his neck and ankle, and even on the Sabbath he had no rest. "Sometimes," says Vina, " 'peared like he would run crazy. But he never got no pity from them whar was the cause of all the trouble. They only laughed at his misery, makin' out like thar's nuthin' bad enough for runaways."

One wet morning in the summer, Burton told Abram, a blacksmith, who was then headman of the hoe hands, to go to one of the hills to scrape cotton, as the bottom was too wet. Abram accordingly led his hands to the hill which he supposed Burton meant, and they all fell earnestly at work. Soon they saw the overseer coming with his grey horse at full gallop. "Why in h—l did n't you go where I told you?" shouted he to Abram.

"I thought this yer de place, Sir."

"You thought! You're not to think; you're to do."

Abram attempted to explain, but Burton grew furious; and at last he drew forth his pistol and shot the slave through the leg—thus crippling him for many months.

The master "*cursed and blustered a heap*" about this, but he was so sure that such a *tight fellow* must be a first rate overseer, that he could not think of turning him away.

Yet even he at length grew weary of the sight of his ragged, filthy people. "I say, Burton," said he one day, as he rode through the field, "how the devil can you work such a miserable gang of niggers? Why don't you make them wash and mend their clothes?

"D—n 'em; I don't care how they look;" replied the overseer. "If they only work, I don't care if the lice eat 'em alive."

"Well, I do; and by G—d, they look too bad. I say, if they don't wash and mend their clothes, you give them the devil."

Vina stood near and listened with indignation to

this order. "When we gwine wash?" cried she.
"We got to work every day, Sundays and all; we
ain't got no time to wash nor mend."

"What are you all doing nights, d—n you?"

"We's a workin' for you, sir, all the time, day and
night; and drove and whipped till we's half dead, any
how."

He turned away. "Burton," said he, "you might
as well give the women *two hours by sun* of a Saturday
to wash, for by G—d, they're too d—d filthy."

The next Saturday, just as the sun was going behind
the trees, Burton dismissed the women to go home and
wash. But they would not please him by accepting
that for "two hours by sun," and so on Monday morning they went out in the same tattered frocks—the
rags sailing in the wind. They had every week washed
their under garments by night—but this they kept a
secret. They were determined to look as badly as they
could, until their master should give them at least their
Sundays to work for themselves.

The effect of Burton's constant whipping and crip
pling the hands was manifest in the fields. So many
of the people were driven to the woods, or otherwise
unfitted for their usual labors, that the corn was
choked, and the cotton could scarcely be seen amid the
tall, rank grass.

This unpromising state of his darling crop at length
opened the master's eyes. He rode through the field one
day when Burton was not there. "What the devil ails
you all?" said he; "I never was in the grass like this."

"No wonder," replied one of the boldest men,
"reckon you'll never git out de grass long 's you keeps
ole Burton yer. He knows nuthin 'bout farmin,' no

how ; he des beats your people, and cuts 'em up constant; dat dar's all he know.   Dem whar's able to work at all can't do past half a day's work, kase dey's all so bruised and cut up."

"'Pears like," says Vina, "this teched his heart. He's mons's 'shamed o' bein' in the grass so much wuss 'an all his neighbors."

Soon after the angry old man cursed the overseer, and ordered him off the place, and though Burton swore he would not go till he was ready, yet after a few weeks he departed.

For the discharge of this inhuman monster the master received no thanks. His servants knew he cared not for their sufferings, but only for the grass which waved so boldly in his fields of corn and cotton. To use the words of Vina, " when it come to that, they didn't try to git him out o' the grass. He done kep' that mean ole Burton thar all the forepart of the year, and let him cut 'em up 'cordin' to his own mercy, and now they wasn't gwine try to make a crap. So that year we didn't make corn enough to last till June. We had to go half fed, and the mules got so poor they'd fall down in the plough. They didn't git nuthin' but fodder, for it come mons's hard to have to buy corn."

The next overseer was the reverse of Burton. " The people all liked him mightily, and he made an elegant crap without any fuss." The stocks were empty, the runaway's irons laid by to rust, and the cowhide was almost wholly idle. But this did not suit the master : and before the year closed he was discharged. Mr. McKiernan declared that his niggers were "all free, and going about kicking up their heels ;" he must get somebody that would be "*tight.*" "*Niggers must be kept down.*"

CHAPTER XXV.

FIRST FOUR YEARS IN TUSCUMBIA.

At the beginning of the year 1842, Peter was hired to Mr. James A. Stoddard, at that time teacher of the boys' school in Tuscumbia. He was á New England man, an elder in the Presbyterian church, and an exception to the often-quoted rule, that "persons who have been *raised* in the free States make the worst masters."

The peaceful home of Mr. Stoddard, with the light labor which devolved upon him, formed a pleasant contrast to the plantation where he had spent the preceding year. He was now well-fed; and was furnished during the year with four suits of clothes, which was one more than he had been accustomed to receive. These suits consisted each of a coarse cotton shirt, with roundabouts and trousers of blue jean. They were not rich, nor costly, it is true, but they were always clean.

During this year, he went regularly once in two weeks to see his family, and on these occasions he was often able to carry them some little comforts. These he earned by performing little services for others at times when Mr. Stoddard had nothing for him to do. Sometimes he went on foot to the plantation, twelve miles distant, but often some kind gentleman lent him a horse; and then with the little package of coffee and sugar, or perhaps with a comfortable jacket for one of his beloved sons, he rode along with a hopeful heart.

Eagerly did his three boys, with their little sister, watch for their father's coming; and when they heard his approaching footsteps, although the night was dark, they bounded forth to meet him with shouts of joy. Ah! they knew he brought the sunshine in his heart.

In October of this year, Miss Sarah Gist, the second daughter of his deceased master, was married to young John H. Hogun, a son of her mother's husband. The eldest daughter, Mary, had died about two years after the second marriage of her mother.

A division of the property was now made. The slaves numbered thirty-four, but to one old man, Uncle Pompey, the guardians of the estate granted his liberty. The remaining thirty-three were examined and appraised by a committee of five men; and then, after being divided into three lots, they were drawn by the agents of the three heirs.

The lot in which Peter was placed was drawn by Miss Sarah's agent; and the guardianship of his affairs was consequently transferred to her father-in-law. He took charge of the property of his children until they should become of age, the young bridegroom at his marriage being but eighteen years old, while the bride was only sixteen.

Uncle Pompey, who was kindly set free on this occasion was about eighty years old. His wife was the property of Rev. Mr. L. of Leighton. The poor old man was not wanted there, and for some time he wandered to and fro, a prey to the cruelty of patrols and other ruffians who abounded in that region. By these he was persecuted and beaten till Miss Sarah, pitying his sufferings, took him home and cared for him during the remainder of his life.

Great was the consternation among the slaves that were drawn by Miss Sarah and her young husband, when they learned that the elder Hogun was, at least for a time, to be their master. They knew his character, and feared that he might take them home to work on the plantation. He, however, allowed them to remain where they were during the year, and at Christmas time, he hired them out again.

Mr. Stoddard was, throughout the year, a kind friend to Peter; and at its close, he recommended him so warmly to his pastor, the Rev. Mr. Stedman, that he hired him for the ensuing year of Mr. Hogun. Mr. Stoddard soon after quitted teaching, and re-opened his store in Tuscumbia, where he still remains—a highly respected merchant, and one of the best citizens in town.

To Mr. and Mrs. Stedman, Peter soon became ardently attached. In all their dealings with him they respected his humanity; and no effort on their part was spared that could promote his happiness.

His duties were various, and required all his time; but he performed them cheerfully, for his heart was in his work. He took the whole care of the Church— kept it clean, rang the bell, and built fires when they were needed. Then he hauled all the wood for the family, and prepared it for the fire; "hauled water" from the spring for two families besides his own; and performed also the duties of waiter and errand boy. If the cook chanced to be sick a day or two, he took her place, and filled it with ability—in short, he

spared no effort that could conduce to the comfort of
those who showed by their steady kindness, that they
regarded him as *a man*.

Morning and evening, when they knelt at the family
altar, the servants were called in, and as the man of
God poured forth his petitions to the Great Father, the
heart of the lowly slave was lifted upward, and from
the loving household band a pure offering of thanksgiving ascended to the throne of the Invisible.

Mrs. Stedman was a native of New England, and
from her conversation and manners, Peter received his
first impressions of life in "*the* North." Oh! how
ardently he wished that he might one day behold that
wondrous land where all are free!

The Christmas Holidays arrived, but Peter instead
of going, as was the usual custom, to spend them with
his fellow-servants at his mistress' home, remained in
town with his good friend, Mrs. Stedman. She had
need of his services until the end of the year, and
though his time for that week was his own, he had no
wish to leave her.

His failure to come out with his fellow-servants, Mr.
Hogun construed into a sign of increasing independence of his master's family. Such an offence must
needs be punished. He therefore hired him for the
next year to Mr. John Pollock, a merchant of Tuscumbia. He knew this would be distasteful to Peter,
because he would naturally choose to remain in the
service of the kind Pastor; but when the slave ventured to express this preference, he received only
curses, and an assurance that he "asked no odds of a
nigger." "You've got mighty independent all at
once;" said he, "couldn't come out Christmas to tell

me where you wanted to live; so now you shall go where I say, d—n you."

On New Year's Day, 1844, Peter went to Mr. Pollock's. Here, too, he was kindly treated, and his labor was not severe. He filled vacancies among the house servants, worked in the garden, and was drayman for the store, where he slept whenever the clerk chanced to be absent. He was diligent and faithful; and his employer ever after spoke in his praise.

In August of this year, Mr. Pollock, at Peter's request, hired him out to go as cook with a company of gentlemen to the Whig Mass Convention at Nashville.

The party numbered sixty-three; and they were well supplied with tents, provisions, and various conveniences for camping out on the road. They had quantities of bread and bacon, with a store of meal for the indispensable hot corn cake.

At about nine o'clock on the morning of the fifteenth day of August, the procession passed gaily through the town. At the doors and windows, bright eyes were beaming, and fair hands waved hopeful adieus to husbands, sons, and lovers; and though the day was intensely hot, the merry band responded in high spirits.

Many of the gentlemen rode their own horses, while others went in the wagons; and conversation, mirth, and song, enlivened all the hours. They stopped occasionally to rest their horses, and to enjoy for a little while the delicious shade at the bright springs which sparkle here and there in the pleasant Valley of the Tennessee.

Just before sunset, they reached Blue Water, a quiet

little stream, that flows between banks of softest green into the lovely river. Here they encamped for the night. The gentlemen proceeded to put up the tents, while the servants built a fire, and prepared the supper. The cooking devolved on Peter, and a man belonging to Mr. W——, of Florence; and while they vied with each other in displaying their knowledge of the elegancies of their art, the two remaining servants were sent to the neighboring Whig farmers to bring straw for the floors of the tents.

Forked sticks were then driven into the ground to support two or three long planks which had been brought in one of the wagons. These formed their table, on which were set the bread and bacon, and the hot coffee which had been prepared in a great kettle over the fire.

Each of the party was supplied with a little tin plate, which he filled himself, and with this he seated himself on a stump or on the soft green turf. Here he enjoyed his simple supper with a relish unknown to those who pine for appetite beside the heavy-laden board of luxury.

After supper, wine, cards and merry conversation filled the hours, till as sleep began to steal over their senses, they sought their tents, where on the clean straw were spread their mattresses and blankets, inviting them to gentle slumbers.

The early morning found them all astir. Hot coffee steamed on the rude table, and a hearty breakfast was soon dispatched. Then the tents were struck, and, with the blankets and cooking utensils, the slaves replaced them in the wagons. The horses, which after being well fed, had been hitched to the trees at night, were soon prepared for motion, and, with a loud "Hurrah!" the party commenced their second day's journey.

At every town through which they passed, they were greeted with welcoming shouts. Ladies waved their hands as they passed by, and little children raised their tiny flags, and cried, "Hurrah for Clay!"

They reached Nashville on the eighteenth, at noon. The Convention was already in session; and the white tents of other visitors dotted the green fields and groves in the suburbs, while in the wood southeast of the city, were set long tables for the entertainment of the guests from abroad. These tables were abundantly furnished by the Whigs of the city with substantial viands, suited to the taste of all. Bands of music enlivened the groves, and it seemed a universal gala day.

Stands for speakers were erected at various places in the city; and wordy politicians talked themselves hoarse on the beauties of high tariffs, and the disastrous consequences that would follow the election of Mr. Polk. Banners with full-length portraits of the great Kentucky statesman were borne in front of processions through the streets—though Mr. Clay himself sat in his quiet home.

The Tuscumbia delegation pitched their tents on a hill near the city, and at once entered heartily into the excitement. Their four servants also, keenly enjoyed these lively times, which formed a variation in their monotonous existence; and to this day the stirring scenes and noisy crowds of the great Convention form the basis of many a tale, which beguiles the dreary hours of toil.

They spent a week in the city; though the Convention adjourned three days after their arrival. The remaining time was spent by the gentlemen in visiting friends, or in such other amusements as were suited to their various tastes and habits.

Peter had hoped that, during his stay at Nashville, he might find some chance to escape from slavery; and it was with this purpose in his heart, that he asked leave to go. He had brought with him his little stock of money—only fifteen dollars, it is true, but it seemed to him a large sum, and he was sure it would do him "a heap of good" if he were free. Thoughts of leaving his dear wife and children made him very sad; but the idea of freedom was mighty; and he resolved to try.

He walked in the evening down to the river, but on no boat could he espy a corner where he might hide and sail away to the far land of the free. He could not be long absent from the camp without being missed by some of his many masters; and when the week had passed away, and the company were about to return, he had been able to discover no avenue of escape. So he aided in the preparations for the homeward journey; and smothered in his heart those wild longings for liberty that had so long been struggling there for breath.

The gentlemen all noticed with approval his active industry, and enjoyed the comforts which they owed to his quick perceptions of order and fitness in the arrangement of their few conveniences; yet not one of them guessed what a brave, true heart he bore; or how that heart, like a caged bird, was even then beating and struggling to be free. Their return home was gayer even than their outward journey. Jests and merriment abounded.   Amusing experiences during their sojourn in the city were reviewed; and none noticed or cared that the servant was less happy than his masters.

Arrived once more at home, Peter moved on in the old channels.   His failure to escape from thraldom had not caused him to despair; and as each day he fulfilled his round of duties, the hope was strong within him that a brighter morn would yet appear.

On the first day of 1845, Peter entered the service of Mr. Michael Brady, a wealthy Irishman, also a merchant of Tuscumbia.   He was a young bachelor of pleasing manners and strict business habits.

Peter had now better opportunities than he had ever before enjoyed for gaining general information. He was employed about the store, in waiting on his young master, and doing errands; and he was frequently an interested listener to conversations which they did not dream he had the sense to understand. He had also many opportunities of becoming acquainted with the citizens of the town, and his habits of close observation tended to his rapid advancement in a knowledge of human nature.   Even at this time few more correct judges of character could be found in town than this quiet, docile slave.   He seemed to see beneath the surface, and to glance deep at the motives of the heart.

Mr. Brady, although extremely kind to Peter, had some peculiar notions.   He paid for his board at a hotel, instead of letting him earn it by waiting on the table, as was the custom with young men who hired a slave; and he positively forbade Peter's performing the slightest service for any person except his partner and himself. In this prohibition Peter felt the galling chains of slavery. He loved to do a kindness; and it was so natural to bring a bucket of water, or to black a pair of boots for some young gentleman who addressed him kindly, that he could scarcely avoid offering such little services, though he knew that thus he should incur the displeasure of his young master.

But Mr. Brady was firm. He did not intend that his servant should need favors from others. He preferred supplying his wants himself; and often, when Peter was going on Saturday night to make his accustomed visit to his family, the young man gave him some little present for them from the store.

For all these kindnesses Peter was duly grateful, but they did not sweeten the slave-cup. It still overflowed with bitterness; and in his heart he spurned the draught, and vowed he would be free.

CHAPTER XXVI.

PETER HIRES HIS TIME.

THE next year, 1846, the young master, John H. Hogun, having become of age, assumed the control of his wife's property, and hired Peter to Mr. Allen Pollock, a bookseller of Tuscumbia.

Mr. Pollock had, some weeks before Christmas, proposed to Peter that he should live with him the ensuing year, and hire his own time. He had not much for him to do, he said, and after cutting his wood, putting his store in order, blacking his boots, and doing such other small jobs as might be necessary, he could get work elsewhere in town; and all he earned above the eighty-five dollars hire which Hogun must receive, should be his own. True, this arrangement was against the law, but if it were kept secret, it could do no harm.

For a long time Peter hesitated. Mr. Pollock was said to be a close, penurious man, and our student of human nature doubted the disinterestedness of his motives. Still there was a *chance* that he might succeed in saving something; he might, at least, procure more comforts for his family than they had yet possessed; and he at length resolved to try.

So the bargain was concluded; openly with Mr. Hogun, privately between Mr. Pollock and the slave; and Peter entered, trembling, upon the new year. He had never before occupied so respectable a position. The eighty-five dollars must be earned, and that was a great sum to be raised by dimes and half dimes, for doing little jobs about town.

At a short distance from the store was Major Pope's hotel, where he engaged his board, for which he was to pay by waiting on the table. He then looked about for work; and was recommended by some friend to the teachers of the Ladies' School, as a neat and careful man, who would be capable of keeping the rooms in order, and of performing any other labor that might be required about the building. He was immediately engaged for this service, which occupied him two or three hours each day.

He also, now and then, found whitewashing to do; and when extra servants were wanted on occasion of a wedding or a party, he found profitable employment. If a cook was sick, he was competent to take her place; and when some weary child of earth had finished his short pilgrimage, Peter was called upon to hollow his lowly grave.

He was at the same time hired by the month to take care of several stores—to sweep, black boots, take up ashes, and bring water; and thus he became well known to most of the business men in town.

The young gentlemen frequently gave parties at the Franklin House, then the principal hotel in town. They furnished the refreshments and table furniture, merely occupying the rooms of the hotel for which they paid a reasonable sum. On these occasions, Peter was invaluable. He prepared the rooms and arranged the tables, and the pleasures of the evening were never marred by neglect or carelessness in his department. Then he had a quiet way of keeping things in place, and of seeing that the guests were supplied with all conveniences throughout the evening; and after the gay company had dispersed, he returned all borrowed articles, and re-arranged the furniture of the rooms in its accustomed order.

His ready kindness, and his promptness in executing his employers' wishes, won him the confidence and esteem of all he served; still, these numerous cares and diverse occupations were extremely fatiguing. All the day long, and often till late at night, he was in active exercise of mind and body, yet though his limbs grew weary, his energies of spirit never drooped.

Thus passed the year away. Every week or two he paid his hire to Mr. Pollock, who several times proposed to act as his treasurer. These offers Peter declined, excusing himself by saying that he spent the most of his money to buy things for his wife and children, and so he had not much to keep.

"I don't see, then," said the gentleman, "any use in your hiring your time, if you spend all your money."

"Oh! that's what I work for," replied the slave, "to buy comforts for my family."

At the end of the year he had saved seventy-five dollars, besides having spent thirty-five dollars, during the year, on his wife and children. But this was a profound secret to all but Vina. No one in Tuscumbia knew even that he hired his time. It was understood, by those for whom he labored, that Mr. Pollock permitted him to make his own bargains, and that to him he paid in all he earned.

His success this year was an astonishment to himself. It opened a new world before him. Hitherto, his only hope of escape from slavery had been in flight; but now came other thoughts. " Seventy-five dollars in one year! How long would it take to buy myself if I could get the same chance every year? Oh! if I could be free!"

Towards the close of the year. Mr. Pollock proposed to his master to hire Peter again; but Mr. Hogan declined making a second bargain with him until he had consulted Peter.

" Well, boy," said he, a few days before Christmas, " do you want to live with Mr. Pollock again next year?"

" No, Sir," replied Peter, " I don't keer 'bout livin' with him."

" Why, I reckon he's used you well this year, and he offers to pay me up now for your hire. I reckon you'll do as well with him as any where. It's not often that a man offers to pay money before it is due."

" Well, Sir, if you hire me to Mr. Pollock, I shall have to stay with him; but there's Mr. Joseph Friedman—he'll pay you as well as Mr. Pollock, and he'd like to hire me for next year."

The young master immediately called on Mr. Friedman, and learning that what Peter had told him was correct, he hired him to the Jew before he left the store.

The Jew! Yes; Joseph Friedman was a German Jew, who had resided in Tuscumbia for six or seven years. He came there at first with a small stock of goods and opened a store, and by untiring industry and strict economy he had now accumulated a handsome little fortune.

He was small in stature, with the black hair and keen dark eyes peculiar to his race. Associated with him in business was his younger brother, Isaac, who was taller and handsomer than Joseph, but scarcely his equal in sagacity and force of character.

At the commencement of their sojourn in Tuscumbia, these Jews, the first that had ever settled in that region, were regarded with suspicion and dislike. But as their stern integrity and manly independence of character became known to the citizens, the prejudice excited by their peculiarities of religion and manners gradually subsided. As business men, they gained the confidence of the public, and though they never mingled freely in society, they were no longer exposed to rudeness or neglect.

Peter during the past year, had been mysteriously attracted towards these somewhat isolated brothers. His thoughts had been intensely occupied in devising some method by which he might yet taste that liberty, which, notwithstanding he had been forty years a slave, he still felt was his *right*. Day and night he had pondered this subject; but one great difficulty was ever present to his mind. He knew not *a man* whom he could trust. If he dared to breathe, in human ear, his wish for freedom, the bold thought might be reported to his master, and from that moment he would be looked upon as unsafe property. The consequence of this *might be* a sale, and a journey to the low country; and then the light of hope would be forever quenched.

And even if his master should be willing to sell him to himself, what security could he have that he would not deceive him, and while he took his hard-earned ransom, retain *him* also in his iron grasp? His long acquaintance with slavery in every guise had made him wary. He remembered Spencer Williams of Lexington, who three times paid the price of his own redemption, and was at last sent to the hated South in chains. No wonder that Peter trembled at the thought of such a blighting of his budding hopes. No wonder that he weighed each word that fell upon his ear, in order to discern the spirit of the speaker. Oh! that he knew a man of soul so brave that he could safely confide to him his heart's great secret! There might be many such in town; but how could he distinguish them from those whose flattering words proceeded from the deep, dark caverns of deceitful hearts?

While his ear was thus eagerly bent to catch the breath of honesty, some chance remarks of Mr. Friedman drew his attention. The Jew made no display of his opinions, or declaration of his principles; but uttered merely some careless sentence, which revealed his sympathy with the suffering, and his hatred of injustice and oppression. Peter had often performed slight services for the two brothers, and whenever he was in their presence, although no word respecting himself was uttered, he felt that he was regarded as *a man.*

It was this feeling which induced him, before his year expired at Mr. Pollock's, to ask Mr. Friedman to hire him for the ensuing year. If he could persuade him to do this, he could have an opportunity to become more thoroughly acquainted with his character;

and perhaps—oh! how the bare idea thrilled his frame!—perhaps he should thus discover the path to liberty.

To Peter's request the Jew readily assented, and, as before related, the bargain with his master was concluded.

On the first day of January, 1847, Peter commenced his labors under the protection of Mr. Friedman. According to their private contract, he was to board and clothe himself; and then, whatever he earned above his hire should be his own. He waited on the table at a hotel, as during the previous year, to pay his board; and his clothing cost him very little—as the Friedman brothers gave him all their cast-off clothes, as well as occasionally the material for a new garment from the store. Besides these, he frequently received presents of half-worn clothing from other young men whom he was always glad to serve; or from married ladies, of discarded articles from the wardrobe of their husbands.

These clothes, however, he never wore, but sold them to slaves from the surrounding plantations—receiving in payment, eggs, chickens, or any little products of their patches, which they brought into town for sale. These articles he conveyed to the hotel, where they were always in demand, and so were speedily converted into money. He always appeared in the same attire—blue roundabout and trowsers, with strong shoes; and a more respectable looking servant could not be seen in all the town.

At the opening of this year, Mr. A. E. Sloan, formerly of Syracuse, N. Y., who had purchased the interest in the school of the former Principal, established the Tuscumbia Female Seminary. Mr. Sloan was a

gentleman of agreeable personal appearance, scrupu-
lously neat in his dress and surroundings, and orderly
to fastidiousness. He determined at once to establish
in the school a new system of order and discipline;
and soon made inquiries for a person competent to
carry out his plans in the arrangement of the school-
rooms. Peter was the first one named to him, and he
immediately secured his services. This measure he
afterwards found no reason to regret, for so quiet was
he, and yet so prompt and regular in the performance
of his duties, that soon his presence, for a few hours
each morning, seemed indispensable to the comfort of
the school. A few weeks later, Mr. G. H. King, of
Northampton, Mass., came on to teach music. He,
too, soon learned Peter's excellent traits of character,
and gave him employment whenever he had pianos to
move, or any work to be done which required careful-
ness and promptitude.

He was now employed about the school-rooms a
much greater proportion of his time than he had been
during the preceding year. His grateful love for Mrs.
Stedman had predisposed him in favor of Northern
ladies; and as at the Seminary he ever received kind
looks and pleasant words, he soon became warmly
attached to all the teachers. Yet he never confided to
one of them his secret. They regarded him as an embodiment of good humor and content; never imagining that the idea of freedom had been struggling in
his breast for years. Once or twice, he says, he was on
the point of opening his heart to one of the young
ladies, but when he tried to speak the great hope that
was swelling in his breast, something seemed to choke
him, and he could not utter it. He took an oppor-

tunity however, to sound Messrs. Sloan and King on
the subject of slavery; and they represented the condition of the slaves as so far above that of the free
blacks at the North, that he judged it would be idle to
look to them for sympathy in his one engrossing hope.

"Why, Peter," said Mr. King, "negroes in the
North do not fare half as well as you, and they are not
so well thought of. Few people will employ them or
trust them they are shunned and disliked. To tell
the truth, most of them deserve no better treatment;
for they are an idle, worthless set of fellows."

All this did not discourage Peter. A voice within
him whispered, "Toil on! Heed not such words as
these! Liberty is before you; and you have drunk
too deep in slavery to believe that freedom would render you less happy, or less worthy of esteem."

The confidence between the worthy Jew and his
faithful servant was constantly on the increase; yet, as
the year drew near its close, and Mr. Friedman made
no advances towards hiring him for the next, Peter
became uneasy. Several other persons had proposed
hiring him, but he had told them all that he thought
Mr. Friedman wished to keep him another year.

At length, when Christmas was very near, he one
day saw his young master across the street, and he resolved to terminate his suspense So he approached
the Jew. "Look yer, sir," said he, "ain't you willin' to do the same by me next year that you have
done?"

"Yes, Peter."

"Well, are you satisfied with the way I have done
this year?"

"Yes;—are *you* satisfied?"

" Yes, sir, to be sure I am : and if you're willin' to do agin like you've done this year, why don't you go and hire me ?   Thar's my master, over yon."

" I see him there, but I will not run to speak to him."

" Well, sir," exclaimed the delighted slave, " I'll tell him you want to hire me ; and we shan't have no new bargain to make; if you'll do like you have done, so will I."

The conference ended, and soon Peter was hired for another year to Joseph Friedman.

CHAPTER XXVII.

PETER BUYS HIMSELF.

PETER commenced the year 1848 with high hopes. His last year's gains had greatly encouraged him, for he had laid up, besides expending over thirty dollars for his family, one hundred and five dollars; which, with thirty dollars which he had saved before he hired his time, and the seventy-five that he had accumulated while with Mr. Pollock, made two hundred and ten dollars now in his possession.

The hope of being free he had thus far communicated to none but his true-hearted wife; but now, as he had become satisfied that Mr. Friedman was his friend, he determined to seek his co-operation in his plan. This resolution was not formed without the most careful consideration; and yet, when he approached the counting-room for the purpose of opening to the Jew his cherished plans, his heart throbbed painfully, and his knees trembled so that he could scarcely walk.

"Mr. Friedman," said he, "I've got something I want to tell you, but it's a great secret."

"Well, Peter——"

"I've been a thinkin', sir, I'd like to buy myself; and you've always dealt so fa'r with me, I did n't know but you mought buy me, and then give me a chance."

The Jew's countenance brightened. He had become much attached to Peter, and had often wished in his heart that by some means the faithful fellow might be free, but such a plan as this had not occurred to him.

"Can you get the money, Peter?"

"I reckon I could, if you did n't pay too high for me. Mars, John Henry ought n't to ask a great price for me, no how, when I've served the family so long."

"How much shall I give for you?"

"I think, sir, five hundred dollars is as much as you ought to pay."

"Hogun will not sell you for that price," said the Jew. "John Pollock offered him six hundred, and he laughed at him. Some men in town would give eight hundred dollars for you—not because you are worth so much, but because they know you."

"Well, sir, I have served the family for thirty-five years. I have earned 'em a heap of money, and have been mighty little trouble or expense. They can afford to sell me for five hundred dollars."

"Yes:—well, I will speak to Hogun."

The proposition of the Jew received, at first, but little favor. Peter was an old family servant, and they intended to keep him in the family as long as he lived. They did not wish to sell him.

"Well," said Friedman, "I would like to buy him. He has a cough, and if he belonged to me, I would try to cure it, but while he is your property, I can do nothing for him. I will give you five hundred dollars."

Hogun turned away. He did not want to sell the

boy; if he did, that was no price for him. He would bring twice that sum.

A few months after this conversation, Joseph Friedman went to the "Red River Country," where he opened a store; leaving his brother Isaac in charge at Tuscumbia. This made no change in Peter's condition. He toiled on as before, steadily adding to his precious gains, while the great hope of freedom grew stronger in his heart.

Soon after his brother left town, Isaac renewed to Mr. Hogun the proposition to purchase Peter, but with no more success. The young mistress did not want him sold; especially to a *Jew*, who had no higher wish than to make money. He would probably soon sell him again: for what use had he for a servant ?—and then, perhaps, the poor old fellow would be carried away to the "low country."

After several attempts to purchase him had been unsuccessful, Peter determined to try the power of his own eloquence. Accordingly, during the last week of the year, he went out to the plantation.

His young mistress had gone with her husband to town; but they soon returned. Peter met them at the gate, and "Miss Sarah," after shaking hands with him, went in; while the young master remained in the yard to inquire after his health. His cough was particularly troublesome whenever any of his master's family were near, and now it annoyed him exceedingly. "Ugh! ugh! Mass'r John Henry, I come to see you 'bout Mr. Friedman buyin' me. I like to live with him; and he said he done named it to you."

"Yes, he did; but he didn't offer any price for you—only five hundred dollars."

"Well, Mass'r John Henry, aint that thar enough for me?"

"No—I can get a thousand dollars for you any day."

"Ugh! ugh! I think you mighty hard to ask such a big price for me when I been in your service so long. Miss Sarah done got all my arnins ever since I belonged to her great uncle, Mars Nattie Gist. Now when I'm a'most fifty years old, ugh! ugh! ugh! I think five hundred dollars is enough for me; and 'pears like, sir, you oughtent to ask no more."

"Well, Peter, you know people like to get all they can for their property; and it makes no difference to you, any how, whether I sell you for a big price or a little one."

"Yes, sir, it does, Mass'r John, kase if a person gives a thousand dollars for me, he 'lows he's gwine to work it out of me; but Mr. Friedman just wants me to wait on him about the store; and he says he'll cure my cough, too—ugh! ugh! He can't afford to pay a big price for me, and then doctor me up."

"Well, go 'long—I don't want to sell you any how; I'd rather bring you home to wait on your Miss Sarah, and to drive the carriage than to sell you for any such price."

"Yes, sir, if you and Miss Sarah was a livin' by yourselves, I'd like that; but I don't never want to come back to work on the plantation—ugh! ugh! I couldn't stand that now. But I belong to you, sir, and of course I must do just as you say. What shall I do, Mass'r John?"

"Go back to town, and stay till I come to see about you."

"Good bye, Mass'r John. Ugh! ugh! ugh!"

Thus he coughed himself out of the yard. All the way back to town he walked with a heavy heart. If his master would not sell him, all his bright hopes would yet be blasted. He had, however, done all in his power. He had used every argument that would be likely to influence him in whose young hand his destiny was held—now he could only wait with patience the result.

When the young master was next seen in town, the Jew hired Peter for another year, and with his wonted cheerfulness of demeanor, the disappointed slave entered upon the labors of 1849. Was there no sublimity in his patience?—no grandeur in his maintenance of Faith and Hope against the giant forces of Despair?

It was not long before the young master's aversion to sell an old family servant was suddenly removed. On the tenth of January an auction was held in town of certain goods—the property of his late uncle—"Old Jimmy Hogun." Among these "goods," were ten choice negroes, two of whom were boys about sixteen years old. These boys, young John Henry wished to own; and before they were put up, he called upon the Jew.

"Look here, Friedman," said he, "you want Uncle Peter, and I want those boys that are for sale to-day. If you will go in and bid off one of the boys for me, I will let you have Peter in exchange."

"I will think about it. How high will the boys go?"

"I don't know,—they're not worth as much as a tried hand like Uncle Peter. Step in, and see how the sale goes on."

He left the store, and Mr. Isaac immediately held a consultation on the subject with Peter himself. The wary slave objected to the plan. "You are not used to dealing in slaves," said he, "and you'd best not buy the boy. There'll be some game about it. If young master wants to buy him, he'll come round, I reckon."

Soon the young gentleman called again to learn the decision of the Jew. Isaac renewed his former offer for Peter, but declined to buy the boy.

"Five hundred dollars is no price for such a servant; you may have him for six hundred, though he is worth more."

"No—I will not pay six hundred."

Away way went Hogun to the auction. The two boys were soon to be put up. He grew more and more and more anxious to buy them, and at last determined to make one more effort to bring the Jew to his terms.

"Well, Friedman," said he, as he stepped into the store, "you may have Peter for five hundred and fifty dollars."

The black eyes of the Jew twinkled with delight, but he was firm.

"I will give you five hundred dollars," said he, "my brother authorized me to pay that sum."

"But," argued Hogun, "he is a great favorite in town—I have been offered six hundred dollars for him."

"I say I will give five hundred; not one dollar more."

The sale was going on—Hogun grew desperate. The boys he wanted would not wait for bidders, for they were choice fellows.

"Well," said he, as he walked towards the door, "you may have him for five hundred; but it's a shame to sell him so."

"Then he is mine!"

"Yes."

"For five hundred dollars!"

"Yes."

"Very well, your money will be ready when you want it."

Hogun hastened back to the auction. The boys were just going up. He bid off the youngest for seven hundred and fifty dollars, and the other became the property of a planter, named W——, a few miles south of the town.

It was night. At his desk sat the young Jew, reviewing the business of the day. Cautiously the door was opened, and Peter entered the counting-room—pausing to listen before he closed the door lest some chance visitor might be approaching. All was still.

"Now, Mr. Friedman," said the slave, while his voice trembled, and his whole frame was agitated, "I've come to pay you that money; and I reckon you wont cheat me. I've worked mighty hard to get it. There's three hundred dollars in this yer bag."

So saying, he drew the precious treasure from his pocket, glancing instinctively towards the corners of the room, to be sure that no spy was there concealed. He proceeded to untie the bag. It was made of leather—about twelve inches long, three inches wide at the bottom, and half that width across the top.

It contained pieces of silver of all sizes, and now and then, as they came forth with a melodious clinking, a piece of gold glittered in the lamp-light.* When the bag was about half emptied, Peter paused. It would be so easy for him to lose it all, and he had known so many slaves defrauded of their hard-earned gains, that it seemed impossible for him to trust. "But," thought he, "I've knowed Mr. Friedman a long time, and I never knowed him to do a mean trick. If I can't trust *him*, the Lord help me! I can't never be free without trustin' some person, any how."

He emptied the bag upon the table, and both counted it twice. It was right—three hundred dollars.

Mr. Friedman wrote a receipt for the money, and signing it, handed it to Peter. Poor fellow! He could not read it; but he believed it genuine, and a load was lifted from his heart. After all, he might be deceived. He was in this man's power; but he resolved to trust, and to go to work with all his might to earn the balance of the sum required to make him *a freeman*.

The next day Mr. Hogun received the stipulated five hundred dollars, and gave a bill of sale, of which the following is a copy:

" $500. For the consideration of five hundred dollars, paid to me this day, I have sold to Joseph Fried-

---

* It was Peter's custom, when he saw a piece of gold in the hands of a gentleman whom he had served, to ask him if he would not like change for that. If he received an affirmative reply, he would bring from his precious bag the amount in small silver coin. The writer knew him at one time to get ten dollars in five-cent-pieces, changed for gold. His habits of industry were so well known that such a request excited no suspicion—the small amount thus changed at once was presumed to be the sum of the poor fellow's wealth.

man a negro man named Peter. I bind myself and
heirs to defend the title of said negro, Peter, to the said
Joseph Friedman and his heirs against all claims whatever.

Given under my hand and seal this 15th January,
1849.   JOHN H. HOGUN."

Great sympathy was felt in Tuscumbia for " poor
Uncle Peter." It was so strange that Hogun would
sell such a faithful old man to a Jew. *Of course*, Friedman wanted to make money out of him; and when he
became no longer profitable, he would not scruple to
carry him off and sell him.

Thus spake gentlemen and ladies; and soon their
children caught the tone. " Don't you think," said
one bright eyed little girl to another, as they walked
to school, " Uncle Peter is sold !"

" Sold ? I'm so sorry ! Who's bought him ? Are
they going to carry him off ?"

" No—no not now. Mr. Friedman 's bought him;
and 'ma says he's a *Jew*, and she says *Jews will sell
their own children for money*. Pa says he don't doubt
that Mr. Friedman will sell him the very first chance
he gets to make money out of him ; and then, perhaps,
he'll be taken off to the rice swamps."

" Oh ! that will be too bad ! Aunt Milly says that
in the rice swamps they don't care no more for killing
black folks than they do for pigs and chickens. Oh !
I'm so sorry for poor Uncle Peter ! But what did
they sell him for ? He did'nt run away—nor his master did n't die."

" I don't know what made them sell him, his master
wanted the money, I reckon. Oh ! I wish my **Pa**

owned him—he would n't sell him, I know. Ma says she thinks it's a pity for black folks to be sold at all, but sometimes it can't be helped."

" Well, I think it ought to be helped, for they feel so bad to be carried away off from everybody that loves them. Just think—if Mr. Friedman should sell Uncle Peter away off where he never could come back —Oh! would n't it be too bad ?"

Said a gentleman, " Why did't you let me know, Peter, that your master wanted to sell you ? I'd not have let that Jew get you. He'll sell you again ; or, perhaps, work you to death."

" No, sir, I reckon not," replied Peter; " Mr. Friedman's always been mighty good to me, and I reckon he'll use me fa'r. Leastways, I belong to him now, and he'll do just as he thinks best."

Such was the judgment pronounced upon the noble-hearted Jew by men and women who had bought and sold, and beaten, and oppressed the poor until their cry had gone up to heaven. They considered it *their right* thus to trample on their darker brethren. They were born slaveholders, and when their servants neglected their duties, or so far forgot their station as to speak improperly to their. superiors, they must be beaten, though their heads were grey. Money, too, was sometimes "tight," and then the sale of a few of the young negroes that were " really in the way about the kitchen" would help to fill the purse. These were *their rights under the Constitution ;* but for a Jew to have such power over a choice old servant was quite too bad. " A foreigner too ! How could he know the feelings of tenderness cherished by a true Southerner for his slave?"

Meanwhile the despised and suspected Jew was arranging, with the object of all this sympathy, their future relations to each other. "You may work, as you did before," said he to Peter, "but you may keep your earnings. When you get two hundred dollars more, I will give you free papers, and you shall go where you like. I do not want your work—get all you can for yourself."

Did the heart of the slave bound at these words? Did the tears of gratitude sparkle in his eye? and the bright beams of hope irradiate his countenance? Ah! there is One "who seeth not as man seeth," and in His eye the generous truthfulness of the slandered Jew outshone the gaudy hypocrisy of his traducers.

Peter continued his usual labors with a light heart. He had now no hire to pay—his earnings were all his own.

The night after paying his three hundred dollars to Mr. Friedman, he went out to make his usual semi-monthly visit to his wife. How her heart throbbed when he told her all! Again and again she asked him if he were sure Mr. Isaac would be true. The children, too, had their hundred questions. Their father was very dear to them; and now he possessed new dignity, even in their eyes. "Just think, he would soon be free!" No selfish dread that thus he might be lifted above them dimmed their transparent hearts. They loved their father, and they could not doubt him.

A few months later, a heavy sorrow fell upon this loving group. The third son, William, who, at Peter's solicitation, had been hired, as waiter, to Captain Bell, in Tuscumbia, was found drowned in the Spring Creek, just below the town.

It was a warm morning in July, and he had obtained permission to go out fishing. Several boys were near him bathing, but after a while they all left him, and went some distance down the creek. Here they continued their play till about dinner time, when, as they came up, one of them noticed a boy's clothes on the bank. "They're William's clothes," said two or three at once. "Where is he?" Alas, they could obtain no answer to their question, and they ran up to town and gave the alarm. A crowd of men and boys hastened to the creek; and after diving for some time, they found him at the bottom.

That night the sorrowing father conveyed the lifeless body of his son to the cabin of his wife, whence he was buried beside the little ones that in their infancy had sunk to happy slumbers.

Poor Vina's heart was almost crushed by this affliction. William was her darling; indeed he was a favorite with all who knew him. "Oh!" sobbed his mother, "I could a seen him die if I'd thought it was the Lord's will; but to think o' his strugglin' and goin' down thar all alone, 'pears like, it's more'n I can b'ar."

In September of this year, Joseph Friedman returned from Texas; and soon after, Peter paid to him one hundred dollars, which he had earned since January. The Jew seemed delighted at the success of his humble friend, and congratulated him on the prospect of soon becoming free. Only one hundred dollars was now lacking, and that, if he were prospered, he soon could earn; and then he should be free.

Patiently he toiled on. His brow was all unruffled, and no trace of care was visible on his cheerful face. He moved so quietly in his accustomed course, that men forgot their jealousy of the Jew, and little maidens ceased to pity "poor Uncle Peter."

Late in the evening of the sixteenth of April, 1850, Peter sought, once more, the counting-room of Mr. Friedman. His hand might well tremble as he raised the latch; for his all was now at stake, and he was helpless. He entered. There sat the little Jew, looking at him with his keen black eyes. Timidly he drew forth his leather bag, and commenced counting out the money.

A footstep approached. Mr. Friedman quietly laid a pile of papers over the coin, and Mr. S——, the auctioneer, walked in.

"What, Peter," said he, "are you paying up?"

"Yes, sir. Mass'r Joe make me pay him up close"

"How much do you have to pay?"

"Well, sir, he makes me pay him half a dollar a day."

"That's pretty *tight*, but it's the best way, after all."

"Yes—that is so—I like to keep all close. Peter must pay me promptly."

When the neighbor's chat was ended, and they heard his receding footsteps on the sidewalk, they finished counting the money. How beautiful it looked to Peter! that little heap of coin, as he shoved it towards the Jew, and felt that now his fate hung entirely on the will of the little man before him.

Mr. Friedman took up his pen, and wrote a receipt in full, together with a Certificate of Freedom, as follows:

Received, Tuscumbia, January 26th, 1849,
of my boy Peter, three hundred dollars . $300 00
                              Jos. Friedman.

Recd. Sept. 1st, 1849, of my boy Peter, $88 00
Eighty-eight dollars and twelve dollars 12 00 100 00

Recd. March 29th, 1850, of Peter, sixty dollars, 60 00
                                                  ———
                      Jos. Friedman, $460 00

Received, April 16th, 1850, forty dollars,   40 00
                                                ———
                                          $500 00

For, and in consideration of the above five hundred
dollars, I have this 16th day of April, 1850, given
Peter a Bill of Sale, and given him his freedom.
                              Joseph Friedman.
Tuscumbia, Ala., April 16th, 1850.

Precious was this paper in the eyes of the self-ran-
somed slave, and yet he felt not all secure. The habit
of doubting that truthfulness of which he had so seldom
seen an illustration, could not at once be overcome.

He had five dollars left, with which he bought a
trunk of Mr. Friedman; and then in one old silver
dollar, which he had kept for many years, consisted
all his store.

Mr. Friedman had charged him no interest on the
two hundred dollars which he had advanced to purchase him of Mr. Hogan, and during the last year he
had bestowed upon him many little presents. Jew

though he was, and sometimes quoted as a miser, yet he knew the happiness of being a blessing to the poor.

Immediately after receiving this last payment from his servant, Joseph Friedman started for California, leaving Peter in the care of his brother Isaac. The whole transaction was still a secret, no mortal save the two brothers, and Peter's own family were aware that he had even wished for liberty.

He was one day engaged in cleaning the church, when two or three ladies came in to superintend his labors. Among them was Mrs. D. one of the most excellent ladies in town. "Peter," said she, when she had finished giving him some direction, "you ought to be free. You have been a faithful servant for a great many years; and now that you are getting old, you deserve to have your freedom, instead of being sold to those Jews."

"Oh!" replied he, "what use would it be for me to be free?"

"Why then you could do as you chose, and go wherever you liked."

"What! now I've got to be an old man, a'most fifty? I've got no house nor garden; and if I was free, I'd have to hire a house, and buy my own clothes; and then if I should be sick, there'd be nobody to take care of me. No, ma'am 'taint no use for me to think of bein' free. I'm too old to be turned off to take care of myself."

Thus carefully did he conceal his real feelings, lest he should place in greater peril that freedom which he had so dearly won.

At the approach of summer, Mr. Isaac Friedman decided to sell out his stock of goods in Tuscumbia, in order to remove to Cincinnati, where his brother Levi then resided.

Peter no sooner learned this plan, than he requested leave to accompany him as far as Louisville. In all his intercourse with the Jew, he had never revealed to him his early history, or breathed to him his own great wish—that of seeking his parents, and his childhood's home. But he had often talked of Lexington, and now he said he should like once more to visit "the old place."

Mr. Friedman readily assented, and Peter commenced his preparations for the journey. His earnings since he had finished paying for himself, together with his receipts from the sale of a few articles which he no longer needed, amounted to eighty dollars. That he thought, would be sufficient to meet his expenses on the way.

The Tuscumbians again became excited. Some gossiping oracle "*reckoned*" that Joseph Friedman had failed, and straightway that important *reckoning* was announced to be a fact. *Joseph had failed, and Isaac was about to sell off his goods at auction, and quit the country. Uncle Peter, too was to be dragged off and sold, or, as some said, to be hired out upon a steamboat, and thus exposed to all the frightful sickness that then raged upon the Western rivers.* "Now Uncle Peter," said one, "if you find out that those Jews are about to sell you, just let me know, and I will buy you."

"It will be too bad for them to speculate out of you," said another, "but I *expect* that is what they bought you for."

To all these kind expressions of interest in his welfare, Peter had but one reply. "Mass'r Joe and Mass'r

Isaac always has been good to me; and any how, I belong to them, and they can do what they like."

"What a contented old fellow he is!" said one who listened to this quiet answer. "I'd like that some of the abolitionists should hear him talk, they would be obliged to own that *niggers' pining to be free* is moonshine."

The Saturday before Mr. Friedman intended to leave town. Peter went out to pay a farewell visit to his family. To them he unburdened all his heart. His great hope had been, if he could once be free, to find his own relations, whom he always thought of as living in or near Philadelphia. Then, if they were able, perhaps they might assist him in the purchase of his wife and children, and so, at last, they could all dwell together.

This hope had so inspired the little family at Bainbridge, that their grief at parting with their beloved father was lost in the bright vision of a speedy reunion in the dwelling of the free. They knew nothing of the difficulties to be encountered; or of the time requisite to perfect such a work, even if their father were successful in his search. *He had bought his freedom;* and in their eyes, such an achievement proved him equal to the attainment of any end. Not thus sanguine was their father; but he was strong in his fixed resolve to work while he had breath for the redemption of his loved ones.

In sweet, though somewhat mournful, conversation passed the hours of this precious visit. They were all too short for the utterance of the many last fond words; and on Monday morning, when the father was obliged to leave them they had not found time for half they wished to say.

The loud horn called them to their labors, and the children said "Good-bye," and hastened out—but Vina lingered. Oh! it was hard to see him go away alone —but still she would not bid him stay. She mounted her mule, and rode toward the field, while Peter walked for a short distance by her side.

His heart was very heavy, but he uttered not his gloomy thoughts. He would fain leave her cheerful; for he knew that ere his return, her heart would oftentimes be shadowed. So he spoke hopefully of the future, and bade her never fear for him. "I will come back," said he, "whether I find my people or not—I will come back, and let you know. Now take care of yourself and the children; and mind they don't tell the secret."

Too soon their paths diverged. When they came opposite the half-plowed field they stopped. "Well Peter," said the brave-hearted wife, "*this yer's your road, and yon's mine. Good-bye.*" One pressure of the hand—one last earnest look—and they each pursued a separate road; the one to slavery's dreary labors, the other toward that Paradise of hope—*The North.*

" Well Peter, this yer' s your road, and yon' s mine.   See page 236.

CHAPTER XXVIII.

JOURNEY TO PHILADELPHIA.

ON the twentieth of July, all preliminaries being arranged, Mr. Friedman and his servant took the boat for Louisville.

"Now, Peter," said Dr. W——, as he shook hands with him upon the sidewalk, "mind what I tell you; if those Jews go to sell you, just telegraph to me."

"Thank you, sir, I will; but I reckon they ain't gwine to sell me, any how."

Several other gentlemen, as he passed along, gave him similar assurances; and with the kindest wishes of all the citizens, he left the town.

"That is outrageous," said a kind hearted gentleman, who watched the faithful servant as he passed out of sight—"for that Jew to carry off such a fellow as old Peter, and to have a right to sell him whenever he likes."

Peter paid his fare to Louisville by working on the boat—The Greek Slave—Captain Francis. When they reached that city, the cholera was raging fearfully; and Mr. Friedman thought best to make no stop, but to hasten on to Cincinnati. Thither also, Peter obtained permission to accompany him; and at six o'clock on the morning of the twenty-sixth of July, the free soil of Ohio was pressed by his weary feet.

Now, for a time, he threw off his pretended bonds, and gave way to his emotions of delight. Springing from the boat, he clapped his hands in ecstasy, shouting, "I'm free! *I'm free!* This is free ground! The water runs free! The wind blows free! I am a slave no more!"

"Hush! Peter," said Mr. Friedman, "people will think you are a fool!"

That day, in the house of his brother, Levi Friedman, Peter revealed to his late master the story of his life. He told him all that he remembered of his early childhood—of his being stolen, of his brother's life and death, and of the one hope which had animated all his labors—that of returning to the spot where he was born, to find, if possible, his kindred, and to see his mother's grave.

Friedman listened with astonishment; and when Peter described, as well as he was able, his early home, which he located at Philadelphia, the Jew could not believe the tale. "No, no," cried he, "you came from Kentucky—your master told me so."

"Yes," replied Peter, "so I did come from Kaintucky; but I was stole and carried there when I was a little boy. I remember the Delaware river—it was not far from my mother's house; and that river is at Philadelphia—leastways, so people has told me. And now I want to go and see if I can find my relations."

The wonder of his auditor was intense. He could not comprehend how, during all these years, so cruel a wrong had been suffered to go unredressed.

"I do not like to have you go away alone," said he to Peter. "The cholera is raging on the river, and you might be sick and die among strangers."

But his fears could not detain the enthusiastic free-man. "Never mind," said he, "if I die, nobody don't lose nuthin by me. I'm my own man, any how, but I reckon I won't die. 'Pears like, now I've got so fur, my work ain't gwine to be lost."

After spending a day and a half at a colored boarding house in Cincinnati, where he had his clothes all put in order, he started for Pittsburg. A cousin of Mr. Friedman accompanied him to the wharf and saw him on board the boat.

How anxious was his heart as the steamer dashed away. He was all alone, and utterly ignorant of the perils he might meet. But he trusted in the Lord, and kept a cheerful countenance.

His characteristic caution prompted him to observe closely the movements of his fellow-passengers, and one of them soon absorbed his attention. This was a short dark man, with a disagreeable expression of countenance. Peter remembered seeing the same man on the boat from Louisville to Cincinnati, where he had made several attempts to draw him into conversation, without, however, learning anything further in answer to his questions than that Peter was going to Cincinnati. Now he renewed his advances, striving to draw him into conversation, and at last asked him if his owner were on board.

"I don't need any," said Peter, as he walked away.

Soon an elderly gentleman, very genteelly dressed, approached him, and asked if his master were on board.

"I have no master," replied he, "who said I had a master?"

"But you are a slave," persisted the gentleman, "or at least have been one. I knew it as soon as I saw you. Where are you going?"

"I am gwine to Pittsburg, and then to Philadelphia; and I am a free man. Who said I had a master?"

"Where did you come from?"

"From Cincinnati."

His interrogator left him in no pleasant mood. Two colored barbers on the boat had told him that the short dark man was watching all his movements. He was whispering, too, they said, among the other passengers, that he knew that fellow was a runaway; and he would take him up, if he had not other business to attend to. He was hunting, he said, for a rascal who had escaped from prison; and he could not undertake another job."

When the boat approached Wheeling, several individuals came to Peter, and offered their advice. The short dark man kept his eye upon him, but said nothing. One young gentleman with a pleasant countenance stooped down and said in a low voice, "Now, my friend, there are a great many watching you; and if you are free, stand to it. Don't leave the boat;—just say that you are free." Seeing some one approaching, the young man rose up, and walked to another part of the boat. "I thought," said Peter, as he narrated this incident, "that the Lord sent that young man, and that he was a true friend; so I determined to take his advice."

Soon came another. "See here, my friend," said he, "the people tell me that you are running away. Now, I am a friend to colored people. Here is five dollars—you'd better not stop in Wheeling, for they talk of taking you up. You take this five dollars, and walk across the bridge—and you'll be in a Free State, where they can't hurt you."

"No, sir, I thank you," said Peter, "I have paid my passage to Pittsburg, and I shall not leave the boat. Let 'em take me up if they like; I can telegraph to my friends in Cincinnati, and I reckon they can make 'em pay for the time I'm hindered. Yes; let 'em take me up, if they think best."

Notwithstanding the bravery of his bearing, he felt extremely uneasy; and as Mr. Friedman had given him no instruction respecting the proper method of procedure in such cases, he was forced to rely alone upon his own judgment. He readily suspected the hypocrisy of the *very kind friend* who offered him five dollars, and advised him to hasten across the bridge. Had he accepted the gift and counsel, he would tacitly have acknowledged himself a runaway, and so he might have become an easy prey to the vultures that pursued him.

But he was not arrested. He saw groups of men whispering together in different directions—and he knew they watched him constantly; but he seemed to regard them with such cool indifference, that they did not venture to attempt the execution of their plots.

The boat arrived at Pittsburg early in the morning; and Peter was conducted by a colored fellow-passenger to the house of a friend of his, where they took breakfast. After remaining about five hours in the city, he took the stage to cross the mountains. He was anxious to reach Philadelphia as soon as possible, for he was told in Pittsburgh that there would be a great turn-out of the colored people there on the first day of

August; and that, he thought, would be a favorable time to seek his kindred.

He paid for a seat inside the stage; but it being crowded with passengers, he was requested to ride outside. He accordingly seated himself beside the driver, where he rode all day. The grand scenery of the mountains was new to him, and wonderful. Wife and children were behind. He could hear their voices, now sad, now trustful, as they talked of "father," while their mother cooked their scanty supper. Subdued were the tones of their dear voices, for on no strange ear must fall the cherished secret that *he* was free. They little dreamed that he was riding now over these wild rough mountains. How strange the scene! The tall hemlocks which sheltered the highest peaks, seemed stern and unloving—but the warm sun looked down upon them all. The same sun even then was shining upon his toiling loved ones; and oh! perhaps it also shone upon the graves of all those whom he had come so far to seek.

Such were his thoughts as, hour after hour, he gazed upon the ever-varying grandeur of the Alleghanies.

After travelling by stage about twenty four hours, he took a seat in a rail-road car. This was another wonder. His previous ideas of rail-roads had been gained from the only one he had ever seen—that extending the length of the Muscle Shoals, and connecting Decatur and Tuscumbia. On that he had been accustomed to see, once a day, two or three little rickety cars come jolting into town, loaded chiefly with freight, but occasionally bringing also a few tired passengers. These cars were drawn by two or three sleepy-looking mules or horses; for the *snake's-heads* were so numerous upon the road, that the wheezing old locomotive, which sometimes came down with freight alone, rendered the journey too perilous for passengers.

What a contrast to all this was now before him! The bright locomotive, the long trains of elegantly furnished cars, and the smooth, level track of Pensylvania road, astonished him; while the frequent villages he passed, the highly-cultivated fields, and the substantial farm-houses, with their great stone-based barns, impressed him with still greater wonder.

On the afternoon of the first day of August, the train reached Philadelphia. Peter sprang to the ground; and, getting possession of his trunk, he stepped aside, and stood an amazed spectator of the noisy scene. Porters accosted him with—" Where want to go, sir?"

"I don't want to go no further than yer."

The crowd began to scatter. Friends met friends, and departed in their company; every one seemed in haste; he only was alone and purposeless. Far away on every side stretched the great city—the goal of all his hopes, perhaps their grave.

He stood still by his trunk, till his fellow-passengers had all dispersed. He knew not where to go. He had been advised, while in Pittsburg, to go to a certain boarding-house in Philadelphia; but the name he could not now remember. "Suppose," said he to himself, "some Abolitionist should come along now, mighty friendly, and tell me where to go, and so I should be entrapped and sold again. I must be careful."

After he had stood alone for more than half an hour, an elderly colored man came up, and kindly accosted him. "Do you wish to go to some part of the city, friend?"

"Yes," replied Peter, "I was recommended, in Pittsburg, to go to a boardin'-house, kept by a Christian man, a preacher; and I would like to find it."

"What is his name?"

"I can't think. I've been a studyin' all the time since I stood here, and I can't remember it. I only heard it once in Pittsburg; but he is a Christian man, and a minister."

The stranger suggested many names, and at last mentioned "Dr. Byas."

"Thar—that's the man—I knowed I should remember it, if I heard it spoke."

"Well," said the stranger, "I know where he lives, and I will carry your trunk there for a quarter."

Peter assented, and followed him. With the trunk upon his shoulder, the stranger led the way through the handsomest part of the city; but the beautiful buildings which they passed scarcely won a glance of admiration from Peter. His dear dead brother's features were in his mind's eye; and, in the face of every colored man he met, he looked to find their counterpart. He gazed in vain. No lineament of that well-remembered face could he discover among the passersby, and he was glad when his guide stayed his steps before the modest residence of the good Doctor.

CHAPTER XXIX.

THE KIDNAPPED BOY RESTORED TO HIS MOTHER.

MRS. BYAS herself answered the bell. She was a bright mulatto woman, with a kind smile and a pleasant voice. Dr. Byas, she said, was not at home—he had gone to Cincinnati. Peter explained to her that he was sent there by some friends in Pittsburg.

" Oh, well, then, come right in," said she, " I can take care of you."

He entered the house, and sat down, while the good woman proceeded to explain to him the cause of her husband's absence. To this he hearkened not. " Do you know how fur it is to the Delaware river?" said he.

" Why, yes—it is right down here at the wharf."

He sprang to his feet. " That is just the river I'm a huntin' for. I was born on that river ; and I want to go down and find the old house where my father and mother lived—right on the side of the hill."

" Oh, stay till I get you some dinner," said Mrs. Byas, " and then I will show you the way to the river."

" No, no—I must go now—I believe I can find the house."

But she prevailed on him to sit down and eat a lunch; and then, according to her promise, she directed him to the river; giving him at the same time her street and number, so that he might find his way back.

When he reached the river he walked a long way up the stream looking for the well-remembered woods upon the hill-side. But the city stretched a long way up the river, and as far as he could see, the bank was dotted with the costly dwellings of the rich;—no humble cottage like the one in his memory, met his eye; and when thoroughly wearied in the fruitless search, he returned disappointed to the residence of his kind landlady.

She was much interested in the stranger, and to aid him in his efforts, she sent a man with him into the streets, directing him to inquire of any aged colored people he might meet for *a man named Levin, and his wife, Sidney, who lost two children about forty years before.*

This search was unsuccessful; and at night Peter turned, with weary feet, towards his boarding-house.

Early the next morning he arose, and with new strength and energy, re-commenced his search. He found one old man who had lived in Philadelphia fifty-three years. He told him that he knew of sixty colored children that were missing from that vicinity in one year; and in another year forty were carried off, of whom no trace was ever found. Yet he had never known the *Levin and Sidney* whom Peter sought.

Hour after hour he continued these fruitless inquiries; and at last he was forced to abandon this method of search, and to return to Mrs. Byas for further counsel.

Towards evening the good woman devised another plan. She told Peter that at the Anti-Slavery Office were kept old records of colored Churches; and that, as he was sure his parents were religious people, it was quite possible that their names might there be found. She thought it best for him to go there immediately, and ask them to search these records.

He did not hesitate to follow her advice; and, with the same guide who had previously accompanied him, at about six o'clock, he started for the Office.

The guide who had been sent by Mrs. Byas had no confidence in Peter. His story seemed to him improble; and he suspected him of being a spy sent out to hunt for fugitives. This distrust soon became mutual. Peter dreaded the Abolitionists of the North, of whose decoying people away and selling them at the far South he had so often heard; and as he noticed that the guide spoke frequently in a low voice to those he met, he feared some net was spreading for his feet.

At last they reached North Fifth street, and as they passed a window of the Anti-Slavery Office, they saw a young colored man within, writing at a desk.

"Did you ever see a black man doing that at the South?" asked the guide.

"No, indeed," replied Peter, "if a black man thar knowed how to write, he'd best keep it a secret."

They entered the office. The young clerk whom they had noticed through the window was there alone. He was graceful in his bearing, and dressed with extreme neatness.

"Good evening, sir;" said the guide. "Here is a

man from the South that says he is hunting for his people; and he wants to make me believe he was born in Philadelphia. Mrs. Byas sent me here with him— she thought possibly you might find the names of his parents on some of your books."

"What were you parents' names?" asked the young man of Peter.

"I was stolen away from the Delaware river," said he, "with my brother Levin, when I was about six years old. My father's name was Levin, and my mother's name was Sidney; and we had two sisters— one name 'Merica and the other Charity; though my brother always said that 'Merica was our cousin. One day when our mother was gone, as we thought, to church, a man came along in a gig, and asked us if we didn't want to ride. He told us he would carry us to our mother; so we got up with him. But in place o' carryin' us to our mother, he taken us off into Kaintucky, and sold us. We used to talk a heap about our mother, but nineteen years ago my brother died in Alabama; and now I've bought my liberty, and come back to hunt for my relations."

The young clerk listened with much apparent interest, and when Peter had ended his simple story, he requested him to wait till he had finished putting up those papers for the Post Office, when he would render him any assistance in his power.

Peter constantly grew more uneasy. He could not shake off the idea that some snare was here laid to entrap him, and while the young man was busied at his desk, he slipped along a little nearer to the door, in order that he might escape if any violence should be attempted.

When the papers were all prepared for the mail, the clerk sat down near him, and entered into conversation. "It will take sometime," said he, "to look over those old papers, and this man may as well go home. I will show you the way back to Mrs. Byas'."

The guide rose to depart,—and Peter prepared to accompany him. "I'll go, too," said he.

"No, no,—stay;" said the clerk, "I will do my best to find your friends."

"Yes, stay—by all means;" added the guide,—if he will look for them, it isn't worth while to go away now."

Peter was greatly frightened. He thought he could detect a mntual understanding between the two, to keep him there till night, that they might commit some outrage upon his person; but he knew no way of escape, for he was a stranger. Trembling, therefore, he consented to remain; but seated himself as near as possible to the door, and watched intently every motion of the young man whose treachery he so much feared.

When they two were left alone, the clerk questioned him further respecting his early memories of home and mother; and then, looking him in the face, he said, "Suppose I should tell you that I am your brother?"

Had a thunderbolt fallen at his feet, he could not have been more astonished. But the doubt was uppermost in his mind, and with an incredulous look he answered, only, "Supposin' you should?"

"Well," continued the young man, "from all you have told me, I believe that you are a brother of mine. My father's name was Levin, and my mother's name is Sidney; and they lost two boys named Levin and

Peter, about the time you speak of. I have often heard my mother mourn about those two children, and I am sure you must be one of them."

The young man's voice trembled as he spoke; and Peter, more frightened than ever, knew not what to say. He did not believe one word the clerk had said; for had he not merely repeated his own story! At last he spoke: "I want to ask you one question—is your father and mother a livin'?"

"My father has been dead some years," replied the clerk, "but my mother is still living."

"Well, sir," said Peter, "then your mother is not my mother; for my mother must be dead. My brother said, before he died, that he was sure she was dead; and that is nineteen years ago. Yes, my mother must be dead. I don't expect to find her alive, but I thought I mought find her grave."

In vain the young man strove to convince him that they might both be sons of the same mother. In vain he related little incidents connected with their loss, which he had heard from his mother's lips. Peter still believed that he was merely constructing a tale to match his own. "Oh!" thought he, "what a fool I was to tell him, any how!"

"Where does your mother live?" asked he, after some minutes spent in painful thought.

"She lives in New Jersey, but I have two sisters living in this city.

"*New Jersey!*" Where could that be? It must be a great way off, for he had never heard of it. Perhaps it was across the sea. "New Jersey," said he aloud, "how far is that from yer?"

"Oh, it is just across the river. My mother lives

fifteen or twenty miles from the city. Come, go with me to my sister's; one of them lives quite near. She is several years older than I, and can tell you much more about our family."

"No, sir; if you please, show me the way to my boardin'-house. It is night, and I'd ruther go thar."

But the young man urged him so strongly, that he at last consented to accompany him to see his sister Mary, an unmarried woman, who taught a little school, and kept a few boarders.

She was engaged, when they entered, in removing the tea-things; and, as she supposed Peter was some stranger who was going home with her brother, she took no special notice of him. Soon she started to go into the basement, and the young man followed her. Peter heard them talking, in a low tone, upon the stairs, and all his worst fears returned. He had heard of houses kept by infamous women in cities; and of strangers being beguiled into them to be robbed and murdered. He had heard, too, of kidnappers, that employed colored agents to ensnare their victims; and the perspiration started from every pore, as he fancied himself thus entangled. He could not flee, for he knew not where to go; and if he made inquiries for his boarding-house, he might fall into other dangers.

After a few minutes, which seemed an age to Peter, the brother and sister returned into the room, and sat down. "Sister," said the clerk, "here is a man who tells a strange story. He has come to Philadelphia to look for his relations, and I should like to have you hear what he has to say."

She turned to Peter. "For whom are you looking?" said she.

"Oh," he replied, *I'm a lookin' for a needle in a hay-stack: and I reckon the needle's rusty, and the stack is rotted down, so it's no use to say any more about it.*"

"But tell her," said the young man, "what you related to me in the office."

He proceeded to repeat his story; but when he spoke the names of his father and mother, his listener could sit still no longer. Seizing the candle, and holding it near his face, she cried, "O Lord! it is one of our lost brothers! I should know him by his likeness to our mother. Thank God! one of our brothers has come!" Then checking herself, she turned to the young brother, "O William, this will kill mother!"

Peter was still more agitated, yet not convinced. He was so unprepared for such a joyful greeting, that he could not believe they were sincere. He promised, however, to come again in the morning, and to go with her to see an older sister, who resided in another part of the city.

After spending a few minutes in further conversation respecting their family, the clerk, according to his promise, accompanied Peter to his boarding-house.

"Good evening, Mrs. Byas," said he, as he entered the neat parlor; "did you send this man to the Anti-Slavery Office this evening?"

"Yes, sir. I thought he might find some account there of his people."

"Well, he is my own brother."

The good woman looked amazed.

"My parents," continued the young man, "lost two children over forty years ago; and from this man's story I am convinced that he is one of those brothers. And now I have brought him back here, as I promised at the office; but I want him to go home with me and stay all night. In the morning I will take him to see other members of our family.

"No, sir," said Peter, who could not yet fully trust his new-found brother, "I'd as lief stay here to-night; and then I can go with you in the morning."

Mrs. Byas, however, joined in urging him to go home with *Mr. Still;* assuring him that he did resemble him in looks, and that she doubted not they were really brothers. At last, after much persuasion, he reluctantly bade his kind landlady "good night," and departed with the clerk.

"*Still,*"—thought he as they walked along—"it seems this man's name is William Still. Then if he is my brother, that must be my name, too. I wish I knowed. And his mother has always loved the boys she lost, and talked a heap about 'em. Well, this is an oncommon case. 'Pears like they all believe this man's tale; but I can't think my mother's a livin' yet, and that I've come right on to one of her children. It seems mighty queer that they all are so ready to own a stranger, any how. Well, I shall know more about it to-morrow, when I come to see the other 'ooman; but I'd a heap ruther staid with Mrs. Byas this yer one night. Thar's no knowin' what'll happen afore mornin'."

Thus, full of doubts and fears, he walked silently beside his young companion towards his home. This was a substantial three-story brick house, situated in a retired, though pleasant part of the city.

Mrs. Still was absent on a visit to her husband's relatives in New Jersey; and after eating their supper the excited brothers separated for the night.

Peter, when left alone in his chamber, gave way to his long-pent grief. Oh! why had he thus exposed himself to every danger? Why did not Mr. Friedman give him more instructions with regard to his future course. Did he not know that his path would be beset with dangers? Then came thoughts of poor Vina, and the children; and he knew they were thinking of "*father*," and feeling sure he must be happy now that he was free. Ah well, he was glad they could not know the dangers which surrounded him. What could these people intend to do? Oh! if he should find after all that their tale were true—but it could not be. Perhaps they were all Abolitionists, and had contrived a plan to carry him off and sell him.

For fear that he might fall asleep and be surprised, he piled the furniture of the room against the door; looking first under the bed, and examining carefully every corner, to be sure that no enemy was concealed in his chamber. He then lay down; and after wearying himself with striving to devise some plan of escape from the imaginary dangers which encompassed him, he fell asleep. Even then he found no rest, for soon his room was stealthily entered by armed men. Starting from his slumber, he listened to hear their footsteps,—but all was still. Then he was about to leave Tuscumbia with his master; and all his clothes were gone. Again he was in the little cabin where Vina cared for his children, and prayed for their father, and ruffians came and tore him from their arms. All night his dreams were gloomy horrid; and in the morning he was unrefreshed. Yet the light of a new day was welcome; for he was anxious to learn more of these strange people who claimed him as a brother.

After breakfast he returned to his boarding-house; where he had a long conversation with Mrs. Byas. She was utterly unconscious of the existence of his doubts and fears; yet her frankness of manner, and her evident confidence in the integrity of "Mr. Still" went far to remove them from his mind.

At twelve o'clock he went, according to appointment, to the house of Miss Mary Still, in order to accompany her in a visit to other members of her family. She received him with sisterly affection—manifesting not, by word or look, a doubt of his being indeed one of her own lost brothers; and the two soon started for the residence of the other sister who lived in the city.

Her name was Kitty. She was several years older than her sister Mary, and was, at this time, a widow. Her daughter was standing near the door as they entered, and inquired for her mother. Away she ran to call her.

"O mother," cried she, "Aunt Mary has come and brought a man with her that looks just like my grandfather. Come, quick, and see him."

"Kitty," said Mary, as her sister approached, "here is one of our lost brothers. He came to William last night, and I am going right away with him to see mother."

Kitty asked no explanation. She saw in him a striking likeness to both her parents; and after the first burst of joy was over, she prepared to accompany them. "Yes, I'll go too;" said she. "How glad I am! What will mother say?"

The small steamboat, as it left the wharf that afternoon, bore no more interesting group than this. The two sisters alternately questioned and congratulated their new-found brother; and he—his heart was full. Now, for a moment, he believed that it was real—that they were indeed his sisters; and then his doubts returned. The joy was greater than his brightest hopes had promised.

But of one thing he was sure. He was upon the Delaware river—that beautiful stream which had ever been the pole-star of his hopes. He blessed its bright waters, and its verdant banks. They had been beautiful in his mind's eye, and now he felt that even if this new hope were all delusive, he must yet be near the home of his childhood. He strove to recall the look that his mother wore when last he saw her face, and then he wondered how he could for a moment hope to meet her again in life.

Thus between hope and fear, between confidence and doubt, he wavered, till they reached Long Bridge, about ten miles above the city. Here they landed, and took seats in the stage for Medford; near which town resided their brother—Dr. James Still.

When they arrived at his house, it was nearly dark, and they thought best to remain there all night, and go to see their mother the next morning. "There," said one of the sisters, "is brother James now walking towards the barn."

He turned, and looked towards them, and the moment Peter saw his face, his doubts departed, to return no more. He was so like poor Levin, that dear brother who lay low in Alabama, there could be no mistake. The full tide of joy rushed over his soul. He had found brothers and sisters! His mother lived! He should yet see her face.

For a short time after their arrival, all was excitement and confusion; the sisters who had accompanied him both talked at once, and all the family pressed eagerly forward to greet him who had come, as it were, from the dead. His resemblance to their family was so striking that they hesitated not for a moment to receive him as a brother.

In relating incidents of the long years of his bondage the evening passed away—that pleasant evening, long will it be remembered by each member of that little circle.

Peter's heart was now at rest. He had realized the dream of his boyhood—the great hope of his riper years. "Oh," thought he, "if poor Levin could be with us now; and if Vina and the dear children were only free, I shouldn't know what more to ask for."

Early the next morning, Dr. Still, with his new found brother, and the two sisters set out to visit their mother, who lived eight miles distant. On the way they agreed, as far as possible, to avoid surprising or exciting their mother, as on account of her great age (she was nearly eighty) they feared that by a shock, even though it were a joyful one, she might be overcome.

The venerable woman lived with Samuel, the oldest, except Peter, of her sons, upon the farm which had been owned by her late husband. When her children, arrived, she had just risen, and was standing in the door. Peter's first impulse was to spring from the wagon, and to clasp the precious form of his mother to his heart, but his sisters' caution sounded in his ears, and he struggled to control himself. Forcing back the flood of tenderness which came gushing up from his throbbing heart, he walked with placid face behind his sisters, who advanced to greet their beloved parent.

"Mother," said Kitty, "you know it is the custom, when one of your daughters marries, for her to come home, and bring your new son-in-law. Now which of these would you rather take for your son?" pointing as she spoke to Peter, and to the man who had been hired by her brother James to drive them out. The mother answered with a smile, and the party entered the house.

Peter chose a seat near his mother, and subduing his emotions, gazed earnestly upon her aged face. There was the same mole concerning which he had so often disputed with his brother Levin, who always maintained that it was only a dark spot upon her face. His thoughts were busy with the past. Ah! how well he remembered the time when his young lips had pressed that mother's cheek, when all his childish griefs had been forgotten while he lay folded to that loving breast.

He remembered too, the kindnapper, with his slimy, lying tongue; his transfer to Kentucky, and the heavy blows by which they strove to crush out from his young heart the memory of his mother's love, all his long years of weary, unrequited toil—a sad procession, passed before him as he sat apparently a calm spectator of the joyous greetings of his kindred. His brother also, he remembered, and that brother's grave, a far-off, unmarked grave, and all that brother's sorrows. Yes, he remembered all the past. The host of cruel wrongs which he had suffered rushed at once into his mind, and from the stand point which he had now gained, the heartless acts of his oppressors, looked a hundred fold more hateful than before.

But he was not long left to his own thoughts. The excitement of their arrival having subsided, he said to his mother, " Are all these your children."

" Yes," she replied, " the most of them are mine."

" You have a large family."

" Yes, I have had eighteen children."

" How many have you livin'?"

" I have buried eight, and I have eight living."

" I thought you said you had eighteen—eight livin' and eight dead would make but sixteen."

The breast of the aged woman heaved as with long-pent anguish! " Ah!" said she, " them two boys have been more trouble to me than all the rest of my children. I've grieved about them a great many years."

" What became of them?" asked Peter.

" I never knew what became of them. I left them asleep in the bed, the last time I ever see them. I never knew whether they was stole and carried off, or whether they was dead. I hope though, they're in heaven."

At that moment, her oldest daughter, Mahala,* who lived very near, came running in. " Do tell me," cried she, half out of breath, " what is the matter? Is any body dead?"

No one replied. She glanced around the room. " Who's this?" cried she, talking to mother. " Who is he? Isn't he one of mother's lost children? He

---

* Peter remembered her as 'Merica. The little Charity he also remembered, was the daughter of his mother's sister.

favors the family, and I'm sure he must be one of them."

" Who ? me ?" said Peter.

" Yes; mother lost two children a great many years ago, and you must be one of them."

" I'm a stranger from Alabama," said he.

" I can't help it," cried the excited woman. " I am sure you are one of mother's children, for you favor the family."

One of the other sisters then approached the mother, and broke to her the joyful news. The aged woman sat for a moment bewildered by the strange scene— then rising, she walked into the next room, where she knelt in prayer.

In a short time she returned, trembling in every limb, though her face was calm. "Who are you ?" said she, approaching the stranger.

" My name," said he, " is Peter, and I had a brother Levin. My father's name was Levin, and my mother's name was Sidney ———."

The mother raised her tear-dimmed eyes to heaven. "O, Lord," she cried, "how long have I prayed to see my two sons ! Can it be that they have come ? Oh ! if you are my child, tell me *how d'y'* once more !"

The long-lost son was blest. He clasped his mother to his warm, full heart, and joyful tears stole down his dusky cheeks.

One week he spent with his new-found kindred. As he related to them the history of his years of bondage, and described the strangely varied scenes through which his path had led, his listeners were never weary; and when he told of all poor Levin's sorrows, of his years of patient suffering, and of his peaceful, happy death, the spirit of their departed brother seemed to hover near the little circle, and to whisper to each weeper there—" Dry now your tears, for where I dwell are neither bonds nor tortures—sorrow and sighing are unknown."

Peter soon discovered that the habits and condition of his relatives differed widely from those described in the South as universal among "free negroes." They were all industrious and frugal; and consequently, in comfortable circumstances.

He did not envy them, but, as he noticed their intelligence, and saw the comforts by which they were surrounded in their own homes, he could not avoid the thought that *slavery had kept him ignorant and poor.* "But times will change," thought he, "and if ever I get my family, my children shall have a chance to know as much as others."

CHAPTER XXX.

PETER'S FAREWELL VISIT TO ALABAMA.

GLADLY would his friends have retained Peter in their midst, but his plan was fixed. He determined to return immediately to the South, that he might acquaint his family with his success, and arrange some plan for their redemption. He felt that he could not himself enjoy the blessings of freedom, and the sweet society of those who loved him while his own wife and children toiled in hopeless bondage.

To his proposed return his friends, at first, refused to listen. They could not bear to lose him now, when they had just learned to love him, and they felt sure that if he went again to Alabama they should see his face no more.

It would be far better, they said, for his family to gain their liberty by flight, and perhaps if he would remain, some one would go and aid them to escape. It would be so hazardous for him to venture where, if his secret were discovered, he might be thrust into jail, and sold upon the block. But he was firm. He knew the dangers which awaited him, yet he had promised his family that he would return; and he would rather lose his life than forfeit his word to them. He knew how anxiously they would watch for his coming; he knew how their hearts would faint if he delayed;—ah! he knew that his love was the one blessed light which shone upon poor Vina's darkened path. From his own lips she should first hear of his great happiness, and together they would try to devise a plan by which herself and children might come to share his joy.

Perhaps he could purchase their freedom. This had ever been his hope; and though his friends believed it was impossible, they failed to shake his confidence in the wisdom of making the attempt. *He had rescued himself from bondage,* and he knew "no such word as *fail.*" "I can die," said he, "but I cannot live without tryin' to do something for my family—I must go back."

With many tears, the affectionate circle bade him adieu. "O, my child! my child!" sobbed his aged mother. "I never shall see your face again. You can't get back; and your poor old mother will go down to the grave a mournin' for her son. May the Lord bless you wherever you go, and deliver you from every danger!"

On the eighth of August, Peter left Philadelphia, on his return to Alabama. He feared that if he remained longer in that city, he might meet some merchant whom he knew; as at that season they were accustomed to come on for their Fall goods. If a Tuscumbian should see him there, the news would swiftly fly, that he had run away from Mr. Friedman; and then he could not return, even with free papers, to complete his cherished plan.

A kind Providence, however, attended him; and he reached Cincinnati without meeting a familiar face. Strangely commingled were his emotions, as he returned. The regretful voices of his brothers and sisters still sounded in his ears; and the memory of all their kindness during his short stay, was warm within his heart. He rejoiced that he had found them. Even if he should never be able to return to them, the dark uncertainty which had so long hung over his parentage, and had shrouded all his life in gloom, was gone. Not less did he rejoice in the character of his newly-discovered kindred. They were evidently honest people—trusted and respected by the surrounding community. They had enjoyed great privileges too, for they were all well educated; yet they were not proud. Ah, well, it was some satisfaction that he had ever done the best he could. He had risen above all who had been his companions in bondage, and he felt that, though he was ignorant of books, his friends had no cause to be ashamed of him.

Arrived at Cincinnati, he related to his former master all his success, and communicated also his plans for the future. The Jew was both astonished and delighted at the good fortune of his humble friend, and readily promised to aid him, if possible, in negotiating for the purchase of his family.

Peter remained in Cincinnati a week, waiting for his free papers. These he was anxious to possess on his return to Alabama, as something might occur which would render it necessary for him to prove his freedom. At last he obtained the valued certificate, of which the following is a copy:

" State of Ohio,
City of Cincinnati. } *ss.*

" Be it known that before me, Henry E. Spencer, Mayor of said City, personally appeared Isaac S. Friedman, who being duly sworn, deposes and says: that he has been acquainted with a colored man named Peter Still, alias Peter Friedman, for the last five years: that the said Peter was formerly a slave belonging to John H. Hogun, residing about three miles from Tuscumbia, in the State of Alabama: that Joseph Friedman, of Tuscumbia, hired the said Peter for about two years of the said John H. Hogun, and afterwards bought him, and held him as a slave for about two years longer, when Peter bought his freedom from his master, the said Joseph Friedman, brother of this deponent, by paying him the sum of five hundred dollars; as fully appears from a bill of sale given by said Joseph Friedman to said Peter, and dated Tuscumbia, Ala., the 16th day of April, 1850, which bill of sale this deponent fully recognizes as genuine.

" And further this deponent sayeth not.

" ISAAC S. FRIEDMAN."

" The foregoing affidavit of the above-named Isaac S. Friedman, to the freedom of the within-named Peter Still, having been duly sworn to and subscribed before me,—

" I therefore do declare the above-named Peter Still, alias Peter Friedman, to be a free person, and entitled to all the privileges of free persons of color, according to the laws of the State of Ohio.

" Said Peter Still is about forty-nine years of age,

is five feet seven and a half inches in height, of a brownish black complexion, and without any marks or cuts.

"Given under my hand, and the Corporate Seal of the City of Cincinnati, this 22d day of August, 1850.

"H. E. SPENCER,
"Mayor."

Peter was now a man. His years of patient toil for noble objects had not made him such—his warm, unselfish heart had never proved him worthy of the ennobling title—*but he possessed free papers.* Guard well the treasure, Peter; for *the papers lost,* you may again be bought and sold—a thing of merchandise—*a slave.*

Immediately after receiving his papers, he started for Tuscumbia. He wore not proudly his new honors, but laying the precious certificate in the bottom of his trunk, he travelled meekly as a slave upon a "pass" from Mr. Friedman. This *pass* was directed to Mr. Alexander, of Tuscumbia, a gentleman who had once before acted as his guardian, during the temporary absence of both the Friedman's. It requested this gentleman to permit Peter to stay at Tuscumbia as long as he should wish to do so; and to send him back whenever he should be ready to return;—as his labor could be made profitable on a steamboat, and his owner could also take better care of him if he had him near himself.

Nothing of interest occurred on the homeward journey. The boat reached Tuscumbia Landing on the evening of the last day of August; and early the next morning, Peter walked up to town.

Many were the friendly greetings he received as he passed through the streets that day. Many questions were asked him concerning Mr. Friedman—his business prospects, etc. To all these Peter replied as he had been instructed. Mr. Friedman would be there before Christmas, and if Peter worked till that time on a steamboat, he should then come with him. Mr. Friedman said he could earn him more money upon a boat than any where else, and had promised to give him something for himself if he did well.

Many gentlemen questioned him very closely respecting the Free States; how he liked Cincinnati, and whether he saw there any *Abolitionists.*

His ideas of these "*desperate characters*" had been greatly modified during the week which he had spent among his relatives; but he answered in accordance with his old ideas—ideas which are carefully inculcated in the minds of slaves. He was "mighty skeered," he said, all the time he was in Cincinnati; and did not dare to go out "after night." One night, he "reckoned" he heard the "Abolitionists fightin' in the streets;" but he was away up stairs, and "too badly skeered to come down."

To all these questionings he answered as truly as he could, and keep his secret; but they made him very uneasy. He saw that the moment he should speak a word in favor of the Free States, he would be suspected, and all his movements watched. Then, if the secret of his freedom should be discovered, his kind friend, the Jew, would be drawn into trouble, as the citizens would at once accuse him of sending back a *free negro* to poison the minds of the surrounding slaves. So he represented the black people of Cincinnati as being wretchedly poor; and the contrast which he drew between the laborers of that city, and the *happier slaves* by whom he was surrounded, would have delighted the author of the "South Side View."

The same day on which Peter arrived in town, a letter came from Mr. Sloan, Principal of the Seminary. He was then spending the Summer vacation at the North; and he wrote to request Peter to whitewash the Seminary, and to put the whole building in complete order, for as he intended to bring on a new corps of teachers, he wished to find the place prepared for their reception.

This was most fortunate for Peter. He entered, at once, upon this work, and soon fell into the old channel of promiscuous labors. His cheerfulness remained unchanged—indeed he was the same industrious, respectful, obedient servant; and those of the Tuscumbians who had most jealously watched his movements, at last decided that not even a trip to Cincinnati could spoil Uncle Peter—he had too much sense to be carried away with the folly of the Abolitionists.

The Saturday evening after his arrival in town, Peter rode out to Bainbridge. He would have gone sooner, for he was most impatient to see his beloved family; but he had determined to resume his old habits, and to do nothing which could betray the least unusual excitement of his feelings.

As he rode along the lonely road, his thoughts were busy. Only six weeks had passed since last he saw his dear ones, but even in that short time what a wealth of experience had he gained! He had seen— had tasted—liberty;—yet he could not enjoy it. He could never, indeed, be really free, while those he loved so well were slaves. But how should he get them? He knew not what course would be the best, but he knew how to trust in that Good Father, who had thus far prospered him in all his ways. He resolved to work hard, and earn all he could, for whatever plan he might adopt, money would never fail to be of use.

But perhaps even now, and his thoughts grew sad, —some one of that little number had gone down to the grave. The sickly season was at its height; and Death, within the last few weeks, had entered many a lowly cabin, and many a lofty hall.

He hastened on, yet it was quite dark before he reached the plantation. He halted at the door of Vina's cabin, and glanced anxiously at the group within. They were all there. Vina was preparing to cook the supper, and the boys were busied in making a fire for her. Thank God! they all lived!

His approach was not long unperceived. "Yes, it is father!" burst at once from the lips of the two sons, and after the first joyful how'dy', they took his horse and led it away.

"O Vina," whispered Peter. as he still held her by both her hands, "I've found all my people. I've seen my mother! Vina, my mother's a livin', and I've got five brothers and three sisters!"

Soon the boys came in, and then the history of the journey, with its glad results, was narrated to them all. How they marveled as he described to them the great cities through which he had passed, and all the new strange sights his eyes had seen! But still greater was their wonder at the story of their far-off kindred, to whom their father had come as from the dead. And then to think that father's people were all free! Ah! how the faint hopes they had cherished of joining their father, at some future day, in the happy home he would provide for them, away off where all were free—how these hopes grew and strengthened in their hearts till they could scarcely refrain from shouting them aloud! Yet they were silent. All these bright visions of the coming joy they shut closely in from the curious eyes of their outside companions—in their mother's cabin only, and even there with caution might they give utterance to their joyful hopes.

Peter's return caused much excitement among the slaves on the plantation. It was whispered around that he had been to Cincinnati, and they were all eager to learn what he saw there; and how the people lived in a Free State. The mistress also questioned him concerning his new manner of life upon a steamboat— how he enjoyed it, etc. He replied, that he liked the business very well; and that his master was very kind to him.

"Mass'r Isaac says he'll buy my family, if I do well," added he, "do you reckon old Mass'r would sell 'em, Ma'am?"

"I don't know," replied the lady, "he thinks a great deal of them all, and I reckon he would ask a high price for them. I don't believe less than three thousand dollars would buy them all, if indeed he would consent to let them go at all."

To his wife and children Peter revealed all his plans for their redemption. He would work, he said, in Tuscumbia, till he had earned enough to bear his expenses back to Philadelphia. He dared not stay in Alabama longer than was necessary, for fear something might occur which would compel him to reveal his cherished secret. While there his liberty was all the time unsafe.

On his return to the North, he intended to set diligently to work to earn money to buy his family; and he hoped his brothers would be able to advance a part of the price. This could soon be refunded to them, when they were all free and able to work together. He mentioned to them, also, the suggestion which some of his friends had made with regard to sending a man to assist them to escape. "My people told me," said he, "that folks are runnin' away *constant*, and gwine to Canada, a place away to the North, where they never let the masters go to hunt them." But still there were so many chances for them to be taken and carried back before they could reach that distant haven, that he decidedly preferred to purchase them. Yet, "if they do send for you," said he, "you must be ready—and do the best you can." They were all willing to do whatever he thought best. The bright hope of freedom *with their father* illumined all the paths which Fancy painted in the future.

Early on Monday morning, Peter returned to town, and resumed his accustomed labors. His first business was to put the Seminary in order, according to Mr. Sloan's request. His manners and appearance were all unchanged. He wore his blue jean roundabout and trousers; and as he stood among the waiters in the dining-room of Mr. Horne's hotel, none of the boarders dreamed that he was that despised and hated biped—"a free nigger."

For two months and a half he remained in Tuscumbia; and during that time he earned sixty dollars. Once in two weeks, as had been his custom for many years, he went to see his family. He would have gone every week, now that he was so soon to leave them, but he dreaded to excite observation by any change in his old habits; and besides, he would have to hire a horse to ride, and that would diminish his gains.

On Saturday, the ninth of November, Peter rode out to the plantation for his last visit. He had sold every article he possessed, except his necessary clothing, and such articles as he knew would be useful to his family. With these last his horse was now loaded, and at sunset he rode up to the cabin door.

His family were expecting him, and they knew this would be his last visit. Its hours were, therefore, doubly precious. Oh! if they should be the last which the whole family might ever spend together!

He renewed his promise to buy them, if possible, and charged them to hold themselves ready. "Now, boys," said he, "you'd best not marry till you hear from me, for if I live, I will get you all, sure. And be good and kind to your mother, for she'll have no one to take care of her now but you. Get every thing you can to make her comfortable;—and you, Catharine, dont you do any thing that will make your mother ashamed of you,—for she has a heap of trouble, any how, and you all oughtent to give her no more. Behave yourselves well; and then people will trust you, and you will be well thought of by every one."

About five miles above Bainbridge, in the Muscle Shoals, is an island containing about two hundred acres, which belongs to Mr. McKiernan. Here young Peter and Levin were to be employed during the week; and, as the cotton-picking season was then at its height, they were obliged to go with their week's allowance on Sunday evening, that no time might be lost on Monday.

After the boys had gone, Peter's friends—and he had many on the place—all called to say, "Good bye," till Christmas; when they expected he would come, as usual, to spend the Holidays.

These partings over, he was left alone with his wife and daughter. Poor Vina! she possessed not the buoyant hopes that filled her children's hearts—she was not so young as they;—and though she lacked not confidence in her husband's truth, yet she could not quell the fear that this was the last evening they should ever spend together. She selected from her simple wardrobe two or three articles of clothing which he had been accustomed to see her wear, and gave them to him. "When you want to see something that looks like me," said she, "you can look at these yer. They'll make you think of Vina."

Monday morning came, and Vina and Catharine must go early to the field, while the husband and father was forced to return to town to complete the arrangements for his final departure. They all arose at dawn and in the dim morning twilight — they parted.

Peter lingered a moment at the cabin door. How could he say "Good bye!" There stood his wife and daughter—and great tears were in their eyes. How gladly would he shield them from every breath of sorrow!—but now he could not stay. Once more he kissed them both—ah! was it for the last time? He could not speak, but with one long pressure of their hands, he tore himself away, and mounted his horse, which stood already at the door.

How the sobbings of these loved ones resounded in the depths of his fond heart! For a moment he almost wished he had not thought of becoming free; but then the great glad hope of saving them returned, and he rejoiced that he had power to make the effort.

Heavy were the hearts of the mother and her children, as they traversed the long cotton rows that day; but their fingers must needs be light. The overseer's whip takes no note of aching hearts. The baskets must be filled.

The light of hope soon returned to her children's eyes, but Vina was still in darkness. Accustomed to the helplessness of slavery, she could not realize that it was possible for her husband to be safe, "'way off yon' by himself, without anybody to take care of him."

The next Wednesday morning, November 13th, Mr. Alexander, to whose guardianship Peter had been consigned by Mr. Friedman, placed him on board the stage for Eastport, a small town at the foot of Colbert's Shoals, about thirty miles below Tuscumbia. (The water was, at this time, so low in the river, that boats could not pass these shoals.) Here he took passage on a small steamboat, with the Captain of which, Mr. George Warren, he was acquainted.

This boat, however, went no further than Paducah, at the mouth of the Tennessee, and there he was obliged to wait for a boat to ascend the Ohio. Soon one came along—a Cincinnati boat—bound homewards from St. Louis.

Peter stepped on board and inquired for the Captain, while two boys from Captain Warren's boat were bringing on his trunk. The boat was again under way, before the Captain could be found. " Here," said the clerk, as at length his superior officer appeared, " this man wants to go to Cincinnati."

" Why didn't you name it before ?" cried the Captain in a passionate voice; and, turning to the pilot, he ordered him to land and " set that fellow ashore."

" But," said Peter, " I did inquire for the Captain—"

" Never mind, never mind, step right off."

" I have got a pass and other papers, and I want to go to Cincinnati, or leastways, to Louisville."

" Never mind—step right off—step right off."

Captain Warren seeing the distress of his humble friend, called out to the Commander of the Cincinnati boat—" It is all right—let the boy go. He has a pass, and everything regular."

But the little great man was inflexible. " Step right off—step right off "—was his only answer ; and Peter was obliged to go ashore and wait for another boat.

This was Saturday evening, and here he remained till eleven o'clock on Sunday night, when Captain Francis' boat came down from Louisville. This was a Tennessee River Packet, but on account of the low water, she could not go up the river, and so made only short trips between Louisville and Paducah. Captain Francis having resided many years in Tuscumbia, knew Peter well, and therefore hesitated not to take him up the river on his boat.

They reached Louisville on Wednesday morning, and as he would have several hours before the Cincinnati boat went out, he went to see Dr. Williamson Fisher, a son of his old master, John Fisher, of Lexington.

This gentleman received his father's former slave with great kindness; though he was so young when the two boys were sold to old Nattie Gist, that he scarcely remembered them. He had, however, in his possession the bill of sale which his father received at the time he bought them.

This short visit was highly enjoyed by Peter. The days of his childhood came vividly to his recollection; and though they were not free from hardships, yet the sunshine of youthful hope had never ceased to gild their memory. What were the buffetings he then received compared to the anguish which he had suffered in later years. As a " *little negro*," he rose each morning from his ample couch—the floor, with supple limbs, and heart unmindful of the old day's sorrows, and ate with a keen relish his homely breakfast of corn cake. He thought of his far-off mother, and longed to return to her—but his attention was easily diverted by surrounding objects, and he was, after all, a merry child. During his manhood he had suffered few of the physical ills of slavery—but *the iron had entered his soul.* He had seen his fellows crushed—his brother beaten, even by the master whom he loved, because he could not stifle the pure affections of his heart; his own loved wife had been insulted—and well nigh murdered, because she would not submit to the vile wishes of a remorseless ruffian; and yet he had not dared to raise his voice, or lift his own right arm in their defence.

All these remniscences of other days crowded his memory as he stood in the presence of him who, when an infant in the cradle, was his "little master," and who had inherited from his father the price of his young nerves and sinews. And then came the sweet thought, that by his own exertions, through the blessing of that Father who had never yet forsaken him, he was no more a slave.

Dr. Fisher gave him much information concerning his early companions in Lexington; from many of whom he had not heard since he left there in his youth; but before he was half satisfied with listening to these interesting details, his time was spent, and he was forced to leave.

He next went in search of a young Mr. Johnson, from Tuscumbia, to whom Mr. Alexander had sent a letter bespeaking his assistance, if necessary, in procuring a passage for the bearer to Cincinnati. This gentleman was pursuing the study of medicine in Louisville; and Peter went to the Medical College, and to various other places in the city, but failed to find him. He was now at a loss what to do, for he had learned from his experience at Paducah how little favor his pass would gain from the Captains of the Cincinnati boats.

He walked down to the wharf, and the first man he met there was a young Mr. McFarland, from Tuscumbia, who had formerly been clerk on Captain Francis' boat. Mr. O'Reilly of the Telegraph was also there, and he immediately recognized Peter, having employed him during the time he spent in Tuscumbia to take care of his office. These two gentlemen kindly procured a passage for him on the boat to Cincinnati, and with many thanks for their friendly assistance, he went on board.

He had now bid a final adieu to slave-land, still his heart was not at rest. For himself he had little fear. His free papars were safe, and he was at length beyond the necessity of affecting any relationship to slavery. But his family—ah! when he thought how long a time might pass before they could be loosed from bondage, he could only trust in the power above, and pray for patience.

He was disappointed in his hope of finding **Mr.** Friedman in Cincinnati, he having gone to Illinois. Peter therefore hastened on to Pittsburg, and thence to Philadelphia. His free papers he carried in his pocket, but as no zealous negro-catcher chanced to fix upon him his greedy eye, he had no need to show them on the way.

CHAPTER XXXI.

THE ESCAPE.

LATE at night, on the thirtieth of November, Peter reached his brother's house in Philadelphia. He trembled not now, as when at first his feet approached his kinsman's threshold. A sense of personal security rested upon his heart, and the light of quiet happiness beamed from his smiling face.

During the few days which he spent with his brother William, the idea of sending a man to rescue his family was again suggested. Many of his brother's friends were earnest advocates of such a plan. It would take too long to raise the sum requisite to purchase them, and besides, the offering of money for their ransom would in some sense recognize the *right* of the slaveholder to claim property in human flesh. "We are anxious," they said, "to aid your loved ones in escaping from bondage, but we cannot bear to give gold to him who has so long defrauded the helpless laborers of their hire."

To all these arguments of his friends, Peter opposed the dangers of their scheme. It would, he said, be very difficult for them to escape; and then, if they should be pursued and taken, the sufferings of their whole past lives were nothing to the punishment they might receive. And worst of all, they might be sold; and then all chance of getting them would be for ever lost.

But those to whose proposal he objected were educated men, while he was but a poor emancipated slave, who never in his life had read a book—and their persuasions triumphed. He described to them, though with reluctance, the location of the premises where his family might be found, and also the persons of his wife and children.

He then left these friends to mature their plan, while he went to visit his mother. He was deeply anxious concerning the result of the deliberations then going on in Philadelphia, for he could not yet give up the idea which he had so long cherished—that of attempting the purchase of those whose safety he prized above all other objects.

Many people in the vicinity of his mother's home had heard of the return of the long-lost son and brother, and now, when they learned his anxiety to redeem his family they kindly volunteered to aid him. He accepted with a grateful heart the contributions which they offered, though *how* they could be made available was still a question.

When he had been two weeks in New Jersey, he received a letter requesting his immediate return to Philadelphia, and he hasted to obey the summons. He had already received one hundred dollars as the beginning of a fund to ransom those he loved, and that he took with him to the city.

During his absence, a man named Seth Concklin, who had heard of his case, had offered to go to Alabama, and bring his wife and children. He asked no further equipment for the journey than sufficient money to defray his necessary expenses, and some sign whereby the family would recognize him as a friend.

Peter's heart trembled. To the proposal of his friends he had assented; but then it was indefinite, and he doubted the possibility of their finding a man who would face the dangers of such an undertaking. He had all the time cherished a secret hope that they would yet abandon this project, and aid him in accomplishing the plan which he so much preferred. Not that he thought it would be unjust or wrong to aid them to escape. Ah, no! He had never yet become so thoroughly enslaved in spirit as for a moment to recognize the *right* of man to hold his brother man in bonds; but merely as a matter of policy he had chosen to purchase their freedom—though to do so would cost him both toil and patience.

Now, however, the scheme was all arranged, and these good friends had manifested so warm an interest in promoting his happiness that he could not refuse them all the aid which it was in his power to give.

He accordingly gave Concklin an accurate description of Mr. McKiernan's place, with directions concerning the best methods of approaching it. He told him also the names and ages of his family; and gave him a cape of Vina's—one of the articles of dress which she had given him as a keepsake. "When she sees this," said he, "she will know that you are a friend; but please, sir, be careful and don't get 'em into trouble. It 'll go mighty hard with 'em if they try to run off, and Mr. McKiernan cotches 'em."

The one hundred dollars which Peter had received

in New Jersey was now devoted to defraying the cost of this expedition, and early in January, all the arrangements having been completed, Concklin entered upon his perilous undertaking.

We subjoin the account which is given by Rev. Dr. Furness, of Concklin's introduction to the friends of the slave in Philadelphia, and also of the first steps that were taken in this daring enterprise.

" Of this remarkable person, whose history, and heroic tragedy, must not be suffered to die, but very little was known at that time. He was not a member of any Abolition Society, nor was it known that he had any fixed residence. A man, plainly dressed, and slightly built, but evidently active and vigorous, with a face expressive of great decision, had come occasionally to the Anti-Slavery Office in Philadelphia, to inquire about Mr. Chaplin, then in prison in Maryland, for aiding certain slaves in an attempt to escape from the District of Columbia. The stranger manifested a deep interest in Mr. Chaplin's fate, contributed a small sum monthly to the Chaplin fund, and on one occasion produced a statement in writing of a plan, which he had devised, subject to the approval of Mr. Chaplin's friends, whereby he offered to go to Maryland, liberate Mr. Chaplin, and bring him safely into the Free States; requiring only a moderate sum to defray his expenses. The scheme was striking for its boldness and sagacity, but all participation in it was declined by the agents of the Anti-Slavery Society, on the obvious ground that it was not by such methods that they were seeking the Abolition of Slavery. (It is not an object of the Society to assist, directly or indirectly, in the abduction of slaves.) The proposals, however, on the part of Mr. Concklin, served to show the character of the man. It was made apparent that he was an Abolitionist on his own account. He was understood to be one of those few men in whom the hatred of slavery has become a ruling passion. He was a whole Abolition Society in himself; with very limited pecuniary means indeed, but with what is infinitely better than uncounted gold, a single and commanding purpose, which danger could not shake, but only animate. His subsequent history, and all that was afterwards ascertained of his previous life, only corroborated the impressions received of his character upon the occasions of these visits to the Anti-Slavery Office. He was a man whose constitutional love of adventure, exercised from early boyhood by a series of privations and trials that would have broken down any ordinary man, had come to be consecrated to the knightly office of succoring the miserable; and especially the enslaved, as of all men the most to be commiserated. In contrast with his tried heroism, the wordy chivalry of the South shows as rags and tinsel.

"As soon as he was informed of the condition of Peter's family, he offered, with the help of a small sum to defray his travelling expenses, to go to Alabama, and bring them into the free State of Pennsylvania. He asked for no companion, and no compensation; only for the means of paying the expenses of the journey, and for credentials to satisfy Peter's wife that he came from her husband.

"A daring enterprise, indeed! It is not easy to conceive of an undertaking more hazardous, or one that more peremptorily demanded, in him who should attempt it, all the qualities that give the world assurance of a man.

" The plantation that Seth Conklin was to reach lay in the north-western part of Alabama, eight hundred miles from Cincinnati. He was to traverse two slave States—Kentucky and Tennessee. To penetrate thus deep into slave-land, at a time when the ferocity and the fear that guard it had been startled from their long slumber by the far-off coming of the step of doom, for the purpose of plucking therefrom a poor bondwoman and her children, outdoes all the fabled feats of old knighthood.

" Our hero took with him neither pistol nor bowie-knife, although he knew how to use them, for, as has since been learned, he had been a soldier. ' He should be tempted to use them,' he said, ' and then he should be sure to be overborne.'

" His first object was to explore the route, to discover safe hiding-places, and to ascertain who in the border free States would be willing to befriend and aid him, when he should have succeeded—if he should succeed—in escaping with his *protégées* from the slave States. At Cincinnati, he met with devoted friends, who appreciated all the hazards of the attempt. But he soon ascertained that his perils would be far from being at an end when he should have got, on his return, beyond the limits of Kentucky. Indeed, when he entered the slave States, it was under the impression that the chief hazard of the undertaking, as the result most fearfully proved, would be encountered in the bordering free States. In seeking to provide places of refuge in Illinois and Indiana, he found the southern boundaries of these States, free as they claim to be, infested with men thirsting for the rewards offered to those who are willing to cast aside their humanity, and do the work of bloodhounds—hunting the outcast, and seeking and dragging back the fugitive. 'Searching the country opposite Paducah, Ky., I found,' he wrote, in a letter dated Eastport. Miss., Feb. 3d, 'the whole country, fifty miles around, is inhabited by Christian wolves. It is customary, when a strange negro is seen, for any white man to seize him, and convey him through and out of the State of Illinois to Paducah, and lodge such stranger in Paducah jail, and then claim such reward as may be offered by the master.'

" Failing in the attempt to secure friends on the borders of Illinois, to meet him upon his return, yet, trusting, nevertheless, to his own address, and to a good Providence, he crossed to Paducah, and took a steamboat on the Tennessee river for South Florence, the final point of his journey. This was a little town, four hundred miles up the river, containing about twenty families, and a post-office, *but no school!*"

This place he reached on the twenty-eighth of January, having been four days coming up the Tennessee.

Soon after his arrival at South Florence, Concklin made his way to the plantation of Mr. McKiernan, and succeeded in obtaining an interview with Vina. It was a cold, dark night. Trembling, the faithful wife went forth from her cabin to the place where it had been intimated to her she should hear from her husband. Every few steps she stopped and listened, for fear some curious neighbor had watched her exit, and would follow her, or—what was worse—report her absence to the overseer. And then she grew afraid to venture forward, lest some trap were laid for her unwary feet.

At last, however, the thought of Peter, and the hope of hearing of his welfare, conquered all her fears, and she walked on. Soon she discerned a figure at a little distance, but the darkness was so intense that she could not tell whether it was friend or foe. She paused. "Is your name Vina?" said a strange voice.

"Yes, sir," she whispered.

"Are you Peter Friedman's wife?"

"Yes, sir, I's his wife."

"How would you like to go to him?"

"I'd like it mons's well, sir, if I could git thar."

"Well, I have come on purpose to take you to see him. Do you believe me?"

"I don't know, sir."

"Can you see me, so as to know me if you should meet me again?"

"No, sir, it's so dark; I can't see your face good."

He held up one hand. "Do you see my hand?"

"Yes, sir."

"Well, if you see me again, you will know me by that hand. You see that half the forefinger is cut off?"

"Yes, sir."

"Do you believe that I came from Peter?"

"I don't know, sir."

He drew forth from his pocket the gingham cape which Peter had given him as a sign. She could see its form, and she recognized it in a moment. That moment her doubts of his sincerity were gone.

Yet she hesitated. She well knew the difficulties

and dangers that would attend an effort to escape; especially when a family of four should make the attempt together; and nothing but her deep love for her husband, and her faith in his discretion could have tempted her to dare it. "But," thought she, "he never would 'a'sent a man 'way here to help us if he didn't think we mought git off. Leastways we'll try. He knows best what we can do, for he's done took the journey twice."

"When does you want us to go?" said she aloud.

"Just as soon as you can get ready. How long will it take you, do you think?"

"I don't know, Sir. I don't believe we could git ready short o' four weeks."

"Well, I can wait. I must go back to Louisville to do some business before I take you on. But I want first to see the boys, where are they?"

"Oh, they're off on the Island, they won't come home 'fore Saturday night."

"Well, you tell them to come down to the landing on Sunday. I will be there walking about, and if I see two young men, I will keep this hand in sight. You describe it to them, that they will know me. Now, good bye. Don't be afraid. I will do all I can for you, but you must help yourselves."

Vina returned to her cabin. Her heart was full. One moment the hope was strong within her that they should all escape in safety. She saw the face of her husband, she listened to his voice; again she heard the fierce pursuer on her track, and felt herself dragged back to meet a tenfold darker doom than she had yet encountered. "*I couldn' b'ar*," she says, "*the idea of totin' a scabby back from one year to another*, and sometimes, 'peard like I couldn't tell whether to go or not. One mind say, yes, and t'other mind say, no but at last I des' thought I would start, any how, whether I prevailed or not.

The next Sunday, Peter and Levin walked down towards the river, and when about half-way to the landing, they met a stranger. He wore an old pair of low quarter shoes without stockings, and his pantaloons were rolled up half-way to the knee. Altogether his appearance was that of the "poor white men," who inhabit the mountainous districts back of the rich plantations. As he approached they noticed the mutilated finger, but they did not speak, they would not appear too hasty.

The stranger stopped. "Do you know me?" said he.

"No, Sir."

"Did you ever see me before?"

"No, Sir."

"Your name is Peter, is it not?" said he, addressing the oldest.

"Yes, Sir."

"And yours is Levin?"

"Yes, Sir, but how did you know it?"

"I know you by your resemblance to your father."

"Where did you see our father?"

"I saw him only once, in Philadelphia."

They then turned aside into the woods, and there, seated upon a log, they held a long consultation concerning the best means of escape. Concklin told them all his plans, and listened patiently to their suggestions, and then, lest some wanderer in the woods should discover them in council, they separated.

The next Wednesday the stranger left the neighborhood on board the boat for Louisville. On the same boat Mr. McKiernan started for his usual annual visit to New Orleans; but as Concklin appeared in humble garb, and neither drank nor gambled, he came into no contact with the planter.

This trip down the Tennessee confirmed Concklin in the opinion he had already formed—that it would be unsafe to depend upon escaping with his poor helpless friends upon a steamboat. He procured a skiff, and early in March he returned, having made all possible arrangements for their speedy transport beyond the bounds of slavery's domain.

For two weeks he was obliged to wait for them to complete their preparations, or rather, for an opportunity for the whole family to leave the place without exciting suspicion. At last, on Saturday night, the boys obtained of the overseer passes to go to South Florence on Sunday, to buy sugar and coffee for their mother. Vina and her daughter also procured passes to go to Mrs. Jackson's, a few miles distant, where they were to remain until the boys returned. They asked for the passes at night in order, as they said, that they might start *soon* in the morning, and get to Mrs. Jackson's before breakfast.

When all was still throughout the quarter—and "it seemed that night as though some of the people never would go to bed," the little family went out into the night. Vina locked the door, and gave the key to a young girl named Susanna, desiring her to go in and prepare supper for them the next evening.

The mother and her children walked away in silence, and at first with stealthy steps. Their hearts quaked with fear, but they had gone too far to recede. Choking down the sobs that strove to break the midnight silence, they pressed each other's hands to renew their courage, and hastened on.

The clear sky hovered lovingly over the trembling fugitives, the stars, all silent, shone upon their pathway; but they saw neither sky nor stars, one faint dim hope beamed on them from afar, but the thick clouds of terror often obscured its light.

With timid steps they approached the river, and walking along the bank, they soon descried the skiff. Levin whistled. No answer. Could it be that Concklin had disappointed them?

They turned and walked down the stream thinking perhaps he had gone in search of them. " Thar!" said the mother, " this yer jaunt's a gwine to turn out bad, for nobody has good luck when they turns back after they's started on a long journey." Failing to perceive the object of their search in this direction, they returned to the skiff, and stooping down, saw Concklin lying fast asleep in the bottom. He had waited for them till he was weary, and Levin's timid whistle had failed to waken him from his first sound slumber.

It was now nearly three o'clock, and entering the skiff, they hastened off. The two boys, as well as Conklin, knew how to use the oars with skill and power, and they fairly flew over the water.

At daylight they passed Eastport, distant about forty miles from Bainbridge Landing. Just below that town they met a steamboat, but by the direction of a kind Providence, she kept on the south side of a small island in the river, while Concklin guided his skiff towards the north bank, and thus they escaped the notice of the crew. Upon that boat was Mr. McKiernan, then on his return from Louisiana; and had the skiff been noticed, he might easily have recognized the two boys, who were both at the oars.

"During Sunday," wrote Concklin to a friend, "we were hailed once by half a dozen men on shore, to know where we were from, where going, &c. There being a strong head-wind, I appeared as if I could not hear them. I know not what they would have done if they had had a good skiff. Several parties of men gazed at us along the river. I had previously informed myself of the scarcity of good skiffs on the Tennessee river, on which thing alone rested a part of my safety. I stood at the helm whenever we were in sight of anybody, keeping Levin and Peter at the oars. At all other times, and during the nights, I was principally at the oars. In the daytime I caused Vina and Catharine to lie under the blankets, so as not to be seen. They had a hard time of it. Having a strong head-wind, the water dashed into the boat, so as to keep the blankets all the time wet. Peter and Levin got sleepy Sunday evening, and were so by times all the way through.

"At five o'clock, Monday evening, for the first time, I lay down under a blanket, when the boys said two men were calling to us in a skiff near the shore, and coming towards us. I ordered that no effort should be made to run. The two men came alongside, eagerly demanding where they were going, and 'whar from? Are you all black men a'board?' My boys replied in Southern phrase, 'White Massa lyin' thar, sir. When I arose on my knees, partly throwing off my blanket, and staring my assailants in the face, they bowed, with 'How de do, sir.' I returned the compliment. They demanded where I was going, and from whence I came.

I dignifiedly replied, 'To Paducah, and from Eastport.'
They bowed, gave my boat a scrutinizing look, and
retired.

"During Monday night a squall of wind came near
dashing our craft to pieces against the large trees, but
by good management I succeeded in getting between
the trees to the shore, and there remained one hour
before we could start. Arrived on the Ohio at sunrise
Tuesday morning—fifty-one hours time. It should
have been done, under favorable circumstances in
thirty-six hours. The current of the Tennessee is very
stiff. On the Ohio I intended to travel exclusively
at nights. Circumstances were against me, and I was
compelled to travel as much by day as by night. One
half of two nights it was so dark, that I could not
navigate. My crew murmured in consequence of the
hardships. They did not seem to understand that they
were to work for themselves and for their lives. I had
no fair wind from the time I started till I arrived at
Harmony. It would be impossible to describe the
difficulties I have encountered."

At ten o'clock on Sunday morning March 23d, they
landed at New Harmony, Ia. Seven days they had
rowed in that frail skiff, exposed each moment to the
danger of discovery and seizure by some one of Slavery's
numerous spies. Seven nights had chilled their limbs,
and well nigh exhausted their energies, both of mind
and body, for except the mother, they were all unused
to patient labors. Theirs had been years of toil without
an object, and they were at this time scarcely capable
of self-imposed endurance of fatigue.

Now, although their feet pressed the soil of a Free
State, their perils were not passed, and they pursued

their way on foot towards the North with anxious hearts.

Concklin, who had assumed the name of Miller, had doffed the shabby garb which he had worn before, and now appeared neatly and comfortably clad. The boys wore pants of Kentucky jean and black cloth coats, while Vina and her daughter in their plaid shawls and comfortable hoods would scarcely have been recognized, even by those who had often seen them at their labor, as field hands from McKiernan's place.

All day they travelled on the public road; and though they "met a heap of people," they were not questioned. There was nothing, indeed, in their appearance to excite remark, except that they were dark in hue and journeying towards the North. At night they reached the house of a *friend*, where they were received most kindly. A bountiful supper was quickly prepared for them, and they soon lay down to peaceful slumbers. All the next day, too, they rested, for in their future journeyings, it was deemed wisest to accept the friendly guidance of the stars.

After supper on Monday night came another *friend* to carry them northward to his home. He brought two horses which the women rode; while himself and Concklin, with the two re-animated brothers, walked beside them. At three o'clock on Tuesday morning they reached their second resting place, where they remained till Wednesday night. They then resumed their journey, and travelled all night on foot. Cheerfully they walked along, for every hour their hope became stronger as their old master's success in overtaking them grew more and more improbable. At late breakfast time on Thursday they reached another *station*, where they rested till Friday morning. They were then so far from the river that Concklin thought they might venture to travel in the day-time, so he proposed to continue their journey. But Vina had awaked that morning with a burdened spirit. She "had bad dreams all night," and she feared to start by daylight. "'Pears like," said she, "something will happen if we starts to-day. You can do as you likes, sir, but if I was you, I'd put off this yer jaunt till night. 'Pears like 'taint safe, no how." But Concklin was naturally hopeful and bold, and the presentiments of the ignorant slave woman he regarded as mere idle superstition. They were so nearly out of danger, that he felt extremely anxious to push on.

Vina started with reluctance. The kind friend at whose house they were, lent her a horse for a few miles, and sent his son to ride the animal back. Soon the rain began to fall, and all day long "it rained constant." All day, too, they journeyed on, for they dared not stop where they were not sure of finding friends.

Late in the afternoon, as with dripping umbrellas and weary feet they walked along, a spotted horse which had escaped from a field by the road side, came galloping before them. His owner called upon the travellers to stop him, but Vina, in a low tone, bade the boys go on. Peter, however, naturally obliging, caught the horse, and delivered him to his owner. A little further on they passed a saw-mill, in front of which a large man stood gazing at the little company. "How d'y', Aunt Lucy," cried he, "which way are you travelling?" No answer was given as they hastened on, but their hearts beat quick with fear.

Just before night they approached the dwelling of the *friend* where they were next to rest. His son lived in a small house close by, and here Concklin bade them "run in out of the rain," while he went on to the main station to announce their coming.

They obeyed, and soon they were all seated beside a cheerful fire. The bright blaze imparted new life to their chilled and weary limbs; and from their hearts ascended a silent thanksgiving to Him who had brought them safely to the end of this day's journey, ——when suddenly the sound of many horses' feet was heard.

CHAPTER XXXII.

THE CAPTURE.

ONE glance at the window sent a shudder through the little party—for there, halting at the gate, were seven men on horseback.

"They done come after us;" hoarsely whispered one of the boys.

"Yes," answered their mother, "I'll lay anything we're gwine to be tooken now."

The men dismounted and tied their horses to the fence. Foremost was *the owner of the spotted horse*, upon the very animal which Peter had delivered into his hand, and next was he who had accosted "*Aunt Lucy*" but an hour or two before.

What to do the helpless creatures did not know. Concklin was away. Oh! why did he leave them? The house was small, and the only place of egress they could discover was the door by which they had just entered, and this their foes were even then approaching. They saw no place to hide, and the young man and woman, whose house they had so recently entered, stood petrified with amazement, and gazed upon the scene.

The seven men entered the little dwelling. Three or four of them remained near the door, while the others advanced into the middle of the room and opened a conversation with the boys. The heart beat wildly beneath each dark-hued breast, but they strove to look indifferent while they replied to the questioners as they had been previously instructed.

" Where are you going ?"

" To Springfield, Sir."

" Do you belong to the man that brought you here ?"

" Yes, Sir."

" Where did you come from ?"

" From Kaintucky, Sir. Mass'r died last year, and left us to his brother, and now he's a takin' us on to his farm."

" What did he bring you through here for ? Did n't he know that it was against the law ?"

" Don't know, Sir, reckon he 'lowed 'twas right."

" I'll be d—d if I don't believe he stole you all."

The brave seven then stood aside and consulted for a few minutes, and then one of their number went out. Soon he returned with a half-gallon jug of liquor, and a wagon. The besieging party then took a drink all round to raise their courage. They offered, too, to treat Levin and Peter, but the boys declined the honor.

Another brief consultation was held, and then, producing ropes, these zealous priests of the Moloch of Slavery, proceeded to bind their victims for the sacrifice. How the boys longed to resist!—but they were all unarmed, while their assailants carried both bowie-knives and pistols. Besides, their host, who stood silent by, would, for aught they knew, join with their enemies against them. It would be idle to attempt to fight against such fearful odds ; so they stood still while their hands were tied behind them, and then, obeying the orders of the foreman of the band, they climbed into the wagon.

The women followed in silence. Despair was written on their faces, but their captors had no pity for their helpless woe. The coarse jest, and the blasphemous oath went round, while now and then a burst of boisterous laughter came from the "*law-abiding*" band that guarded their return towards the "land of chivalry."

When they had proceeded a short distance, Concklin came running after them. Oh! that he had never left them! then had they been safe. He sprang into the wagon, and commenced untying the captives. But he was soon discovered by the ruffians in attendance, who, pointing their pistols at his head, swore that they would blow out his brains if he did not desist.

He remained in the wagon, however, until they reached the jail at Vincennes. It was very late. The lights were extinguished in all the houses, and the jailor was asleep. "Ho! Hallo!" cried the leader of the band.

The jailor at length appeared.

"Do you want some more stock?"

"I don't know; that depends on what sort it is."

"Well, its a sort you've not had here lately. Take them in; they're tired, and want to go to bed."

The jailor held up his light and took a survey of the captives. "Well," said he, "if they're tired, I don't think they're sleepy; say, are you sleepy, old woman?"

"No, Sir," replied Vina, "I don't feel like sleepin'."

"So I thought; I should'nt if I were in your place."

After some further conversation with the chief of

the band, he took the prisoners in and locked them up. "But he acted," Vina says, "like he felt mighty sorry for us; and I believe, if we had'nt been watched so close, he mought 'a' let us go."

In the jail they were visited every day by Concklin, who came and talked with them through the window; and daily Vina begged him to leave them there and seek his own safety. "Now you can't do us no good, Sir, no how, and 'pears like you best take care o'you-self."

"Oh," replied he, "I don't feel at all uneasy."

"Well, Sir, I feels oneasy about you, and you best not stay round yer no longer. It wont make it no better for us, and you'll git into trouble, sure."

But some dream of rescuing them haunted his mind; he could not bear to leave them. It was something new for him to be foiled in any undertaking; and he had set his heart upon delivering this family to the husband and father, who he knew was waiting, with trembling heart, to welcome them.

Immediately after lodging them in jail, the chief of the marauding band had telegraphed in all directions to ascertain if four negroes, answering the description of these had anywhere been missed; and also what reward was offered for their capture. The "lightning postboy" hasted to execute their mission, and soon returned them answer. "Four likely negroes had been stolen from Bernard McKiernan, near South Florence, Ala., and their owner had offered a reward of four hundred dollars for the property, and six hundred for the apprehension of the thief, and his delivery in South Florence."

Upon the receipt of this information, Concklin was seized, and thrust into prison. Still his brave hopeful spirit bore him up—" 'peared like he couldn't feel discouraged."

It was night; and night in prison is never lovely. Catharine and her brothers were asleep, but Vina's eyes closed not. Her thoughts were busy picturing the sorrows to which they were returning, the tortures that awaited them, and all the hopelessness of their future lives. Never more should the voice of her husband greet her ear—never more should his smiles gladden her heart. And her children—henceforth they would be branded as runaways, and thus exposed to grievous ills, to which, thus far, they had been strangers. No one would trust them now.

Suddenly she started. Wheels approached, and stopped in front of the jail. Did she know that voice? Yes, she could not be mistaken.

"I wish you would let me in. I would like to see them."

She heard the jailor in reply, and soon footsteps approached their cell. Vina roused her children. "We'll git toted back now. Old McKiernan's a comin.' He's a talkin' out yer."

Soon the key turned in the lock, and the jailor entered with a light, followed by a stranger, and the "old master." His cane was in his hand—his face looked redder than usual, and his eyes hastily searched every part of the room. He approached the bed on which his slaves were still lying, and for a moment looked down on them in silence.

"Ha! boy, what are you doing here?" said he to Peter.

No answer.

"Speak! you rascal, or I'll knock you in the head with this stick. Don't you know me?"

"Yes, sir."

"Aint I your old master?"

Reluctantly Peter answered, "Yes, sir."

"Didn't I raise you all?"

"Yes, sir."

"Well, d—n you, what are you doing here?"

"Don't know, sir."

"*Don't know!* I'll make you tell a different tale from that when I get you home. You, Levin, don't you think this is a devil of a caper?"

Levin was silent, and the master turned to his mother. "See here, girl, how came you to leave home?"

No answer.

"Aint it d—d astonishing you all can't answer when you're spoken to?"

Still no answer came, and he turned to his companion. "Ah, that huzzy! she's at the bottom of all this. If it hadn't been for her, and that rascal Peter, they never would have left me in the world."

"What Peter is that?" asked the man.

"Why, he is this girl's husband. He got in with a Jew, and persuaded him to buy him; and a few months after that, Peter bought himself. This scrape was in the bargain at first, I'm certain."

"Where are this Peter and his master now?"

"I don't know exactly—but if they ever show their heads in Tuscumbia again, I'll have them hung sky-high. Peter is at the bottom of this; but he never had sense to do it alone—he's had help, I'll swear. Some d—d abolitionist has had a hand in it. I believe there's some of them in Franklin county, and if I can hunt them out, they shall be burnt, or I'll have their heads —one."

He then proceeded to question the family concerning their escape; and to shield Concklin, they told a story which they had previously prepared for an emergency like this. They declared that Concklin, or as they called him, Miller, did not bring them away at first, but that four persons took them, and delivered them up to him. Who these persons were, they could not tell; but they described "*some sort o' men that they had never seen.*" "Yes, yes," said the master, "d—n them, *I've seen four such looking fellows in Tuscumbia.*"

After a while he left them, and went into the next room, where Concklin was confined. There they heard his voice for a long time; at first in moderate tones, but when his passion rose, his words could easily be distinguished. "It's d—d astonishing that you won't tell who started you in this business. Would you be such a fool as to be carried back in irons, and lose your life for the sake of saving other people?"

"It is of no use for you to question me about them," replied Concklin. "You have me now, and it is not worth while to bring other people into trouble."

"Well, d—n you, how do you feel in them irons?"

"I suppose I feel better than you will at some future day in consequence of causing them to be put on me."

"How is that?"

"You will have plenty of time to find out."

Finding that he could get no satisfactory answer from the "*thief,*" he returned to the room where his property was confined. Here he remained about an hour, alternately cursing and asking questions; but he could not make them tell who started them on their way. At last he left them and went out.

Early in the morning, he returned, and ordered them to get ready to go home. They rose immediately, but were scarcely ready when the stage came to the door.

After they were seated in the coach, Concklin was brought out in irons, and put in with them. He still looked brave and cheerful; but the slaves, alas! there was no light in their downcast eyes—no hope in their disappointed hearts.

When the stage stopped to change horses, they alighted to take breakfast. They all sat down together, but only the master and his companion* had appetites for food. Vina only drank a cup of coffee, and the boys ate very little.

" Why don't you eat, girl?" demanded the master.

"I don't keer 'bout eatin'," she replied.

" Well, if you all had staid at home, you'd been able to eat."

They were soon re-seated in the stage, and none of them left it again till after dark, when they reached Evansville. Here they spoke of putting the captives into jail for safe keeping; but it was whispered that if they did so they might not find them in the morning; and at last they took them to a private house, where, after giving them their supper, they locked them up all together in a room in the second story. The master of the house, who, they understood was a brother-in-law of their master's escort, sat all night on the stairs to watch them.

* Emison. See Memoir of Concklin.

Concklin had now become alarmed, and during the night he was much excited. He tried the windows of the room, and was about to jump from one of them, when Vina interposed. "Oh!" said she, "don't go out thar'. You'll be dashed to pieces, sir, jumpin' out o' that ar high winder. Oh! if you had tuck my advice, and run off when they first cotch us, you'd 'a' been safe now, and it would n't 'a' been no worse for us."

This was a gloomy night. None of the prisoners felt inclined to sleep. Liberty—the precious goal which they had almost grasped, was now beyond their reach—forever lost. "Well chillern," said the mother, "you all 's got to cotch it now. You wont be the best hands on the place no more, and everything 'at's done wrong 'll be laid to you. But it can't be *hoped*—we's done the best we could, and now the Lord's all the friend we got."

Morning dawned at last, and after an early breakfast, Mr. McKiernan came with his attendant, Emison, to conduct them to the boat.

How the sinews of Levin and Peter ached for a race! If their mother and sister had been safe, would they have walked quietly down to the river, on whose bosom they were to be borne back to slavery? No, no—they would at least have made one desperate effort to escape. But they could not desert those who were so dear to them; and so they meekly followed their old master, while they knew his footsteps led to the scene of cruel torture—perhaps even to death.

Once on board the boat—the "Paul Anderson," the negroes were deemed safe; still, whenever the boat landed they were closely watched. Concklin was kept confined in a state-room, where his poor friends had no chance to speak to him. They lay at night upon the cabin floor, and *the young people* slept. Their mother, too, several times grew drowsy, but the horrid dreams that came soon frightened sleep away. She heard every footstep; and towards morning, they were all aroused by people hurrying to and fro with lights, and calling to each other in every direction. The master came to Vina. "Where are the boys?" said he.

"Yon they lie, sir."

"Well, that rascal's gone."

"Is he?" Such was her only answer; but her heart beat quick with the hope that he had by some means, escaped in safety. The boat was searched in every part, but no trace of him was found.

Early in the morning, Mr. McKiernan, with his property, landed at Paducah, to wait for the "Greek Slave," which was expected to pass that day on her home trip from Louisville.

The mistress of the hotel where they stopped, took a great interest in the returning fugitives, and begged Mr. McKiernan to sell her the old woman and her daughter. He did not, however, seem anxious to dispose of them.

"How would you like to live with me?" said the lady herself to Vina.

"I don't know, ma'am; you mought be hard to please. I've had one hard missus, and I don't care 'bout changin' for a worse one."

"Well," said the lady, "I give you my word, I would be kind to you. You may ask any of my servants if I am hard to be suited."

But the old master listened with impatience to all her arguments. "I *raised* this family myself," said he, "and even if there is danger of their running off again, I may as well hold bad property as anybody else."

Such was his usual feeling whenever any one proposed to purchase one of his people. He disliked to part with them; not because he loved them—for we have seen that his heart knew no pity for their sufferings; but *they were his*, and he would rather buy than sell.

At about ten o'clock in the morning, the "Greek Slave" appeared, and the melancholy company were soon ascending the Tennessee. The lonely quiet banks looked gloomy to them now, notwithstanding the trees were clothed in their freshest green, and wild flowers of every form and hue were nodding to their lovely images in the bright water. There was no Spring-time in their hearts. Darkness, like the shadow of Death, hung over their spirits, while the bright sunshine and the glad notes of a thousand birds but mocked their misery.

CHAPTER XXXIII.

PETER PLANS TO REDEEM HIS FAMILY.

As soon as Mr. Concklin left Philadelphia, Peter returned to his mother's house, and there remained, restless and anxious, for many weeks. At last his brother William, who had received a letter from Concklin, dated Princeton, Ia., March 24th, wrote to him that his family had arrived in a Free State. Immediately he hastened to Philadelphia, his heart swelling with the hope of soon embracing them; but the day after his arrival, alas! these glorious visions of approaching joy suddenly faded away.

" O, Peter, said his sister Mary, as he entered the room where she was sitting, " have you heard the news ?"

He noticed that her voice trembled, and that her eyes were filled with tears; and his heart interpreted but too faithfully her emotion. Still he answered calmly, " No."

" Sit down," said she, " and I will read it to you." She had the " Ledger" in her hand, and she read several extracts from Indiana papers, giving an account of the seizure of four slaves who had escaped from Bernard McKiernan, of South Florence, Ala., and also of a white man, calling himself Miller, who had them in charge.

Peter listened in silence. "It is just what I expected," said he in a hoarse voice, when she had finished, "just what I told them all. Oh! if they had heard to me!

For a time he seemed discouraged. His thoughts followed the trembling fugitives on their return, and under every torture which he had been accustomed to see inflicted upon runaways, he fancied that his dear wife and children, even then, were groaning.

A boy belonging to a *pious* man, near Tuscumbia—a class leader in the Methodist Church—was, at the time Peter came away, wearing a heavy iron collar upon his neck, and a band of the same metal around his body. A rod of iron was welded to each of these upon his back, and extended further above his head than his hands could reach. Rods of iron were also fastened to the collar on each side, and at the point of each shoulder they were bent up, and reached higher than his head. To the highest of these rods a bell was fastened, which tinkled constantly. In the morning the boy was locked to the plough by a chain which was fastened to the band around his body, and thus he was obliged to plough till noon. The headman then unlocked the chain, and led the mule away; leaving his fellow-slave to follow to the house. All the long afternoon he was forced to plough in the same manner; and at night, the head-man locked him in a cabin alone, and left him to cook his scanty supper and to get what rest his torturing irons would allow. For several months he had already worn these cruel badges of the runaway—and now the father shuddered, as in imagination he saw his own beloved sons enduring similar punishments.

Another man, belonging to Mr. B——, of Tuscumbia, died not long before Peter left that town, from wearing an iron collar in hot weather. It rubbed the skin off the poor fellow's neck, but his master swore he should wear it till he died. Soon was his threat fulfilled, for the flesh mortified under the heated iron, and when the sufferer uttered his last groan, the inhuman instrument was still upon his neck.

He knew also that even the women on McKiernan's place had learned to wear the irons. Well he remembered Mary—a beautiful woman, and a special favorite with her master, as all the pretty women were. She had received so much abuse from her mistress that her life was hateful to her, and at last she resolved to escape, for a time at least, from her persecutions. Accordingly she fled to the woods. The next Sunday morning the order was issued that no allowance should be given out till all the hands had been out to hunt Mary. Peter was there that day visiting his family, and as Vina was obliged to go, he joined the hunt, well knowing that such a course would gratify the master. They soon found her track, with here and there traces of corn and onions which had appeased her hunger. But few of the slaves, however, had any desire to find her, and those few were easily sent by the others in a wrong direction. When night came, therefore, Mary had not been taken. All day they had rambled in the woods—fasting—except that some had now and then seized a roasting ear as they passed by a field of corn; they were delighted therefore, when, as the shades of night approached, they were suffered to go home, and to receive their week's allowance.

But notwithstanding the failure of this day's hunt, the search for Mary was at divers times repeated, and after having spent three or four months in the woods, she was brought in. Then came the punishment for her heinous crime. First, her master gave her a cruel beating, and then the overseer inflicted upon her naked back a like " correction ;" and after that, for a long time, she was daily stripped and beaten by her mistress's orders. This system was continued until she became so weak that they feared she would be "*ruined*," and then the irons were brought in requisition. The collar was welded on her slender neck, and a heavy band of iron upon her ankle. To this latter, one end of a heavy log-chain was attached, the other end of which was brought up and locked round her waist. Month after month was the poor woman forced to wear these galling irons. Peter, himself, had often seen her coming from the field at night, " lookin' every minute like she would drop down to the ground with the weight of her shackles. She was raggetty and dirty too, for she hadn't no spirit left to wash and mend her clothes."* The image of this tortured wo-man would rise before him now—the clanking of her heavy chain would rack his ears. No wonder that he

---

* Vina says, " Mary done took so much whippin' that the flesh between her shoulders inflames nigh 'bout every year, and the skin looks like a dry brown crust. Then they has to send for the doctor, and he takes out a strip o' flesh five or six inches long. After a while her back heals up again, and she gits well enough to work. They done quit 'busin' her now, and she works all the time in the field, 'cept they has a heap o' company, or there's some great hurry o' sewin' gwine on. Then they brings her in for she's a ele-gant seamster, and understands all sorts o' house service."

could not rest. No wonder that all labor and privation seemed as nothing if he could yet gain the ransom of his loved ones.

Peter started immediately for Cincinnati, in the hope of finding his late master, and obtaining his assistance in this, his pressing need. But he was disappointed. Mr. Isaac Friedman was still in Illinois. His brother Levi, however, warmly espoused his cause, and would have gone himself to Tuscumbia, to try what could be done for the relief of the family, had he not been kindly warned that such a step would be both hazardous and futile. A friend of his in Franklin county, wrote him that the citizens of Tuscumbia were highly incensed against both his brother and Peter, as in consequence of what the latter had said to Mrs. McKiernan, concerning Mr. Friedman's partial promise to buy his family, they regarded them as instigators of the escape.*

But this did not discourage the anxious husband and father. He had brought from Philadelphia a letter

* That this feeling was not, however, quite universal among the citizens is evident from an incident which occurred on board the " Greek Slave," as she lay at Tuscumbia Landing, having on board the captured family. " Well, Old Woman," said a gentleman from town, who came on board to see them, " are you sorry for running away ?" " No, Sir, I don't feel sorry;" replied Vina. " I think any person else would 'a' done like I have." " Yes, that's so," replied he, " I would have done the same thing myself. Peter is a good fellow too, and your master is an old rascal. Look here, if he takes a notion to sell you all, I'd like to buy you, for I believe you're an honest family, and I don't think the less of you for this." " I can't remember his name," said Vina, as she related the incident, " but he spoke mons's kind, and he's as fine looking a man, nigh 'bout, as ever I see."

of introduction to Levi Coffin, a worthy Friend, residing in Cincinnati. This he delivered, and Mr. Coffin soon made his case known to several benevolent gentlemen in town. One of these, Mr. Samuel Lewis, at Peter's request, addressed a letter to Mr. L. B. Thornton, of Tuscumbia, requesting him to ascertain from Mr. McKiernan, whether or not he would sell the family, and at what price he valued them, and asking him to write the result of his inquiries to William Still, of Philadelphia. (Mr. Thornton was a young man much esteemed—a Virginian, who had for some time taught the boy's school in Tuscumbia, while he pursued his law studies. Peter had often performed slight services for him, and always regarded him as one of his best friends.)

One day during his stay in Cincinnati, as Peter was standing upon the sidewalk, striving in his own mind to devise some means to hasten the release from bondage of those he loved, a pale lady, seated in a carriage, beckoned him towards her. He approached the carriage, and the lady asked him if he would like employment, and if he could drive. He replied in the affirmative, and was soon seated on the box. For several hours he drove her carriage about the city, and so kindly did she address him, that at last he told her all his grief. She listened with much interest to the story, and after expressing her sympathy with his sorrows, she told him that her husband was a friend of the unfortunate, and that perhaps he could assist him in his efforts to buy his family. She accordingly directed him to her husband's office, and entering, he found himself in the presence of Hon. Salmon P. Chase.

This good man, after hearing his simple tale, readily

offered to do anything in his power to aid him. Peter then told him that to Mr. John Gist, of Kentucky, a brother of his former master, Mr. McKiernan was largely indebted; and that as he was an old servant of the family, he thought it possible that Mr. Gist would be able and willing to assist him in the purchase of his family. Before he left the office Mr. Chase wrote a letter to this gentleman, asking for information with regard to the best plan for getting the family and also if he could in any way aid the poor man in his efforts for their purchase.

From this letter Peter never heard, although he staid in Cincinnati more than three weeks after it was despatched.

Towards the last of June, he returned with a heavy heart to his friends in New Jersey. He had done all he could, but nowhere could he discern a ray of hope. Yet he could not be idle; and as it seemed useless at that time to attempt any further steps towards the accomplishment of his one absorbing wish, he settled himself at service in Burlington, New Jersey.

His mistress, Mrs. Mary A. Buckman, treated him with uniform kindness, and with her aid and that of her two daughters, he commenced learning to read. We have before related his resolute attempts to learn the mysteries of letters during his few visits to the Sabbath School in Lexington, but that was long— long years ago, and though he had then mastered the wondrous alphabet, and even learned to spell a few little words, he had never, since that time, been able to make the least advance in erudition. But now when through the kindness of these ladies, he became able to read, though but imperfectly, the precious words of the New Testament, he felt that his arduous efforts to be free had not been all in vain.

Sometime in the ensuing August came the following letter from Mr. McKiernan, to whom Mr. Thornton had referred the one which had been written to him from Cincinnati:

"South Florence, Ala., 6th August, 1851.

"MR. WILLAM STILL, NO. 31 NORTH FIFTH STREET, PHILADELPHIA.

"SIR a few days sinc mr Lewis Thornton of Tuscumbia Ala shewed me a letter dated 6 June 51 from cincinnati synd samuel Lewis in behalf of a Negro man by the name of peter Gist who informed the writer of the Letter that you were his Brother & wished an answer to be directed to you as he peter would be in Philadelphia. the object of the letter was to purchis from me 4 Negroes that is peters Wife & 3 children 2 sons & 1 girl the Name of said Negroes are the woman viney the (mother) Eldest son peter 21 or 2 years old second son Leven 19 or 20 years 1 Girl about 13 or 14 years old. the Husband and Father of these people once belonged to a relation of mine by the name of Gist now Decest & some few years sinc he peter was sold to a man by the Name of Friedman who removed to Cincinnati ohio & Tuck peter with him of course peter became free by the voluntary act of the master some time last march a white man by the name of Miller apperd in the nabourhood & abducted the bove negoes was caute at vincanes Indi with said negroes & was thare convicted of steling & remanded back to Ala to Abide the penelty of the law & on his return met his just reward by Getting drownded at the

mouth of Cumberland River on the ohio in attempting
to make his escape I recoverd & Braught Back said
4 negroes or as You would say coulard people under
the Belief that peter the Husband was acsessery to the
offence thareby putting me to much Expense & Truble
to the amt $1000 which if he gets them he or his
Friends must refund these 4 negros here are worth in
the market about 4000 for tha are Extraordenary fine
& likely & but for the fact of Elopement I would not
take 8000 Dollars for them but as the thing now stands
you can say to Peter & his new discovered Relations
in Philadelphi I will take 5000 for the 4 culerd people
& if this will suite him & he can raise the money I will
deliver to him or his agent at paduca at mouth of
Tennessee river said negroes but the money must be
Deposited in the Hands of some respectable person at
paduca before I remove the property it wold not be
safe for peter to come to this countery

"write me a line on recpt of this & let me know
peters views on the above

"I am Yours &c

"B. McKiernan"

"NB say to peter to write & let me know his views
amediately as I am determind to act in a way if he
dont take this offer he will never have an other ap-
portunity

"B. McKiernan"

This letter was soon circulated among those friends
who had become interested in accomplishing the re-union
of the family, and so enormous was the price demanded
for the slaves that few persons deemed it possible for
Peter to procure the means to ransom them. But his

courage did not falter. He could not live in freedom, surrounded by his friends, and supplied with every comfort, and yet make no effort to redeem those he loved far better than life, *or even liberty*, from the cruel bondage which they endured. But for a time he hesitated as to the means that would be safest and most speedy in effecting his purpose. Give it up, he would not—that was settled.

He thought of going from place to place to solicit aid, but then he was unknown, and even the benevolent in heart would hesitate to contribute towards so large a sum, while they were unacquainted with his previous character. It would be useless to write to any of his old friends in Tuscumbia for testimonials concerning the uprightness of his former life—for there he was believed to have originated the plan of running off his family, and he knew that notwithstanding all his years of honest, patient, persevering toil he was now branded as a *negro thief.*

After pondering the subject for some weeks, he bethought him that after all, he might have a friend in "the North" who had known his character. He remembered that one of the young ladies, who had taught in the Seminary at Tuscumbia, returned home about the time he finished paying for himself; and he resolved, if possible, to ascertain her residence. He had heard the teachers, in conversation with each other, mention New York and Syracuse, and he believed the latter place had been their home. Yet he had no certain knowledge, for he had cautiously refrained from asking any questions about the North, lest he should be suspected of undue curiosity respecting the dwelling of the Free. He soon communicated to his friends his hope of obtaining some testimonials of good character from these ladies, if they could be found, and a letter of inquiry concerning them was immediately written by Mr. McKim, of Philadelphia, to Rev. S. J. May, of Syracuse.

This letter was promptly answered, but from some unknown cause the reply was not received by Peter. So he quietly continued at his service, performing his regular duties to the satisfaction of his mistress, though all the while his mind was racked by alternate hopes and fears.

Thus passed the winter of 1851–2; but in the spring his anxiety to *do* something for his family became so intense that he resolved to go out and try his success in collecting funds for their ransom. He acquainted Mrs. Buckman with this design, but, just after she had engaged another servant to take his place, an incident occurred which revived his hope of finding yet a friend. He heard a gentleman who was visiting at the house speak of his home in Syracuse, and he took an opportunity to inquire of him if he had ever known the ladies of whom he was so anxious to hear. To his great joy Mr. —— knew them both, and informed him that although one of them still remained in the South, the other had returned, was married, and resided a few miles from Syracuse.

This cheering news Peter communicated to his mistress, who, at his request, wrote for him to his friend. He now determined to remain in Burlington until he should receive an answer to this letter, and accordingly, he entered the service of Judge Boudinot, one of the principal citizens of that place.

About this time the idea occurred to him, that, perhaps, it would be best to buy his wife and daughter first, and afterwards to try to raise a sum sufficient to purchase the two boys. He determined at least to learn what chance of success he would have in case he should obtain the means to do this; and for assistance in making this inquiry, he applied to Dr. Ely, of Medford, N. J., who wrote for him a second letter to Mr. Thornton of Tuscumbia. To this came in due time the following answer:

"Tuscumbia, Ala., August 19th, 1852.

"H. N. ELY—Dear Sir—Your letter has remained unanswered for so long because I have not been able to have an interview with Mr. McKiernan on the subject about which you wrote. I have just seen him. He says he will not separate the family of negroes, and the lowest price he will take under any circumstances is $5,000; and if that is placed in my hands, or with any responsible persons for him, he will let the negroes go.

"I would like Peter to get his wife and family, and think this amount a high price: but it is the lowest, I know.   Very respectfully,

LEWIS B. THORNTON."

The letter written by Mrs. Buckman failed to reach its destination; and after remaining in Judge Boudinot's service for five months, Peter resolved to go himself to Syracuse, and find his friend, if indeed he had one in that vicinity. If he accomplished this, he would then try his success in collecting money. He had already saved from his wages since he had been in Burlington, one hundred dollars, which he determined should be the first contribution towards the $5,000.

CHAPTER XXXIV.

"HOW DID HE GET THE MONEY?"

PETER received from his friends at parting but small encouragement to hope. The sum required was so enormous, and the idea of paying gold to him who had already robbed them of the earnings of long years was so repugnant to the feelings of the best men, that it seemed almost useless to attempt to raise the money. A few days before he started, his brother William said to him, "You ought not to feel so uneasy—so perfectly restless because your family are slaves. There are thousands of people as good as they who are in the same condition. Do you see that woman across the street? She is just as good as you are, and she has a mother and sisters in slavery. You cannot expect people to give you five thousand dollars to buy your family, when so many others, equally deserving, are just as badly off."

"Look here," replied Peter, "I know a heap of men, as *good*, and as *smart* as I am, that are slaves now; but—*I've bought my liberty, and my family shall be free.*"

On the eighth of November, 1852, he left Burlington on his travels, carrying with him the kindest wishes of all who knew him, and also the following certificates from those whom he had served in that city.

"Burlington, November 6, 1852.

"Peter Still (a colored man), has lived in my employ for some months past, but I have known him for two years.

"It affords me much pleasure in being able to recommend him, as an honest, sober, industrious and capable man, perfectly trustworthy and ever willing to make himself generally useful, either about the house or stable. I part with him reluctantly; he leaves me, to make an effort to redeem his wife and children from slavery.

"E. E. Boudinot."

"The above named Peter Still, was in my employ ten months, during which time he fully sustained the character given him by Mr. Boudinot. It gives me pleasure to add my name to this recommendation.

"Mary A. Buckman."

"Judge Boudinot is one of our principal citizens, and I have entire confidence in his recommendation of Peter Still.

"Cortlandt Van Rensselaer.

"Burlington, N. J., Nov. 6, 1852."

Peter went first to Brooklyn, where he visited his brother John, who by his advice and sympathy did much to cheer him on his way. "Now, Peter," said he, "you can call on me at any time for fifty or a hundred dollars, and whenever you need clothes, or anything else that I can furnish you, just let me know.

And be careful whom you trust. You will find plenty of friends, if it is known you have a little money. Be careful, and watch well for rogues.

On the sixteenth of November, he reached Syracuse, and delivered a letter of introduction and recommendation from Mr. McKim, of Philadelphia, to Rev. Mr. May. This lover of humanity listened with great interest to his thrilling story, examined his papers, which gave ample testimony to the integrity of his character, as well as to the truthfulness of his tale; and the next day sent him to the residence of the friend whom he had come to seek—the writer of this narrative. Here he remained until the nineteenth, when, with a letter to Mr. May, corroborating such facts in his statement as had come to her knowledge, and certifying to his character for truthfulness and industry while a slave, he returned to Syracuse.

He was now thoroughly furnished for his arduous undertaking; and with letters of introduction from Mr. May to various co-laborers in the work of benevolence, he left Syracuse, and journeyed westward.

His first stop was at Auburn, where a letter from Mr. May, together with his other papers, and above all, his modest earnestness of manner, won him a favorable reception. He visited first the clergymen of the different churches, to some of whom he brought letters; and they commended him to the charity of their people. Here, in Rev. Mr. Millard's church, on Sunday evening, he appeared for the first time before the public. "I was mighty skeered," said he, "when Mr. Millard took me with him into the pulpit, and told me I must stand up, myself, and tell my story to the people. 'Peared like I could n't stand, no how; but I said a few words, and Mr. Millard, he helped me out; so I got along mighty well."

He remained a week in Auburn, and received while there fifty dollars. This success encouraged him, and he went on to Rochester, stopping by the way at Waterloo, where also he received some assistance.

At Rochester he staid two or three weeks, and was kindly entertained at the houses of worthy citizens, and about the middle of December he returned to Syracuse with two hundred dollars. This, Mr. May deposited for him in the bank, and giving him letters to Messrs. William Lloyd Garrison, Theodore Parker, T. Starr King, and others, in Boston, bade him hasten thither, in order to be there before the Holidays.

As soon as he had delivered his letters of introduction from Mr. May, in Boston, he sought Andover, for the purpose of visiting the Author of "Uncle Tom's Cabin," to whom also he had a letter of recommendation. Mrs. Stowe received him cordially, and after heading his subscription list in Andover, gave him the following brief letter, which, he says "*helped him mightily.*"

"Having examined the claims of this unfortunate man, I am satisfied that his is a case that calls for compassion and aid.

"Though the sum demanded is so large as to look hopeless, yet if every man who is so happy as to be free, and have his own wife and children *for his own*, would give even a small amount, the sum might soon be raised.

"As ye would that men should do for you—do ye even so for them.

H. B. STOWE."

A contribution was also taken for him at the Free Church in Andover, and during his stay in that town he received about forty dollars.

On his return to Boston, he presented the following letter, which he had brought from Burlington, to Rev. John P. Robinson.

"Burlington, N. J., Oct. 5, 1852.

"DEAR COUSIN JOHN:—Peter Still, who carries this note, is one of the most estimable of men. He wishes to have access to the great hearts of some of the good people of your city, who have great purses.

"Please get from him his history, and his object, and direct him what to do. His integrity may be relied on.   "Affectionately,

"JOSEPH PARRISH."

"The above letter is from Dr. Joseph Parrish, a distinguished physician of New Jersey, and well known by his profession in Boston.

"JOHN P. ROBINSON.

"Boston, January 3, 1853."

A day or two later, the following notice appeared in one of the morning papers, which has been copied in the papers of almost every New England town which Peter afterwards visited:

"Boston, January 3, 1853.

"The bearer, Peter Still, was kidnapped in early childhood, on the borders of Delaware river, in New Jersey, and carried thence to Kentucky, and subsequently to Alabama. After being held in slavery more than forty years, he succeeded in purchasing his freedom; and being obliged, consequently, by the laws of Alabama, to leave that State, he came North to Philadelphia, where, by a strange coincidence, he became acquainted with his brother and family, from which he had been so long severed. He has left a wife and three children in Alabama, whom he naturally and ardently desires to bring into freedom, and have with him at the North. For this purpose he now appeals to the sympathy of the benevolent for such pecuniary aid as they may be disposed to give him.

" We, the undersigned, have carefully examined his letters and papers, and have obtained knowledge of him. From this examination, we are satisfied that his story is true in all its particulars; that he is himself a worthy and virtuous man, whose extraordinary history gives him a strong and peculiar claim upon the public sympathy and aid.

" Any contributions for the object above named may be forwarded to any of us.

> " S. K. LOTHROP,
> " ELLIS GRAY LORING,
> " EPHRAIM PEABODY,
> " WM. J. BOWDITCH,
> " J. I. BOWDITCH,
> " JOHN P. ROBINSON,
> " THOS. STARR KING."

In Boston and neighboring towns he remained till the last of March, when, having deposited four hundred and sixty dollars in the hands of Ellis Gray Loring, Esq., who kindly acted as his treasurer, he received numerous letters of recommendation from gentlemen of distinction here, and went to Portland, Me. The following will serve to illustrate the spirit cherished by these noble sons of New England towards the dark-hued victim of oppression. Among his papers are many others which breathe the same tender sympathy, the same warm human love.

" Boston, March 28th, 1853.

" I desire to certify that I am acquainted with Mr. Peter Still, have examined all his papers, and am entirely satisfied with the truthfulness of his story and the worthiness of his claims upon the sympathy and beneficence of the community. It does not seem possible that any further commendation of a Christian brother's appeal to the charity of men should be needed than the fact that he desires to be the owner of his own wife and family. So far as any words of mine can help him, I most cordially recommend him to the favorable consideration of the humane.

" T. S. KING."

At Portland Peter's subscription list was headed by Hon. Neal Dow ; and during the eight days he spent in that city, he received one hundred dollars. Thence he proceeded to Brunswick, Bath, Saco, Biddeford ; Portsmouth, N. H.; Hampton, Newburyport and Garretson Station ; and on his return to Boston, about the last of May, he deposited four hundred and ninety dollars in the hands of Mr. Loring ; making in all nine hundred and fifty dollars which he had received during the five months he had spent in New England.

He now decided to return to New Jersey and to visit Philadelphia for the purpose of further conference with his friends. As he passed through New York, on his way thither, he presented a letter to Thomas Foulcke of that city, from Dr. Parrish of Burlington, and though he staid but a short time, a few friends there presented him seventy-five dollars.

At Burlington he allowed himself a few days rest. He had been absent seven months, and had visited more than twenty different towns. His mind had been constantly excited—the theme of his discourse wherever he went, was the liberation of his family. He had no doubts concerning the result. When asked what he would do with the money he had gained, if after all, he failed to accomplish his object, his reply was, "'Pears like the Lord wont let me fail." Such was his simple, earnest faith, and to this his actions corresponded. His dress was neat, but strictly economical, and though he was not mean, yet every dollar he received was precious.

Notwithstanding his success thus far, his friends in New Jersey and Philadelphia had no confidence in his being able to raise the whole sum demanded by the tyrant; and Mr. Dillwyn Smith, of Burlington, who from the first, had taken much interest in his case, wrote for him to his former mistress, Mrs. Hogun, of Alabama, to solicit her influence with Mr. McKiernan, in the hope of procuring some abatement of the price.

For two weeks Peter waited there for an answer to this letter, but none arriving, he grew impatient to proceed with his great work; and once more bidding adieu to his kind friends, who had, during his stay, presented him forty-five dollars, he left them and went again to Brooklyn.

There he spent the fourth of July with his brother

John, and then he went to Syracuse, where, in a few days, he received one hundred and twenty-five dollars. Thence he went to Peterboro', and spent a night at the home of Gerritt Smith. He had frequently heard, since he had been free, of the great wealth of this distinguished friend of Man, and he had expected to find him inhabiting a princely dwelling, abounding in all the luxuries that gold can buy. But to his astonishment, his residence was a plain and quiet home, and his manners and style of living entirely free from pomp and ostentation. Mr. Smith gave him the following letter, together with a generous sum for the furtherance of his all-engrossing object.

"I am, and have long been deeply interested in the case of the bearer, Peter Still. I hope he may meet with generous friends wherever he shall go.

"GERRITT SMITH.

"Peterboro, July 27, 1853."

Peter now returned to Boston, arriving there the last of July, and on the third of August, he was in New Bedford. Here he remained till the twelfth, when he returned to Boston with one hundred and fifteen dollars, which he deposited in the hands of Mr. Loring. Next he visited Lowell, whence he returned on the second of September, with one hundred and eighty-five dollars. This also he placed in the care of his kind treasurer. Somerville gave him thirty-six dollars, Cambridge nineteen, and next he found himself at Worcester, where soon after his arrival the following notice appeared in the "Spy."

"Worcester, September 8, 1853.

"We would take this method of commending to the attention of all Christians and friends of humanity, the bearer, Peter Still. We heard his story, and examined his letters of introduction when he first came to Boston, in December last, and are satisfied of his worthiness to be encouraged and helped as he needs. He has been welcomed to many hearts in New England, and he will be to many more. All ye who can, give him aid and comfort.

"J. G. ADAMS.
"A. HILL.
"EDWARD E. HALE."

In Worcester he remained about two weeks, and then once more returned to Boston with one hundred and seventy-five dollars.

Next he journeyed southward; visited Plymouth, Kingston, and Fall River, and in every town found friends ready and willing to aid him in his work. From Fall River, Rev. Asa Bronson commended him in the following letter to Providence, to which place he immediately repaired:

"To the disciples of Christ and the friends of humanity in Providence, R. I.

"I have carefully examined the various letters and documents of Peter Still, and I fully believe that he is entitled to the entire confidence, cordial sympathy, and generous aid of the Christian public. We have assisted him in Fall River and vicinity to the amount of about $200.

"Help him if you can. 'He that hath pity on the poor, lendeth to the Lord.'

"With due respect,

"Yours,

"Asa Bronson.

"Fall River, October 26th, 1853."

In Providence, Peter remained during the month of November, and on looking at his book, in which were registered the gifts he there received, we find that one hundred and forty separate individuals contributed to his aid. Besides what he then personally received, collections were taken up for him in four churches in the city on the seventh of November. In Worcester, one hundred and fifty-four individuals contributed, and when we consider that to most of these persons, he of course repeated a sketch of his history, we cannot but wonder that his energies flagged not. We must, at least, admire his industry.

He received in Providence two hundred and fifty dollars; and then after making a short visit at Woburn, he returned to Boston, having gathered during the ten weeks he had been absent, six hundred and thirty dollars. Here he remained, visiting occasionally at Roxbury, Charlestown, Cambridge, and other neighboring towns, until about the middle of January, when, placing in the hands of his treasurer two hundred dollars more, which he had gathered since his return from Providence, he started homeward.

On the twentieth of January, we again find him in New York. He brought from a kind friend in Salem the following letter, which he immediately presented:

"Salem, First Month 12th, 1854.

"MY DEAR FRIEND: I take the liberty of giving the bearer, Peter Still, a letter to thee. He is the colored man, whose story I partly related to thee in Boston.

"I think there is that in his story that verifies the proverb, that 'truth is stranger than fiction.'

"I do not doubt the truthfulness of Peter, and he can tell thee his own story, which unfolds a phase in the history of slavery strongly illustrative of its evils, its oppressions, its injustice, and its opposition to all that is good, and kind, and Christian.

"I have ventured to tell Peter that I think he will find sympathizing friends in New York, and among them the kind friend I now address.

.   .   .   .

"Thy sincere friend,
"STEPHEN A. CHASE.

"ROBERT J. MURRAY."

This kind friend was right. Peter found sympathizing friends in New York, and before the middle of February he had received in that city and Brooklyn $1,146 45.

He then went on to Burlington, and in that city and its neighborhood, he remained until May. His heart now beat high with the hope of a speedy reunion with his loved ones; and even those among his friends who, at first had been furthest from uttering words of vain encouragement, now cheered him on. They looked upon him with wonder. All unlettered as he was— but four years out of slavery—they could hardly credit his strange success, while hearing from his own lips the story of his travels.

Peter was not spoiled by his good fortune, and never presumed upon the indulgence of his benefactors. Everywhere his manners were the same—modest and respectful, yet full of earnest dignity—the result of virtuous self-respect. " In every place I go," said he, "I aim to associate with the best people. I never knowed nothing gained by going into low company." And he was right. The best men in every place he visited opened wide their doors at his coming; and at their tables, notwithstanding the prejudice—once well-nigh universal—against color, he was a welcome guest.

Early in May, he again departed on his travels; and earnestly did he hope that this tour would be the last, before he should be ready to start in another direction —to meet those for whose ransom he had become a wanderer.

He went directly to New York, where he received the following letter from the senior editor of the Tribune, which he hastened to deliver in Albany.

" New York, May 10, 1854.

" MY OLD FRIEND: Peter Still, who will hand you this, was born free in New Jersey; kidnapped thence when six years old, with his brother, two years older, and sold into slavery; served forty years in Alabama; finally bought himself free, leaving his wife and three children in the hands of the scoundrels who had robbed him of forty years' work; and he is now begging money to buy them out of bondage. His chivalrous robber only asks him $5000 for his own wife and children. It is robbery to pay it, but inhumanity to refuse; and, as the time has not yet arrived for paying such villains with lead and steel, rather than gold, I wish you could help him raise a part of the money among those you know.

"Yours,

"HORACE GREELEY.

"George Dawson, Esq.,
"Albany Evening Journal Office."

Here, too, Peter found friends. Thurlow Weed, after contributing generously to his aid, gave him a letter expressive of his confidence in the integrity of his character, and, during the few days which he spent in the Dutch Capital, he received seventy-five dollars.

Thence he went to Pittsfield, Mass., where he received one hundred and five dollars, and then, without loss of time, he journeyed on to Springfield. Here one hundred dollars was added to his fund, and on the twenty-second day of June, we find him at New Haven.

Soon after his arrival here, he waited on Rev. Leonard Bacon, to whom he brought a letter of introduction. Mr. Bacon examined all his papers, and immediately entered with great zeal into the work of aiding his endeavors. He gave him the following letter of recommendation to his townsmen; and in divers ways, proved himself one of that noble band who delight in works of mercy for the mercy's sake.

"The case of this poor man, Peter Still, is a hard one. Kidnapped in his youth, and by unlegalized fraud and violence reduced to slavery, he has borne the yoke for many years with exemplary patience. He became a husband, in the sense in which a slave can be a husband; and children—his by the law of nature and of

God, but another man's property by the atrocious laws of Alabama—were born to him in the house of bondage. At last he became free by the consent of his owner. He purchased his freedom by the slow accumulation of what he could earn when all the service exacted by an absolute master, from day to day, had been performed. His wife and three children attempted to escape from slavery, and were re-captured. Meanwhile, he himself, returning to the region in which he was born, has found his yet surviving mother and his numerous brothers and sisters, who are living in and near Philadelphia. He has also found friends and benefactors, as he has travelled from place to place, in the enterprise of collecting the exorbitant sum which is demanded for the liberty of his wife and children.

"I have examined his papers and am convinced of their authenticity, and of his entire honesty and reliableness. The letter from the legal owner of his wife and children is especially worth studying.

"LEONARD BACON.
"New Haven, 23d June, 1854."

In New Haven, Peter remained until about the middle of July; and we find, by referring to his registry, that he received donations in that city from more than two hundred and fifty persons. In the list of his benefactors—Heaven bless them all—we find "*Carpenter's Millinery Help,*" "*Ladies in Shirt Factory,*" "*Workmen in Clock Factory,*" "*Young Ladies of Miss Dutton's School,*" "*Lancasterian School,*" "*Ladies of the Rubber Factory,*" and "*Pupils of Webster High School.*" We also find one contribution set down as— "*Money Lent.*" Yea, verily, "HE *that hath pity on the poor lendeth to the* LORD ; *that which he hath given will he pay him again.*" In the same long list we see "*Anti-Abolition,*" and then, "*A Slaveholder,*" and again, "*A Slaveholder patterning after Abolitionists.*"

After receiving three hundred dollars in New Haven, our traveller went up to Hartford, and there, also, he received three hundred dollars. Thence, with a grateful heart, he went to Wethersfield, where he remained three days, and collected twenty-one dollars. August seventh, we find him at Middletown, Ct., where in one week, he received one hundred and twenty-six dollars.

While in Middletown he encountered a lady who in consequence of marrying a Northern man, had been transplanted there from South Carolina. She assured Peter that the slaves were far better off than free negroes. "Indeed, I know all about it," said she, "for my mother owns plenty of them, and not one of them is obliged to work so hard as I do myself. Here the free negroes are begging around, many of them half-starved, and some of them stealing and going to prison."

" Yes, ma'am," answered Peter, " they do that, both white and colored. It is not the colored people alone that beg and steal; and I have been told that there are more white people in the prisons than black ones, any how."

" Well, that may be, but they are better off in the South, where they are all taken good care of."

" So I came away and left her," said Peter, as he related this incident, " but I couldn't help wishin' I knowed whether she'd like to be a happy, well-fed slave herself."

The next week he spent in Meriden, where he collected eighty dollars; and August 22d we find him at Bridgeport. Here, also, he found many friends; though at one house where he called, he met a violent rebuff. The master met him at the door; and Peter, as was his custom, modestly proffered his request—presenting at the same time his papers. The *gentleman* did not wait to examine these, but proceeded in a loud voice to curse him "mightily." "I know," cried he, "it's all a d—d lie. There's a parcel always coming round telling their lies. I don't believe one word you say. You ought to be arrested. There's a lazy pack of you that make it a business to go around whining about having families in slavery. It's time it was stopped." So saying, he turned his back upon the the suppliant; and Peter quietly walked down the steps and into the street.

On mentioning this incident in town, he learned that this gentleman himself *had property in slaves.* Another slaveholder in the same town he called upon, who received him kindly, and assured him that, *though slavery was not so bad after all as he imagined, yet he was not to blame for wishing to get his wife and children.*

Notwithstanding these slight ripples on the surface of the waters, Peter received in Bridgeport one hundred and thirty-six dollars; and on the fifteenth of September, he had found his way to New London. Here the friends of humanity contributed one hundred and fifteen dollars for his aid; and the good people of Norwich, whose charity he next besought, gave him one hundred dollars.

The first of October found him at Northampton, and though he staid not long, yet those in that town who "*had pity on the poor*" gave him forty-five dollars.

Once more Peter directed his steps toward Syracuse. How different were the emotions that now swelled his heart from those which dwelt there when he first approached that city, may be inferred from the following extract from a letter written at this time by a friend, who from the first had watched his progress with the deepest interest:

"It seemed almost a hopeless undertaking. The idea of raising five thousand dollars, by the simple recital, in his own uncultured words, of his strangely interesting story was certainly not probable; and, but for the wonderful Providences that had restored him to his mother, and for his earnest faith in the success of his project, it would have seemed like mockery to encourage him to go on. But that simple faith was mighty, and he went out. Wherever he met noble generous natures, there he presented his plea for aid— and not in vain. Many of America's proudest names are enrolled among those who delighted to encourage his true heart by kindly words and generous gifts. The blessing of the All-Merciful rest upon them! He who has said, 'Inasmuch as ye have done it unto the least of these, my brethren, ye have done it unto me,' will not forget their labor of love.

The $5,000 is ready. It is a great price to pay the mean man, who has appropriated to himself all their past years of hard labor. But they are his property— *constitutionally;* and he must be well paid for all the *care and watchfulness* which he has exercised in their behalf. How long! Oh! how long shall such mockery exist!

But little more, we trust, remains for our patient friend to do before he shall have all things arranged for the exit of those loved ones from the house of bondage. There are no doubt kind hearts that will still find pleasure in assisting to raise the sum necessary to defray their travelling expenses.

"Oh! that the journey were commenced! That journey which will end in such a joyful embrace of husband and wife, father and children; so hopelessly separated—so rapturously met. Beyond the power of the master—far from the sound of the overseer's whip; *free!* FREE ! *and all together !* Heaven speed the hour that shall bring them release !

In Syracuse he received letters from Rev. Mr. May to Rev. G. W. Hosmer, Buffalo, also to Rev. Dr. Willis, T. Henning, Esq., and Rev. J. B. Smith, of Toronto, C. W.

The eleventh of October saw him in Buffalo, where, through the kind offices of Rev. Dr. Hosmer, and Peter's friend, Mrs. Legrand Marvin, who had known him well during a previous residence of several years in Alabama, he received eighty dollars. On the thirteenth, he crossed to Toronto—not for the purpose of soliciting funds but merely " to see how his brethren (the fugitives from slavery) prospered," and " to enjoy the pleasures of treading for once upon *free soil*." Here he spent the Sabbath, visited two colored churches, and gratefully received a present of fifteen dollars.

The next Sabbath found him at the little village of Camillus, N. Y. Here he had many friends, who had long been watching his career, and praying for his ultimate success. He had not previously called on them for contributions, but at this time collections were taken up for him in both the churches. " He can suc-

ceed without our aid," said Rev. Mr. Bush, of the
Methodist Church, "*but we cannot afford to lose this opportunity.*" To this sentiment each heart responded.
During the day he received sixty-three dollars; and
heartfelt prayers were offered for his speedy re-union
to those for whose ransom he had so faithfully labored.

He now resolved to return to Burlington, and thence
to Philadelphia, for the purpose of completing the arrangements for the purchase of his family before the
coming of winter. Negotiations had been opened,
some months before, by Mr. Hallowell, a wealthy merchant of Philadelphia, with Mr. John Simpson, of
Florence, Ala., who had agreed, as soon as the requisite funds should be forwarded to him, to buy the
family for Peter. Accordingly, soon after Peter's return to Philadelphia, his friends in that city having
contributed the balance of the sum necessary to defray
the expenses of their journey, a clerk of the house of
Hallowell & Co. was sent to Florence with the money;
and with instructions to receive the family, and to conduct them to their future home among the free.

CHAPTER XXXV.

EXPERIENCE OF THE RETURNED FUGITIVES.

BEFORE noon on Saturday, the fifth of April, 1851, Vina and her children returned to their deserted cabin. Through what an age of anxiety and suffering had they passed during the three weeks which had elapsed since they forsook the shelter of its lowly roof. Then the hope of liberty had caused their hearts to throb, and their dark eyes to gleam with an unwonted light; now their hearts were hard, and still in their deep anguish, and a heavy shadow dwelt beneath their downcast eyelids.

The best of the furniture and clothing which they had left, had all been stolen and conveyed away during their absence, but this they heeded not in their despair. True, many hours of tedious toil, by night, had been required to purchase these few comforts, but now that *liberty* had been rudely snatched from their eager grasp, they had no tears to shed for minor losses.

At noon, the people came in from the field. Most of them looked wistfully upon the captured fugitives, and when they said "*Howd'y*," their voices had a mournful tone. Others, however, were glad they had been brought back, " bekase," they said, " dey's nuthin' but niggers, no how, and dey's allers so mighty good, and never gits de cowhide; now dey'll des find out how good it feels to git a cuttin' up."

After dinner, the family were sent out with the other hands to plant cotton. Ah! their labor just then was greatly needed, and for that reason, probably, the day of vengeance was postponed. They knew it was not forgotten; for dark hints were often uttered in their hearing, and threatening looks were cast upon the runaways.

In gloomy silence they pursued their regular labors, till Wednesday morning, when Mr. McKiernan, attended by Smith, the overseer, entered the field. Vina knew their errand, and her indignation rose—but she was helpless. She saw them approaching the spot where young Peter was at work, and heard them order him to strip. Poor fellow! he was wholly in their power, and he obeyed.

There stood the mother and counted the two hundred heavy lashes that fell upon the naked back of her first-born son. He bore his torture bravely. Not one cry for mercy did he utter; not one imploring look did he vouchsafe the fiends, who sought to bend his spirit; and not till they had finished, did he speak. "This is the last time," said he then to the overseer, "that you shall ever strike me. I never will be whipped again by any man."

"Hush your mouth, you d—d rascal," cried his master, "or I'll have as much more put on you."

They left the young man, and came to his mother. Smith attempted to tie her. "No, sir," said she, "I don't belong to you, and you aint gwine to whip me. Yer's my mass'r—I belong to him, and he may kill me if he want to; but I'm not gwine let you tie me nor whip me. You don't like me, and I never did like you no how. If my mass'r wants me beat, he must do it hisself."

Mr. McKiernan was sitting on his horse, but at this he dismounted, and bade the overseer give him his whip. Smith complied, and the *chivalrous* master ordered her to take off her *coat*. He then tied her hands, and gave her less than a hundred blows, a slight punishment for a runaway. He did it *very gently* too, for the skin, though sorely bruised, was not cut by the cowhide.

This done, the two worthies repaired to the blacksmith's shop, where Levin was at work; and then his manly form was bared, while the fierce lash of the overseer whizzed through the air as though it loved the sport.*

Catharine escaped the cowhide. Her master questioned her minutely concerning her knowledge of the plan of the escape, but she appeared so ignorant that he told the overseer it was not worth while to whip her. "It's that devilish Peter that's been at the bottom of all this," said he, "and I believe the Jew has done the work. There's Catherine, she didn't understand any of their plans; but her mother—d—n her, she's

---

* Neither the stocks nor the runaway's heavy irons were called into requisition, why, we know not, unless their very success in once reaching the Free States warned their master against provoking another attempt at flight. The influence of this overseer was also opposed to such exhibitions of barbarity. "Smith," Vina says, "was mons's hard to chillun, and them women whar was afeard of him, but to the rest o' the hands, he was as good as any o' the overseers."

got sense enough. It would be just like her to try it again, but she'll never go and leave her daughter. She's always doted on her girl, and I'll be d—d if I blame her, for Catharine is a devilish likely wench. So it's best to keep one of them on the island, I reckon the old woman. She wouldn't be long starting off again d—n her, if she took it into her head. She was always bound to have her own way, though to tell the truth, she's as clever a woman as ever I owned."

The next Sunday, Vina received the order to prepare to go to the island. It did not seem to move her. "I don't keer whar they sends me," said she, "any place is better 'n this yer." So with desperate promptness she packed up the few articles necessary to furnish the cabin which she was to inhabit there, and that very day she departed.

"I liked stayin' on the island a heap the best," she says, "out o' sight mostly of both mass'r and Missus. Me and them had fell out, and I didn't never want to make friends with 'em no more. I didn't keer about bein' called in every time any person was took sick, and I just determined that if they ever sent for me agin, I wouldn't go without they driv me like a dog."

Of all the beating hearts on the plantation, none thrilled with such a commingling of delight and grief at the return of Vina and her family, as did that of a maiden named Susanna.

She was a bright mulatto, the daughter of "Aunt Patsey," who for the last few years, had taken charge of the young children. Susanna was a quiet well-behaved girl, that had been *raised* on the place, and ever since they were children, young Peter and herself had loved each other. But when his father went away, and left to his family the assurance that if he lived they should be free. Peter determined to obey his counsel; and so the union of the devoted pair was postponed for an indefinite period.

Now that their great effort to achieve their liberty had failed, the young man's heart would whisper that perhaps his father would consider his request no longer binding. Yet he kept these thoughts hid deep in his own breast, for he saw that in his mother's heart, all hope of freedom was not yet extinct.

But the master's watchful eye had long noticed their attachment, and, imagining that if Peter had a wife he would be less likely to run off again, he determined that now they should be married. No favorable opportunity however occurred for him to urge the matter, until the crop was laid by in August; when, according to his annual custom, he gave his slaves a barbacue. Then he determined that the marriage should take place.

The long trench was duly prepared with its bed of glowing coals, over which were roasting numerous pigs and chickens, with the flesh of sheep and oxen in abundance. Peter was aiding in the preparation of the feast, when he was summoned into the presence of his master.

"How would you like to marry Susanna, boy?"

"I don't care about marryin' any body now, Sir."

"But Susanna says she loves you, and you ought to have her."

"No, Sir, I don't care about marryin' without my people's willin'."

"It's no matter about your mother, boy, I give you

leave, and you needn't ask her anything about it. Go and dress yourself."

"I've got nothin' to dress in."

"Well, go and put on clean clothes, any how, and then come back to me."

Peter went to his mother's cabin. For a time he hesitated, but his master's command was absolute, and he had bid him hasten. His long-years' love for Susanna was not silent, but that voice he knew how to quell at duty's bidding. His mother, he could not bear to vex her.

Half undecided what course would be the wisest, he dressed mechanically in clean working-clothes. (He had a suit of Sunday clothes which he had bought himself, but these he would not wear to please his master) His toilette completed, he sat down again to think. He could not long defer his decision, for his master would be as angry at his delay, as if he should refuse obedience to his orders; so at last, scarcely knowing whether he was doing right or wrong, he left the cabin, and approached the spot where he had left McKiernan.

Susanna, having previously received an order from her master to dress and come to him, was already there.

One of their fellow-slaves, a preacher, named William Handy was now called to marry them; and in a few minutes they were marching around the field at the head of a troop of their young companions, who with gay songs and merry laughter were celebrating the marriage of their friends.

Vina soon heard what had occurred; but she was one of the cooks, and she continued quietly to baste the meat, though every moment her wrath was rising higher. Levin stood by her side, and he, too, was indignant. Soon the master approached. " Why don't you march with the others?" said he to Vina.

" I aint a soldier," replied she, " and I don't know nuthin' about marchin'."

" Why, what is the matter with you?"

" Nuthin' more'n common; and things that's common yer is shockin' to strangers."

" What's that?   Say that again."

She repeated her words. " There's not a plantation in a million o' miles whar thar's such works as thar is yar."

" Better mind how you talk, girl, or I'll give you a slap."

" I don't keer what you do. I would n't keer if you killed him and me too. You've done made a heap o' matches, and none of 'em never prospered, no how."

" Oh, I was so mad!" she says, " every time I looked down, 'peared like I could see sparks o' fire a comin' out o' my eyes. Then he went to the house and told the missus I was powerful mad. She 'lowed he ought to be ashamed o' himself, kase she said he'd done me mean, and she did n't blame me if I was mad. Well, he said, when they wanted to marry, nobody should n't hinder 'em. He'd marry 'em hisself when he liked."

The young people lived in the cabin with Aunt Patsey, and for some time the current of their lives flowed calmly on. After about a year, a little boy was folded to Susanna's breast—a fine, " peart," healthy child. She named him Edmund; and he soon became very dear to the hearts of all his kindred. But Vina, now that the tide which had whelmed her in despair had fallen, lived in hourly expectation of a summons to her husband; and she was sad at the advent of this little one. She, too, loved the baby dearly; but she knew it formed another tie to bind the young father fast to slave-land.

When little Edmund was a few months old, he was seized with whooping-cough, and then he needed his mother's care. But she was forced to go each morning to the field; and though Aunt Patsey was not heedless of her little grandchild, yet she had so many children to look after that she could not always watch him. So he took cold, and then his cough became worse; and week after week, he continued to grow weaker, till it was plain that he could live but little longer.

Oh! how his mother longed to stay in and nurse him for the last few days! But in vain she begged this privilege of the overseer—and when, in her sorrow, she sought her mistress, who had seen four of her own little ones laid in the grave, the lady sharply bade her "Go out to work." "It's no use," said she, "for you to stay in—you don't know how to take care of children—if you did, your baby never would have been so bad."

A week later, a messenger was sent to the field to bid Peter and his wife *come and see the last of their child;* and, first obtaining permission of the overseer, they hastened to the cabin. The baby did not know them now—and though the young mother fondly kissed his lips, and breathed his name in tenderest accents, she could awake no answering smile. A fierce convulsion shook his little frame—it passed—the child was dead.

Fond mother, who hast watched thy little one by day and night, until the angels bore him from thy arms, rememberest thou the anguish of that hour? What torture would have rent thy heart if thou hadst seen him wasting—dying, and all for lack of care — while thou wast forced to toil for the gain of a remorseless tyrant! God pity the mother who is doomed to live—a slave!

" Ah, well," said the mistress, when they told her that Susanna's child was dead—" it will be better off. My life is nearly worried out of me by sick children, and I am sure I wouldn't care if they were all dead. It is just as well for Susanna, for it never would have done her any good if it had lived."

Early in the spring of 1854, another son was born unto them, and this they called Peter. Vina had now come down from the Island, and had resumed the office of general nurse, which she had filled for many years; and when little Peter was five weeks old, the master asked her if she thought Susanna was well enough to go out.

" No, Sir," replied she, " she aint over and above strong, no how, and she oughtent to go out when the weather's so bad."

" Well, if you think so, I will give her another week."

But the overseer was " pushed," and before three days, Susanna was sent out to the field. A heavy rain came on soon after, which was followed by a chilling wind.

" Please, Sir," said the young mother, " may I go to the house? I'm mighty cold, and my side aches powerful."

"No, no; you used to be smart enough, but now you're always complaining, and getting to be no account. Go 'long to your work."

A week longer she labored, but by that time she became so very ill that they could force her to go out no more. The doctor was called, but he could do but little to relieve her.

Month after month she lay in the cabin a patient sufferer, and watched with a mother's interest the growth of her little Peter. Poor baby, he was weak and sickly, and she often wished that she might take him with her to that better land, where there is neither toil, nor pain, nor sorrow.

"Don't stay long," said Susanna, as she saw Peter going out of the cabin one Sunday morning in August, "it's lonesome when you're gone."

He returned and sat down by her side. All day she talked sweetly to him of that blest home to which she was hastening; for "Susanna was a religious girl," and her long, lonely days of sickness she had spent in thinking of the happy land above. "I'm gwine away from you now, Peter," said she, "but I shall leave our little baby with you. You'll take good care of him for my sake—won't you? O Peter, you'll be lonesome when I'm gone, but you must think I'm happy; and it wont be long before you'll come too."

Her eyes grew very bright as she thus strove to comfort her sorrowing young husband; but when the sun went down her eyelids closed—*she had gone home.*

CHAPTER XXXVI.

"THEY TAKE GOOD CARE OF THEIR PROPERTY."

For more than two years after her return from "*dat dar jaunt to de Norf*," Vina remained upon the island. Sometimes both of her sons were with her there; but Catharine was kept constantly upon the home place.

"Well, girl," said her master, some months after her return, "do you remember the road you travelled when that rascal carried you all off?"

"Yes, Sir," replied Vina, "I remember every inch I went; and I could go over it again with my eyes shot."

The boys also were questioned concerning their knowledge of the route, and they gave similar answers; "though to tell the truth," says Vina, "I should n't know no more about it when I got off o' the river, than if I was blind."

Their prompt assertions that they knew "every inch of the road," did not diminish their master's fear that they might repeat the attempt to escape, and he determined to take every possible means to prevent another trial. But he could not control his own base passions; and though Vina never smiled, and seldom spoke cheerfully in his presence, his evil nature impelled him

to make one more effort to accomplish the base purpose in which, years before, she had so signally foiled
him. Her gloom, the consequence of disappointed
hope and stern resolve to make another effort to escape
his hated rule, he construed into the effect of shame at
her disgrace; and now, if ever, he deemed he might
succeed in depriving her of her honor.

It was winter. She was upon the island engaged in
picking up trash and burning it to prepare the land for
plowing.

The master came, and sat down by the fire. She
took no notice of his approach, but continued picking
up the rubbish, and adding it to the heap.

"Vina! O, Vina!"

She did not answer—there was something in his
tone that made her angry.

"Girl! O, Girl! Come here!"

She turned her head towards him, but continued her
work.

"Here—this fire don't burn much."

"No, sir—its just kindled—it'll burn to-reck'ly."

"Well, you bring some more trash to crowd in
here."

She brought him a handful of sticks.

"Look here, Vina," said he in his most insinuating
tone, "I intend to stay here on the island to-night—
won't you come to my house, and stay with me?"

"What you mean, sir, by askin' me such a thing as
that? *You mought as well sing a psalm to a dead cow
as to name such a thing as that to me.* I hav n't forgot
how you've used me and my chillern just bekase I
done what any person else would do. I did n't do no
wrong, and I ain't ashamed o' goin' off; but you ought

to be ashamed, sir, to talk to me this way—after my knowin' all about you that I do."

"Well, now look here," urged the *gracious* master, "I've forgiven all that—it's all dead and buried."

"No, sir, it ain't buried so but what I can scratch it up, and it never will be forgot—not by me."

"Well, won't you come to my house? If you will, I'll do all I can for you; and you never shall want for anything."

"No, sir, I never will come to your house. Thar's a little old hut yon', that you built for me, whar don't keep the rain out nights; I cun stay thar like I has done. You think I done forgot seein' poor Lydia, only a few months ago, bucked down afore that very door o' yourn, and all the five hundred blows the poor thing tuck just for you?"

"Well, I did n't do that."

"No, sir, but your son did; and your wife sent him the note tellin' him to whip her till he just left the breath o' life in her, and Aunt Lucy heard him a readin' the note. Thar in the mornin', when thar's a white fross on the ground, she was stripped by your son—a right young man, not of age yet, and beat with whips and an oak paddle as thick as my hand till the breath was a'most gone out of her body. That too, after you'd whipped her yourself for killin' her child. She would n't a killed it only 'twas yourn, and she knowed what she'd suffer about it if it was seen.* You mighty good—it's all honey till you gits girls into trouble, and then you walks off—and leaves 'em to

---

* The whole history of the affair here referred to is in the possession of the writer, but it is too horrid for publication.

b'ar all the 'buse they gits. And it's good enough for 'em if they'll be fooled by you when they knows you so well. Now, would n't it be mighty strange if I did n't hate you, knowin' so much about your ways as I does. I tell you, sir, I never did like you, and I never shall."

"The devil! Don't you stand there, and tell me you don't like me."

"Well, sir, it ain't no hurt to tell the truth; and that is so—I don't like you, and I don't want to hear no more such talk as you talked to me to-day."

"Well, you think of it," said he, returning to his softest tone—"and you'd better do as I want you to."

"It's no use talkin'—I'll never put myself in your power while I live."

"What's that girl's name of yours?"

"What girl?"

"Why, your daughter, there."

"You knows her name, sir, just as well as I does. You done knowed her from the day she's born. Her name Catharine—why, what you gwine say 'bout her?"

"I say she's a devilish likely girl, and I ——"

"Now, mass'r I wants to tell you—if you ever comes a foolin' round her, you'll be sorry. You know I never said I'd do a thing, but I done it, or least ways, tried; and if my girl ever consents to your mean ways, I'll kill her or you—one. I ruther die a peaceable death 'an to be hung, but just as sure as you meddles with my daughter, I'll do what I say. I ain't gwine to see her like the other girls yer, whar you been the means o' gettin' all cut to pieces."

The master walked away. He had listened to such

a lecture as he seldom received ; and from that time he ceased to torment the resolute woman that dared to speak the truth even to his face. Vina was very impudent. He might have killed her on the spot; but she knew he would not strike her. Her just and fearless words, slave though she was, shielded herself and the daughter that she loved from further insults.

Notwithstanding that during their absence their cabin had been robbed of nearly all its comforts, yet on their return from their unfortunate journey Northward, Vina and her family resumed their former industrious habits. The boys cultivated their patches as had been their custom, and saved every penny which they gained, in order to fulfil their father's injunction — to provide every thing needful for their mother's comfort. Meantime, Vina and Catharine labored faithfully both nights and Sundays, and the well-mended garments and warm stockings that the brothers wore testified to the skill with which their fingers wrought.

During the summer of 1853 the patches yielded well, and the people had all their little crops secured before Christmas. They were obliged to sell them to their master, as had ever been his rule; and when they were all ready, the overseer weighed the corn and cotton they had raised, and promised them to see that *all was right*. The master affected to rejoice in their success ; and told them to come to him *the first day of Christmas*, and he would pay them.

Accordingly, when Christmas came they all, accompanied by the overseer, went to the house to receive their money.

" Well, well," said the master, " I havn't got the

money now; but I'll tell you what I'll do. Every one
of you, big and little, that wants to go to town, may
go to-morrow,—and I'll go too, and pay you all in
town. I've got the promise of some money that is
due me there to-morrow."

"Aha!" said Vina, as they came away, "I know
how it will be—you all won't git no money to-morrow.
He aint gwine pay no money, and I wont go."

But her companions could not believe that their
master would thus deceive them; and the next morning the whole plantation force climbed into the huge
wagons and took the road to Tuscumbia.

To one unused to *Christmas sights* in slave-land a
more grotesque spectacle than was presented by these
loaded wagons could scarcely be imagined. There
were old women with red and yellow turbans—stiff-
starched and tall—and a score of boys and girls—some
with bare heads, and others glorying in comical old
rimless hats and bonnets, in styles unknown to Paris
milliners.

Then there were sage uncles and prim young girls
who were anxious to show off their best behavior
"gwine to town"—and these sat up stately and stiff;
while those less dignified, with laugh, and song, and
frolic, and grimace, reminded them that "*Christmas
time*" would not last all the year.

The master met them as he had promised at the
store of Mr. N—, and there, instead of paying them
the money he selected a lot of poor damaged calico,
and called the women to choose each of them a dress.
They looked at each other in consternation. Here
was the fruit of all their toil! Nights and holidays
they had spent for this—a few yards of mean thin

calico, that would not pay for making up. Their eyes rolled angrily and their lips pouted the displeasure which they dared not speak; and so the calico was measured off, though in their hearts they scorned the mean-spirited wretch who could thus stoop to cheat them.

One or two, however, rebelled. Catharine went quietly and selected something for herself. " Ugh!" said her master, "that's too dear."

" Well," said she, "if I can't have that, I don't want none at all."

He finally yielded and allowed her to take what she had chosen. But when Amanda, a middle-aged woman, followed her example, and sought such goods as would make comfortable clothes for her children, he swore she should take such as the others had, or none at all.

"No, sir," said she, "I wouldn't walk out de store with such stuff as dat dar. I done worked hard all dis year to make a crap, and I don't want to be cheated now. I got a house full of chillern, and dey's all mighty nigh naked, and I want something decent to make clothes for 'em.''

" Hush your mouth! you huzzy!" cried her master, "you shall take what I give you."

" Well, sir, if you dont git me what I want, I'll git it 'fore de year's out. If I can't git full pay for my crap one way, I will another."

He raised his hand to strike her.

" I don't keer if you does whip me. I'm gwine to have my rights if I cun git 'em."

This *peculiar* shopping ended, the whole company returned home in ill humor. " I told you so," said

Vina, "I knowed he wasn't gwine to pay you all for yer craps. He didn't have no money promised him in town, no how. That's the reason I wouldn't go. I wasn't gwine to foller him off to town for money, when I knowed he wasn't gwine to give it."

Vina had not been many months on the island before her mistress began to wish for her presence on the home place. She was an excellent nurse in sickness, and for many years she had been called in to wait upon any of the white family that chanced to be ill; and so faithful and competent was she, that when Vina was in the sick-room the mother felt no uneasiness. Among the slaves her field was wider, for there, unless in extraordinary cases, she was both doctor and nurse.

At last Mrs. McKiernan told her husband that they must get Vina back, or they never should raise any more children. "The trouble with them commenced," said she, "when Vina and her family first ran off, and since that time there has been nothing but bad luck with both the women and children. There's Delphia might have been alive now if it hadn't been for those fools of doctors."

"Well, Vina," said the master, when she had been more than two years on the island, "how would you like to go back to the low place?"

"I don't keer 'bout gwine back, sir."

"But your mistress says she would like to have you back. Several of the women will be sick soon, and she wants you there."

"I don't want nuthin' to do with 'em, sir; you done sent me off yer out o' spite, and now the sick ones may

take care o' their selves.   I ain't gwine to be runnin'
after 'cm."

"Well, if you don't go now, you may not get a
chance when you do want to go."

"I don't keer nuthin' 'bout it, sir; I don't want to
go thar, never."

After a few weeks, however, she packed up the few
cooking utensils which she had there with two or three
other articles of furniture, and went home to the cabin
which Peter had built for her so many years before.
Still she was dark and gloomy—her heart had lost its
light; and though she did not quite despair, yet her
chance of meeting her beloved husband seemed to
lessen day by day.   But now there was much sickness
on the place; and in sympathy with the suffering of
her sisters, she found transient forgetfulness of her own
griefs.

Delphia, to whom reference was made by Mrs. Mc-
Kiernan, died a few days after Vina ran off; and her
story, though it reveals a course of cruelty too base
even for savages, shows but another phase of slavery.

Smith, the overseer, at that time, was severe, as has
before been stated, only towards children, or those
women who were afraid of him.   "He knowed," says
Vina, "the people mostly would fight him if he tried
to beat 'em, and so he managed to do without much
beatin'.   But them whar's feared of him fared mons's
hard—'pears like he never knows when to stop, if he
gits mad at one o' them kind."

Smith had a great deal of company on Sundays;
and as the overseers are furnished by their employers
with corn and bacon for their families, as well as flour,

coffee, and sugar, so many guests were quite expensive to Mr. McKiernan.

One Sunday afternoon, he walked down to the quarter, and saw two horses hitched at the overseer's gate.

" Whose horses are these ?" asked he of a group of women that stood near.

Delphia chanced to reply.

" Smith has a heap of company, don't he?" said the master.

" Yes, sir," said Delphia, " last Sunday thar was six horses hitched to his fence, and every one of 'em was carried off, and fed."

Some evil-minded tale-bearer took the first opportunity to report this conversation to the overseer; and he was enraged.

A few days after, the master plainly expressed his opinion to Mr. Smith respecting the number of his guests, adding that he knew it was so, for he saw them there himself.

" You did not see them," said Smith, " you were not in sight when they were here. Some nigger has told you; and it is no other than that lying, tattling wench, Delphia."

From that hour he vowed vengeance on the poor woman; swearing at the same time there were other ways to kill a cow besides shooting her or knocking her in the head.

Thereafter, he never gave Delphia a moment's rest. She was one of the plow women; and though she was not in a condition to bear extreme fatigue, he compelled her day after day to plow with her mule in a trot. She dared not stop, for his eye was ever on her;

and when the other women told her she was killing herself, she only replied, " You know how Smith hates me, and he will beat me to death if I don't mind him."

Thus week after week, she ran all day in the plow, till at last she was forced to stop, and she went, with her mule, to the quarter.   Smith was at his house, and he saw her coming.

" What are you there for ;" cried he.

" I'm sick, sir, I can't work."

" No, you're not sick.   You need n't put out your mule—tie him there ; and in just two hours you shall go out again.   I'll give you that long to rest."

She went into her cabin, and in less than two hours the doctor was sent for.   Before night, poor Delphia lay still and cold in death, with her dead baby by her side.

As two of her fellow-slaves were digging her grave the overseer came up.   He jumped down into the narrow house they were hollowing for his victim— " There," said he with an oath, " this is the place where all liars and tattlers ought to go."

But that not the overseers alone were spiteful and even murderous in their barbarity, may be inferred from the following incident, which occurred soon after Vina went home from the island.

A woman, named Leah, was taken sick in the field, and her master being near, she went to him for permission to go to the house.

" What the devil do you want to go to the house for ?"

" I'm sick, sir."

"Sick, d—n you! go to work; and if I hear any more of your complaining, I'll give you something to complain about." So saying, he gave her a few cuts with his cowhide, in token of what she might expect if she repeated her request, and she went back.

But she grew worse; and not daring to leave the field without permission, she went again to her master.

"It's a devilish lie. You are not sick; if you are, I can cure you." With these words he flew at her, and beat her cruelly; after which, with kicks and curses, he sent her back to her work.

It was impossible for her to remain much longer. She started to leave the field, and Vina, who had been a witness of the scene, followed her to her cabin. We give what followed in her own words.

"In about a half hour, her child was born, and such a sight as that child was would make any person cry that has any heart at all. * * * * *
* * * * * * * * * *
The overseer's wife was thar, and she was shocked mightily. She called her husband, and he come and looked at it; and two gentlemen, whar was thar a visitin' him, they see it too; and they all 'lowed they never see nuthin' like it in all their lives.

"Well, I staid, and done all I could for Leah, and dressed the baby—for it was livin' after all, and when I got all done, I went up to the house to tell Missus. Mass'r was a sittin' by, but I never stopped for him— I told her the whole story, and all about the beatin' too. She hated it mightily, partic'lar when I told her 'bout the overseer and them other two white men seein' it. 'That's just like you,' says she to Mass'r, 'you're always bringing some disgrace on this plantation. The report of this will go all over the country.'

" 'Why, I did'nt know she was sick,' says he.

" ' Yes, you did know it, she told you she was sick, and if she had not, you might have known better than to beat her so, and she in such a state. You did it on purpose to disgrace yourself, and the plantation, it is just like you. I'll order my carriage, and go away till the talk about this is over. It is just the way you always do—just like you.'

" That's all the comfort Leah got from Missus. She was mighty sorry to have folks know such works was a gwine on, but she didn't never do much for them whar was a sufferin'. If she could keep cl'ar o' the disgrace, that thar was all she cared for.

"Leah's baby lived a week, and I reckon it was a good thing it died, for 'peared like it suffered a heap all the time. Oh ! it aint no wonder so many o' their chillun dies, its more wonder that any of 'em lives when the women has to b'ar so much."

CHAPTER XXXVII.

THE RE-UNION.

Towards the close of the year 1854, their being no immediate need of Vina's presence on the "low place," she went back to the island. Susanna had died during the summer, and now the boys were both with their mother, leaving Catharine sole tenant of the old *home cabin*.

"The island," although it was five miles above the home plantation, was not a lonely place. There were good neighbors on the river bank opposite, and with some of these, the slaves who were kept here, formed lasting friendships; even Vina, though she had been so morose and sad during these last years, had not been unmindful of the sympathy of her own people.

On Sunday morning, December seventeenth, as she was sitting alone in her cabin, a woman belonging to Mr. Hawkins, who owned a plantation on the North bank of the river, came over to pay her a visit.

"What do you think, Vina?" said she, as soon as she was sure there were no listeners, "I heard a great secret in town last night."

"Oh, I don't know what I thinks till I yers what it's about," replied Vina.

"*Well, Peter's sent for you all! and dar's a man in*

town whar's come from some place 'way off to de Norf dar, to tote you all off."

"How does you know?" asked Vina, her eyes dilated, and her whole frame trembling with excitement.

" Why, I's to town last night to Mr. Simpson's store, and I yer Mr. Simpson say so hisself. Dey all's a makin' out de papers, and dey'll send for you 'fore many days."

The visitor soon departed, and Vina sat down to think, but her brain whirled, and she was glad when her sons came in, that she might share with them the great joy that was swelling in her heart. She did not for one moment doubt the truth of the report, for it was what she had expected. O poor faithful loving heart! thou hast borne grief with patience, wait but a little longer, and thy joy shall overflow.

The mother and her sons now held a consultation on the most judicious course for them to take; and they determined to say nothing on the subject until they should hear more. Catharine they could not see before the next Sunday. Oh, how they wished that she could share this joy.

On Monday morning, they went to work, as usual. The bright glad hope with which their hearts were warm shone not in their dark faces, they had schooled their features to wear ever the same calm look. Full well they knew that any change of countenance might be construed into a token of some hidden hope. Slaves must not seem to hope for aught save Christmas Holidays, though they may laugh, and dance, and sing, so they evince no *thought* beyond the present.

Soon after midnight the next Wednesday, the island people were all called up. They were to kill hogs that day, and every one upon the place was obliged to be in motion.

Great fires were built here and there for scalding the fated animals, and sharp knives, gleaming in their strange light, seemed impatient to begin the sport. Soon all was noise and bustle. The merry butchers talked and laughed, their victims squealed, and grave old women scolded at the trifling of the youngsters; for though the day's work was no trifle, it was a change in their monotonous life, and fun and frolic reigned.

About ten o'clock in the morning, Vina, who amid all the confusion, was watching for a messenger, saw her master coming up the hill from the river. He walked towards the cabins, and soon called—"Vina! O Vina!"

She strove to quell the tumultuous throbbings of her heart, and she succeeded in subduing all appearance of emotion—so that when she reached the spot where the master stood, her face was calm, and her voice was clear as usual.

" Well, Vina," said he, " how would you like to see Peter ?"

" Mons's well, Sir," replied she.

" Do you know where he is ?"

" I reckon, sir, he's in Cincinnati."

" No—he lives in Philadelphia, and he's bought you all."

" *Bought us ?*"

" Yes, he's bought you ;—how would you like to go to him ?"

" Why, if it's true, sir, I'd like to go mighty well."

" *If it's true ?*—don't you believe it ?"

" I don't know, sir, whether I believes it or not."

"Well, don't you suppose I can sell you if I choose?—Don't you belong to me?"

"Yes, sir, I know you can."

"Well, if you want to go, make haste and get yourselves ready; for I've got to carry you all over to Florence to-night. There's a man there, who has come for you—he can tell you all about Peter. You ought to have been there before now, but you are all so devilish hard to hear that I had to hallo there for a boat, 'till I'm right hoarse."

"We didn't hear you, Sir—the hogs kept such a fuss."

"I know—I know—but you all must hurry yourselves now."

He then went to the boys, and told the news to them; but they, too, made strange of it, and seemed to doubt his words.

"Well," said he, "you all act like you don't believe me—now, I'm no ways anxious to sell you, and if you don't want to go, you can stay. But if you do want to go, you must get ready devilish quick, for I must have you in Florence to-night; and we must cross the river before dark."

The mother and her sons entered their cabin, and hastily gathering up such of their things as they could carry easiest, they hastened to the river. Among their fellow-slaves were many whom they counted friends, but even to these they had no time to say "Good bye." Crossing to the main land in a canoe, they sprang into the wagon which waited for them there, and drove toward home, the master riding by their side.

As soon as they arrived at the quarter, he called the

overseer. "See here, Smith, get on your horse, and go quick and tell Catharine to come here. Ride fast; for I'm in a devil of a hurry."

Away went the overseer to the clearing, where he found Catharine busy chopping down a tree. "Here, Girl," cried he, "give me your axe—go quick to the house—you're sold, and your master sent me for you in a hurry."

Half bewildered, yet guessing the truth, Catharine walked as fast as possible towards the quarter. Her mother's figure was the first that met her eye. Then her pulse beat quicker—she bounded towards her.

"Mother, what is it?"

"Why, yer father's sent for us, chile—leastways Mass'r says so."

"Has he done bought us?"

"Yes; so your Mass'r says."

"I don't want no more!" cried the girl, as with eager hands she assisted her mother in their hasty preparations.

The master remained in sight, and every minute shouted to them to hurry, or they could not cross the river; thus confusing them so that they could think of nothing. Vina wished to see her mistress, who owed her about three dollars for chickens, and had promised her the money on Christmas. Vina knew that *she* would not refuse to pay her now, but Mr. McKiernan would not let her go. "Never mind," said he, "I'll pay you when we get to town."

"Wouldn't you like to take your little grandchild with you?" asked the master.

"Yes, sir," said Vina, "if I could—how much you ask for him?"

"Oh, a trifle!" replied he, "I'd sell him to you for a trifle—perhaps a hundred dollars."

"Well, Sir, here's all my things; they cost a heap o' money, and, if I had time, I could sell 'em all."

"I'll pay you for them when we get to town: but come—hurry yourself."

Vina understood the value of his promise to pay her for the goods she left behind; but she was helpless. She threw a change of clothes for each of them into her trunk—she had no time to select the best—and tying up her feather bed which Peter had bought for her nine years before, she said "Good bye" to a few mothers, who chanced just then to come in from the field to nurse their babies, and left her cabin—to return no more.

Notwithstanding all their haste, they were not in time to cross the river before dark; and so they staid at Mr. Wm. Jackson's till morning, when they went into town.

They stopped at Mr. Simpson's store, where the papers were to be signed; and here they saw the young gentleman who had been sent for them.

It was a cold raw, day, and the slaves were shivering in their plantation clothes. "I wish, Sir," said Vina to her master, as they stood in the chilling wind, "you'd give me money enough to buy me a thick shawl."

"Why, Girl," said he, "I could n't do it. I came from home in such a hurry, that I did n't have time to get any small change—I have nothing with me less than a ten-dollar bill."

"Seems to me," said his son-in-law, who stood by, "these niggers are poorly dressed to be for sale; you might get her the shawl now, and pay for it some other time,"

"Oh!" said Mr. McKiernan, " they've got better clothes, but they won't put them on."

Vina thought of his promise to pay her for the chickens, and also for the goods she left behind ; but she determined not to ask him again, herself. So when she saw a crowd of gentlemen standing around, she sent Peter to tell him that she wanted the money for the chickens.

" Why, Boy," said he, feeling in his pocket, "I have no money smaller than ten dollars."

Vina was listening. " Yes," cried she, when she heard his answer, " so I thought when you would n't let me stop to see Missus. I knowed you was n't gwine pay me in town."

"McKiernan, d—n it," said one that stood by " why don't you give your servants something? You ought to give them a present for the good they've done you."

He muttered something to himself, but made no answer.

After awhile Peter went to him again, and asked him *how much he would take for his baby.* Poor Susanna's dying words rang in his ears, and it seemed as if he could not go and leave her child, that she had so solemnly committed to his charge.

"The baby, eh? Oh, you may have it for two hundred dollars."

The young father's hopes were dashed. He could not raise so large a sum as he had learned that the funds sent by his father were barely sufficient to defray the travelling expenses of the family.

"I say, McKiernan," said a gentleman in the crowd, who pitied the distress of the slave-father, "I think you ought to give that old woman her grandchild— I heard you say she has always been a good servant—that you never struck her a lick, and that she never deserved one—and that her family have always behaved themselves well. Give them the little one for good measure."

"Oh, I'll sell the child cheap to them."

"Ha! sell it! They've no money to buy it. Give it to them—that would be no more than fair."

Said another, "Where in the world did Peter get the money to buy his family?"

"Oh," replied McKiernan, "he's got rich relations; his friends are all wealthy. I saw one of his brothers last year in Philadelphia—William Still is his name. He is rich, and a devilish likely fellow too. He keeps the Anti-Slavery Office. I was in there twice, myself, and I saw him write a hand that I could n't beat, nor you either."

"What office, did you say?"

"The Anti-Slavery Office. Ha! ha! I was as good an Abolitionist as any of them while I was there. I tell you—that William Still is a fine fellow. Another of the brothers has a store, and Peter I believe owns half of it."

The business was at last concluded, and soon after the stage drove up that was to convey them to Eastport. There they were to take the boat which could come up no higher on account of the low state of the water in the river.

"When we got in the stage," says Vina, "I felt free. 'Peared like I didn't weigh no more'n a feather."

" Aha !" said Catharine, looking down with ineffable contempt upon her soiled and tattered garb, " reckon when I git whar father is, I'll drap off these old duds."

" Why ?" said her mother, I don't reckon he's got any new clothes for you."

" But didn't Mass'r say he got a store ?"

" Pshaw ! child, don't believe all he says."

" I believe that, for he never would have said such a thing, if it wasn't so."

The young gentleman who had them in charge was closely questioned by the Captain of the boat, and by sundry other officious persons at Waterloo—a little village on the north side of the river, nearly opposite Eastport. He was, however, allowed to go on board with them, and they were glad, for soon they had their supper—the first food they had tasted since daylight in the morning.

All went smoothly till they reached Paducah. Here they were obliged to change boats, and again was their young guardian subjected to a series of impertinent questioning, as to what he was going to do with the negroes, &c. He at length succeeded in transferring his charge to a Louisville boat; but the captain of this was exceedingly uneasy about the slaves—he having seen them when Mr. McKiernan was conveying them back to slavery—nearly four years before. This young man was evidently from the North; indeed he did not scruple to confess it; *and if he should be running these niggers off, and if his boat should bear him on in the commission of such treason against the Constitution and the Union,* alas! what ruin would ensue. Yet he had straight papers, and did not act in the least like an Abolitionist so after much deliberation, he concluded to let them come on board; but at the same time he resolved to watch them well, lest the fellow should play some *Yankee trick.*

They arrived at Louisville in safety, and lost no time in seeking a boat for Cincinnati. But lo! the valorous captain of the packet they had just left was there before them, and his sage warning procured from the commander of the Cincinnati boat a stout refusal to take them on. Their young guardian was now sorely perplexed; but fortunately he recollected that he had an acquaintance in Louisville, who was a merchant of some note. To this gentleman he hastened in his extremity, and by *his* influence with the cautious captain, he at length secured a passage for himself and the four ransomed slaves to Cincinnati.

The nearer they approached the end of their long journey, the more restless and impatient grew the mother. She had learned to bear suspense and sorrow. She had waited and been patient; but this rapid and sure approach towards the fulfilment of her hopes was strange and new. She could not eat nor sleep for very joy. The attention of her children, however, was more easily diverted by surrounding objects, and as the boys found occasional employment on the boat, the hours to them were far from wearisome.

They all suffered exceedingly from cold. Their clothes were thin and old; but what cared he who clutched in his hard grasp the avails of all their years of toil, beside the five thousand dollars for their ransom?—what cared he if they should perish by the way? *He held the gold.*

It was the morning of the Sabbath—the last day of

the year 1854. Peter rose very early, and walked down to the wharf. He had been in Cincinnati for a week, waiting to greet his loved ones—how long the hours had seemed while his heart trembled between hope and fear. One hour he felt sure that he should soon clasp in his fond arms the precious forms of wife and children—the next, a hundred fears arose that all his hopes, even now, were doomed to disappointment. He had not heard from them since from the papers he had learned of their return to slavery, perhaps—Oh! how the thought now shook the fabric of his hopes— perhaps to torture and to death. Four summers had passed since then—four seasons where fearful sickness is wont to make its annual visits to the dark, unhealthy quarters of the slave.

But on this holy Sabbath morning, these fears no longer vexed him; for but a few hours had passed since the telegraph had brought him tidings of the safe approach of those for whom he waited.

He stepped on board the "Northerner," and the first man he met was the agent of Mr. Hallowell. A moment more, and wife and daughter—both were clasped to his true heart, while on each side his manly sons, with grateful reverence, gazed upon their father's face.

In that embrace no toil or sorrow was remembered; their swelling hearts had only room for love and gratitude, and praise to Him who had not betrayed their trust.

At the home of Levi Coffin the ransomed family were welcome; and as that good man himself received them there, his kind heart thrilled with a delicious joy, in which the angels sympathized.

Rest ye, poor hunted ones. No more shall "Christian wolves" prowl along your pathway, for the golden hand of charity hath taken from their cruel fangs the power to do you harm. Aye, ye are free! How changed from the poor trembling fugitives that so lately feared the echo of your own unequal footsteps. Rejoice! for gold hath power when justice fails. Be glad! for mercy lives, though on the fairest portion of our country's wide domain her hands are chained—her tongue is silent.

The news of this glad re-union spread rapidly among the citizens of Cincinnati, and on two successive evening, public meetings were held for the benefit of the shivering strangers. Gifts of warm clothing, and of money to defray the expenses of their journey onward, were gladly offered by those who love to "clothe the naked," and who rejoice in the "setting at liberty of those who were bound." Many worthy persons also proposed to entertain the family at their houses, but being already settled at Mr. Coffin's, they deemed it wisest to remain there during their stay in town.

On the third of January they left for Pittsburg. There, also, they were received with joy; for Peter's story had found interested listeners in that city, as he had passed to and fro between Cincinnati and Philadelphia.

While they remained at Pittsburg, a meeting was held for them in the Bethel Church, at which the whole family appeared in the clothes they wore from the plantation. The grateful joy of the father, which beamed so brightly from his smiling face, and the shrinking modesty of those who had been redeemed from bondage through his patient efforts, will be long remembered by those kind friends who there offered them the greetings of the free.

On the tenth, the travellers reached Philadelphia, but here they made no stop. Poor Vina was, by this time, quite worn out by excitement and fatigue, and all the family were suffering from colds contracted on the river. So they hastened on to Burlington, where Peter had previously made provision for their reception in the family of a colored friend.

Often, during Peter's weary wanderings here and there, while collecting money for the ransom of his family, was the momentous question asked, "*What will they do when they are free?*" To answer this important inquiry is all that now remains.

The first few days were spent by the re-united family in resting from the tedious journey, and in rendering themselves presentable to the new relatives and friends that longed to greet them. Then came the delightful visit to Peter's aged mother. She had heard of their arrival in Cincinnati, and had been, for some days, expecting them at her home.

We need not picture the glad meeting of the venerable woman with the wife and children of her long-lost son. The sight of their happy faces filled her heart with holy gratitude; for in each form so lately released from slavery's hated chains, she saw a living witness of her Great Father's love. Year after year her heart had sorrowed for her sons; and now, like Israel to Joseph, she could say, "I had not thought to see thy face, and lo, God hath showed me also thy seed."

But even in that glad circle beat one sorrowing

heart. Young Peter turned sadly from the joyful greetings of his new-found kindred, for the sound of a little voice rang in his ears. "*I am not there, my father!*" was the wailing cry—and the last parting gift of his dying wife seemed stretching forth its little hands to claim a place among the free. Poor baby! God forbid that thou shouldest live—a slave! Let us trust that in His good Providence this little one may yet be brought to share the blessings of that liberty which, without his presence his young father can never half enjoy.

Early in February, Catharine went to reside with her uncle, William Still, in Philadelphia, for the purpose of attending school, and also of receiving instruction from her aunt in the practical duties of a free woman.

Young Peter has obtained an advantageous situation in the service of Mr. Richard Ely, at New Hope, Bucks county, Pa.; and Levin is perfecting his knowledge of the blacksmith's trade in Beverly, N. J.

The father and mother, during the summer (1855), have been at service in a large boarding-house in Burlington; and though they are not yet entirely settled, the arrangements are nearly completed by which, for the first time in their lives, they may enjoy the comforts of their own home.

We must not omit to mention a novel marriage that has occurred in the family since their emancipation. The previous relation of the parties, as well as the motives which impelled them, may be gathered from the subjoined Certificate.

"This is to certify that *Mr. Peter Still* and *Lavinia,*

his wife, having solemnly testified to their lawful union in wedlock, which took place twenty-nine years ago, the twenty-fifth of last June, while in the bonds of Southern Slavery, in the State of Alabama, having now obtained their freedom, and having no certificate of said union, being desirous of again solemnizing their union in the sacred nuptial ties, were solemnly *re-united* in the bonds of marriage, on the eleventh day of March, in the year of our Lord one thousand eight hundred and fifty-five, by me, a duly authorized Minister of the Gospel.

"WASHINGTON BARNHURST.

" Burlington, Burlington Co., N. J."

Our task is done. We have sought truthfully to portray the various phases of slave-life which are illustrated in the history of the subjects of these "Recollections." The facts are from the lips of Peter and his wife; and are in all cases given substantially as narrated by them to the writer. If their record shall in any wise subserve the cause of Justice and Humanity; if the perusal of these pages shall increase the reader's hatred of slavery, or win one manly voice or vote for Freedom, our labor is not lost.

APPENDIX.

SETH CONCKLIN

WAS born February 3, 1802, at Sandy Hill, N. Y. Previously to her marriage his mother had been a teacher in the schools of Vermont. His father was a mechanic, who was accustomed to go South in search of employment. He died in Georgia, leaving his widow with five children, of whom Seth, then about fifteen years of age, was the oldest. He was not wholly without property, but what little he had, he left in charge of a man, who defrauded the family of every cent of it and fled to Canada. They became dependent upon the boy Seth, who took up the business of a pedlar, and so procured a livelihood for his mother and sisters. It is remembered how careful he was to save every penny for them, how he went upon long journeys, being absent for weeks at a time, how anxiously his return was watched for, how highly he was thought of, not only by the little ones of his own household, but also by the children of the neighbors; how the children, when they descried the weary young pedlar returning after a long tramp, ran to meet him and quarrelled for his hand and hung upon his coat.

After a while, Mrs. Concklin was induced by some

relatives to go to Canada. There was a more promising prospect for her in that country. Seth procured a situation in a lumber yard, where his employer esteemed him so highly, that in order to keep the lad contented, he took into his family a little sister of Seth's, Eveline. The lumber man, Mr. W——, treated him with uniform confidence. This man was subject to violent fits of intemperance, when he would fasten up his house and keep his wife and children in the utmost terror by his wild and frenzied proceedings. At such times Seth was the only person who had any influence over him. Again and again he seized his gun and threatened to shoot Seth, whom he charged with colluding with the family against him. But the lad, as his sister well remembers, stood calm and unmoved by the threats of the madman. So fearful was Mr. W—— in his sane moments, of being forsaken by Seth, who, he knew, wished to join his mother, who had sent for him, in Canada, that he caused the little Eveline, Seth's sister, to be locked up in a chamber up stairs, so that her brother could communicate with her only by climbing a tree which stood near her window. He seized an opportunity when his master was unable to rise from his bed, to take his little sister away. He did not go without bidding farewell to Mr. W——, who paid him his wages and shed tears at parting with the youth. "I shall go to utter ruin now that Seth has left me!" the master exclaimed.

The boy and girl set out on foot for Canada. They met with much kindness. Sometimes a kind woman, a mother, would take them in, give them food and shelter, wash the little girl and comb her hair. From others they received harsh words, and thus they trudged on. They were observed and spoken of as "the children." For though Seth was some seventeen years of age, his appearance was very boyish. The country was then new and wild, and log houses were the principal habitations to be seen. In one place in the neighborhood of Watertown, a good woman living in a neat frame house, surrounded by a large farm, a Mrs. Coles, treated the young travellers with especial kindness, took a fancy to the little Eveline, wished to retain and adopt her, as her own children were all grown up and married; and made Seth promise that if he returned to the States, he would bring Eveline to her, and let her have the child. At this stage of the journey, the little girl fell sick and was worn down by fatigue, and grew fretful and cried a good deal, but Seth was anxious to reach Sackett's Harbor; and he coaxed and threatened her. She remembers how they used to sit down by the road-side to rest, and how her brother used to cry, and she thought it was because his pack was so heavy, and she wanted him to let her take it, although it was beyond her strength.

At last they reached Sackett's Harbor one afternoon. Seth found that the steamboat fare was higher than he could pay. He took his sister to a public house, bade her go to bed and sleep till he called her the next morning. The weary child slept till ten o'clock the next morning, and upon waking and not finding Seth, grew frightened and thought he had left her; but he soon came. He had engaged a man with a small sail-boat (a smuggler), to take them across the Lake to Gravel Point, which they hoped to reach that same evening. It was September. The weather was cold, with flurries of snow. They had been out on the Lake hardly an hour when a rain-storm arose, and the waves grew angry and dashed into the boat, so that it required constant bailing, and there was nothing to bail with but a leaky old coffee pot, and that was soon lost overboard. The little girl was very much frightened. She screamed and took off one of her shoes to bail out the water. The boat made little or no headway till dark. They were all drenched to the skin, the water going over them all the time. Seth's sister remembers their getting round a dangerous point called Pillar Point. The opposite shore, which they were approaching was apparently uninhabited. But, although the others could not see it, the little girl descried a small log hut in the distance. They gained the land at last, and the man and boy set themselves immediately to gather sticks and wood to make a fire to warm and dry themselves, and keep off any wild beasts. Eveline, however, entreated them so earnestly to go in the direction in which she insisted she had seen the log hut, that at last they yielded. After walking some distance, it appeared in sight, and they found that she had not been mistaken. At the hut they found a young married couple, squatters, who had been settled there only a few months, and who received them with a hospitable welcome. The woman said she had seen their boat while it was daylight, and had watched it for some time. This couple had their chief dependence for food upon game. The only eatable they had in the house was some wheat flour. The woman made bread for them and for their supply on the morrow. She divided her bedclothes with them. The hut was so low that a man could hardly stand erect in it. There was no chimney; a fire was made at one end, and the smoke found its way out through the roof.

The next day they started by the lake for Gravel Point, and arrived at sunset. The weather had cleared. As they were approaching land, they saw a two-horsed wagon just starting for Kingston, some four or five miles distant. Seth was so anxious to secure a seat in the wagon for his sister, that when they got into shallow water, he bade her take off her shoes and stockings. They both jumped into the water and ran to overtake the wagon. There were a number of men with it, but they refused to let her ride, as, they said, the road was new and very bad, scarcely a road—they were carrying rails to prop and lift the wagon—they doubted whether they should be able to go through. They took no notice of Seth and his sister. The mud was so deep—Seth sinking into it over his boots—that he took the little girl in his arms, who with his baggage made a heavy burthen. She begged to be put down. At last she was allowed to walk, and tried to jump from log to log, but she fell again and again into the mud and was completely covered with it. It began to grow dark. They got to Kingston, however, before the wagon. At the ferry a fat, good-natured old woman insisted upon taking off the child's clothes, giving her a good washing, and wrapping her up in a buffalo skin.

The young travellers reached Kingston at two o'clock in the morning; and with the assistance of a watchman, found the dwelling of a Mr. Roleau, with whom their mother lodged. She received her two children with great emotion, laughing and weeping hysterically. She had been sick, but was on the recovery. During her illness her business, keeping a small shop, had gone to ruin, and she was earning bread for her children with her needle.

Eveline was ill for three months, from the cold and fatigue of the journey. Seth took to peddling again, through the approaching winter and the following summer. But the winter after that, the second in Canada, he became discouraged. One day he brought back such a pittance that he threw down his pack, and said he would never take it up again. He knew not what to do. Occasionally he found some transient employment. He searched the newspapers diligently to seize upon what might offer. One day, in looking over a newspaper, he found something about a haunted house. "Here's a ghost story!" he said to his mother and brothers and sisters, "come, let me read it to you." It turned out to be an advertisement of a house in Sackett's Harbor, which had the reputation of being haunted, and in which the owner was willing that any one should live, rent free, until the place should get a better name. Seth exclaimed: "I'll go take that house, and we shall have nothing to pay." He started instantly for Sackett's Harbor, with the consent of his mother (they had no fear of ghosts), and returned in three days, having found and engaged the house in the suburbs of the place; large and commodious, originally built for an hotel.

While the family were preparing to leave Kingston, a robbery was committed on the money-drawer of the shop, adjoining the house where the Concklins lived. Seth was arrested and put in jail on suspicion of being the thief. The sole ground of the charge, thus brought against him by the shopkeeper, was that Seth being well acquainted with his two sons, had often been in the shop and knew where the money was kept. The family felt keenly the shame of such a charge; and some of their best friends grew cool. Seth, however, fearless in the consciousness of his integrity, was convinced that he would be acquitted, and begged his mother not to be detained by his trial, which was not to take place for some weeks; but to go immediately to their new residence in Sackett's Harbor. Accordingly she started; it was the spring of the year; the snow was all gone. But just as she had got on board the vessel with all her baggage, and with her five children, a man came running to inform her that Seth was to have a hearing, and she must return. There was nothing to be done but to let the children (the oldest of whom was a girl of about twelve years of age), go alone with the baggage. The mother gave this child some money and every possible direction, and the strictest charges to make no fire and light no candle in the house till she came. They were to live on bread and milk. One of the children, a little boy, was sick, and had to be carried in the arms of his little sisters all the way. The party of little ones reached Sackett's Harbor in safety, attracting much curiosity and kindness on board the boat. The haunted house belonged to a Mr. Comstock, but a person by the name of Parker had care of it. Lydia left the other children in the boat and went to look after the house. In about a couple of hours she returned with the key, and a man and cart to take their baggage. As they were on the way to their new tenement, an old man met them who proved to be a quack doctor, who, struck by the youth and unprotected condition of the little group, carrying with them a sick child, stopped and questioned them, took the sick one in his arms, and went with them to the house. It soon became dark. The children had no supper. The old doctor said they must have a light. But the children would not listen to it. It would be against the express commands of their mother, who feared probably that they might catch the house or themselves on fire. The doctor expostulated, but to no purpose. Mother had forbidden it. He was, it seems, an oddity. His speeches set the children a laughing. He suspected, he said, that the house really *was* haunted, and that these little things were the ghosts—they were so afraid of light. He guessed they had an *invisible* mother.

Three times a day for ten days, till the mother joined her children (Seth having been fully acquitted), the good man visited them, bringing them soup, etc., and nursing the sick child. As soon as their mother arrived, she unpacked her trunks and furniture, and made the place a good deal more comfortable. As she was seated at her first meal with the children, in came the doctor, and stood staring at the party without saying a word. "I was wondering," he said at last to Mrs. Concklin, "whether you were a ghost or a real woman."

The mother brought to her children the cheering intelligence that Seth would be with them in three weeks. Eveline, then about eleven years of age, with her little brother George, kept watch on the shore of the Lake, as the time drew nigh for the coming of Seth. At last they recognized his figure, before they could see his features, on board of a vessel that was approaching, and on which he worked his passage. At this period the family was tolerably comfortable and happy. Seth got work. They lived in "the haunted house" one year. Then, as the owner considered the good character of the place established, he required them to pay rent. It was too high for their means, and they removed.

Seth, recollecting his promise to Mrs. Coles, the good woman who had been so kind to him and taken such a liking for the little Eveline when they stopt at her house on their way to Canada, advised his mother to send Eveline to that lady. She acceded, and the child was sent by the stage, and received by Mrs. Coles with the most cordial of welcomes, and adopted as her own, and taught many things. The child was happy here and the next winter, Mr. Coles, a worthy and elderly man, took her in a sleigh to see her mother. Upon her visit home, Eveline found Seth a soldier. Her mother was declining, and Seth, having the offer of a place as a substitute, enlisted for one year, nine months, nineteen days in Company B. By cooking for the company, Seth greatly increased his income, and was better able to assist his mother. As he was not allowed to leave the garrison, Mr. Coles took Eveline to see Seth and she recollects how the old man who was a methodist gave Seth his blessing for being such a good son and brother.

The next fall, of the eight hundred men in garrison at Sackett's Harbor, four hundred were drafted to go to St. Mary's (understood to be a thousand miles off,) and Seth being young and unmarried, among the number. He endeavored to be excused but without success.

The hope was cherished that he might be induced to re-enlist when his time was out. His mother parted with him with a heavy heart. She told the children she should never see him again.

With the help of her eldest daughter, the mother was enabled to do something for the support of her children, making sun-bonnets. Seth sent them nearly all his wages, and kept them so well supplied with money that when his mother shortly after fell sick, and after an illness of eight weeks, died, there was money enough in the house for all the frugal wants of its inmates, and for the expenses incurred by her sickness and burial. In this her last illness, she talked only of her absent son, and her dying injunction to her little ones was to obey Seth in all things.

Upon the decease of Mrs. Concklin, the unprotected state of the orphans was published in the newspapers, so that their kindred might come and take charge of them. Seth saw the papers. They gave him the first news of the death of his mother. He succeeded in obtaining a discharge. His mother died in April, but he was not able to reach home till August. He found the children in the care of an aunt. His interest had been awakened in the Shakers, and he conceived the idea of putting his brothers and sisters in the charge of a Shaker community.

With this intention he visited the Watervliet Shaker settlement not far from Albany, and was so much pleased with it, that he took the little ones, now every where known as "Seth's family," and enrolled them and himself as members of that community. The Coles, having had a daughter with five children come home to live with them, gave up Eveline who joined the Shakers also. Seth remained with the Shakers three years, the children for a longer period.

Upon leaving the Shakers, Seth went from place to place, finding employment now here, now there. He followed the business of a miller for some time in Syracuse and in Rochester and other places, never, in all his wanderings, losing sight of "his family," keeping always in correspondence with them. Everywhere he was accounted a singular man, eccentric, silent, "in the way of bargain, cavilling for the ninth part of a hair," and yet generous as the day. Whenever any attempt was made to cheat him, he instantly appealed to the law, and, it is said, he never lost his suit. At the same time he would turn his pockets inside out to relieve the destitute. On one occasion his attention was arrested by a poor Irishwoman with a number of children, who told him how they had been turned into the street for rent, her husband being in jail on the same account. He asked the amount, and, upon learning it, gave her what she wanted, but it was nearly all that he had. The woman immediately fell at his feet in the street and clasped his knees, and poured out, with Irish volubility, such a torrent of blessings and thanks that quite a crowd collected. Seth, much annoyed, turned to get rid of her, and at last finding he could not silence her, he shook her off, exclaiming in a way that was characteristic of him: "Get away, you d—d fool!"

From time to time, he visited his old friends the Shakers. (His youngest sister remains with them to this day.) Although, according to their rules, members who quit them, lose their membership, yet exceptions occur. And Seth, in consideration of his worth and eccentricity, was allowed again and again to return into full communion with the Society of Watervliet. It impressed him very strongly in favor of the Shakers that they did not recognize the distinction of color.

It was after "his family" was settled among that people, at the very beginning of the abolition movement, that Seth Concklin began to take an interest in that odious cause. And it may be doubted whether it has ever yet had a more devoted adherent. He recognized it as the only hope of the Slave. He saw clearly, and from an early period through the Colonization scheme, how it concedes to the inhuman prejudices of the country. He abhorred it as heartily as Mr. Garrison himself does.

In a letter, dated July 20, 1830, written from Syracuse to his sister Eveline, he says, "Lest you might be deceived by that wicked spirit of the American Colonization Society, I take the liberty to inform you that the American Abolition Society is the only thorough good spirit which maintains the rights and privileges of colored people. Be not deceived by the Colonization Society,

"They are as cunning as the devil can invent.

"They rivet the chains of Slavery.

"They put beneath them all mercy.

"They deceive many honest white people by saying that they are friendly to the black population, and raise funds to send from this land of freedom and religious liberty all free persons of color whom they can influence. Be not deceived by that dreadful demon spirit."

All that he earned, beyond the means of his own

frugal subsistence, was given to the abolition cause. I find receipts of sums of five dollars and ten dollars from Seth Concklin, acknowledged in "the Emancipator." Sometimes he gave fifty dollars at a time, and once one hundred dollars. Once in Syracuse, and again in Rochester he was mobbed for taking the part of black men against white rowdies, and had to run for his life, and absent himself for days till their infuriated passions had cooled. At Rochester he dashed like lightning through the crowd and levelled the ringleader who had got a rope round a poor colored man and was otherwise maltreating him, thus diverting the wrath of the mob to himself. That more than one such case of the persecution of the colored people should have occurred years ago in Western New York, will seem improbable to no one who recollects, as many not very old persons may remember, what a time-honored custom it was, not very long since, in the enlightened city of Boston to drive all "the niggers" off the common on a certain State-Election holiday that occurred in the spring of the year.

On one occasion, early in the history of the Abolition movement, the people of Syracuse were outraged by the sudden and mysterious appearance among them of some Anti-Slavery tracts: no one knew whence they came. The place was thrown into as great an alarm as if combustibles and lighted lucifers had been found under every door. A public meeting was held to devise "summary proceedings." It was suspected that some emissary of Satan had alighted in the town. With the leaders of the meeting Seth Concklin was on terms of familiar acquaintance. He attended on the occasion; but retired before the meeting was brought to a close. Upon returning to their homes, the officers of the meeting, and all who had taken any conspicuous part in it, found the accursed tracts had been thrown into their doors, while they had been so patriotically engaged in seeing to the safety of the community. Wrath mounted to the highest pitch against the incendiary, who, it was rumored, was a stranger putting up at the Syracuse House. Judge Lynch was invoked. Tar and feathers were got in readiness. No suspicious stranger was to be found; but it was ascertained that the offender was an acquaintance of theirs, Seth himself, who very wisely took care to retire from the scene. In a few days the excitement died away. Considering that the offence had been committed by no impudent stranger, but by one of their own neighbors, and by no other than so odd and honest a fellow as Seth Concklin, the people recovered their composure so completely, that when he shortly returned among them, they shook hands with him over his escape.

The subject of this brief memoir appears to have been a man who had " swallowed formulas." He was a law to himself. He took and kept his own counsel. On one occasion, a colored man, professing to be an agent for the Wilberforce Colony in Canada West, visited Western New York, collecting moneys from the charitable. He every where showed a book, imposingly bound in red morocco, in which the names of those who contributed to his object were recorded; among them were the names of men well known and eminent. This book served as his passport and recommendation, and secured his success in the towns which he visited. Our friend Seth, having some suspicion of this man's honesty when he came to Syracuse, watched him closely, and became convinced that he was an impostor. Resolved that the community should be duped no longer, Seth disguised himself and followed the fellow, and overtook him in the neighborhood of Seneca Falls, and there, without being recognized, offered him a subscription, and when the red book was handed to Seth to put down his name, he took possession of it, and refused to return it to the owner. The man complained of him before a magistrate; Concklin was held to bail for his appearance at the next General Sessions to answer to the charge of abducting this book, the property of another. His friends in Syracuse came promptly to his aid, and abundant testimony was furnished to his character for integrity and general correctness. The prosecutor, however, never appeared against him; and Concklin was considered as being right in his estimation of the man, and as having done the community a service, although he adopted a perilous and illegal way of arresting the depredations of an impostor.

Not long after this transaction, Concklin spent some time in the West, visiting St. Louis, and residing awhile at Springfield, (Ill.). His chief business then and there, a business which took precedence in his regard of all other matters, was aiding the transit of passengers on the Under-Ground Railroad. He acted, however, very little in concert with others. In a time of uniformity and conformity, when the tendency and fashion everywhere is to ride in troops, Seth Concklin was a man by himself. He went on his own hook. His fearless speech brought him into frequent peril. On one occasion, he was condemning the "Patriarchal

Institution," in such strong terms, that one of his hearers struck him a heavy blow with his fist; for which outrage Seth caused him to be arraigned before the Church to which the offender belonged, and compelled him to make confession of his fault. Although thus fearless, our friend was very cautious in communicating with the slaves. He gave them no hope of his assistance, until he found that they were resolved upon obtaining their freedom: then he gave them all possible information as to time of starting, and the places to which they should go, adding a small pecuniary gift, and bidding them never to be taken alive.

While he thus felt for others, it was equally characteristic of him that he was resolved to see for himself. He has been known to go miles to ascertain the actual state of the case in any important matter. In 1838–39, the western part of New York was in a state of great excitement, caused by what was dignified at the time by the name of the "Patriot War," a border outbreak. Concklin, true to his character, determined to go and see what it all amounted to. He knew that Canada was the refuge of the fugitive slave, and he was anxious that that refuge should be preserved for the oppressed. Leaving his business, he went straight to the frontier, crossed over to Navy Island, where the head-quarters of the Patriots then were, and enlisted with them, under the command of the so-called Gen. Van Ranssalaer. His purpose was to discover the designs and strength of the Patriots, and make them known to the Canadian authorities. After looking about him and satisfying himself as to the character and objects of the Patriot army, he desired to be dismissed from the service. But this was not permitted. His taciturn manners, his evident disinclination to associate familiarly with the people among whom he found himself, caused him to be suspected as a spy, and closely watched. Finding his situation more and more uncomfortable, he determined to escape from the island at all hazards. He waited one day till nearly dark, and, when the sentinel's back was turned towards him, he unfastened a skiff at the landing, and with no other oar than a piece of board, watched his chance and pushed off. He knew that if he should lose his paddle, he must be carried down the Niagara river and over the Falls, an appalling contingency. Scarcely had he started when he was seen and fired upon. The ball struck his paddle, nearly knocking it from his grasp. He succeeded, however, in reaching the American shore, at Schlosser, in safety. At this point a guard had been stationed by the Patriots, and he was forbidden to land. Compelled to acknowledge himself a deserter from Navy Island, he was seized and very roughly handled, and sent back to the island.* There, by order of Van Ranssalaer, he was confined and closely guarded in a log-house, which was so situated as to be exposed to the guns on the Canada side. He could save himself from being hit only by lying prostrate on the ground, as the sentinel

---

* Another account says, that Concklin was taken by the American troops under Col. Worth, stationed, professedly to guard the neutrality of the United States, on Grand Island, which lies so near to Navy Island, that the "Patriots" called to the American forces and informed them that Concklin was a deserter ; and he was sent back, the United States' officer stipulating only that he should not be hurt.

who stood guard over him threatened to shoot him when he sought the protection of the breastwork, to which the sentinel himself had recourse. Several shots passed over him, within two or three feet of him, through the upper part of his prison. The Patriots said they intended the British should kill their own spy.

On the evacuation of the Island by the Patriots, which took place about a week after Concklin was put in confinement, he was left behind—the only man in the place. It was the month of January. His sufferings from cold and hunger were severe. He was the last twenty-four hours without food. He tied his handkerchief to a pole, and took his station opposite the Canadian side. The signal was observed; and very soon a boat came off and took him in, and conveyed him to Canada. There he was subjected to a very close examination by a board of officers. In answer to their inquiries, he gave them a minute account of all that had occurred from his leaving Syracuse up to the hour of his examination. His statement was committed to writing by several different persons. The examination was repeated two or three times. He was well treated, and kindly provided for during the few days he remained on the Canada side. When the investigation was ended, and he was about to return to the States, it was proposed to him that he should swear to the truth of what he had stated. To this proposal he readily acceded. His affidavit was published in the papers at the time. When he arrived in Buffalo, he published a statement of his treatment by the United States officers on Grand Island in one of the leading journals of that city. And he also made complaint at the War Department in Washington, forwarding to the Secretary a copy of his publication in the Buffalo paper. The Secretary of War directed the District Attorney of the Northern District of New York to look into the case. That officer, living at a distance, caused some inquiries to be made in Syracuse in regard to the veracity of the complainant; and honorable testimonials to his uprightness were presented. The case, however, was never followed up. Concklin was, for a time, quite a lion at Buffalo, on account of his prominence in those border difficulties.

Not many months after the affair at Navy Island, Concklin's interest was awakened in the events which were transpiring on our Southern border. He wanted to know what the United States Government was doing in Florida among the Indians there. The newspapers had much to say of our arms in that quarter. Without consulting with any one, he resolved to visit that part of the country. As the best way of getting there, and learning what he wanted to know, he enlisted in the United States service. The first intimation of his whereabouts, which his friends in Syracuse received, was in the shape of a letter directed to one of them, which we here transcribe:

" Talahasse, Middle Florida, May 9, 1840.

"JOSEPH SAVAGE: My object in writing to you is that it may be known in Syracuse where I am; and I request that you write to me. I have heard nothing from Syracuse in a year. Direct your letter to Talahasse, Middle Florida. Should you receive this, and the postage not be paid, let me know it. I am now fifty miles from the post-office.

"Last fall I came from Pittsburgh, by way of New Orleans and the Gulf, to St. Marks, and eighty miles east of St. Marks, on the 6th of January, and entered on the campaign with the 1st and 6th Regiments, United States Infantry, a few dragoons and several companies of volunteers, on their way through all the hammocks in Middle Florida to the Suwannie river, hunting Indians. Near the end of January our forces met on the Suwannie river, below Old Town (formerly an Indian Village destroyed by Jackson), opposite Fort Fanning, East Florida, having driven before us a few Indians, discovered in the Old Town hammocks. All the companies (now the 1st February) were directed back on their trails, scouting through to keep down the Indians. There does not seem to be any very formidable force of Indians in Florida; and I believe that a part of the murders charged on the Indians are committed by the white settlers, and many of the public (official?) reports of the whites and the Indians being killed or taken are untrue.

"Nearly all the white male settlers in Middle Florida, over twelve years of age, receive from Government twenty-two dollars per month and rations. There is now a report that a man found in a hammock five Indians in the act of torturing, by fire, his son. He killed four of them, and the fifth ran away. Should this be published, you must believe it without proof. I believe these reports are only pretences to keep up this shameful war.

"March 21st, I left a post near Old Town Hammock alone, unarmed, and travelled one hundred miles through the plains and hammocks without seeing a human being in five days. This circumstance alone would convince uninterested people that there are not many Indians.

"But I have further proof that no great danger is apprehended from the Indians, from the fact that a company of United States Infantry near Old Town Hammock, one of the most interior towns in Middle Florida, frequently send out scouting parties through the hammocks without loaded guns and without ammunition, though they carry their guns with them, but as a mere matter of form. I do not know that the blood-hounds find any Indians; though it appears that in East Florida the dogs, the Spaniards, and our soldiers have captured one old Indian.

"SETH CONCKLIN."

In another letter of the same date, addressed to a brother-in-law in Philadelphia, he repeats the same particulars, and gives, in addition, some brief and striking instances of his observation. "I have seen," he writes, "some of the slaves on the north border of Middle Florida. They are much more intelligent than their owners, probably from their being from farther north."

The following winter, Concklin appeared again unexpectedly in Syracuse. From that time till he went upon the chivalrous enterprise which cost him his life, he is believed to have resided principally in Troy, occasionally visiting "his family" and his sister Eveline married, and resident in Philadelphia. More than once he made the journey from Syracuse to Philadelphia, all the way on foot. He appears to have commanded the confidence of all who knew him. He was a man of an "incorrigible and losing honesty," abhorring deceptions and injustice, and making every injured man's cause his own. Altogether he was a man of heroic character. His life was a romance— an heroic poem.

A gentleman of Syracuse, with whom Concklin lived two years, states, that on one occasion he sent Seth fifty miles from home for a horse. He was provided with money to defray his expenses to and fro by boat or stage. His employer was greatly surprised to see him returning leading the horse, instead of riding him. The saddle and a bag of oats were on the horse's back. He returned nearly all the money which had been given him for the expenses of the journey. It appeared that he had walked to the place where the horse was to be obtained in one day, on returning he took two days, as being *encumbered with a horse*, he could not walk so fast as without one.

It is unnecessary to repeat here the story of the humane and daring enterprise in which he lost his life. Various accounts of it went the rounds of the newspapers at the time. We give the following from a Pittsburgh (Pa.) journal, bearing date, Thursday morning, May 29, 1851 :

" A SINGULAR ENTERPRISE.—During the last trip of the steamer *Paul Anderson*, Captain GRAY, she took on board, at Evansville, Indiana, a United States Marshal, having in custody an intelligent white man, named J. H. MILLER, and a family of four slaves— mother, daughter, and two sons. Captain GRAY subsequently learned from Mrs. Miller that he had been

employed by some persons in Cincinnati to go to
Florence, Alabama, and bring away this family of
slaves—the woman's husband being in a free State.
For this purpose, with a six-oared barge, procured at
Cincinnati, Miller had gone down the Ohio and up the
Tennessee River, to Florence, there laid in wait till an
opportunity occurred, and privily taken away the
family of slaves. The barge was rowed down the
Tennessee, and up the Ohio, to the Wabash, and up
that river till within thirty miles of Vincennes, where
the party was overtaken and captured by the Marshal.
The unfortunate Miller was then chained, to be taken
back to Florence for trial and sure condemnation, by
Alabama slave laws. The *Paul Anderson* having
landed at Smithland, mouth of Cumberland River, Mr.
Miller made an attempt to escape from her to the
steamer *Mohican*, lying alongside, but, encumbered by
his manacles and clothing, was drowned. The body
was recovered and buried about a week afterwards.
The slaves went back to bondage. The barge was
rowed down the Tennessee 273 miles, up the Ohio 100
miles, and up the Wabash 50 miles, before the party
were overtaken. Mr. Miller, we learn, had a sister
and other relatives in or near Philadelphia. He was
a mill-wright by occupation, and owned property in
the neighborhood of Vincennes."

So far the public press. As these accounts are very
imperfect, a person was found who offered to go to
Indiana and make such inquiries as might relieve, in
some measure, the painful anxiety of Mr. Concklin's
relatives and friends, and to obtain his remains, or, at
least, if practicable, cause them to be disinterred and

examined. We subjoin a copy of the written statement made by this agent of Mr. Concklin's friends.

Statement.

Mr. Chandler (I think), at Evansville, in answer to a question as to his knowledge of Miller and the abducted negroes, said, I could obtain information of John S. Gavitt, the former Marshal of Evansville. He (?) himself believed and told the parties at the time, that the proceedings by which Miller was taken out of the State were illegal, and if such things were to be tolerated, no white man was safe.

I next called upon John S. Gavitt, who treated me very respectfully, and seemed not only willing but anxious to impart every information. He told me that he had Miller and the negroes in custody, and that he delivered them on board the steamboat, in care of Mr. John Emison, of Evansville, to be delivered to the authorities in Florence, Alabama. I asked him by what authority they were taken. He said he had the writs in his possession, made out by Martin Robinson, Esq., of Vincennes. I asked to see them. He showed them to me. I asked for the privilege of copying them. This he would not permit, for the reason, he said, that he believed, "We've all been guilty of *illegal proceedings*, and if it's brought out, I don't want to give our enemies any advantage." He said, it was no more he than others. "I believe," said he, "we've *all* done wrong." The writ for the apprehension of Miller was based upon an affidavit by the aforesaid John S. Gavitt, before Squire Robinson, in which he swears that Miller abducted from B. McKiernan, of Florence, Ala., the four negroes. And the writ ordered the said Gavitt to take the said Miller and safely deliver him to the Sheriff in said Florence, to be dealt with *according* to law. The authority quoted, I think, was, Sec. 1, No. 62 of the Statutes of Indiana. (I wrote from memory, not being permitted to copy.) The other writ for returning the negroes was made, I think, upon the affidavit of James M. Emison, the man who first took them up on suspicion. The said James M. Emison is not an officer.

I asked Gavitt how he could know the circumstances stated in the writ well enough to make such an oath? He then stated substantially as follows: That on or about the 28th of March last, he received a dispatch from Vincennes, stating that four negroes had been taken up on suspicion, with the man Miller. He in turn telegraphed South, and soon got returns describing the negroes and Miller. He started at once for Vincennes, and drove the whole distance (55 miles) in six hours. He says he made the oath because he was convinced from the *description by telegraph*, and from conversations with the boy Levin, that they were the same. There seemed to be an indistinctness and confusion in Gavitt's statements, and though I conversed with him two hours, and he freely answered all questions, I did not fully rely on him. For instance, he would state at one time that he believed Miller perfectly honest and conscientious in his course; yet, at another time said, that Miller owned to him that he was to get $1,000 for the job. He says, his main effort, while Miller was in his charge, was to get him to turn State's evidence, and upon that condition agreed to let him go. This Miller positively refused to do, though he confessed that there were four others con-

concerned with him. He said Miller offered him $1,000 if he would let him go. The reward offered for Miller, he said, was $600, and $400 for the negroes. The story that Miller told him was, that the negroes were his—his brother in Henderson (Kentucky) having emancipated them after they should have worked upon his farm near Springfield (Illinois) a certain length of time. He says Miller had shaved his whiskers, and cut off his hair after he was first discovered by James M. Emison. When he was about putting him on the boat, Miller called him aside and told him he would give the names of his accomplices if he would let him go. He told him it was too late then, upon which Miller became a perfect picture of despair, and walking suddenly to the side of the boat, he thought, with a determination to throw himself overboard, but was caught by John Emison. Understanding that while Miller was in custody of Gavitt, he was kept at the house of Mr. Sherwood (a relative), the present Marshal of Evansville, and that he had conversation with Gavitt's mother, I requested to have her called in. She said she felt very sorry for him, and tried very hard to get him to turn State's evidence ; but he said, nobody was to be blamed in the affair but himself, and that he was not at all sorry for what he had done ; he had done his duty—a Christian duty—and felt a clear conscience. Gavitt said that McKiernan told him that Miller should be hung if it cost him $1,500.

Further evidence was procured from the office of the Evansville Journal.

From Evansville to Princeton, and thence to Vincennes, I went in company with Col. Clark and son, of the latter place. He (the Col.) gave a statement of the affair, which made it take quite another direction from Gavitt's story. He placed Gavitt in no very enviable light. *He said* that there was a jar between him (Gavitt) and the Emisons about the *spoils*. Of course the sending back of the " d—d Abolitionist" to Alabama, was all right with him (the Colonel).

Having been directed by Gavitt to call on Mr. John Emison, in Vincennes, I did so. He was pointed out to me in the street as the stage agent, or, perhaps, proprietor. I called him aside, and told him that, having some business in Vincennes, I had been requested by a friend of Miller's friends to make inquiry concerning him; upon which the said John Emison broke forth in a strain like the following : " Now, my friend, you'd better be pretty d—d careful how you come into this place and make inquiry about such men as Miller." " You've waked up the wrong passengers." " And you might get yourself into the Wabash river." " If you'll take my advice as a friend, you'd better leave town on pretty d—d short notice." " We don't allow any G—d d—d Abolitionist going about *this* town," &c., &c., with many other extras too numerous to mention. I told him my object in making inquiry of him was a specific one —solely to gratify, or rather to satisfy, Miller's friends, and if such a course was likely to produce a disturbance in the place, I was very sorry. But out of respect to those who entrusted the inquiries to me, I felt bound to learn what I could. Emison partially apologised for his haste, and said he was mad at the d—d Abolitionists on the *Paul Anderson*, who threatened to throw him overboard. (See *Evansville Journal*, p. 27.) He said he felt for Miller, as deeply as anybody could—that he was courageous, and that anybody that was bold enough to jump overboard deserved to get away. " But," said he, " he's dead and buried— he's gone to —— with his manacles on, so you'll know him when he comes up in the resurrection." He said he would let me have a letter, which he had received from the young Mr. McKiernan, containing further evidence of Miller's death, in addition to the letter from Hodge.

Mr. Chandler, of whom I first spoke, told me that he was informed by Gavitt that the lawyer, who had taken a fee from Miller of some $50, or $80 (as some said)—when Miller was brought into court, said lawyer refused to undertake his case—having received a fee of $25, from the other party. I asked Gavitt about this: he said it was true, for he had paid him the $25 himself, though he could not tell me *what the man's name was*.

William T. Scott, sheriff and jailor of Knox Co., told me the slaves were brought to the jail in the morning (Friday, I think), and the request made by James Emison, that they should be put in: he admitted them, though he told me he knew he had no business to do so. Said Emison & Co. told him they had taken the negroes the previous morning about daylight, as they were crossing a bridge. Miller soon came up, and claimed them as his—they had been liberated by his brother, in Henderson, Ky., and were to serve for him a certain time near Springfield. They took the negroes and bound them, and upon Miller's threatening them with law, they took him also, and bound him and put him in the wagon with the rest. After riding five or six miles, and listening to the logical reasoning of Miller, they began to be alarmed, lest they might be doing something wrong in thus binding a *white man*, without due process of law, so they untied him and let him go. He, however, still continued to follow the wagon, and, it being still dark, before they were aware, Miller was in the wagon untying the negroes. When they discovered this, they threatened to shoot him if he should again attempt it. Miller still followed the wagon to Vincennes, where the slaves were committed to jail as above. A telegraphic dispatch was sent to Gavitt aforesaid, at Evansville, and by him sent South, from whence he obtained an answer as before- stated. Gavitt went to Vincennes, with evidence sufficient to warrant their being sent back; but would not give the evidence, or make any move in the premises, till Emison & Co. had agreed to give him *one half of the reward*. This agreed, the oath was made, and Miller arrested, under a law of the State, for detaining fugitives from their lawful owners. Previous to this, and I think on the same day, Miller had taken out a *habeas corpus*, under which the slaves were said to be delivered; but Judge Bishop, associate judge for the circuit, *remanded them to jail till the next day at* 12 *o'clock*—of course without any claim to law, but (with) merely a suspicion that by that time evidence might be obtained that they did not *belong to themselves*. When Gavitt arrived, and Miller was taken as aforesaid, his lawyer, Allen, appeared in his behalf, and the proceedings against him were quashed. After this, *Miller was remanded back* to jail, though Allen says it was done by his (Miller's) own request, that he feared the mob, &c. While Miller was thus in jail, the owner arrived, and found his work all made ready to his hand. True, a little more swearing was needed to prove Miller the abductor of the negroes, but it was readily furnished by Marshal Gavitt. Scott says that a young man now in jail, and with whom Miller talked freely, says, he (Miller) had a quantity of gold coin quilted into the collar of his coat. Scott thinks it was not so, as he himself searched him. Scott says, Miller told him that he had only one thing to regret in the transaction, and that was that he had not pursued his own course, and refused to listen to the advice of others. He says the negroes were well trained, and all told the same story with Miller until the master came, when they owned him—at least all of them but Peter. Upon Miller's second sham trial, he owned all the facts in the case, and pleaded justification. He was asked why he undertook the work without being armed: he said, if he had carried weapons he should have probably felt a strong inclination to use them, and in that case would certainly have been overcome; consequently, he had not allowed himself even a penknife.

I went to see C. M. Allen, Esq., to inquire about *the two fees*, and other matters. I told him that in justice to himself, some explanation should be given. He stated in substance as follows: "That on the morning of the day on which the negroes were brought into town, Miller came to his house very early—before he was up—he told the same story that he did to the captors about the slaves of his brother, at Henderson, &c.; and wished Allen to take out a *habeas corpus* to liberate the slaves. He told Miller that it was a trouble-

some case, and if he undertook it he should charge
him a heavy fee. Miller asked, how much? The reply was, one hundred dollars. Miller promptly said,
'I won't give it.' As Mr. Miller was about to leave
him, he called him back and told him it was a hard
case to be placed in such a situation, and with but little
means. He showed his purse and counted his money
before him. There was forty dollars, or perhaps a
little over, in gold, silver and bills. Miller told him
if he would undertake his case he would give him
fifteen dollars. There followed a parley about the fee,
and Mr. Allen did not tell me how much he received;
but he said he told Miller, if he had not told him the
truth, that he should abandon his case at any time,
whenever that should appear. So when Miller was
brought into court, after the arrival of McKiernan, he
refused to act for him, because the evidence seemed so
strong that Miller had misrepresented the thing to him.
Allen, it appears, acted for Miller, in taking out the
habeas corpus for the negroes, and also in Miller's trial
on the indictment for breaking the law of Indiana;
both of which resulted in Miller's favor. Upon quash-
ing the proceedings in the last named case, Allen made
a request of the judge that Miller should be remanded
back to jail, upon *his own* request; that he probably
had his own reasons for such request. The judge told
him that he did not know that he had any right to do
so—if he would show him law for it, he would do so.
Allen replied that he did not know that he could—it
was only Miller's request. The judge complied. Allen gave it as a reason that he feared the violence of
the mob, as the whole place was in a high state of excitement. While thus in jail, Gavitt came with his

telegraphic evidence and made the necessary oath to have Miller apprehended, and remanded to Alabama, as a fugitive from justice.

Gavitt (who, it seems, had been into the jail, and tried to extort a confession from the negroes), told me that he stated to the court ('Squire Robinson), that he was aware that the testimony of colored persons was not admitted by law on such occasions, but wished to know if the court would do him the favor to listen to the statement of the boy Levin ?   He ('Squire R.) *said he would.*   The boy then owned in answer to questions put to him, that he was the slave of 'Master Kiernan,' and that he had come with Miller from South Florence, Ala.   I asked Gavitt which he thought had the most weight with the court, his affidavit or the negro's statement?   His reply was : ' The nigger's story *was what done it.*'   I went to see 'Squire Robinson, and asked him to let me see the law by which Miller was remanded.   He said there was a law shown him at the time, but he could not now tell what or where it was, as he kept no minute of the proceedings.

A great many other little incidents were narrated during the four days that I was in Evansville, Princeton, and Vincennes, that might be elicited by questions ; but I have given the most important, or at least that which I considered so.   From the feeling manifested, I saw it would not be safe for me to go to Smithland to disinter the body, so I wrote to Mr. Hodge for the verdict of the Coroner's jury, and any other particulars as to identity which he might be able to give.   Have not yet received an answer.

(Signed),   E. JACOBS.

Cincinnati, June 11, 1851.

From these statements there can be no doubt that the body taken from the Ohio river, near Smithland. in irons, and buried in irons, was the body of Seth Concklin. But of the manner of his death, there is no direct evidence. Of all the conjectures that may be formed, the least probable is, that he was drowned in an attempt to escape. Daring as he was, he was nevertheless a man of too much sagacity to have dreamed of escaping by the water, cumbered as he was with manacles. The most probable state of the case was that, seeing how utterly hopeless the prospect was for him, if he once entered the Southern country, he tore himself from the savage clutch of cruel men, and threw himself upon the mercy of God. The suspicion of foul play which is involuntarily awakened, is put at rest by the consideration that his captors had no temptation to murder him. They knew perfectly well their own Slave laws, and must have been only too eager to carry him back alive and make an example of him, to the terror of their slaves and of all who should think of helping them to escape.

Although he was buried as he was found, in chains, and was branded with the name of "negro thief," and his captors exulted in their blood-stained rewards, yet in the sight of Truth and of Heaven, he is joined to the noble and heroic company of the martyrs, the martyrs of Freedom and Humanity.